PEOPLE AND ISSUES IN LATIN AMERICAN HISTORY

THE COLONIAL EXPERIENCE

Sources and Interpretations

Edited by

LEWIS HANKE and
JANE M. RAUSCH

University of Massachusetts, Amherst

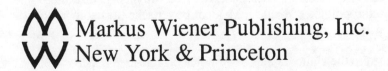

Markus Wiener Publishing, Inc.
New York & Princeton

For information write to: Markus Wiener Publishing, Inc.
114 Jefferson Road, Princeton, NJ 08540

Library of Congress Cataloging-in-Publication Data

People and Issues in Latin American history. The Colonial
    experience/Lewis Hanke and Jane Rausch, editors.
    Rev. ed. of: History of Latin American Civilization. Vol. 1,
The Colonial experience. 2nd ed. 1973.
    Includes bibliographical references.
    ISBN 1-55876-061-X
    1. Latin America—History—to 1830. I. Hanke, Lewis.
II. Rausch, Jane M. , 1940- . III. History of Latin American
civilization. Colonial experience.
F1412.P383 1992   92-25817
980.012—dc20   CIP

The photographs in the text are reproduced courtesy of the following sources: Library of Congress; University of California Library, Berkeley; The Peabody Museum, Harvard University; Instituto Nacional de Anthropologia e Historia, Mexico; Bayerische Staatsbibliothek, Munich.

Printed in the United States of America on acid-free paper
by Princeton University Press.

PREFACE

This reader on colonial Latin American history makes available once again materials originally compiled by Lewis Hanke in 1967 and published by Little, Brown and Company as *History of Latin American Civilization: Sources and Interpretations,* Volume 1: *The Colonial Experience.* In 1973 Hanke revised the volume for the second edition published under the same title, and a year later he prepared an abridged version entitled *Latin America: A Historical Reader.* For this new volume, Sections I, II, and VI have been taken from the 1973 second edition, while Sections II, IV, VII, and VIII with slight revisions follow the 1974 abridged version. Wherever possible, I have retained Hanke's lively introductions to the sections and individual selections. The only new unit is Section V, "The Introduction of African Slavery in Spanish America," which I have added to reflect the enormous scholarly output on this topic since the 1960s. Finally, I have updated the bibliography and listed titles of readily accessible 16 mm films and videotapes that can provide a visual dimension to the printed word.

Unlike the companion volume, *People and Issues in Latin American History—The National Era* (New York: Markus Wiener, 1991), where five of eight sections are focused on representative personalities rather than issues, *The Colonial Experience* remains faithful to Hanke's original design by highlighting eight important topics debated by historians. Nevertheless, within these pages students will meet Bartolomé de Las Casas, the stout defender of the Indians in sixteenth-century Spanish America, and Antonio Vieira, his seventeenth-century counterpart in Brazil. They will read of the exploits of Juan Garrido, a black conquistador in Mexico; Francisco de Toledo, Viceroy of Peru; Johan Maurits, the humanist Dutch governor of Recife; Sor Juana de la Cruz, "Supreme Poet of the Seventeenth Century Spanish World"; and the German savant and scientist, Alexander von Humboldt. They will also learn of the nameless men and women—Spanish, Portuguese, Indian, and African—whose collective stories make the history of three hundred years ago more comprehensible to our twentieth-century mentalities.

I am grateful to Professor Hanke for his permission to reprint these essays; I believe that today, as much as in 1967, they continue to exemplify his belief that Latin American history must be taught not as a "crisis" subject, but as "the unfolding story of a culture, a civilization both interesting and worthy of attention in itself, (and) as a significant and fascinating part of the history of mankind."

Jane M. Rausch
Amherst, June 1992

CONTENTS

SUGGESTIONS FOR FURTHER READING AND VIEWING

THE COLONIAL EXPERIENCE

An Indian Experiment to Determine Whether Spaniards Were Mortal. Many strange and wondrous fantasies were held by Spaniards as they conquered America (Reading 3). In the early years, they attempted to find out whether Indians "could live like Spanish farmers" by a series of sociological experiments.

Indians also experimented on Spaniards, and in 1508 some Puerto Rican Indians decided to find out whether the Spaniards were mortal or not. If immortal, as was suspected, why bother to war against them? So the Indians held several conquistadores under water in the river to see whether they would be drowned. Then they hauled the lifeless Spaniards to the bank, explaining it was all a joke — for they apparently were convinced the Spaniards were really immortal. But after three days, "when the bodies began to stink," the Indians realized the truth, declared war, and almost wiped the Spaniards out.

The Flemish engraver and book publisher Theodore de Bry (1528–1598) depicted this remarkable experiment.

The Transit
of Civilization

THE INFLUENCE OF EUROPE

Why have so little effort and imagination been spent on determining what
ideas, institutions, values, and ways of life the Portuguese and Spaniards
carried to America during their more than three centuries of colonial rule?
More particularly, why has such minor attention usually been given in Latin
American history courses to the European scene, the background from which
the conquerors and colonists came?

One answer can be given easily: there is simply too much material on
Spanish and Portuguese history, and what interest historians have displayed
in the subject has been too narrowly focused on the specific ethnic, cultural,
and institutional elements the mother countries transplanted across the Atlantic from 1492 on. Charles Julian Bishko of the University of Virginia, who
has been a major figure in enlarging our views of Iberian background studies,
would emphasize the period from 711 when the Arabs first swept into the
Iberian peninsula until the death of Philip II in 1598, which marks the end
of "the basic epoch of the discovery, conquest, and colonization of the
Spanish and Portuguese Indies." But he also states: "broadly speaking, from
the chronological standpoint, the Background stretches from the first human
habitation of the Peninsula right down to present-day Spanish and Portuguese
influence upon Latin America."

To this enormous chronological scope, Professor Bishko would join an
equally all-embracing approach:

> First, the subject should be studied not merely in terms of politico-mili-
> tary history and biography, but as broadly as modern historians treat
> Latin America itself, in its social, religious, economic, cultural and

3

juridical aspects. Second, the overworked mechanical formula of tracing Ibero-American ideas or institutions to their metropolitan ancestors
should be expanded to include the larger problem of why, how, and
from what general context these and not other forms were adopted for
use in the Indies. Third, interpretations of the Background should
recognize in medieval and early modern Spain and Portugal highly complex, unstable societies moving, in the midst of violent internal change
and conflict, from an original dynamic diversity towards the more static
ethnic, religious and constitutional uniformity and centralization of the
arteriosclerotic seventeenth century, to which, not to earlier periods, so
many of our glib generalizations about Spain and Portugal really apply.[1]

Given the size of the task, is it any wonder that Latin Americanists, pressed
to cover a large New World history in a short time, have tended to devote
scant attention to the Old? Fortunately for students who wish to pursue
Iberian background studies further, there has recently appeared a valuable
one-volume survey that for the first time provides a solid basis of readings in
English.[2]

Another explanation of the special problem faced by Iberian background
studies is the influence that present politics sometimes exert on the writing of
history. Since the sixteenth century, arguments have been loud and bitter
on the correct interpretation of the role of Portugal and Spain in the New
World. Grand generalizations still flourish.[3] For some, these Iberian nations
redeemed a wilderness of savages and brought them into a Christian, Western
way of life; for others the institutions and ways of life brought from Europe
were largely destructive and were almost wholly responsible for all the ills
Latin America has suffered from 1492 to today. The historical study of these
important and enduring influences in the lives of Latin Americans has been
hampered by the passion and dogmatism engendered all too often by political
considerations.

THE IBERIAN BACKGROUND

We must remember that conquest and colonization was not a simple process,
for it varied somewhat from region to region. Moreover, early modern Eu-

---

[1] Charles Julian Bishko, "The Iberian Background of Latin American History: Recent Progress and Continuing Problems," *Hispanic American Historical Review*, 36
(1965), pp. 50–80. The quotations from this article appear on pp. 53–55.

[2] H. B. Johnson, Jr., ed., *From Reconquest to Empire: The Iberian Background of
Latin American History*, Borzoi Books on Latin America (New York: Knopf, 1970).

[3] See the author's "A Modest Proposal for a Moratorium on Grand Generalizations:
Some Thoughts on the Black Legend," *Hispanic American Historical Review*, 51
(1971), pp. 112–127. For a rebuttal see Benjamin Keen's article, ibid., pp. 336–355.

rope in the era of the Renaissance and Reformation carried medieval elements as well as some modern ideas into an already populated continent whose cultures had been evolving for centuries with few outside contacts. There were also differences between the history and life styles of the Portuguese and Spanish peoples, even though they shared the same peninsula, cherished the same faith, and had much in common. Less has been written on the Portuguese background, but Professor Stuart B. Schwartz provides a succinct and interesting overview (Reading 1).

Spanish precedents for institutional developments have been studied,[4] but the subject of specific medieval survivals in the New World has received less attention. Dr. Luis Weckmann's broad-brush treatment (Reading 2) is therefore particularly welcome. Ideas are sometimes underestimated by "practical" historians, but no one can ignore the influence of the fancies and speculations as the Spaniards came into contact with an unknown continent and its puzzling people (Reading 3).

Plants and animals are also an integral part of history, and James A. Robertson has compiled one of the few general descriptions of Spanish contributions in this field (Reading 4). Here indeed is an important topic worthy of further study, for the early chroniclers recorded remarkably sharp and detailed observations of flora and fauna. Carl Sauer stated that perhaps no other part of the world has an equal wealth of such data for that time.[5] A recently discovered Aztec map now in the Library of Congress indicates that the Indian leader Don Carlos Chichimecatecotl as early as 1536 began to develop orchards in Mexico, both by introducing Spanish apple, pear, and quince trees and by grafting them onto native stocks.[6]

Spaniards embarked upon their conquests in America at the very moment when Antonio de Nebrija had produced the first modern grammar of any Eu-

---

[4] See Robert S. Chamberlain's *Castilian Backgrounds of the Repartimiento-Encomienda* (Washington, D.C.: Carnegie Institute of Washington, 1939) and "The *Corregidor* in Castile in the Sixteenth Century and the Residencia as Applied to the *Corregidor*," *Hispanic American Historical Review*, 23 (1943), pp. 222–257.

[5] *Handbook of South American Indians*, vol. 6 (Washington, D.C.: Government Printing Office, 1950), p. 487.

[6] Howard F. Cline, "The Oztoticpac Lands Map of Texcoco, 1540," *Quarterly Journal of the Library of Congress*, 23, no. 2 (Washington, D.C., 1966), p. 106. Indians were knowledgeable about plants, as may be seen from Margaret A. Towle's *The Ethnobotany of Pre-Columbian Peru* (Chicago: Aldine Publishing Co., 1961), an excellently documented account of the utilization of wild and domesticated plants in the prehistoric culture of the Andes. See also Pedro Armillas, "Gardens on Swamps: Archeological Research Verifies Historical Data on Aztec Land Reclamation in the Valley of Mexico," *Science*, 174, no. 4010 (November 12, 1971), pp. 653–661. "The material foundations for Aztec imperialism were established by the farmers who had conquered the swamps." *Ibid.*, p. 660.

ropean language, the *Gramática Española* (1492), and they raced over the great stretches of the New World while the printing press was being intensely developed in Spain. The books that Spaniards brought to their colonies for pleasure or instruction, or for converting the Indians, are an impressive tribute to their love of the printed page and their conviction of the need to communicate through books. Their record of printing in America, as the Chilean scholar José Toribio Medina has abundantly shown, is most impressive. The sheer quantity of research on printing and books in the Spanish colonies makes it impossible to present a brief selection that will do justice to this aspect of Iberian culture transfer. Many good works exist for the interested student.[7]

NEW WORLD INFLUENCE ON THE OLD

The effect of America on Europe has been even less thoroughly investigated than the transit of civilization westward across the Atlantic. The most immediate and dramatic effect was to be seen in Sevilla, the Andalusian port town that was converted into a thriving international metropolis. The discovery of America doubled its population within fifty years to make it the largest city in Spain, and the fabulous riches that arrived from the New World attracted such a horde of wealth seekers that Lope de Vega generally referred to Sevilla as a "new Babylonia." Professor Ruth Pike eloquently describes the change in the city's tone and values:

> In the sixteenth century Sevillian society underwent a profound transformation. New and economic values were created and old ones discarded as a result of the city's new position as chief port for the Indies. Traditional beliefs emphasizing virtue and valor as the basis for nobility fell into disuse. An acquisitive society was emerging, and a spirit of gain overwhelmed the city. Greed for money and dissatisfaction with social and economic status became the common affliction of all Sevillians. The riches from the New World cast a spell over the whole town.[8]

Another obvious and significant effect was the inflation caused by the great influx of minerals, especially silver, which Professor John Lynch has competently analyzed. Spain was primarily an exporter of raw materials and an importer of manufactured goods, and she used American silver to make up for her unfavorable trade balance. Spain also "lavished more and more on foreign

---

[7] On one important development see Lawrence S. Thompson, "The Libraries of Colonial Spanish America," *Bibliotheca Docet: Festgabe für Carl Wehmer* (Amsterdam: Verlag der Erasmuss-Buchhandlung, 1963), pp. 257–266. For a more general view see Irving A. Leonard, *Books of the Brave: Being an Account of Books and Men in the Spanish Conquest and Settlement of the Sixteenth-Century New World* (Cambridge, Mass.: Harvard University Press, 1949).

[8] Ruth Pike, *Aristocrats and Traders: Sevillian Society in the Sixteenth Century* (Ithaca: Cornell University Press, 1972), pp. 1, 21.

enterprise," and the result was a sharp increase in prices, which raised the cost of living for all Spaniards.[9] Since the classic work on Spanish prices by Earl J. Hamilton a generation ago, much attention and some criticism have been directed toward his explanation that American silver caused the price revolution. Recently a Hungarian historian, Tibor Wittmann, has suggested that internal conditions in Spain were perhaps even more influential than the influx of American silver.[10] But another survey of the enormous literature on Spain's decline confirms that her economy was indeed adversely affected by riches from the New World.[11]

Except for treasure, the influence of the New World on the Old has had an uncertain effect, which Professor John H. Elliott sets forth in a persuasive way (Reading 6). Since the sixteenth century the question has been raised in Europe whether the discovery of America was a boon or bane for mankind. In the eighteenth century, prize contests were organized in France for the best essay on the subject, and generalizations pro and con flourished among the Enlightenment philosophers.

The Pacific Ocean as well as the Atlantic was a highway that moved ideas, plants, silks, and spices back and forth between Spanish America and the Orient. There is much documentation, mostly in rare printed chronicles and manuscripts, on trans-Pacific influences, but only a beginning has been made toward telling the full story.[12] Another study requiring more attention is the influence of America on Africa. We must not forget the migration of food plants to Africa. As Philip D. Curtin has emphasized, "at least two new-world crops were introduced into Africa in the sixteenth century: manioc and maize spread very widely and came to be two of the most important sources of food on that continent." [13]

Did colonial Brazil exert an influence on Portugal? Professor James Duffy of Brandeis University has been working on this interesting but little-known subject and has reached some tentative conclusions:

Portugal's overseas enterprise left a distinctive impression on the small nation's personality. As a result of Portugal's dramatic thrust into new

[9] Earl J. Hamilton, *American Treasure and the Price Revolution in Spain, 1501–1650* (Cambridge, Mass.: Harvard University Press, 1934).

[10] Tibor Wittmann, "Apuntes sobre los métodos de investigación de la decadencia castellana (siglos XVI–XVII)," *Nouvelles Études Historiques publiées à l'occasion du XIIe Congrès International des Sciences Historiques par la Commission Nationale des Historiens Hongrois* (Budapest: Académie des Sciences de Hongrie, 1965), pp. 243–259.

[11] John H. Elliott, "The Decline of Spain," *Past and Present* (London), no. 26 (November 1961), pp. 52–75. For a more general view see Elliott's brilliant *The Old World and the New, 1492–1650* (Cambridge, England: Cambridge University Press, 1970), and "The Discovery of America and the Discovery of Man," *Proceedings of the British Academy,* 58 (1972), pp. 3–27.

[12] Pablo Guzmán-Rivas, "Geographic Influences of the Galleon Trade in New Spain," *Revista Geográfica* (Rio de Janeiro), 27, no. 53 (July–December 1960), pp. 5–81.

[13] *The Atlantic Slave Trade: A Census* (Madison, Wis.: 1969), p. 270.

and distant lands — Africa, America, India and beyond — cultural values were changed and then crystallized in the sixteenth and seventeenth centuries. . . .

I believe that the pattern of Portuguese culture, certainly more than that of any other European nation, has been shaped by the consciousness of expansion. . . . A large part of Portuguese historical and artistic writing has concerned itself with overseas themes. Portuguese art and architecture reflect the same preoccupation. The Portuguese Catholic Church has long seen itself as a militant missionary force. Portuguese folklore has been enriched by motifs from one part of the remote world or another. Even Portuguese science has more often centered its attention on colonial phenomena than on those of the metropolis. This constant interest in the overseas world has contributed to the formation of the unique Portuguese personality.[14]

A FINAL QUESTION

Why were some Iberian customs, ideas, and institutions accepted or modified in America and others rejected? As the anthropologist George Foster emphasizes, Spanish forms were welcomed by Indians in the field of material culture and techniques when they were recognized by the Indians as useful, and when there were no indigenous counterparts or where Spanish forms represented a significant extension of their indigenous forms. But in the broad field of folk culture — dietary patterns, superstitions, folk medicine, folklore, and music — "Spanish traits found themselves in competition with indigenous traits, and often with no clear advantage." [15] As George Kubler described the process in Peru:

> Indian populations under colonial pressure retained powers of selective choice, accepting certain European subsistence activities, and rejecting others. In Peru, these patterns of selective choice were governed, on the whole, by environmental limitations and by antecedent Indian needs and habits. Most interesting are these latter. Once a European food plant, for instance, had weathered the transportation to an American climate, that import was doomed to failure unless it found Indian acceptance. Examples in Peru during the sixteenth century were European squashes and gourds and beans; rice, and gardening vegetables; grapes and orchard fruits; barley and rye. If cultivated, these species were grown only for

[14] Statement by Professor Duffy, March 3, 1960.
[15] George M. Foster, *Culture and Conquest: America's Spanish Heritage* (Chicago: Quadrangle Books, 1960), p. 229.

European use, and never came to dominate Indian subsistence. On the other hand, Indians accepted and exploited horse- and cattle-breeding, pigs, sheep, and goats, as well as cats; chickens; sugarcane, mustard, garlic, and alfalfa. In the absence of specially intense pressures, therefore, the Indian communities could pick and choose among the new subsistence activities. Their choices were governed by certain simple considerations. They were not interested in European species that closely resembled their own or provided analogous satisfactions. European squashes illustrate the point: a plantfood insufficiently distinguished from Indian varieties. Indians were also disinclined to cultivate plants from which few by-products were available, or which required large amounts of land: orchards and vineyards are examples. They also refused species whose cultivation entailed radical changes in the ceremonial organization of labor. Thus wheat, barley, and rye, which require careful, continuous cultivation, cannot be grown by the traditional, easy-going communal methods of Andean corn-agriculture. The Indians long avoided these crops, even in favorable climatic and geographical conditions.

But horses and cattle, unlike the native livestock (llama, alpaca, vicuña), could be used as draft animals, and their hides and fats were useful by-products. The Indians accepted them, even at the expense of giving over arable land to alfalfa and other fodder crops. Sugarcane, to take another case, yielded a prized sweetening, a welcome addition to Indian diet, as well as fuel from the discarded fiber. Mustard and garlic finally, competed successfully as condiments with Indian peppers, and entailed no basic changes in the methods of agriculture.[16]

It also appears that "cultural crystallization" took place in the early years of the conquest: "The early decades in America were decades of decision, a time when new adjustments and colonial cultures were roughed out and the basic outlines set." [17]

The readings in this section will indicate some important and constant flow of ideas and materials back and forth across the Atlantic Ocean between the Iberian motherlands and their American colonies. Much more research must be undertaken, but enough is known to suggest the extent of this reciprocity in the history of Latin America.

[16] George Kubler, *Mexican Architecture of the Sixteenth Century*, vol. 2 (New Haven: Yale University Press, 1948), p. 419.

[17] Foster, *Culture and Conquest*, p. 234. For a valuable comparison of Spanish American culture traits by a veteran scholar, see Foster's "Report on an Ethnological Reconnaissance in Spain," *American Anthropologist*, 53 (1951), pp. 311–325.

THE PORTUGUESE BACKGROUND

1. Brazil's Portuguese Heritage Should Not Be Forgotten

STUART B. SCHWARTZ

Professor Schwartz is a representative of the vigorous school of younger Brazilianists that has developed during the last decade to bring fresh ideas and research power to the study of Portuguese colonial history. Owing much to the inspiration and example of such *grandes figuras* as Charles R. Boxer, they are, however, contributing their own insights and balanced views to the complicated and relatively unstudied history of colonial Brazil and other topics in the story of the widely scattered Portuguese empire. Here we have an excellent example of his interpretive work, which focuses on the social and cultural heritage transferred to Brazil "not by the government of Portugal, but by the Portuguese people."

There is a famous painting by Maria Margarida entitled *"Tres Meninas da Mesma Rua,"* which is often reproduced in books on Brazil. This painting symbolically depicts three beautiful girls representing each of the three major

Among Portuguese customs introduced to Brazil was the Moorish-inspired tradition that women should be secluded and not appear in public unless properly accompanied. This scene of a Portuguese merchant, followed by his heavily-veiled wife and maid-servant, appears in Murphy's account, Travels in Portugal, *published in 1795.*

From "The Uncourted Menina: Brazil's Portuguese Heritage" by Stuart B. Schwartz, *Luso-Brazilian Review*, 2 (Summer 1965) © 1965 by the regents of the University of Wisconsin, pp. 67–81, passim. Reprinted by permission.

racial components of Brazilian society: Indian, Negro and white. Anthropologists and other social scientists, perhaps lured by the exotic, have ardently courted the first two young ladies in the sense that much attention has been given to the Indian and Negro elements in Brazilian society. The white girl, however, has been neglected. This is especially true of the Portuguese element of Brazil which is obviously so crucial for an understanding of Brazil's past and present. Monograph after monograph can be found on almost all facets of the Negro and Indian contributions to Brazilian culture but information on the Portuguese remains scarce. . . .

The Portuguese heritage of Brazil can be examined on two different levels. One is the administrative, official aspect which amounts to the history of Portuguese colonial control of Brazil. The other is the social and cultural heritage transferred not by the government of Portugal, but by the Portuguese people. The two are at many points difficult to separate, but it is the social and cultural tradition which will be discussed here. What were the characteristics of the Portuguese colonizers? What aspects of Brazilian life are the result of Lusitanian influence? These are the primary questions. Almost everyone who writes on Brazil agrees that the common denominator of Brazilian culture is basically Portuguese. There remains to be studied, however, what these elements are, what changes they underwent, and how they were integrated into Brazilian culture.

Certainly, the starting point of an examination of Brazil's cultural debt to Portugal must be a discussion of the development and character of the Portuguese people. The Portuguese at the time of the conquest of Brazil were not a racially homogenous group and their culture was a result of a variety of contacts and developments. The original Lusitanians had, through contact with Phoenicians, Romans, French and English knights, Moors, Jews, and Negroes, acquired a complex of traditions and values which formed the basis of Portuguese society. In a sense the Portuguese were a people of mixed cultural and racial heritage, a fact that would be important in their settlement of Brazil. . . .

The Portuguese have been called a mixture of dreamers and of men of action who do not lack a practical side to their nature. They can be extremely pragmatic and adaptable when faced with a problem that calls for a practical solution. This plasticity and adaptability has been considered by some to be the basic key to the success of Portugal in creating a lasting civilization in Brazil. As an active dreamer, the Portuguese, if given an ideal, is capable of great efforts through determined and persistent action involving self-denial, sacrifice, and courage. When, however, the task is mediocre and does not arouse his interest, he lacks initiative. . . . It was the stimulation of his imagination and interest for the glory of conquest and battle, the lure of wealth, and the service of religion which motivated the Portuguese in the Age of Discovery.

The heart is the measure of all things for the Portuguese and he is basically human, amorous, and affectionate. The pleasures of the Lusitanian tend to be organic rather than intellectual and the Portuguese have a robust humor that can lead them to "Breughel-like frolicking." Violence and unnecessary suffering are avoided, as is the case in the Portuguese-style bullfight, or *tourada,* in which the bull is not killed. If outraged or dishonored, however, the Portuguese is capable of extreme and sudden violence. As will be shown below, this is especially true when the chastity of the female members of his family is concerned or when his own personal honor is at stake. The Portuguese has a strong belief in miracles and in the stroke of luck, as is evidenced by the popularity of the lottery in Portugal and as has been shown in the past by the cult of Sebastianism. This belief in miraculous solutions appears to have been inherited by the Brazilians, who have developed a "Deus é brasileiro" attitude toward their problems. This attitude has been reinforced, however, by Brazil's own peculiar history, especially in view of its economic cycles and boom-bust-boom experience.

The Portuguese, like his Iberian relatives, is an individualist who places great emphasis on personal relationships. He avoids impersonal, secondary relations and prefers to act within the broad ties of the family, often reinforcing these relations with the *compadrio* system. The "autarchy of the individual" and the emphasis on personality are constants of his nature which he will only renounce for a greater good. The result has often been either anarchy or extreme centralization tending toward dictatorship.

An aspect of Portuguese character which the people of Portugal like to claim as theirs alone in that of *saudade. Saudade* is an untranslatable word which seems to be a combination of sentimentality, homesickness, and nostalgia. This *saudade,* this sadness of character, is a current which runs deeply throughout Portuguese literature. At times it can become fatalistic and even morbid. The soul-rending *fado* heard in Lisbon originated as an expression of the *saudade* of the Portuguese colonizer in Brazil for his homeland. This longing for Europe, for the metropolis, which characterized many Portuguese in Brazil during the colonial period, has been viewed as one of the worst aspects of the Portuguese heritage of Brazil, for its result was the *mazombismo* of Brazil which depreciated things Brazilian and looked toward Europe, first Portugal and then France, for a model. No less a friend of the Portuguese then Gilberto Freyre has said, "since the end of the sixteenth century the Portuguese has lived parasitically on a past whose splendour he exaggerates." *Saudade,* however, in its less malignant aspects, is soft and sentimental — which is quite understandable when it is remembered that for the Portuguese the heart is the measure of all.

The penchant of the Portuguese for display and ostentation has been noted by many writers. Though there might be little to eat at home, there was always an air of pomp and gentry. . . . It seems, however, that this ostenta-

tion was not a matter of personal luxury and comfort but rather of imagination. Jorge Dias has noted that the Portuguese have the hardest beds in
Europe, while the streets are filled with automobiles. Poor people who lack
the least comfort in their home appear in the street in elegant dress. A similar
situation was noted in colonial Brazil and still exists today in rural areas, where
women whose dress at home may be ragged appear at mass in finery to which
all attention is given. This "Sunday best" is known in Brazil as *traje domin-
gueiro* or *roupa de ver-a-Deus*. Gilberto Freyre, using Thorstein Veblen's
term, has called this ostentation "conspicuous waste," and has noted that in
the colonial period women who had so many jewels they could not wear them
all at the same time often put them on the slaves who followed their mistresses
to church.

Coupled with the ostentation of the Portuguese has been his attitude toward
work. There existed, during the period of conquest, a depreciation of manual
labor. Peasants, although they labored hard, shared the *fidalgo* ideal with the
nobility. This attitude was found among the Spaniards as well. The Iberian
hoped to get rich quickly, perhaps to own land, but not to labor. Work was
for the slave. In fact, in Portugal the verb "to work," *trabalhar,* was often replaced with *mourejar,* "to work like a Moor." Perhaps this attitude of antipathy to manual labor was due to the fact that work indicates the submission
of the individual will to an external force, and the Iberian with his emphasis
on the individual could not condone this. The result in Brazil was a "bandeir-
ante spirit" in which all energy was devoted to the quick profit. Even in agriculture the emphasis was on the large profit, and at times the Portuguese
government had to legislate to force plantation owners to grow food crops.
The result of this attitude was the development in Brazil of a "gentleman
complex" which depreciated manual labor and emphasized non-functional
education as a sign of breeding to be coupled with wealth. Even among the
Brazilian lower classes the idea of the quick fortune is pervasive, and men in
the Amazon often desert farming in hopes of a rapidly amassed fortune in
rubber-hunting. In the mind of the Portuguese productive activity has had
much less value than contemplation and love, and a dignified idleness always
seemed more noble than the "insane struggle for the daily bread."

The most important aspect of Portuguese character, or at least the most
often discussed, is his adaptability. The Portuguese lacks the flame and or-
thodoxy of the Castilian; rather, he is a compromiser without immutable prejudices who has been able to adapt to climates, occupations, cultures, and races
in an exceptional manner. The quality of flexibility and tolerance of other
races led in Brazil to miscegenation of an unprecedented extent. This miscegenation and the adaptation of the Portuguese to his new environment has
been the basis on which Gilberto Freyre has advocated a new field of study,
"Lusotropicalism," or the study of Portuguese integration in the tropics.

Much has been written on the capacity of the Portuguese people to mix with other races. As has been noted earlier, they are themselves a mixed race in which Semitic and Negro elements are important. Some writers, like Freyre, have attributed the race mixing in Brazil to Portugal's contact with the Moors, the concept of the *moura encantada* as the ideal and epitome of sex and beauty for the Portuguese being transferred to the darker-skinned Indians. This ideal, plus the social plasticity of the colonizer in which no firm racial lines were drawn, has often been cited as the prime reason for the success of miscegenation in Brazil. It has been pointed out, however, that the scarcity of women may have had much to do with the extent of racial mixing, and in instances of colonization in Brazil in which the colonist was accompanied by his wife, as in Santa Catarina, much less miscegenation took place. Slavery, of course, played a role in the process of race mixture in Brazil.

Whatever the cause, miscegenation did take place in Brazil. Slavery was certainly a cause, but slavery, says Freyre, was inevitable. The result of lasting importance was the creation of a psychological and cultural unity of the Brazilian people. An author less convinced of the benefits of race mixture, especially through illegal unions, has noted the characteristics of the *mestiços* or *mulatos* as, "emotional imbalance, inner discord, insecurity, instability, resentment, marginalism, laziness, melancholy," and a constant search for a father-image. . . .

The family in Brazil has been considered the most important institution in the history of the nation and has played a dominant role in the course of Brazil's history. The Brazilian colonial family has often been thought of as that patriarchal institution depicted in the works of Gilberto Freyre which describe the sugar region of the Northeast. The colonial family seen as patriarchal, extended, multifunctional, and of "towering dominance" has been questioned to some extent, since in Brazil variation between groups in the social strata is enormous. The ecological and economic conditions in Brazil did play a part in the continuance of the extended family, as did the weakness of the colonial government. . . .

The prescribed roles of men and women in both the Brazilian and the Portuguese family are based on the virility/virginity complexes. The woman is expected to lead a secluded life, never appearing in public unless properly accompanied. Freyre has laid this tradition to Moorish antecedents. After marriage the woman is expected to be mother and housekeeper, not a companion to her husband. Virginity is a primary requisite before marriage, and should the bride be found lacking in this respect the groom has proper grounds for annulment of the marriage. Any extra-marital relations on the part of the woman are considered grounds for separation. It is common, however, for a husband to kill both the unfaithful wife and her lover and then claim temporary insanity. This is expected and accepted community behavior.

In contrast to the female role in the upper-class Brazilian family is the virility complex of the male, which encourages sexual contact at an early age, ridicules male chastity, and considers extra-marital sexual relations permissible. With the home, however, the male is expected to act as guardian and protector. The males of the family are also expected to be avengers of the family's honor, especially that of its female members. This attitude in Brazil has been reinforced by immigration from Portugal, Spain, and southern Italy. Thus far, the above description can be applied to both Brazilian and Portuguese upper-class families.

The lower-class Brazilian family places much less emphasis on the virginity/virility complex. Marriage is far less stable, and extended kinship groups are not viewed as of great importance. These facts tend to substantiate Willems' thesis that the patriarchal, extended family lessens in importance as one descends the social scale. A similar situation might be expected in Portugal, but such is not the case. The Portuguese lower-class rural families are based on property, which acts as an adhesive force, holding the family together and reinforcing traditional attitudes. . . . The rural Brazilian family is weak, for it can offer little, and its children tend to leave the paternal home to seek better-paying jobs. It is significant to note that the Brazilian-type rural family is to be found in Alentejo among migratory workers. Here is a case of economic conditions affecting traditional patterns.

Another difference between lower-class Brazilian and Portuguese rural families derives from the tendency of the Portuguese to live in villages or small communities, which act as factors of control and stabilization through community pressure. The more dispersed nature of many of Brazil's rural families means a lessening of community pressure and more individuality and plasticity in family structure. Willems in his studies has shown that the original Portuguese family structure did not remain unchanged in Brazil but was altered to meet ecological, human, and economic conditions, and due to these new changes new structural organizations developed.

The patriarchal family usually attributed in its origins to Portugal must undergo some review, since it has been discovered that in some regions the patriarchal family is not as dominant an institution as had been thought. . . . In parts of the Algarve, the women are the members of the family who take an active part in community life. In Brazil, similar developments can be noted which seem to be exceptions to the patriarchal generalization. Women in São Paulo of land-holding but not of planter-class families often raise their own produce and sell it, keeping the profits themselves. Occasionally, these women engage in speculative loans. These economic activities indicate a degree of independence not usually associated with the Brazilian woman. In both Portugal and Brazil the role of the patriarchal family must be studied further, for it would seem that important exceptions to it do exist. . . .

It is in the everyday life of the Brazilian, especially the rural Brazilian, that the Portuguese heritage is to be seen. The language of Brazil is Portuguese and the style of life of the Brazilian reflects the Portuguese heritage in a hundred ways. For example, the *mutirão*, or mutual work party, although found among Africans and Indians, can be seen in Alentejo, Beira, and Minho. The festivities in Brazil following a *mutirão* are found only in Portuguese origins. Here is but one more example of the duration of the Lusitanian element in Brazil.

The aspect of the Portuguese heritage of Brazil which is most apparent in everyday life and is probably easiest to study is that of the popular folk traditions of Brazilian society. Certainly, the administrative actions of the metropolis during the colonial period played an important role in the formation of Brazilian society just as the Church did in conjunction with the Jesuit Order. But it is the popular rather than the official traditions to which I am referring. . . . Folk tales and folk songs, as well as *louvores populares* to the Virgin, can serve as a basis for tracing the transmission of Portuguese popular cultural elements to Brazil, especially since much work had been done on both sides of the Atlantic in collecting these songs and stories. Théo Brandão in his *Trovas Populares de Alagoas* noted the adaptation of Portuguese *trovas* to Brazilian conditions with modifications due to environment, local expressions, and structural changes. . . . Also, it seems that the custom of the *desafio*, the improvisation of verses by two contending balladeers so clearly explained by Euclides da Cunha in *Os Sertões*, is a Lusitanian custom. . . . From infancy, the Brazilian child is exposed to the Portuguese heritage of his nation. The Brazilian's first games and playthings and even the bogey-men used to frighten him are of Lusitanian origin. The Papão and the Cuca, two such mythical creatures, can be traced directly to Portugal. . . . Even the *lobisomen*, or werewolves, do not stem from any Indian forest spirit but are to be found in Portuguese folk traditions.

The extent to which the Lusitanian folk tradition is dominant in Brazil varies greatly within the diverse cultural regions of the nation. The influence of other cultural elements dilutes the strength of Portuguese cultural tradition while enriching it at the same time. Aside from the obvious cultural differences of non-Portuguese immigrants, other traditions continue to exist, but usually within the basic Portuguese framework. For example, in Rio Grande do Sul the Hispanic influences of the La Plata area are strong, while in the Amazon the economic and cultural patterns show heavy Indian influence. In other areas, particularly the old sugar-producing regions of Bahia and Pernambuco, the cultural heritage of the Negro is evident. Brazilian culture is not Portuguese culture transplanted, but without this element it would be much different than it is.

Certainly, one of the most enduring aspects of Portuguese cultural heritage in Brazil is that of Catholicism: that special brand of Catholicism characteristic of Portugal. The agony-torn Christs of Spain and the soaring Gothic Spanish cathedrals are lacking in Portuguese Catholicism, which was and is a humanistic form of Christianity with anthropomorphic tendencies, often giving special importance to saints associated with love and agricultural fertility. It was the body of Catholic thought which had been softened by long contact with the Moors but which had left a place for saints of the Reconquest. This last aspect can be seen in Brazil in the existence of Sebastianism mixed with other elements in the messianic movements of the Northeast. Religion in Portugal and then in Brazil served a social as well as a spiritual function.

The parallelism and the cultural borrowing of Brazilian Catholicism from its Portuguese antecedents is extensive. The importance of shrines, pilgrimages, and the ceremony of the blessing, all so important in Brazilian Catholicism, stem from the Catholic traditions of Portugal. In both countries the June cycle of the three major saints — St. Anthony, St. John, and St. Peter — is a high point of the religious calendar, even though in Brazil June is a winter not a summer month as it is in Portugal. In Brazil and Portugal St. Anthony is a *santo pândego* or *santo folião,* a patron of revelry, a forgiver of human weakness, and a noted matchmaker to whom ribald songs are often sung. Also, saints' images are often treated like human beings and are punished or rewarded as their case may merit. It has been noted that Portuguese seamen who have prayed for a favorable wind and fail to receive it lash the saint's effigy to the mast and flog it. In Brazil a non-compliant saint's image may be put uncomfortably near a fire or even pounded to dust in a mortar.

The list of particularly Lusitanian features of Brazilian religion, especially in its folk manifestations, could be extended to great lengths. The impact of the Portuguese form of Catholicism on Brazilian religious and social life is undeniable. It must be remembered, however, that contact of Portugal with Brazil was a historical process extending over at least three centuries, and that the element of change is a part of this process. . . . To continue the analogy made at the beginning of this paper, the third *menina* deserves to be courted, for she comes from a fine old family which has left her a rich inheritance.

THE SPANISH BACKGROUND

2. *Spain Transmitted to America Many of Her Medieval Accomplishments*

LUIS WECKMANN

Mexican diplomatist and professor Luis Weckmann is one of the few scholars who has systematically studied the medieval customs, ideas, and institutions that Spain carried to the New World. Though his specific examples are generally taken from Mexican history, his analysis and description may also be applied to other parts of the empire, and help to explain the way in which "Spain was able to transmit to America, as a living product and not as a dead tradition, many of her mediaeval accomplishments."

For the mediaevalist it is interesting to note that there exists a natural continuity between the Middle Ages in Europe — and especially the Spanish Middle Ages — and the early institutional and cultural life of the Ibero-American colonies. As I hope to prove, the Middle Ages found their last expression on this side of the Atlantic, where, after the termination of the mediaeval period in Europe, an appropriate setting for the development of mediaeval ideals existed for an extended period in the Spanish New World while, contemporarily in Europe, the Religious Reformation and the so-termed Italian Renaissance were causing the abandonment of the essentials that sustained mediaeval Christendom.

Although Renaissance thought has its importance in the shaping of early Latin American civilization, and some of the conquerors, notably Cortés, were Renaissance men in their fondness for the visible, material things — grandeur, wealth, fame — it is nonetheless true that some old mediaeval trends, perhaps nowhere stronger than in Spain, the land of the perennial crusading, greatly influenced the early course of Latin American life. That should not surprise anyone. Forced to remain long in the background of European evolution, due to her almost constant state of warfare, Spain realized, later than any other

From "The Middle Ages in the Conquest of America" by Luis Weckmann, *Speculum*, 26 (1951), pp. 130–139, passim. Reprinted by permission of the author and of the Mediaeval Academy of America.

country in western Europe, the flowering of her mediaeval civilization. Thus, Spain was able to transmit to America, as a living product and not as a dead tradition, many of her mediaeval accomplishments. There was no waning of the Middle Ages in Spain as there was during the fourteenth and fifteenth centuries in the rest of Europe. Spain found herself in the autumn of the Middle Ages during the first two centuries of her modern history, when, against insurmountable odds, she strove to keep alive and dominant such mediaeval ideals as those embodied in the *ecclesia universalis* and in the universal empire. The conception of a universal empire, the Company of Jesus, the new mysticism of St. Theresa and of St. John of the Cross, the new scholasticism of Vitoria and Suárez, the romance of chivalry, the *Romancero* and the theater represented the late fruits the Spanish mediaeval spirit produced well into the modern age.

Columbus, the first link between the Old World and the New, stands in a clearer light, perhaps, if we envisage him not so much as the first of the modern explorers but as the last of the great mediaeval travelers. Although there is no doubt that Columbus' mind was affected by Renaissance trends, we can still say that this man, the spiritual heir of Marco Polo, was impelled by mediaeval quests and geographical puzzles towards the exploration of new routes of navigation. Was it not on the basis of Marco Polo's report (on his first voyage Columbus took with him Marco Polo's writings), even if this was complemented by newer works, that he set out to find the fabulously rich islands, off the coast of Asia, so lavishly and imaginatively described by the Venetian? Still other mediaeval legends concerning the existence of islands to the West and current in Columbus' days were known to him and in part impelled him to the undertaking of his voyages. Antillia (whence Antilles), St. Brandan's Isle, Brasil, the Island of Seven Cities, were among those legendary isles. Columbus never outgrew these geographical conceptions. In all his travels, when navigating through the Antilles or bordering the coasts of the American mainland, he thought (as his diary shows) that he was visiting the many islands which, as he said, were depicted in mediaeval maps at the end of the Orient in the vicinity of Cathay. . . .

Perhaps most poignantly mediaeval of all was the conviction displayed by Columbus in the course of this third voyage, when he firmly asserted that he had found nothing less than the Terrestrial Paradise. To support his assertion, he quotes, in genuine mediaeval fashion, the opinions of St. Isidore, of the Venerable Bede, of the "master of scholastic history" (i.e., Petrus Comestor), of St. Ambrose and of Johannes Scotus, all of whom had placed the earthly Paradise in the East. The earth, Columbus claims, is pear-shaped and Paradise lies in its highest summit. He reports that he was able to locate the Terrestrial Paradise after having encountered the mouths of the four rivers of Genesis that proceed from the Tree of Life, when he mistook the delta of the Orinoco river for the paradisiacal streams. The site of Paradise was so rich, asserted the discoverer, that with its wealth he could finance an army of 100,000 infantrymen and 10,000 cavalrymen with which the old mediaeval goal of recovering the Holy Sepulchre could be attained. Columbus also rejoices at the thought that he has found a new land where the Lord can be served by the divulgation of His Holy Name and Faith among so many new peoples, a truly mediaeval attitude. In other minor details, such as in the method of time computations, in Columbus' writings as well as in those of his pilots and staff, and in the diaries of subsequent explorers, mediaeval usages are likewise followed.

The mediaeval world was surrounded by a realm of fable. Beyond the known lands there existed others, populated in mediaeval fantasy (drawn, it is true, from ancient sources, and distorted) by all kinds of mythical beings, monsters, enchantments so charmingly depicted in mediaeval *mappaemundi*. Such were, for instance, the giants, pygmies, gimnosophists, sciopodies, Amazons, cinocephali, boys with white hair, people who lived on smells, headless beings with eyes on the stomach, bearded women, etc., so dear to the mind of St. Isidore, together with griffons, dragons, the Sea of Darkness, the Land of Prester John. As the discoverers of the late fifteenth and early sixteenth centuries came to venture to the edges of the world it was supposed that, sooner or later, they would encounter some of these mythical figures whose existence was, at least for a great number of them, beyond dispute. Of special prominence in the early history of Latin America is the quest for the Amazons, which seemed to have fascinated practically every conqueror and which has left a permanent souvenir in the names of the mightiest river of the continent and of the northernmost of Spain's provinces in America: California. Columbus already, in his second voyage, refers to a certain island, Madanina, inhabited, according to Indian versions, only by women, information that is put down soberly and sceptically by the historian of the Indies. Cortés, in a letter to the king in 1524, refers to what is now Lower California — presumably an island and at that time unvisited by Spaniards — saying that it was inhabited only by women who, at given times, received visits of men from the mainland. Of the issue only female children were kept, the males being disposed of. The very name "California" apparently derives from an island of Amazons, ruled by Queen Calafia and mentioned in *Las Sergas de Esplandián*, a Spanish romance of chivalry and sequel of the famous *Amadís de Gaula*. . . .

Among the other recurrent legends of early American exploration, *El Dorado*, the gilded man whose kingdom was so rich that his subjects painted him every day with gold and washed him off at night, and Quivira and the Seven Cities of Cíbola, founded by seven mediaeval bishops, have conspicuous places, the second legend having led to Coronado's discovery of the American Southwest, where to this day New Mexico's folk plays represent a survival of mediaeval mystery plays. López de Gómara, author of the *Historia General de las Indias*, the first seven chapters of which are in spirit and in form still mediaeval, weighs the reasons advanced by the fathers of the church and by ancient writers for and against the existence of antipodes. After wearisome references to Lactantius, St. Augustine, St. Isidore and others, the author finally accepts the probability of their existence in the New World, after which he passes on to discuss the belief of the inhabitants of Iceland that Purgatory is to be located under their island. Among the fabulous beings which the imagination of the Spaniards places somewhere in America, room is reserved for the Devil himself. According to Gómara, the Devil is the principal god worshipped in a certain island of the Caribbean Sea where he appears many times and "even speaks" to his devotees. To balance this, we also find the Apostle St. James, the Patron Saint of Spain, fighting side by side with the Spaniards in many of their military engagements. The New World is, no doubt, a land of hidden marvels, of untrodden mysteries; the land, as Columbus said, of Alpha and Omega, where the sun rises and where the sun sets, the beginning and end of the earth.

That the Spaniard of the sixteenth century was naturally prone to believe in such marvels can be explained in part by the fact that the romances of chivalry, partially outmoded in the rest of Europe, were still very popular among Spanish readers. Ferdinand Columbus, son of the Discoverer, heads the list of prominent men in the history of the New World who were attracted by this type of reading. When the army of Cortés, after an exhausting march, finally catches its first glimpse of the city of Tenochtitlan, strange and beautiful, mirroring its colors in the lake upon which it was built, Bernal Díaz, the soldier-chronicler of the expedition, merely comments: "We were astonished and told ourselves that this seemed like a thing of enchantment, such as they related in the book of Amadís," after which the conquering army entered the Aztec capital with all the trappings of mediaeval splendor. Later on, when a rebellious soldier is condemned to death he finds no better way to express his disagreement with his sentence, which he attributes to tyranny rather than to justice, than to hope that sometimes, in a better future, the Twelve Peers will rule — a reference to the *Historia de Carlomagno y de los Doce Pares,* a romance of chivalry first published in Spain in (the date is very revealing) 1525.

In some episodes of the civil and urban life of the early colony, such as the dinner offered in 1538 by the first viceroy of New Spain to commemorate the signing of a peace treaty between Charles V and Francis I of France, all the splendor of the most magnificent of all mediaeval courts, that of the dukes of Burgundy, was reproduced. On this occasion, the *pièces de résistance* were huge pastries filled with live quail and rabbits. The *mises en scène,* a favorite device of the Burgundian dukes to entertain their guests and to display their wealth and magnificence, were also continued in New Spain, where, for example, the main square of Mexico City would be converted into a lake and a naval battle fought around a fortress built on an artificial island, the whole episode representing the siege of Rhodes by the Turks. Nothing strange in this, if it is remembered that Charles V of Spain, himself born in Ghent, was the heir of Burgundian policies and of Burgundian grandeur through his father, Philip the Fair.

In the legal and institufional realm of early America the mediaeval imprint is equally patent. The Spaniards of the period retained the ideal of a universal empire, of whose present incumbent they were but servants. Charles V remained for them the *dominus mundi,* the legitimate and God-ordained lord of the world. Sometimes, they found no better reason than this to demand from Indian rulers their submission to the king. Typical is the case of Francisco Pizarro in Peru, and his counsellor, Fray Vicente de Valverde, both of whom informed the last of the ruling Incas that they were the envoys of the pope and the emperor, the lords of the world, who demanded his submission to their authority. In the legal terminology of this and of later ages we find many feudal reminiscences too: the Indians are regarded as "vassals," a somewhat ideal conception badly shattered by reality; in the creation of titled estates with which the conquerors were rewarded, in the terminology used in the documents of donation with their mention of woods, pools, meadows and so forth, all are mindful of feudal Europe. The oath, a basic institution of the feudal age, where it sustained the very fabric of society, plays an important role in appeasement of internal quarrels, and in setting up alliances between the conquerors. When, for instance, Almagro and Francisco Pizarro were reconciled at Cuzco, they attended mass together and, joining hands over the consecrated host, swore not to malign one another, not to send separate reports to the emperor, and to share equally all profits — a scene which recalls the famous story of the oath exacted from King Alfonso VI by the Cid and which proved, may I add, equally ineffective.

The pastimes of the conquerors are still those of a feudal class: tournaments, tourneys of canes (*juegos de cañas*), hawking, etc., all of which presupposed a mounted nobility. When Las Casas had in mind his scheme of colonization in South America, at Cumaná, he founded an order of "Knights of the Golden Spur" to finance it. Other usages, such as the cutting of boughs from trees in token of taking possession of the land and the reservation of hidden treasures to the king, the "royal fifth," are also reminiscent of feudal practices. The *derecho de lanzas* paid to the king by the early *encomenderos* corresponds in general to a feudal scutage. The *encomienda* system itself, by placing a certain number of natives under the protection and guide of a Spaniard, could be considered fuedalistic because conceived in the spirit of patronage, so characteristic of the feudal world. But since land tenure was not included in this system, the *encomienda* was deprived of what could have been its most feudal characteristic. Still, a contemporary Mexican scholar, Federico Gómez de Orozco, thinks it possible to trace the *encomienda* back to mediaeval Spain, where conditions similar to those in sixteenth-century New Spain were created as the Christian kingdoms of the peninsula in their southward expansion were faced with the problem of a newly subjected class of non-Christians, and these new vassals of the crown were placed in trust (*encomienda*) with the military orders which were made responsible for their spiritual welfare. Another thought should be given to the *Capitaneas* or administrative divisions of Brazil in the colonial era that resembles very strongly the type of administration prevalent during the late Middle Ages in the Madeira and Azores islands; and the *sesmarias,* the Portuguese mediaeval form of land grant introduced in Brazil after 1500, cannot pass unmentioned. Also, the mediaeval Spanish institution of the municipality — of ancient extraction but fortified by the role of the townspeople played in the War of Reconquest — the *cabildo abierto,* already obsolete in the peninsula, was revived in America by the conquerors, eager to preserve for themselves and for their descendants a voice in the internal government of the colonies.

Perhaps nowhere else is more visible the imprint of the Middle Ages in America, and especially in Mexico, than in the realm of art. Military architecture in the beginnings of the sixteenth century, the early fortresses and castles built by the first conquerors, with their moats, drawbridges and turrets, such as the castles of Ulúa and Acapulco, are still genuinely mediaeval, and the same can be said of such walled cities as Campeche. In regard to religious edifices, conventual architecture of the first and even of the second half of the sixteenth century might be classified, according to Manuel Toussaint, Mexico's leading critic of Colonial art, as a mediaeval survival. It can be said, adds that authority, that the great fortified temples and convents of this period stand as the final expression of the Middle Ages in the world. . . .

Perhaps the most striking phenomenon in relation to mediaeval architectural survivals in America exists in the construction of Romanesque churches and other buildings of Romanesque type. The church of the Franciscan convent of Pátzcuaro is, essentially, a Spanish Romanesque church which could have been built in the twelfth century. Romanesque chapels and capitals adorn many sixteenth-century churches. This is not as surprising as it may appear: Romanesque constructions in New Spain are not, strictly speaking, afterthoughts but follow a "natural" architectural evolution. Romanesque style took a deep and lasting hold in those European countries that had long been a part of the Roman empire, such as Spain and southern France, regions in which Gothic may be regarded more or less as a foreign intrusion. Old Roman structural devices and constructions remained alive — even though suffering alterations and decay — for many centuries in the Mediterranean countries, and the fact that Spanish *cortijo* basically follows the plan of the Roman *villa,* which likewise is copied in the plantation or *hacienda* of central and northern Mexico, is an eloquent proof of the lasting character that the Roman genius gave to its edifices. The pattern of the unwalled town with a fortified church featuring strong walls, ramparts, merlons, narrow skylights, so familiar in the Mexican central countryside, has its precedent in mediaeval mendicant practices, especially in southern France, like Spain, a Mediterranean land. . . .

The cultural atmosphere of sixteenth-century New Spain represents in many respects an unfolding of mediaeval Spain. In the colleges, and notably in the Royal and Pontifical University of Mexico founded in 1551 — whose constitutions and organization were copied from those of Salamanca, and where graduates gave each member of the cloister "six fat hens, four pounds of cold viands and a pair of gloves" after their reception — St. Thomas Aquinas and Duns Scotus reigned supreme at least until the eighteenth century. In the days of Carlos de Sigüenza y Góngora, the University of Mexico, in its government and curriculum, was still an interesting and curious survival of European mediaevalism. The early Mexican historiographers and, more notably so, the first Spanish historians of America, followed the practice of the mediaeval chroniclers, in transcribing in their writings material from older sources without bothering to acknowledge their debt. There are traces, I believe, of Spiritual Franciscanism in the teachings and writings of Friar Peter of Ghent, one of the first Franciscans to arrive in Mexico and one of the most venerable figurees of the early history of the Mexican church. The councils of that period, needless to say, echoed those of contemporary Europe. . . .

Theology was in colonial days and even beyond, down to the Wars of Reform, the queen and pinnacle of all university studies, with the *Sententiae* of Peter Lombard the undisputed text in that field. Latin remained compulsory for university work throughout the Spanish commonwealth until the days of King Ferdinand VI, and to the study of Latin that of oriental languages and of native languages was added as the result, I believe, of the impulse given in this direction in mediaeval days by St. Raymond Lull. The power and influence of the church in colonial Mexico, especially that of the mendicant orders, was considerable. A distinguished contemporary Mexican historian, Pablo Martínez del Rio, has said "not without exaggeration, of course" that the history of colonial Mexico is the history of mediaeval Europe without the strife of the Investitures. Religious festivities, the holidays *par excellence* until the nineteenth century (and, to a certain extent, even today, especially in rural areas), combined in many instances Christian purposes and pagan ceremonies in a process of syncretism that the practical genius of the church fostered in Europe in the era that followed the Germanic migrations. The old practice of the church in mediaeval Europe of building Christian sanctuaries on the site of heathen sacred abodes, was repeated in Mexico, where many a church of today is built upon a pagan pyramid. Religious theater, especially that celebrated in the *atria* of churches — in many instances today, the *atrium* of the local church, is still the center of town life — is also remindful of mediaeval practices. The dominance of religious themes in colonial painting, architecture and sculpture (and the fact that sculpture was in many cases ancillary to architecture) as well as the noticeable activity of the miniaturists in the sixteenth century and after, are very suggestive. The Inquisition was not suppressed in Mexico until 1812. The great devotion to the Virgin, even today the most cherished form of piety, would have been most pleasing to St. Bernard of Clairvaux. . . .

As I have tried to point out, the study of mediaeval survivals in America is a fascinating field of research, for the better understanding of the early history of the New World and for its later currents and developments where mediaeval ideas and practices are palpable even today, as well as for the better appreciation of the intrinsic vitality and permanence of such ideas and practices which as living forces were able to survive their own atmosphere and their own epoch and to bear magnificent fruits in a different environment beyond the seas in the New World which in many respects came to fulfill mediaeval expectancies. . . .

3. The New World Was a Place of Wonder and Enchantment Populated with Mysterious and Bewildering People

LEWIS HANKE

Fantasy has often exercised a subtle and persistent influence in the lives of men and women. The conquest of America afforded Spaniards a rich opportunity to use their imagination, and also to speculate about the wondrous lands and mysterious people the conquistadors found there. Some classical doctrines, such as Aristotle's views on the natural slavery of certain peoples, were dusted off and applied to the Indians to justify the claims of those who considered them inferior beings fit only to serve the superior Spaniards.

The Spaniards who actually saw America not only became tremendously excited and stimulated but they tended to look at the New World through medieval spectacles. The wealth of ideas and legends developed with such luxuriance during the Middle Ages was transferred at once to America; this medie-

From *Aristotle and the American Indians* by Lewis Hanke (Chicago: Henry Regnery Co., 1959), pp. 3–11, passim. Reprinted by permission of Henry Regnery Company and The Bodley Head, Ltd.

val influence was especially marked during the early years of the discovery and conquest. . . .

Spanish captains went forth to their conquest expecting to encounter many kinds of mythical beings and monsters depicted in medieval literature: giants, pygmies, dragons, griffins, white-haired boys, bearded ladies, human beings adorned with tails, headless creatures with eyes in their stomachs or breasts, and other fabulous folk. For a thousand years a great reservoir of curious ideas on man and semi-men had been forming in Europe, and was now freely drawn upon in America. St. Augustine in his *City of God* had a whole chapter on "Whether the descendants of Adam or of the sons of Noah produced monstrous races of men," and by the end of the fifteenth century a rich body of fantastic ideas was ready for use in America. Trumpet-blowing apes, for example, "formed parts of a loosely defined pictorial cycle combining subjects from the world of fable with the exotic beasts of the Bestiaries and the Marvels of the East." It is not surprising, therefore, to find that the early historian Gonzalo Fernández de Oviedo had heard of a Peruvian monkey that "was no less extraordinary than the griffins," for it had a long tail, with the upper half of its body covered with many-hued feathers and the lower half with smooth, reddish fur. It could sing, "when it felt like it," in the same dulcet tones as a nightingale or a lark.

Wild men also had captured popular imagination during the Middle Ages. They were depicted on the façades of churches, as decorations for manuscripts, and in tapestries, as ferocious beings of wild mien rending lions barehanded or smashing their skulls with trees or mighty clubs. Wild men served as jamb figures on the façade of the fifteenth-century San Gregorio monastery in Valladolid in which Las Casas lived during the 1550 disputation with Sepúlveda. The wildman motif was much used in Spain, crossed the Atlantic with Spanish workmen, and is seen on the façade of the Casa del Montejo in Yucatan, built in 1549. Wild men also supported the arms of Charles V in Tlaxcala. Given this medieval mélange of man, beast, and mythical creature, we are not surprised to find that a 1498 edition of John of Holywood's *Sphaera Mundi* describes the inhabitants of the New World as being "blue in colour and with square heads." One of the earliest pictures of American natives, printed as a wood engraving about 1505, showed the same fantastic spirit. The caption read as follows:

> They go naked, both men and women; they have well-shaped bodies, and in colour nearly red; they bore holes in their cheeks, lips, noses and ears, and stuff these holes with blue stones, crystals, marble and alabaster, very fine and beautiful. This custom is followed alone by the men. They have no personal property, but all things are in common. They all live

together without a king and without a government, and every one is his
own master. They take for wives whom they first meet, and in all this
they have no rule. They also war with each other, and without art or
rule. And they eat one another, and those they slay are eaten, for human
flesh is a common food. In the houses salted human flesh is hung up to
dry. They live to be a hundred and fifty years old, and are seldom
sick. . . .

Fifteenth-century Europeans had assumed their knowledge of the world
to be exact, and the appearance of a vast unknown continent across the seas
shook their confidence in themselves. Ingenious attempts were made to
demonstrate that the early Christian authorities foreshadowed that shattering
event, the discovery of America. If the new lands could be related somehow
to the world they knew, a bridge could be built between the known and the
unknown. The natives of this marvellous new world were, of course, at the
centre of speculation. Even before the first decade had passed, these plumed
and painted peoples — so inevitably and so erroneously called Indians —
had become the principal mystery which perplexed the Spanish nation, conquistadores, ecclesiastics, crown, and common citizens alike. Who were they?
Whence came they? What was their nature, their capacity for Christianity and
European civilization? Most important of all, what relationship would be the
right one for the Spaniards to establish with them?

The popular image, in the first feverish months, of a terrestrial paradise
was soon succeeded by that of a hostile continent peopled with armed warriors rushing out of the tropical forests or strange cities to resist the advance
of the Spanish soldiers and the missionary efforts of their companion friars.
The early suppositions that the lost Ten Tribes of Israel were the progenitors
of the Indian — held by more than one serious writer of the day — or even
the later idea that in some mysterious way the Welsh nation had sent out
these strange shoots — failed to answer satisfactorily the urgent basic
questions: Who and what are these creatures? How shall we treat them? Can
they be Christianized and brought to a civilized way of life? How shall this
be attempted, by war or by peaceful persuasion? The conquistadores tended
to ask rather pointedly: When may just war be waged to compel the Indians
to serve God and the king and us? And the ecclesiastics asked eagerly: How
can the natives be made to change from what they are to what they ought to
be?

Two circumstances were responsible for these questions, which were asked
by no other European colonizing nation with such general and genuine concern. The first was the nature of the Spanish people themselves, a people legalistic, passionate, given to extremes, and fervently Catholic. Three events of

the year 1492 reflect some of the most fundamental characteristics of Spaniards and their history. Granada, the last of the Moorish kingdoms, fell to the Catholic Kings Ferdinand and Isabella on January 2, the Jews were next expelled, and on August 3 Columbus set sail. The final conquest of Granada was the climax of a long national effort to establish Christian hegemony in Spain. This long travail had helped to prepare the nation for larger tasks. Isabella herself discovered this in that same year, 1492, when she bluntly asked the scholar Antonio de Nebrija, as he presented to her his Spanish *Gramática,* the first grammar of a European modern language ever written: "What is it for?", and the Bishop of Avila, speaking on behalf of the scholar, replied: "Your Majesty, language is the perfect instrument of empire."

The second circumstance was the nature of the dominion exercised by the Spanish crown in America, by which the Spaniards felt themselves responsible for the conversion of the natives. The decrees of Pope Alexander VI, the famous bulls of donation of 1493, which were used at first to justify the exertion of Spanish power in the new lands, specifically entrusted to the crown of Castile the Christianization of these lands. Without becoming embroiled, as the Spaniards themselves became, in the legal and moral implications of these papal pronouncements, we may be clear that the Spaniards had, logically, to determine Indian nature and capacity before they could legitimately pursue either conquest or Christianization.

Most Spaniards, no matter what attitude they developed towards the Indians, were usually profoundly stirred by them. Kings and the Council of the Indies instituted prolonged and formal enquiries in both Spain and America on their nature. Few significant figures of the conquest failed to deliver themselves of opinions on the Indian's capacity for Christianity, ability to work, and general aptitude for European civilization. Among the documents which remain to us are not only opinions but also numerous and curious proposals for the protection and welfare of the Indians. Early in his career Las Casas proposed the introduction of Negro slaves to the islands, in order to spare Indians the heavy labour which was destroying them, but later repented and opposed Negro slavery as well as Indian slavery, "and for the same reasons." Spaniards never fought, however, as hard or as consistently against Negro slavery as they did on behalf of the Indians, not even Las Casas. Despite his final rejection of Negro slavery, as late as 1544 he owned several Negro slaves and no document has come to light which reveals any concerted opposition to Negro slavery during the sixteenth century. Why did the consciences of Spaniards twinge more easily for Indians than for Negroes? Perhaps Iberian peoples had become accustomed to having Moslem Negro slaves, and Indians were not only new to them but had never had an opportunity to hear the faith before. The Jesuits Alonso de Sandoval and Pedro

Claver were to work on behalf of Negroes in the seventeenth century but the moral conscience of the modern world was first roused by the plight of the American Indian.

Many men and many methods were engaged in the attempt to help the American Indians. In the same month (May, 1550) that saw the beginning of the famous discussion on the nature of the Indian, a Sevillan named Cristóbal Muñoz obtained a contract from the king to introduce 100 camels into Peru. Why? To spare the Indians the bearing of heavy burdens up and down the Andes. The archives of Spain and America are full of absorbing documentation on what the conquerors thought of the conquered people in this first widespread meeting of races in modern times. The amount and quality of the information available is unparalleled in the records of any other colonizing nation, and constitutes a wealth of material not yet fully exploited by anthropologists.

As the conquerors and clerics moved forward into America in the uneasy partnership which the crown's double purpose of political dominion and religious conversion enjoined upon them, stubborn facts and theological convictions clashed resoundingly. The voices of individuals and of different factions — ecclesiastics, soldiers, colonists, and royal officials in America as well as of men of action and thought in Spain — rose continually during the sixteenth century in a loud chorus of conflicting advice to the Spanish kings and the Council of the Indies. Each man, each faction, held a profound conviction about the nature of the Indians and all generalized about them as though they were a single race. Each made his own views on the Indians the basis of a recommendation for a government policy which he urged upon the powers in Spain as the one true solution which would once and for all set the enterprise of the Indies on a firm and unassailable foundation. The crown considered all these recommendations and ruled above all individuals and all factions, jealous of its prerogatives and determined to prevent the growth of a powerful and turbulent aristocracy such as had just been broken in Spain by the unremitting efforts of Ferdinand and Isabella. It was the Emperor Charles V and his counsellors, therefore, who had to decide eventually what doctrine should be applied to the American Indians. In the feverish days of the early conquest, when even hard-bitten conquistadores suffered strange dreams and the New World was to some men a place of wonder and enchantment populated with mysterious and bewildering people, it is not surprising that even the ancient theory of Aristotle, that some men are born to be slaves, was borrowed from antiquity and found conveniently applicable to the Indians from the coasts of Florida to far-distant Chile.

4. *Spaniards Brought Animals, Fruits, Vegetables, and All Manner of Plants*

JAMES A. ROBERTSON

The late James A. Robertson, the first editor of the *Hispanic American Historical Review* and a pioneer in developing the study of Latin American history in the United States, here describes the fundamental contributions of Spain in introducing plants and animals to America. This was the peaceful side of the conquest, not yet fully understood.

"Very extraordinary," says the good Jesuit father, Bernabé Cobo, writing in 1652, "is the abundance of the increase in this New World of all the animals fruits, vegetables, and all manner of plants which the Spaniards have taken to it since they discovered and settled it." So true was this, continues the same author, that some people doubted that certain things had been transferred from Spain at all, but declared them native to the new lands. A residence of forty years in America, however, and an acquaintance with old men who remembered when certain European animals and plants were not to be found in the Indies, or who remembered, even, when some of them were first brought over, gave Cobo a right to speak with a certain authority on the matter. Induced by friends or officials, the observant Jesuit had the prescience to write down what he knew of the bringing of new forms of life to the Indies, and his chapters on the subject are valuable testimony.

But Cobo, although he will be used largely in this paper, is not the only authority on this phase of Spain's constructive labors in the colonies. Others — and some much earlier than he — left partial records of animal and plant transfers to and from the Indies, among them Cortés, the conqueror, Oviedo, the official, Acosta, the Jesuit (whose books have run into many editions), Herrera, the chronologist, Solórzano, the jurist, and many others. . . . Even a slight study shows that Spaniards thought of other things beside gold and precious stones, and that among the early explorers, discoverers, officials, and others, were persons with a large outlook and some with a scientific type of mind — largely untrained though they may have been in the exact tenets of science. Thus we find the great pioneer Cortés writing:

> I assure your Caesarian Majesty that, could we but obtain plants and
> seeds from Spain, and if Your Highness would be pleased to order them

"Some Notes on the Transfer by Spain of Plants and Animals to Its Colonies Overseas" by James A. Robertson, *James Sprunt Historical Studies,* 19 (Chapel Hill: University of North Carolina Press, 1927), pp. 7–21, passim. Reprinted by permission.

sent to us . . . the ability of these natives in cultivating the soil and making plantations would very shortly produce such abundance that great profit would accrue to the Imperial Crown of your Highness. . . .

Cobo's evidence is especially interesting and valuable. He states that he does not know in all instances by whom introductions were made into each province; yet he remarks the problem is not a very difficult one, for most products were taken first to Isla Española, whence they were transferred to other regions. It is true, however, as he says, that some products were taken to other parts without passing through Isla Española first. Since his acquaintance was more intimate with Peru than any other region, it is not surprising that he confines himself more especially to that country.

On his very first voyage, Columbus noted the lack of European fruits, vegetables, grains, and animals. Accordingly, on his second voyage, he carried animals for breeding purposes, besides seeds and slips of plants. Later expeditions did the same thing, so that, says Cobo, "there are very few plants of all the kinds grown in Europe which have not been transferred to this land." And he makes the same observation that the transfer of animals and plants has been more advantageous to the New World than the immense wealth of gold and silver sent thence to Spain. One may predict, he continues, that every Spanish plant will thrive in the New World. One potent cause for the great increase in plants and trees has been the destruction and change of site of many Spanish and Indian settlements. Abandoned by their inhabitants, gardens have run riot, while cattle reverting to a wild state, have continued to breed and have formed immense herds. Soldiers on entering a ruined city in Chile found veritable groves of various kinds of fruit trees, which bore excellent fruit. The Indians once destroyed a Spanish settlement in the valley of Neyva, situated between Peru and the Nuevo Reino de Granada. They left some of the cattle behind, which continued to breed and within a short time had formed immense wild herds.

On their part the Indians, recognizing the benefits to be derived from the new animals and plants, ere long began to pay their tributes in wheat and cattle. The immensity of excellent grazing lands was a potent aid in the breeding and dissemination of animals; while plants, in addition to human agency (both of Spaniards and natives) were often spread by birds and in other ways.

TRANSFER AND SPREAD OF ANIMALS

The American Indies were astonishingly bare of domestic animals. Dogs of questionable breeds, and cats, were not rare, and there were some wild pigs. The wild buffalo or American bison roamed the plains of North America; in South America, the Indians had tamed the vicuña and llama. But horses and domestic cattle were unknown. Columbus, himself, took the first horses to

Isla Española in 1493. Ponce de León, Narváez, Soto, and Luna y Arrelano had horses in their expeditions to Florida. Cortés took this friend of man to Mexico, where the awestruck natives thought it some sort of powerful god; Pizarro, to Peru; and Coronado, into the southwest. There is no doubt that horses aided very materially in the conquest.

In the first years of the conquest, it was common to pay from 3,000 to 4,000 pesos for a horse, but they bred so rapidly in the New World that the price dropped very materially within a comparatively short time. Very soon also some horses escaped into the wilds where they quickly reverted to a wild state forming as seen above immense herds. Wild herds were no uncommon sight in Isla Española, and they rose to uncommon proportions in the colonies of Paraguay and Tucumán. The immense herds that roamed through our own western country are too well known to need more than mention. These also were often the descendants of horses that escaped from the conquistadores. In Cobo's time the best horses came from Chile, where they had been introduced from Peru.

Shortly after their permanent entrance into the Philippines (1565), the Spaniards also took horses thither, but the sturdy Chinese horse had been there for many years. The small ponies that are capable of drawing such extraordinarily large loads are descended from the Spanish horses (often Arabs or mixed with Arab) and the Chinese horse.

The first cattle were taken to Isla Española at the beginning of the conquest, and to Peru three or four years after Pizarro's entrance. Like the horse, some of them escaped into the wilds and before long they too were formed into large herds in various regions. Indeed, wild cattle were so numerous in Isla Española and other West Indian islands, that it was found profitable to kill them for their flesh and hides. The men who made this their business, most frequently English, Dutch, or French, though the scourings of many other nations gradually drifted into the seas of the Indies, were known as *boucaniers,* a word derived from an old Indian term, *boucan* or *buccan,* meaning the method of drying or smoking the meat; and since the piratical crews which scurried along the Spanish main during the sixteenth and seventeenth centuries were usually recruited from these men, the term "buccaneer," meaning pirate came into the English language. Acosta notes that in 1587, a single fleet carried over 64,000 hides to Spain. The pirate Esquemelin noted the large number of wild cattle in Isla Española and says that the bulls found there were of huge bulk.

The first asses in the New World were taken to Isla Española, whence they spread into other regions, being taken to Peru by Captain Diego Maldonado, who obtained them in Jamaica. But most likely because of the abundance of horses throughout the Indies, neither asses nor their hybrid offspring, the mules, were very abundant in America in Cobo's time. However, asses could be procured in Lima for prices ranging from 10 to 15 pesos; while mules, which were very dear in early days, could be had at reasonable figures in Cobo's time, working mules fetching only 30 to 40 pesos, riding mules, 60 to 100 pesos, and choice animals, 200 to 300 pesos.

The New World had various kinds of wild, but no domesticated pigs. Because of their food value, the early conquistadores were accustomed to take large droves of European swine with them on their explorations and *entradas,* as, for instance, did Pizarro to Peru in 1531 and slightly later, Soto to Florida. Only four years after Pizarro's entrance into Peru, a slaughter house was erected in Lima, the first meat to be sold therein being pork. A decree of the cabildo of Lima, dated August 14, 1536, ordered that a pig be killed daily and the meat sold for twenty reals per *arroba,* and that no other animals were to be killed. In the middle of the seventeenth century pigs could be bought for eighteen pesos in Lima and even more cheaply in other places. Lard had a steady sale and the rendering of it was a fairly profitable business.

Sheep, when transferred from Spain to the warm regions of America (and the same was true of the transfer to the Philippine Islands), did not thrive well. Later, however, it was found that those reared in the highlands of Peru and in Chile fared better, and in those localities it was not long after their introduction before the woolen goods made from their fleece were able to compete with those of Spain. The Spaniards also early took goats and rabbits to the new lands, as well as dogs, although the Indians had plenty of the latter, albeit of poor breeds. The European dogs were used in tracking the poor Indians who fled before the cruelty of their self-appointed masters, and many a victim fell before the ferocity of the great hunting mastiffs and bloodhounds. The classic example of the dog in the early days of American colonization was the animal used by Juan Ponce de León in his conquest of Porto Rico, which shared like and like with the soldiers in all booty and wages. Pizarro took dogs to Peru, and Soto to Florida. Las Casas, the Apostle to the Indians, speaks in scathing terms of the cruelty of the dogs and the curious reader will find many interesting pictures of the dog in the great works published by Theodore de Bry in the latter part of the sixteenth century. There were instances of the dog's reverting to a wild state, and Esquemelin mentions the great, wild dogs of Isla Española descended from those brought in by the Spaniards. . . .

INTRODUCTION OF PLANT LIFE

It was quite natural for the Spaniards on coming to their new lands to look for the plant life to which they had been accustomed; and not finding it, to attempt to introduce it, both to remind them of the land of their birth and to serve as food and for other uses. It was also quite natural for them to transfer the plant life of the colonies to Spain or from one colony to another, but with this phase of transfer we have no concern in the present article. In bringing seeds, roots, and slips from the mother country, it is not surprising that many difficulties were encountered, for methods of packing were generally crude, and in the long voyages in their insecure ships, it was not uncommon for everything to be drenched with seawater, while the intense heat as they entered the tropics caused many of the seeds to rot. The story of the transfer of wheat, for instance, is a thrilling one. Various attempts to bring seed had failed, and it seemed impossible to bring the seed alive to America. At last, however, what it seemed impossible to accomplish by design was brought about by pure accident. It is recounted that a Negro slave of Cortés, while preparing rice for the expeditionaries one day, discovered several grains of good wheat. These were planted in New Spain and grew, and the resultant grains were also planted. In due time, the harvest was sufficient for use. A similar story is told of the introduction of wheat into Peru. Doña Inez Muñoz, wife of Martín de Alcántara — one of the conquistadores who had come to Peru with Pizarro — one day in 1535 while cleaning rice to make some soup for the family meal, found a few grains of good wheat in the rice barrel. Since she was much interested in transferring Spanish products to the new possessions, she recognized the value of her discovery. Accordingly, she planted the grains in her garden. What a gala day that must have been when the first shoots appeared above the ground, for the wheat grew rapidly and yielded abundantly. For several generations the harvest was in turn planted and in 1539 the first flour mill was erected in Peru. Next year, the cabildo of Lima regulated the sale of flour, and on November 19, 1541, bread was sold at one real for two and one-half *libras* (pounds). Other grains, including barley and rice, were early planted in Peru and flourished. . . .

The first cultivated seed or slip of the vine was taken to Lima by Hernando de Montenegro, and so rapid was the development that by 1551 grapes were being gathered in abundance. In that year, being placed on sale, under the auspices of Licentiate Rodrigo Niño, they brought half a *peso oro* or 225 *maravedis* per *libra*. However, Montenegro, to whom the grapes belonged, considered this price too low and appealed to the audiencia of Lima asking that he be permitted to sell at a higher rate. So greatly were the first plants esteemed, says Cobo, that it was necessary to have them guarded by armed men, so that the shoots should not be stolen. The first vines taken from Peru to Chile sold at 3,000 pesos, and the shoots at 100 pesos each. In Cobo's time there was an annual export from Peru of more than 100 shiploads of grapes. The price of the wine made from the grapes dropped to as low as three to four pesos per *arroba*. As time passed most of the Spanish varieties of grapes were transferred to Peru and flourished; and as might be expected, found favor not only with the whites but with the Indians as well. The Jesuit

Joseph de Acosta, writing much earlier than Cobo, bears similar testimony of the vine, but says that this most useful product did not thrive in Tierra Firme or in the islands. The vines bore well in New Spain, however, but the grapes were there used only for eating, no wine being made, because as Acosta conjectures, the grapes did not ripen thoroughly on account of the rains of July and August. On the other hand, he says, excellent wine was made in Peru and Chile; and so great was the increase in those regions that the tithes of the church increased five or six times within twenty years.

The olive was first brought to Peru by Antonio de Ribera, one of the principal settlers of that country. Having been sent to Spain as procurator for the new colony, on his return in 1560, he brought many olive plants from Seville, but only two or three survived the voyage. Planting these in his garden he had them carefully guarded against theft by Indians and dogs. Notwithstanding his care, however, all the plants except one were stolen one night, and taken to Chile where being planted they throve exceedingly. The one left to Ribera became the parent of all the trees in Peru, and in Cobo's time was still living although the garden in which it had been planted had been transferred to a community of nuns. . . .

Sugarcane was first brought to the West Indies by Pedro de Atienza, an inhabitant of Concepción de la Vega in Isla Española, and from this place it spread all over the tropical Indies redeeming much territory that had been considered as only waste. The product was larger than in its former home, and grew so abundantly that sugar was made in great quantities and soon became very cheap, costing only four or five pesos per *arroba*. In Peru, notwithstanding the heavy consumption of sugar, there was a considerable export to Spain.

The first sugar in the Indies is said to have been made by Gonzalo de Vibora, who brought over sugar experts to Isla Española, and who erected a horse mill for expressing the juice. "To him alone," says Oviedo, "are due thanks for the first manufacture of sugar in America." So rapid was the development of sugar growing that despite the heavy capital needed to run a mill because slave labor only was employed, many sugar mills were early established, among mill owners being Luis Colón, Cristóbal de Tapía, Miguel de Pasamonte, Lucas Vasquez de Ayllón, and many others whose names are familiar. Until sugar became an object of export, ships had to return to Spain in ballast. In 1553, so much sugar was made in Mexico that heavy exports were made from Vera Cruz and Acapulco to Spain and Peru. One shipment of sugar to Spain before 1590 amounted to 898 boxes, each presumably of 8 *arrobas'* weight, and this notwithstanding the heavy consumption in the Indies. Sugar, indeed, became the chief product of the West Indian islands, and its abundance created a great demand for confections of various kinds. . . .

Oranges and lemons spread so rapidly that it early became not uncommon to see them growing wild in Isla Española. Acosta, indeed, says that whole forests of wild oranges were found growing in many localities. The first oranges (both sweet and sour varieties) were taken to Isla Española from Spain, and throve wonderfully both inside the city of Santo Domingo and in other parts of the island, and spread very soon to the other islands. The first oranges were taken to Peru by Baltasar Gogo and planted in a garden not far from Lima. Lemons were unknown in Peru when Cobo first went there, but when he wrote they had been flourishing for a score of years.

The mulberry was introduced into the New World by Hernando Cortés, who tried to establish the silk industry in New Spain. The first bananas in the New World, according to Oviedo, were planted in Isla Española in 1516 by Tomás Berlanga, a Dominican priest, who is said to have brought them from the Canary Islands; but Acosta says that they had been known in America before the arrival of the Spaniards. Cobo is probably in error in his assertion that the first bananas were planted in Tierra Firme, but probably correct when he says that the first ones were taken to Peru by a lady of Panama who went to that country.

With regard to the plant life of the New World, Candolle says that of 247 plants cultivated in America, 199 originated in the Old World, 45 in America, 1 in Australia, while the native habitat of 2 can not be determined. It might be well in this connection to repeat Humboldt's warning, lest we get to believing that the New World was poorer in useful plant life than was really the case. He says:

> In general, if one considers the garden plants of the Aztecs and the great number of farinaceous and sugar roots cultivated in Mexico and in Peru, he will see that America was not nearly so poor in food plants as would appear from the untrustworthy evidence advanced by certain savants, who know the new continent only through the works of Herrera and Solis.

And he notes further that, before the arrival of the Spaniards in America, Mexico and the Cordilleras of South America produced several fruits quite similar to those of the temperate climate of the old continent.

On the other side of the globe, the Spaniards transferred various products to the Philippine Islands, both from the American Indies and from Spain. This story may not be taken up in any detail in this paper. Suffice it to say that Miguel López de Legazpi, who made the first permanent Spanish settlement in the Philippines (that at Cebu), in writing his official report of 1565, states that the soil was so fertile that four days after the Spanish forces had taken the native town of Cebu, "the Castilian seeds had already sprouted."

Whatever mistakes the Spaniards made in their colonization of their new possessions, whether in the western or eastern hemisphere, one can indorse much of what Claudio Gay says, namely:

> Never has a nation carried the colonizing spirit to a degree as high as the Spaniards. Although many of them expatriated themselves with the sole object of enriching themselves at any price, the majority had the firm resolution to contribute to the civilizing and evangelizing of semi-barbaric peoples. With this object they carried with them, not only the principal elements of civilization, such as domestic animals, wheat, beans, vegetables, etc., but also a force of goodwill and of perseverance truly wonderful which naught could change.

THE INFLUENCE OF
THE NEW WORLD ON THE OLD

5. The Impact of America on Europe Was Complex and Uncertain

J. H. ELLIOTT

Professor Elliott is an English historian, now at the Institute of Advanced Studies, who has made notable contributions to Spanish history through *The Revolt of the Catalans* (1963) and *Imperial Spain, 1469–1716* (1963). Recently he has turned his wit and his scholarship to assessing the reasons why America puzzled Europeans who found it so difficult to understand the alien civilization across the ocean. In this selection he explains "the uncertain impact" of the New World on the Old. Perhaps this uncertainty may be explained, in part at least, by the fertility of European imagination concerning America. As late as 1774 Pedro Alonso O'Crouley wrote a work on Mexico that included a chapter, "Remarkable Curiosities," on the wonders of the New World, "which ranged from a woman who had borne forty-eight children to the leashing of fleas with minute gold chains, an accomplishment of the Indians of Mexico." *

* *A Description of the Kingdom of New Spain, by Señor Don Pedro Alonso O'Crouley*, trans. and ed. Seán Galvin (San Francisco: John Howell, 1972), p. 110.

Nearly three hundred years after Columbus's first voyage of discovery, the Abbé Raynal, that eager inquirer after other men's truths, offered a prize for the essay which would best answer the following questions. Has the discovery of America been useful or harmful to mankind? If useful, how can its usefulness be enhanced? If harmful, how can the harm be diminished? Cornelius De Pauw had recently described the discovery of the New World as the most calamitous event in human history, and Raynal was taking no chances. "No event," he had cautiously begun his vast and laborious *Philosophical and Political History of the Settlements and Trade of the Europeans in the East and West Indies,* "has been so interesting to mankind in general, and to the inhabitants of Europe in particular, as the discovery of the new world, and the passage to India by the Cape of Good Hope." It took the robust Scottish forthrightness of Adam Smith, whose view of the impact of the discoveries was generally favourable, to turn this non-committal passage into an *ex cathedra* historical pronouncement: "the discovery of America, and that of a passage to the East Indies by the Cape of Good Hope, are the two greatest and most important events recorded in the history of mankind.". . .

Raynal's formulation of his questions no doubt tended to prompt philosophical speculation and dogmatic assertion, rather than rigorous historical inquiry. But this was less easily evaded in 1792, when the Académie Française asked competitors to examine the influence of America on the "politics, commerce and customs of Europe." It is difficult not to sympathize with the sentiments of the anonymous prize-winner. "What a vast and inexhaustible subject," he sighed. "The more one studies it, the more it grows." Nevertheless, he succeeded in covering a great deal of ground in his eighty-six pages. As might have been expected, he was happier with America's political and economic influence on Europe than with its moral influence, which he regarded as pernicious. But he showed himself aware of the concealed danger in this enterprise — the danger of attributing all the major changes in modern European history to the discovery of America. He also made a genuine attempt, in language which may not sound totally unfamiliar to our own generation, to weigh up the profits and the losses of discovery and settlement. "If those Europeans who devoted their lives to developing the resources of America had instead been employed in Europe in clearing forests, and building roads, bridges and canals, would not Europe have found in its own bosom the most important objects which it derives from the other world, or their equivalent? And what innumerable products would the soil of Europe not have yielded, if it had been brought to the degree of cultivation of which it is capable?". . .

For all the interest and importance of the theme, the historiography of the

From *The Old World and the New, 1492–1650* by J. H. Elliott (Cambridge, England: Cambridge University Press, 1970), pp. 1–27 passim. Reprinted by permission.

impact of America on Europe has enjoyed a distinctly chequered career. The eighteenth-century debate was conducted in terms which suggest that the participants were more concerned to confirm and defend their personal prejudices about the nature of man and society than to obtain a careful historical perspective on the contribution of the New World to Europe's economic and cultural development. It was not until Humboldt published his *Cosmos* in 1845 that the reactions of the first Europeans, and especially of the Spaniards, to the alien environment of America assumed their proper place in a great geographical and historical synthesis, which made some attempt to consider what the revelation of the New World had meant to the Old.

Nineteenth-century historiography did not show any great interest in pursuing Humboldt's more original lines of inquiry. The discovery and settlement of the New World were incorporated into an essentially Europocentric conception of history, where they were depicted as part of that epic process by which the Renaissance European first became conscious of the world and of man, and then by degrees imposed his own dominion over the newly-discovered races of a newly-discovered world. In this particular story of European history — which was all too easily identified with universal history — there was a tendency to place the principal emphasis on the motives, methods and achievements of the explorers and conquerors. The impact of Europe on the world (which was regarded as a transforming, and ultimately beneficial, impact) seemed a subject of greater interest and concern than the impact of the world on Europe.

Twentieth-century European historiography has tended to pursue a similar theme, although from a very different standpoint. The retreat of European imperialism has led to a reassessment — often very harsh — of the European legacy. At the same time the development of anthropology and archaeology has led to a reassessment — sometimes very favourable — of the pre-European past of former colonial societies. Where European historians once wrote with the confidence born of an innate sense of European superiority, they now write burdened with the consciousness of European guilt.

It is no accident that some of the most important historical work of our own age — preoccupied as it is with the problem of European and non-European, of black and white — should have been devoted to the study of the social, demographic and psychological consequences for non-European societies of Europe's overseas expansion. Perhaps future generations will detect in our concern with these themes some affinity between the historians of the eighteenth and twentieth centuries. For Raynal and his friends were similarly consumed by guilt and by doubt. Their hesitancy in evaluating the consequences of the discovery and conquest of America sprang precisely from the dilemma involved in attempting to reconcile the record of economic and technical progress since the end of the fifteenth century with the record of the sufferings endured by the defeated societies. The very extent of their preoccupation with the great moral issue of their own times, the issue of slavery, helped to create a situation not without its parallels today. For if their preoccupation stimulated them to ask historical questions, it also tempted them to reply with unhistorical answers. . . .

From 1492 the New World was always present in European history, although its presence made itself felt in different ways at different times. It is for this reason that America and Europe should not be subjected to a historiographical divorce, however shadowy their partnership may often appear before the late seventeenth century. Properly, their histories should constitute a continuous interplay of two distinctive themes.

One theme is represented by the attempt of Europe to impose its own image, its own aspirations, and its own values, on a newly-discovered world, together with the consequences for that world of its actions. The other treats of the way in which a growing awareness of the character, the opportunities and the challenges represented by the New World of America helped to shape and transform an Old World which was itself striving to shape and transform the New. . . .

Gold and conversion — these were the two most immediate and obvious connotations of America, and those most likely to be associated with the name of its discoverer. It was only by slow degrees that Columbus began to acquire the status of a hero. He figured as the central protagonist in a number of Italian epic poems written in the last two decades of the sixteenth century, and in 1614 he at last appeared as the hero of a Spanish drama, with the publication of Lope de Vega's extraordinary play, *El Nuevo Mundo descubierto por Cristóbal Colón*. Lope shows a genuine historical appreciation of the significance of Columbus's achievement when he puts into the mouth of Ferdinand the Catholic a speech affirming the traditional cosmography of a tripartite globe, and scoffing at the possibility that there might exist a portion of the world still to be discovered. At the same time, his Columbus, as a dreamer mocked by the world, has already started on his career as the romantic hero who becomes the symbol of man's unquenchable spirit of discovery.

There were already intimations of this romanticization of Columbus during the sixteenth century. But more commonly he was set within the framework of a providential interpretation of history, which depicted him as a divinely appointed instrument for the spreading of the gospel — and even here he was likely to find himself relegated to second place by the more obviously heroic figure of Hernán Cortés. But not even the mass-conversion of hitherto unknown peoples was sufficient of itself to ensure a firm place for Columbus, or Cortés, or for the New World, in the European consciousness. In some circles — especially certain humanist and religious circles, and in the merchant communities of some of Europe's leading cities — the interest was intense, although partial, and often specialized, in character. But it seems that the European reading public displayed no overwhelming interest in the newly-discovered world of America. . . .

It is difficult not to be impressed by the strange lacunae and the resounding silences in many places where references to the New World could reasonably be expected. How are we to explain the absence of any mention of the New World in so many memoirs and chronicles, including the memoirs of Charles V himself? How are we to explain the continuing determination, right up to the last two or three decades of the sixteenth century, to describe the world as if it were still the world as known to Strabo, Ptolemy and Pomponius Mela? How are we to explain the persistent reprinting by publishers, and the continuing use by schools, of classical cosmographies which were known to be outdated by the discoveries? How are we to explain that a man as widely read and as curious as Bodin should have made so little use of the considerable information available to him about the peoples of the New World in the writing of his political and social philosophy?

The reluctance of cosmographers or of social philosophers to incorporate into their work the new information made available to them by the discovery of America provides an example of the wider problems arising from the revelation of the New World to the Old. Whether it is a question of the geography of America, its flora and fauna, or the nature of its inhabitants, the same kind of pattern seems constantly to recur in the European response. It is as if, at a certain point, the mental shutters come down; as if, with so much to see and absorb and understand, the effort suddenly becomes too much for them, and Europeans retreat to the half-light of their traditional mental world. . . .

How can we expect a Europe so conscious of its own infallibility — of its unique status and position in God's providential design — even to make the effort to come to terms with a world other than its own? But this Europe was not the closed Europe of an "age of ignorance." Instead, it was Renaissance Europe — the Europe of "the discovery of the world and of man." If Renaissance ideas and attitudes played an important part — however elusive it may be to determine exactly *what* part — in prompting Europeans to set out on voyages of discovery and to extend their mental as well as their geographical horizons, might we not expect a new kind of readiness to respond to fresh information and fresh stimuli from a newly-discovered world?

The conclusion does not necessarily follow. In some respects the Renaissance involved, at least in its earlier stages, a closing rather than an opening of the mind. The veneration of antiquity became more slavish; authority staked fresh claims against experience. Both the boundaries and the content of traditional disciplines such as cosmography or social philosophy had been clearly determined by reference to the texts of classical antiquity, which acquired an extra degree of definitiveness when for the first time they were fixed on the printed page. Fresh information from alien sources was therefore liable to seem at worst incredible, at best irrelevant, when set against the accumulated knowledge of the centuries. Given this deference to authority, there was unlikely to be any undue precipitation, least of all in academic circles, to accept the New World into consciousness.

It is also possible that a society which is wrestling — as late medieval Christendom was wrestling — with great spiritual, intellectual and political problems, is too preoccupied with its internal upheavals to devote more than fitful attention to phenomena located on the periphery of its interests. It may be too much to expect such a society to make a further radical adjustment — and one which this time involves the assimilation of an entirely new range of alien experiences. Against this, however, it could be argued that a society which is in movement, and displays symptoms of dissatisfaction, is more likely to show itself capable of absorbing new impressions and experiences than a static society, satisfied with itself, and secure in the assurance of its own superiority. . . .

The obstacles to the incorporation of the New World within Europe's intellectual horizon were formidable. There were obstacles of time and space, of inheritance, environment and language; and efforts would be required at many different levels before they were removed. At least four different processes were involved, each of which raised peculiar difficulties of its own. First of all there was the process of observation, as defined by Humboldt when he wrote: "To see . . . is not to observe; that is, to compare and classify." The second process was description — depicting the unfamiliar in such a way that it could be grasped by those who had not seen it. The third was dissemination — the diffusion of new information, new images and new ideas, so that they became part of the accepted stock of mental furniture. And the fourth was comprehension — the ability to come to terms with the unexpected and the unfamiliar, to see them as phenomena existing in their own right, and (hardest of all) to shift the accepted boundaries of thought in order to include them.

If one asks *what* Europeans saw on arriving on the far side of the Atlantic, and *how* they saw it, much will inevitably depend on the kind of Europeans involved. The range of vision is bound to be affected both by background, and by professional interests. Soldiers, clerics, merchants, and officials trained in the law — these are the classes of men on whom we are dependent for most of our first-hand observation of the New World and its inhabitants. Each class had its own bias and its own limitations; and it would be interesting to have a systematic survey of the extent and nature of the bias for each professional group, and of the way in which it was mitigated or altered, in individual cases, by a humanist education.

One Spanish official in the Indies who transcended many of the limitations of his class, and achieved an unusual degree of insight into Quechua society by dint of learning the language, was Juan de Betanzos. In the dedication to his History of the Incas, written in 1551, he spoke of the difficulties he had met in composing the work. There was such a quantity of conflicting information, and he was concerned to find how differently the *conquistadores* speak about these things, and how far removed they are from Indian practice. "And this I believe to be due to the fact that at that time they were not so much concerned with finding things out as with subjecting and acquiring the land. It was also because, coming new to the Indians, they did not know how to ask questions and find things out, for they lacked knowledge of the language; while the Indians, for their part, were too frightened to give them a full account."

The professional preoccupations of the conquistadores, and the difficulties of conducting any form of effective dialogue with the Indians, are more than enough to account for the deficiencies of their reports as descriptions of the New World and its inhabitants; and it is a piece of unusual good fortune that the conquest of Mexico should have thrown up two soldier-chroniclers as shrewd in their observation and as vivid in their powers of description as Cortés and Bernal Díaz. In Cortés's letters of relation it is possible to see at work the process of observation, in Humboldt's sense of the word, as he attempts to bring the exotic into the range of the familiar by writing of Aztec temples as mosques, or by comparing the marketplace of Tenochtitlán with that of Salamanca. But there are obvious limits to Cortés's capacity of an observer, particularly when it comes to depicting the extraordinary landscape through which his invading army marched. . . .

Even where Europeans in the New World had the desire to look, and the eyes to see, there is no guarantee that the image which presented itself to them — whether of peoples or of places — necessarily accorded with the reality. Tradition, experience and expectation were the determinants of vision. Even a presumably sober official of the Spanish Crown, Alonso de Zuazo, manages to transmute Hispaniola in 1518 into an enchanted island where the fountains play and the streams are lined with gold, and where nature yields her fruits in marvellous abundance. Bernal Díaz, in many ways so down-to-earth and perceptive an observer, still looks at the conquest of Mexico through the haze of romances of chivalry. . . .

It is hard to escape the impression that sixteenth-century Europeans . . . all too often saw what they expected to see. This should not really be a cause for surprise or mockery, for it may well be that the human mind has an inherent need to fall back on the familiar object and the standard image, in order to come to terms with the shock of the unfamiliar. The real test comes later, with the capacity to abandon the life-belt which links the unknown to the known. Some Europeans, and especially those who spent a long time in the Indies, did successfully pass this test. Their own dawning realization of the wide divergence between the image and the reality, gradually forced them to abandon their standard images and their inherited preconceptions. For America was a *new* world and a *different* world; and it was this fact of difference which was overwhelmingly borne in upon those who came to know it. "Everything is very different," wrote Fray Tomás de Mercado in his book of advice to the merchants of Seville; "the talent of the natives, the disposition of the republic, the method of government and even the capacity to be governed."

But how to convey this fact of difference, the uniqueness of America, to those who had not seen it? The problem of description reduced writers and chroniclers to despair. There was too much diversity, too many new things to be described, as Fernández de Oviedo constantly complained. "Of all the things I have seen," he wrote of a bird of brilliant plumage, "this is the one which has most left me without hope of being able to describe it in words." Or again of a strange tree — "it needs to be painted by the hand of a Berruguete or some other excellent painter like him, or by Leonardo da Vinci or Andrea Mantegna, famous painters whom I knew in Italy." But the sheer impossibility of the task itself represented a challenge which could extend the boundaries of perception. Forcing themselves to communicate something of their own delight in what they saw around them, the Spanish chroniclers of the Indies occasionally achieved a pen-picture of startling intimacy and brilliance. What could be more vivid than Las Casas's description of himself reading matins "in a breviary with tiny print" by the light of the Hispaniola fireflies? . . .

Even where the observer depicted a scene with some success, either in paint or in prose, there was no guarantee that his work would reach the European public in an accurate form, or in any form at all. The caprice of publishers and the obsession of governments with secrecy, meant that much information about the New World, which might have helped to broaden Europe's mental horizons, failed to find its way into print. Illustrations had to run further hazards peculiar to themselves. The European reader was hardly in a position to obtain a reliable picture of life among the Tupinambá savages of Brazil when the illustrations in his book included scenes of Turkish life, because the publisher happened to have them in stock. Nor was the technique of woodcuts sufficiently advanced, at least until the second half of the sixteenth century, to allow a very faithful reproduction of the original drawing. . . .

In spite of all the problems involved in the dissemination of accurate information about America, the greatest problem of all, however, remained that of comprehension. The expectations of the European reader, and hence of the European traveller, were formed out of the accumulated images of a society which had been nurtured for generations on tales of the fantastic and the marvellous. . . . The temptation was almost overpoweringly strong to see the newly-discovered lands in terms of the enchanted isles of medieval fantasy. But it was not only the fantastic that tended to obtrude itself between the European and reality. If the unfamiliar were to be approached as anything other than the extraordinary and the monstrous, then the approach must be conducted by reference to the most firmly established elements in Europe's cultural inheritance. Between them, therefore, the Christian and the classical traditions were likely to prove the obvious points of departure for any evaluation of the New World and its inhabitants. . . .

The reverence of late medieval Europeans for their Christian and classical traditions had salutary consequences for their approach to the New World, in that it enabled them to set it into some kind of perspective in relation to themselves, and to examine it with a measure of tolerant interest. But against these possible advantages must be set certain obvious disadvantages, which in some ways made the task of assimilation appreciably harder. Fifteenth-century Christendom's own sense of self-dissatisfaction found expression in the longing for a return to a better state of things. The return might be to the lost Christian paradise, or to the Golden Age of the ancients, or to some elusive combination of both these imagined worlds. With the discovery of the Indies and their inhabitants, who went around naked and yet — in defiance of the Biblical tradition — mysteriously unashamed, it was all too easy to transpose the ideal world from a world remote in time to a world remote in space. Arcadia and Eden could now be located on the far shores of the Atlantic.

The process of transposition began from the very moment that Columbus first set eyes on the Caribbean Islands. The various connotations of paradise and the Golden Age were present from the first. Innocence, simplicity, fertility and abundance — all of them qualities for which Renaissance Europe hankered, and which seemed so unattainable — made their appearance in the reports of Columbus and Vespucci, and were eagerly seized upon by their enthusiastic readers. In particular, they struck an answering chord in two worlds, the religious and the humanist. Despairing of the corruption of Europe and its ways, it was natural that certain members of the religious orders should have seen an opportunity for reestablishing the primitive church of the apostles in a New World as yet uncorrupted by European vices. In the revivalist and apocalyptic tradition of the friars, the twin themes of the new world and the end of the world harmoniously blended in the great task of evangelizing the uncounted millions who knew nothing of the Faith.

The humanists, like the friars, projected onto America their disappointed dreams. In the *Decades* of Peter Martyr, the first popularizer of America and its myth, the Indies have already undergone their subtle transmutation. Here were a people who lived without weights and measures and "pestiferous moneye, the seed of innumerable myscheves. So that if we shall not be ashamed to confesse the truthe, they seem to lyve in the goulden worlde of the which owlde wryters speake so much: wherin men lyved simplye and innocentlye without inforcement of lawes, without quarrelling Iudges and libelles, contente onely to satisfie nature, without further vexation for knowledge of thinges to come."

It was an idyllic picture, and the humanists made the most of it, for it enabled them to express their deep dissatisfaction with European society, and to criticize it by implication. America and Europe became antitheses — the antitheses of innocence and corruption. And the corrupt was destroying the innocent.

But by treating the New World in this way, the humanists were closing the door to understanding an alien civilization. America was not as they imagined it; and even the most enthusiastic of them had to accept from an early stage that the inhabitants of this idyllic world could also be vicious and bellicose, and sometimes ate each other. This of itself was not necessarily sufficient to quench utopianism, for it was always possible to build Utopia on the far side of the Atlantic if it did not already exist. For a moment it seemed as if the dream of the friars and the humanists would find its realization in Vasco de Quiroga's villages of Santa Fe in Mexico. But the dream was a European dream, which had little to do with the American reality. As that reality came to impinge at an increasing number of points, so the dream began to fade.

Francisco de Toledo, Viceroy of Peru (1569–1581). One of the best ways to study the nature of Spanish rule in America would be to examine closely the objectives and accomplishments of this notable viceroy who established Spanish power in Peru. To this end he elaborated laws to regulate practically all aspects of colonial life, executed the Inca Tupac Amaru, concentrated Indians in communities and harnessed their labor for agriculture and mining. He was also concerned to prove that Spanish rule was recognized as just and that Inca rule had been unjust (Reading 4).

SECTION II

Was Inca Rule Tyrannical?

EUROPEAN REACTIONS TO INDIAN CIVILIZATIONS

Spaniards were amazed by the strange peoples they found in the New World, and over the years, as they strove to conquer and Christianize the Indians, they devoted much attention to the many native languages, religions, and cultures. The kind of culture the Indians had attained became part of the verbal battles over their "rationality." Bartolomé de Las Casas, the sixteenth-century Protector of the Indians, attempted in a long treatise, *Apologetic History,* to prove that the Indians were eminently rational beings with such "excellent, most subtle and natural intelligence" that they satisfied all the requirements laid down by Aristotle for the good life.[1] Besides these obviously political reactions, others looked at Indian achievements in art through professional eyes. Albrecht Dürer, the outstanding German painter and engraver

---

[1] For more information on this treatise, see Lewis Hanke, *Aristotle and the American Indians* (Bloomington: Indiana University Press, 1970). As an example of the variety of opinions on rationality, here is a recent one by Dr. Francisco Guerra, the well-known authority on medical history: "Setting aside the legal and theological discussions, and examining only the biological facts, the American Indians had to be found irrational at the time of the Discovery because they acted against natural law on a number of counts: human sacrifices, anthropophagy, sexual relations of incest and sodomy and abuse of drugs producing inebriation. The reports of explorers and historians on these customs were often biased, but on the whole consistent, though what was true for a single area was often credited to the entire continent. These actions, if executed by human beings, had perforce to be judged by the divine, positive, and natural law as unnatural, and consequently as irrational. From a biological standpoint they are exceedingly important, because they reflect an attitude to life and death, to sexual drives, and towards the customary use of drugs affecting mental behaviour, which was very different from what was held as normal in Europe prior to the discovery of America. In other words, for the purpose of a psychological assessment, the pre-Columbian mind, after centuries of isolation, held values for life, sex, and drugs which were aberrant by the standards of the European cultural tradition." See *The Pre-Columbian Mind* (London: Seminar Press, 1971), pp. 4–5.

of the time, visited the first exhibition of aboriginal Mexican art in Europe that took place in Brussels before Emperor Charles V in 1520. Dürer recorded his surprise and delight in his diary on first examining the gold and silver objects wrought by the Indians and dispatched by Cortez to illustrate the greatness of his conquests: "All the days of my life I have seen nothing that rejoiced my heart so much as these things, for I saw amongst them wonderful works of art, and I marvelled at the subtle ingenuity of men in foreign lands." [2] Cortez also sent an Aztec ballet troup to Spain a few years later, which greatly impressed Charles and his imperial court. As described by Friar Diego Valadés, in his *Rhetorica Christiana* (Perusia, 1579), the first book published in Europe by a native-born Mexican: "Their dances are very worthy of mention, since despite such a multitude they sing in the most perfect unison and move in perfect synchronism, whatever the shifts of measure and melody. The invincible emperor Charles V could not believe the report of so great a number of dancers and their rhythmic perfection until he witnessed their performance at Valladolid, where he and a number of his principal courtiers were enthralled by their demonstration an entire morning." [3]

WAS INCA RULE JUST?

Art and music were all very well, but what really interested the sixteenth-century Spaniards was to establish without question the justice of their rule in the New World and the tyranny of the native governments. Questions on the just title of Spain to the Indies were raised in the early days of discovery, and they continued as the Spaniards toppled the Maya and Aztec empires. As the conquest moved to the high Andean regions in Peru, the arguments over the kind of civilization created by the Indians there became more acute and more political. The youthful conquistador Pedro de Cieza de León admired Inca achievements (Reading 1), while the oldest survivor of the conquest in Peru, one Mancio Sierra de Leguízamo, solemnly swore on his deathbed in 1589 that not only were the Incas wise rulers but that the invading Spaniards had corrupted an ideal Indian society (Reading 2).[4] The Inca Garcilaso de la Vega, the son of an Inca princess and a Spanish captain,

---

[2] Robert Stevenson, *Music in Aztec and Inca Territory* (Berkeley, 1968), p. 88.

[3] Ibid., p. 89. In 1528 Cortez took with him to Spain a troupe of native entertainers, including some jugglers from Tlaxcala who performed "in a manner never seen or heard in Spain." Also brought along to impress the court were male and female dwarfs, hunchbacks, and native prestidigitators. See Howard F. Cline, "Hernando Cortés and the Aztec Indians in New Spain," *Quarterly Journal of the Library of Congress,* 26 (1969), pp. 70–90.

[4] A number of other wills on behalf of Indians by conquistadors testify to the influence of Las Casas's demand that restitution be paid to despoiled Indians. See Guillermo Lohmann Villena, "La restitución por conquistadores y encomenderos: un aspecto de la incidencia lascasiana en el Perú," in *Estudios Lascasianos: IV Centenario de la muerte de fray Bartolomé de las Casas, 1466–1966* (Seville, 1966), pp. 21–89.

wrote nostalgically of the civilization his maternal ancestors had created and his paternal kin had destroyed (Reading 3).

Viceroy Francisco de Toledo on his arrival in Peru in 1569 discovered so much uncertainty over the comparative merits of Inca and Spanish rule that he launched a frontal attack on the Inca system (Reading 4).

LATER ECHOES OF THE ARGUMENT

Inca government and Inca history continued to play a political role long after Viceroy Toledo returned to Spain in 1581. José Gabriel Tupac Amaru attempted to utilize the glory of his Inca ancestors to help him during the revolt in Peru in the 1780s, though his aim was to capture Spanish institutions, not to destroy or displace them by others. During the wars for independence in Argentina in the early nineteenth century General José de San Martín and Manuel Belgrano supported the idea of an "Inca Monarchy" to supplant that of Spain, and even had propagandistic handbills printed in the Indian languages Aymara and Quechua for distribution among Indian caciques to arouse sympathy for the revolutionists against Spain.[5] In northern South America, far from Cuzco and other ancient centers of Inca strength, the opponents of Spain continued to invoke the splendors of the Indian past to aid their campaigns. The Liberator Simón Bolívar and his generals "were tiresomely extolled as the final 'avengers' of the fallen Incan Empire." [6]

A century later in Peru, during the early years of President Augusto B. Leguía's administration in the 1920s, Fredrick Pike states: "an increasing number of Peruvian intellectuals turned their attention to Inca history, folklore, and archaeology. In Lima the Society of the Golden Arrow was formed, the purpose of its members being to study the glories of the Inca past. . . . Leguía himself joined in, and liked to be referred to as Viracocha, the white-skinned, culture-bearing deity." [7] Though Leguía did not pursue these Inca interests, other Peruvians such as José Carlos Mariátegui and Víctor Raúl Haya de la Torre did; some of the roots of the APRA [Alianza Peruana Revolucionaria Americana] political party are sunk in the Inca past. In the years between the two world wars Italian fascism found Inca "communism" a useful tool, and the Bolivian revolution of 1952 is said to have been prepared for by renewed interest in Inca studies.[8]

---

[5] Harry Bernstein, *Modern and Contemporary Latin America* (Philadelphia: Lippincott, 1952), p. 199.

[6] David Bushnell, *The Santander Regime in Gran Colombia* (Newark: University of Delaware Press, 1954), p. 175.

[7] Fredrick B. Pike, *The Modern History of Peru* (London: Weidenfeld & Nicholson, 1967), chap. 8.

[8] Benedetto Giacalone, *Comunismo Incaico-araucania-Florida-Colombiano* (Genoa: Bozzi, 1936), and Charles Arnade, "The U.S. and the Ultimate Roots of the Bolivian Revolution," *Historia* (Río Piedras), n.s., vol. 1 (1962), no. 1, pp. 35–50.

Scholarly attention to all aspects of Inca history has grown during the last half century, though it has not produced a consensus. Philip Ainsworth Means, a pioneer student in the United States of Inca history, agreed with the highly favorable accounts of the sixteenth-century Spaniards and concluded: "Such was the unique civilization which Spanish culture, bringing with it Christianity and money culture, was destined to overwhelm and change beyond recognition. . . . The greatest, the fundamental and the universal source of evil brought into Peru by the Spaniards was the money-complex whence arose all the endless misery which has weighed down the Andean peoples ever since the money-less empire of the Incas was shattered." [9]

Later writers, influenced by the swirling currents of discussion in Europe on the proper functions of the state, have characterized Inca culture as "socialistic." [10] A more evaluative note was struck by a Swiss anthropologist, the late Alfred Métraux, who objected to attempts to force the Inca system to conform "to a modern formula: a socialistic, a totalitarian, or a welfare state" (Reading 5). Though "romantic attitudes and unfounded prejudices, glib exaggerations and superficial generalizations have provided the basis for either uncritical exaltation or contemptuous denigration of Peru's aborigines and their historical feats," as Professor Pike declares,[11] a new realism is being brought to bear upon the Inca past. The young Swedish scholar Ake Wedin has challenged previous interpretations of Inca chronology,[12] and John V. Murra has also denounced the practice of classifying the Inca system using terms applied to European economic and political history.[13] He refuses to employ the labels "socialistic," "feudal," "totalitarian," or the concepts implicit in "commoner," "nobleman," or "lumpenproletariat." The most recent author to survey the interpretations of Inca rule reaches this conclusion: "The old sources of knowledge of Inca culture . . . indicate that one cannot speak of an Inca communistic order, nor of a collectivistic system, or a socialist centralization of land tenure. The property tax of 66%, the personal service or *prestación,* the compulsory change of residence, and the impossibility of

---

[9] P. A. Means, *Fall of the Inca Empire* (New York: Scribners, 1932), p. 12.

[10] Louis Baudin, *A Socialist Empire: The Incas of Peru* (Princeton, 1961).

[11] Pike, *Modern History of Peru,* chap. 1.

[12] Åke Wedin, *La cronología de la historia incaica: Estudio crítico* (Madrid: Instituto Ibero-Americano de Gotemburgo, 1963). See also his monographs, *El sistema decimal en el imperio incaico: Estudio sobre estructura política,* (Madrid: Instituto Ibero-Americano de Gotemburgo, 1965), and *El concepto de lo incaico y las fuentes: Estudio crítico,* Studia Historica Gothoburgensia, 7 (Uppsala: Scandinavian University Books, 1966).

[13] John V. Murra, "On Inca Political Structure," *Systems of Political Control and Bureaucracy in Human Societies, Proceedings of the 1958 Annual Spring Meeting of the American Ethnological Society,* ed. Verne F. Ray (Seattle, 1958), p. 30. See also his "Social, Structural and Economic Themes in Andean Ethnohistory," *American Anthropologist,* 34 (1961), no. 2, pp. 47–59.

overcoming social barriers because of the static order of social classes, show very clearly that the Incas and their form of the state cannot serve as a model for our times." [14]

The study of Inca culture, however, holds rich rewards, because one may learn more about a remarkable civilization the Spaniards encountered and may see how cultural history has been manipulated for varied purposes.

A FINAL THOUGHT

One of the conclusions to be drawn from these conflicting interpretations of Indian culture is that "virtue lies in the eye of the beholder." A recent stimulating volume on the ways Aztec civilization has been viewed demonstrates that Inca culture was not the only one to provoke a variety of reactions.[15] A dramatic example may be found in the work of the late George Vaillant, one of the leading American archaeologists of this century. Writing in the dark and uncertain years just before World War II, Vaillant reflected in this way on the meaning of the Aztec way of life for his own time:

> The civilization of the Indian may not offer a direct inspiration to us modern individualists, yet we have profited from their labor in our food plants and the wealth produced by our neighbor republics to the south. In this world, torn with hate and war, adrift without an anchor or a compass with which to chart our course, we may well consider their example. The Indians worked together for their common good, and no sacrifice was too great for their corporate well-being. Man's strength lay in the physical and spiritual welfare of the tribe, and the individual was honored only inasmuch as he contributed to that communal good. The Indian civilization may have been powerless to resist the culture of the western world, but it did not consume itself, as we are doing, in the expression of military power.[16]

Many other examples can be found. Therefore as we read about Indian cultures we should first of all try to understand the perspective from which the author develops his interpretation.

[14] Horst Nachtigall, "El estado estamental de los incas peruanos," *América Indígena,* 24 (1964), no. 2, pp. 93–110.

[15] Benjamin Keen, *The Aztec Image* (New Brunswick: Rutgers University Press, 1971).

[16] George C. Vaillant, *The Aztecs of Mexico* (New York, 1941), pp. 280–281. Keen's comment in *Aztec Image* (p. 493) on Vaillant's statement is pertinent: "That Vaillant, who knew the sources of Aztec society so well, should have shut his eyes so tightly to the abundant evidence of social cleavages and tensions within it testifies to the power of emotive factors in the way we view the past. Vaillant's radiant vision of Aztec civilization undoubtedly reflects his profound discontent with the state of the world in which he lived, a discontent that may have contributed to his tragic death by suicide . . . shortly after the publication of the *Aztecs of Mexico*."

It is unfortunate that Indians left few written records of their views of Spanish culture. We know that many fled away to the hills to escape the invaders, which is one response. Others we are told committed suicide or faded away as they came to realize the gulf between their culture and that of the invaders. And we know that the initial reaction of Montezuma was terror on learning of Cortez and his men on the way to the Aztec capital (Reading 19).

One of the rare testimonies on Indian views is found in the official history of Antonio de Herrera, who reports that one day a Spaniard in Peru enquired of "a discreet Indian" what he considered the most significant contributions of the Spaniards to their life. The reply must have surprised the Spaniard, for the discreet Indian said not a word about the Christian religion, education, or plants. Instead he emphasized the importance of chicken eggs, horses, and candles: "The eggs because they are abundant and fresh everyday, and good for old and young whether cooked or not; horses because they allow one to travel without fatigue and relieve men of burden bearing; and candles because with their light one may live a part of the night." [17]

The most valuable document by a Peruvian Indian on Andean life before Pizarro came from the pen of Guaman Poma de Ayala, who about 1615 wrote what he called "a letter" to the King of Spain. This 1,200-page work, illustrated by the author with 400 drawings, is a unique source: "It was mostly a cry of anguish, a petition to the all-powerful King overseas to look at what his men were doing in America, to look at what they had destroyed. . . . But it also is a constructive document; most of it is devoted to plans for a 'buen gobierno,' a good government Poma thought could still be devised by combining revived Inca social and economic organization with Christianity and some beneficial aspects of European technology, such as growing grapes and making wine." [18]

Poma never achieved his dream of presenting his manuscript to Philip III. But it somehow was saved and finally printed. The splendid article by Professor John Murra, with a number of illustrations reproduced, will introduce students to the most eloquent and most informative testimony by a Peruvian Indian on the past, present, and future of his land.

[17] Antonio de Herrera y Tordesillas, *Historia general de los hechos de los castellanos en las islas y tierra firme del mar Océano,* ed. Antonio de Ballesteros and Ángel Altolaguirre, vol. 2 (Madrid, 1934), pp. 34–35.

[18] John V. Murra, "Guaman Poma de Ayala: A Seventeenth-Century Indian's Account of Andean Civilization," *Natural History,* 70 (1961), no. 7, pp. 34–47; no. 8, pp. 52–63. The quotation comes from no. 7, p. 35.

FAVORABLE ASSESSMENTS

1. *How the Incas Achieved So Much*

PEDRO CIEZA DE LEÓN

This chronicler went to America as a boy of 13, became one of the youngest conquistadors on record, and gathered information as he participated in the conquest from northern South America to southern Peru. He kept a diary of his many experiences and on his return to Spain in 1550 published a *Crónica del Perú* (Sevilla, 1553), a remarkably accurate and detailed work. A second work, *Senorío de los Incas*, was not published until 1880 and is considered an indispensable work on Inca society.

He was a friend and admirer of Las Casas, as his recently discovered will shows, and did not hesitate to criticize his fellow conquistadors harshly, but by the middle of the sixteenth century he felt Spanish government was just: "I remember that when I was in the province of Jauja a few years ago the Indians told me with great contentment and happiness: 'these are happy, good times, similar to those of Inca Tupac Yupanqui'. . . . Certainly, all of us who are Christians should rejoice and give thanks for this to our Lord God, that in such vast areas and lands, so far from our Spain and all Europe, there should be such justice and such good government." *

One of the things most to be envied these rulers is how well they knew to conquer such vast lands and, with their forethought, bring them to the flourishing state in which the Spaniards found them when they discovered this new kingdom. Proof of this is the many times I recall hearing these same Spaniards say, when we were in some indomitable region outside these kingdoms, "Take my word for it, if the Incas had been here it would have been a different story." In a word, the Incas did not make their conquests any way just for the sake of being served and collecting tribute. In this respect they were far ahead of us, for with the order they introduced the people throve and multiplied, and arid regions were made fertile and bountiful, in the ways and goodly manner that will be told.

---

* Bailey W. Diffie, *Latin-American Civilization: Colonial Period* (New York: Octagon Books, 1967), p. 311.
From *The Incas of Pedro de Cieza de León* by Pedro de Cieza de León, trans. Harriet de Onis, ed. with intro. by Victor W. von Hagen. Copyright 1959 by the University of Oklahoma Press., pp. 158-161.

They always tried to do things by fair means and not by foul at the beginning; afterward, certain of the Incas meted out severe punishments in many places, but they all tell that they first used great benevolence and friendliness to win these people over to their service. They set out from Cuzco with their men and weapons, and traveled in careful manner until they were close to the place they were going and planned to conquer. There they carefully sized up the situation to learn the strength of the enemy, the support they might have, and from what direction help might come, and by what road. When they had so informed themselves, they tried in every possible way to prevent them from receiving succor, either by rich gifts or by blocking the way. Aside from this, they built fortifications on hills or slopes with high, long stockades, each with its own gate, so that if one were lost, they could retire to the next, and so on to the topmost. And they sent out scouts of their confederates to spy out the land and learn the paths and find out whether they were waiting for them, and where the most food was. And when they knew the route by which the enemy was approaching and the force in which they were coming, they sent ahead messengers to say that the Inca wanted them to be his kin and allies, and, therefore, to come out to welcome him and receive him in their province with good cheer and light heart, and swear him fealty as the others had done. And so they would do this willingly, he sent gifts to the native rulers.

In this way, and with other good methods they employed, they entered many lands without war, and the soldiers who accompanied the Inca were ordered to do no damage or harm, or robbery or violence. If there was a shortage of food in the province, he ordered supplies brought in from other regions so that those newly won to his service would not find his rule and acquaintance irksome, and that knowing and hating him would be one. If in any of these provinces there were no flocks, he instantly ordered that they be given thousands of head, ordering that they tend them well so that they would multiply and supply them with wool for their clothing, and not venture to kill or eat any of the young during the years and time he fixed. And if there were flocks, but they lacked some other thing, he did the same. If they were living in hills and wooded places, he made them understand with courteous words that they should build their villages and houses in the level parts of the sierras and hillsides; and as many of them were not skilled in the cultivation of the land, he had them taught how they should do it, urging them to build irrigation canals and water their fields from them.

They knew how to provide for everything so well that when one of the Incas entered a province in friendship, in a little while it seemed a different place and the natives obeyed him, agreeing that his representatives should dwell there, and also the *mitimaes*. In many others, where they entered by war and force of arms, they ordered that the crops and houses of the enemy be spared, the Inca saying, "These will soon be ours like those we already possess." As this was known to all, they tried to make the war as mild as possible even though fierce battles were waged in many places, because, in spite of everything, the inhabitants of them wanted to preserve their ancient liberty and not give up their customs and religion for others that were alien. But in the end the Incas always came out victorious, and when they had vanquished the others, they did not do them further harm, but released those they had taken prisoner, if there were any, and restored the booty, and put them back in possession of their property and rule, exhorting them not to be foolish and try to compete with his royal majesty nor abandon his friendship, but to be his friends as their neighbors were. And saying this, he gave them a number of beautiful women and fine pieces of wool or gold.

With these gifts and kindly words he won the good will of all to such a degree that those who had fled to the mountains returned to their homes, and all laid down their arms, and the one who most often had sight of the Inca was considered blessed and happy.

They never deprived the native chieftains of their rule. They were all ordered to worship the sun as God, but they were not prohibited from observing their own religions and customs. However, they were ordered to be ruled by the laws and customs which prevailed in Cuzco, and all were to speak the general language.

And when the Inca had appointed a governor with a garrison of soldiers, he went on, and if the provinces were large, he at once ordered a temple built to the sun and women assigned to it as in the others, and palaces built for the Inca, and the amount of tribute to be paid fixed, without ever making this burdensome or offending the people in any way, but guiding them in the ways of their polity, and teaching them to wear long clothing and live in their settlements in orderly manner. And if they lacked for anything, they were provided with it, and taught how to plant and cultivate. So well was this done that we know of many places where there had been no flocks that had them in abundance from the time the Incas subdued them, and others where there had been no corn that later had more than they could use. Those who had lived like savages, poorly clad and barefoot, after they acknowledged this ruler wore shirts and ribbons and blankets, and their women likewise, and other good things; so much so that there will always be memory of all this. In the Collao and other regions they ordered *mitimaes* to go to the highlands of the Andes to plant corn and cocoa and other fruits and roots, the necessary number from all the settlements. And these and their wives always lived in the place where they planted their crops, and harvested so much of what I have described that there was no lack, for these regions produced so much that there was no village, however small, that did not receive something from these *mitimaes*.

2. *Spaniards Corrupted an Ideal Indian Society*

MANCIO SIERRA DE LEGUÍZAMO

Spanish soldiers often developed mixed feelings about their labors during the conquest and afterward. Because Las Casas and other Indian defenders denounced the cruelty of their fellowmen, it was not uncommon to find conquistadors leaving money in their wills to benefit Indians in order "to make restitution." One of the best known of these doubters of the justice of Spanish rule was Mancio Sierra de Leguízamo, who had participated actively in wars against the Indians for many years. He had become famous throughout Peru for having won as booty the celebrated gold image of the sun in Cuzco.* Possibly some zealous, pro-Indian ecclesiastic actually composed his moving last will and testament and had threatened the dying conquistador with hell fire if he did not sign the document.

Before beginning my will, I declare that for many years I have wished for the opportunity to advise his Catholic Majesty, King Philip, our Lord — seeing how Catholic and very Christian he is and how zealous in the services of our Lord God — of what is necessary for the relief of my soul because of the large part I played in the discovery, conquest, and settlement of these Kingdoms when we took them away from those who were Inca Lords and possessed and ruled them as their own, putting them under the royal crown. His Catholic Majesty should understand that the said Incas had these kingdoms governed in such a manner that in all of them there was not a single thief, nor man of vice, nor idle man, nor any adulterous or bad woman; nor were people of loose morals permitted among them. Men had honorable and useful occupations; uncultivated lands, mines, pastures, hunting grounds, woods, and all kinds of employments were so managed and distributed that each person knew and held his own estate and no one else took possession of it or deprived him of it; nor was there any litigation over it. Military enterprises, although they were frequent, did not obstruct commercial matters, and the latter did not impede farming nor anything else; in everything from the most important to the most trifling, there was order and methodical arrangement. The Incas, as well as their governors and captains, were respected and feared by their subjects as persons of great capacity and leadership; and since we found that they

---

* James Lockhart, *Men of Cajamarca* (Austin: University of Texas Press, 1972), p. 469. He *claimed* this, but apparently fibbed.
From "Testamento de Mancio Sierra de Leguízamo," *Revista del Archivo Histórico del Cuzco*, 4 (1953), pp. 91–102, passim.

were the ones who had the strength and authority to offer resistance, we had to deprive them of their power and goods by force of arms in order to subdue and oppress them for the service of our Lord God and in order to take away their land and put it under the royal crown. Our Lord God having permitted it, it was possible for us to subjugate this kingdom with such a multitude of people and riches, and those who had been lords we made servants, as is well known. . . .

His Majesty should understand that my motive in making this declaration is to unburden my conscience of guilt for having destroyed by our bad example people of such good conduct as were these natives, both men and women, and so little given to crime or excess. An Indian who had 100,000 pesos in gold and silver in his house would leave it open and put a broom or small stick across the doorway as a sign that the owner was not there; with this, according to their custom, no one could go inside nor take anything from within. When they saw that we had doors and keys in our houses, they thought that this was due to fear that they would kill us, but they did not believe that anyone would take or steal the property of another; and thus when they saw that among us there were thieves and men who incited their wives and daughters to sin, they regarded us with disdain. These natives have become so dissolute with their offenses against God because of the bad example we have given them in everything that their former extreme of doing no evil has been transformed, so that today they do little or no good. . . . In addition, those who were kings and lords, wealthy and obeyed, have come to such a low estate that they and their descendants are the poorest men in the kingdom. Moreover, we Spaniards even want to force them to serve as bearers, to clean and sweep our houses, to carry refuse to the dung-heaps, and to perform even lowlier tasks. And to avoid such tasks, these Inca Lords have started to learn shoe-making and similar trades, taking advantage of an ordinance of the Viceroy, D. Francisco de Toledo, that natives who served the public did not have to perform personal service, for Toledo's ordinance has greater influence than their being free men. Many things of this nature are permitted, which His Majesty would do well to realize and correct for the relief of his conscience and those of us who were discoverers and settlers and caused these ills. I can do no more than to inform his Catholic Majesty of these conditions, and with this I beg God to absolve me of my guilt, which I myself confess I am moved to speak because I am the last survivor of all the discoverers and conquerors since, as is well known, there is no other left in this kingdom or outside of it.

3. *"The Incas Had Attained to a High State of Perfection. No Thoughtful Man Can Fail to Admire So Noble and Provident a Government"*

GARCILASO DE LA VEGA

This famous mestizo was born in Cuzco of a Spanish captain and an Inca princess in 1539. He went to Spain in 1560 and there embarked on a literary career. He had learned much about Inca history as a boy in his mother's house, for his father had taken a Spanish lady as wife and married off Garcilaso's mother to a Spanish soldier. His account of the culture of his maternal ancestors, the *Royal Commentaries,* was only one of his notable contributions to Spanish prose, but it became the most widely read and translated source of Inca culture. It was an honest picture, for he does not hide the misery of the masses, but for Garcilaso, Inca rule was perfect, a "Paradise Lost," and he is generally considered an apologist for the Incas.

HOW THEY DIVIDED THE LAND AMONGST THE VASSALS

As soon as the Ynca had conquered any kingdom or province, and established his Government amongst the inhabitants according to his laws and idolatrous customs, he ordered that the cultivated land capable of yielding maize should be extended. For this purpose he caused irrigation channels to be constructed, which were most admirable, as may be seen to this day; both those that have been destroyed, the ruins of which are yet visible, and those still in working order. The engineers led the irrigation channels in directions required by the lands to be watered; for it must be known that the greater part of this land is barren as regards corn-yielding soil, and, for this reason, they endeavoured to increase its fertility as much as possible. As the land is under the torrid zone it requires irrigation. The Yncas supplied the water with great ingenuity, and no maize crop was sown without being also supplied with water. They also constructed channels to irrigate the pasture land, when the autumn withheld its rains, for they took care to fertilise the pastures as well as the arable land, as they possessed immense flocks. These channels for the pastures were destroyed as soon as the Spaniards came into the country, but the ruins may be seen to this day.

Having made the irrigation channels, they levelled the fields and arranged

From *First Part of the Royal Commentaries* by Garcilaso de la Vega, trans. Clements R. Markham (London: The Hakluyt Society, 1st series, nos. 41, 45, 1869–1871), no. 45, pp. 3–29, passim.

them in squares, so that they might get the full benefit of the water. On the sides of the mountains, where there was good soil, they made terraces so as to get level ground, as may be seen at this day round Cuzco and all over Peru. These terraces or *andenes* consisted of three walls of strong masonry, one in front and two at the sides, slightly inclining inwards, as are all their walls, so as to sustain the weight of the earth, which was filled in until it reached the top of the walls. Over the first *anden* they constructed another narrower one, and above that another still smaller. Thus they gradually covered the whole mountain, levelling the ground after the manner of a flight of stairs, and getting the use of all the land that was suitable for sowing, and that could be irrigated. . . . So industrious were the Indians in all work tending to enlarge the extent of the land capable of yielding maize. In many places they led an irrigation channel for fifteen or twenty leagues, to irrigate only a few *fanegas* of maize land, that it might not be lost.

Having thus increased the quantity of arable land, they measured all that was contained in each province, every village by itself, and then divided it into three parts. The first part was for the Sun, the second for the King, and the third for the people. These divisions were always carefully made, in order that the people might have sufficient land for their crops; and it was a rule that they should rather have more than was requisite than too little. When the people of a village or province increased in number, a portion was taken from the lands of the Sun and of the Ynca for the vassals. Thus the King only took for himself and for the Sun such lands as would otherwise remain desert and without an owner. Most of the *andenes* belong to the Sun and to the Ynca, because the sovereign had ordered them to be made. Besides the maize lands which were irrigated, other unirrigated tracts were portioned out, in which they sowed pulses and other crops of much importance, such as those they call *papas, ocas* and *añus.* These also were divided into three parts: for the people, the Sun, and the Ynca. But as they were not fertile, from want of irrigation, they did not take crops off them more than once or twice, and then portioned out other lots, that the first might lie fallow. In this way they cultivated their poor lands, that there might always be abundance.

The maize lands were sown every year, because, as they were irrigated and manured like a garden, they were always fertile. They sowed a seed like rice with the maize, called *quinua,* which is also raised on the cold lands.

THE ARRANGEMENT THEY ADOPTED FOR TILLING THE LAND, AND OF THE FESTIVAL THEY HELD WHEN THEY CULTIVATED THE LAND OF THE YNCA AND THE SUN

They also established a regular order in the tilling and the cultivating of the land. They first tilled the fields of the Sun; then of the widows, orphans, aged, and sick, for all these persons were classed as poor, and, as such, the Ynca ordered that their fields should be tilled for them. In each village, or in each ward, if the village was large, there were men deputed to look after the lands of persons who were classed as poor. These deputies were named *Llacta-camayu,* which means "officers of the village." They superintended the plough-ing, sowing, and harvesting; and at such times they went up into towers the night before, that were built for the purpose, and after blowing through a trumpet or shell to secure attention, cried with a loud voice that on such a day such and such lands of the poor would be tilled, warning those, whose duty it might be, to repair thither. The inhabitants of each district were thus apprised on what lands they were to give assistance, which were those of their relations or nearest neighbours. Each one was expected to bring food for himself of what he had in his house, for those who were unable to work were not re-quired to find food for those who could. It was said that their own misery sufficed for the aged, sick, widows, and orphans, without looking after that of the neighbours. If the disabled had no seed, it was provided from the stores, of which we shall speak presently. The lands of soldiers who were employed in the wars were also tilled in this way, like those of widows and orphans; and while the husbands were serving in the wars, their wives were looked up as widows during their absence. Great care was taken of the children of those who were killed in the war, until such time as they were married.

After the lands of the poor and distressed had been tilled, the people worked on their own lands, the neighbours assisting each other. They then tilled the fields of the Curaca, which were the last that received attention in each village or district. In the time of Huayna Ccapac, an Indian superinten-dent, in the province of Chachapoyas, was hanged because he caused the land of a Curaca, who was a relative of his, to be tilled before that of a widow. He was punished as a breaker of the rules established by the Ynca for the tilling of the land, and the gallows were set up on the land of the Curaca. The Yncas ordered that the lands of their vassals should take precedence of their own, because they said that from the prosperity of his subjects was derived their faithful service to the King; for if they were poor and in need, they would not be able to serve well either in peace or war.

The last fields that were cultivated were those of the King. All the people tilled the lands of the Ynca and of the Sun in common, and they went to them with great joy and satisfaction, dressed in the clothes which they wore on their grandest festivals. These garments were covered with plates of gold and silver, and the people also wore plumes of feathers on their heads. When they ploughed (which was the labour they most enjoyed) they sang many songs, composed in praise of their Yncas, and they went through their work with joy and gladness, because it was in the service of their God and of their King.

Hard by the city of Cuzco, on the slopes of the hill where the fortress stands, there was a terrace covering many *fanegas* of ground, and it will be there still, if it has not been covered with houses. It was called the Collcampata. The suburb which contains it, takes its name from the terrace, and this terrace was the special and principal jewel, so to speak, belonging to the Sun; for it was the first land that was dedicated to that deity throughout the whole empire of the Yncas. This land was cultivated by persons of the blood royal, and none but Yncas and Pallas could work on it. The work was performed with great rejoicing, especially the ploughing, when the Yncas came forth in their richest clothes. All the songs that were sung in praise of the Sun and of their Kings, were composed with reference to the meaning of the word *Haylli,* which in the general language of Peru means "triumph." Thus they were said to triumph over the earth by ploughing it, and turning it up so that it might yield fruit. In these songs they inserted graceful references to discreet lovers and to valiant soldiers, all bearing on the triumph over the land that they were tilling. The refrain of each couplet was the word *Haylli,* repeated as often as was necessary to complete the compass which the Indians made; for they ploughed the land backwards and forwards so as to break it up more thoroughly. . . .

The songs of the Indians and their tune appearing good to the master of the choir of the cathedral church of Cuzco, he composed a chaunt, in the year 1551 or 1552, for the feast of the most holy sacrament, very like the *Haylli.* Eight mestizo boys, school-fellows of mine, came forth dressed as Indians, each with a plough in his hand, to represent the song of *Haylli* in the procession, and the whole choir joined them in the refrain of the couplets, which pleased the Spaniards, and caused great joy to the Indians to see the Spaniards solemnizing the festival of our Lord God, whom they called Pachacamac, with the native songs and dances. . . .

THE TRIBUTE THAT THEY GAVE TO THE YNCAS, WITH AN ACCOUNT OF THE GRANARIES

Now that the method the Yncas had of dividing the land has been described, and how it was cultivated by the vassals, it will be well to explain the nature of the tribute they paid to their kings. Their tribute was to cultivate the lands of the Sun and of the Ynca, to gather in the harvests, and to store them in granaries which were kept in each village. One of the chief crops was the *uchu,* which the Spaniards call *axi,* and for another name pepper.

The granaries, called *pirua,* were built of clay mixed with straw. In the time of the Yncas they were constructed with great care. The blocks of clay were of a size conformable to the height of the wall where they were placed, and were cast in different sizes in a mould. They made the granaries of sizes according to the required measurement, some larger than others, to hold from fifty to two hundred *fanegas*. Each granary was measured so as to be of the required size. It had four walls, and there was a passage down the middle, leading from one granary to another, so that they could be emptied or filled at pleasure. But they did not move them from where they were once placed. In order to empty a granary, they had small windows in front, in eight squares, opening so as to give a measurement of the quantity of grain that was poured out, and thus they knew the number of *fanegas* that had been taken out and the quantity remaining without having to measure it further. Thus they could easily tell, by the size of the granaries, the quantity of maize in each depôt, and by the windows they knew how much had been taken out and how much was left in each granary. I saw some of these granaries, which remained from the time of the Yncas, and they were among the best, for they were in the house of the virgins of the Sun, and were built for the use of those women. When I saw them, the convent had become the house of the sons of Pedro del Barco, who were my school-fellows.

The crops of the Sun and those of the Ynca were shut up in places apart, though in the same depôt. The seeds for sowing were given by the Lord of the land, who was the Sun or the King; and in the same way for the sustenance of the Indians who worked, that they might be maintained each out of his own estate, when they tilled and cultivated their lands; so that the Indians had only to give personal labour as their tribute. The vassals paid nothing to the Ynca from their own crops. . . .

THE VASSALS WERE SUPPLIED WITH CLOTHES. NO BEGGING WAS ALLOWED

As there were regulations for the supply of clothing, in abundance, to the soldiers; so also the wool was given to the Curacas and vassals generally every two years, to enable them to make clothes for themselves and their families; and it was the duty of the Decurions to see that the people were clothed. The Indians, and even the Curacas, had few llamas; while the Sun and the Yncas possessed innumerable flocks. The Indians said that when the Spaniards first came to the country there was scarcely sufficient pasture for the flocks, and I have heard my father and his contemporaries relate the great excesses and waste committed by some Spaniards among these flocks. . . . In the warm country cotton was distributed from the royal estates for clothing for the Indians and their families. Thus they had all that was required for human life, both in clothes, shoes, and food; and no one could be called poor, or require to seek alms. For all had as much as they would have required if they had been rich, but they were as poor as possible in unnecessary things, having nothing more than they required. Father Acosta, speaking of Peru, says briefly and compendiously what we have related with so much prolixity. At the end of the fifteenth chapter of the sixth book he has these words: "The sheep were shorn at the proper season, and each person was given wool to spin and weave into cloth for his wife and children. Visits were made to see if this was done, and the idle were punished. The wool that was over was put into the storehouses; which were full of it, and of all other things necessary for human life, when the Spaniards arrived. No thoughtful man can fail to admire so noble and provident a Government. For, without being religious or Christians, the Indians attained to a high state of perfection in providing all that was necessary, and plentifully sustaining their houses of religion, as well as those of their King and Lord. . . ."

In the following chapter, speaking of the occupations of the Indians, he . . . says what follows, copied word for word: "Another thing which the Indians of Peru practised was to teach each boy all the arts which it was necessary a man should know to sustain human life. For, among these people, they had no special tradesmen, as we have, such as tailors, shoemakers, or weavers; but each man learnt all, so that he could himself make all that he required. All men knew how to weave and make clothes; so that when the Ynca gave them wool, it was as good as giving them clothes. All could till and manure the land, without hiring labourers. All knew how to build houses. And the women knew all these arts also, practising them with great diligence, and helping their husbands. Other occupations, which were not connected with ordinary wants, had their special artizans, such as silversmiths, painters, potters, boatmen, accountants and musicians. Even in the ordinary labours of weaving, tilling, and building, there were masters for special work, who served the Lords. But among the common people, as has been said, each could do all that was necessary in his household, without having to pay another, and it is the same at the present day. . . . In truth, these people were neither covetous nor wasteful, but were contented to pass their lives in great moderation, so that surely if their mode of living had been adopted from choice, and not from habit, we must have confessed that it was a very perfect state of existence. Nor were the seeds wanting for the reception of the doctrine of the Holy Gospel, which is so hostile to pride, avarice, and waste. But the preachers do not always make their acts agree with the doctrine they preach to the Indians." A little further on he says: "It was an inviolable law that no one should change the peculiar dress of his province, even if he moved to another; and the Yncas held this rule to be very conducive to good government. The custom is still observed, although not so strictly as it was then." So far the Father Acosta. The Indians wonder much at the way the Spaniards change the fashion of their dress every year, and attribute it to pride and presumption.

The custom of never seeking alms was still observed in my day; and up to the time when I left Peru, in 1560, throughout all the parts that I travelled over, I never saw an Indian, man or woman, begging. I only knew one old woman in Cuzco, named Isabel, who begged, and her habit was more to go jesting from house to house, like a gipsy, than to seek alms from necessity. The Indians quarrelled with her, and spat on the ground, which is a sign of contempt and abhorrence; so that she never begged of the Indians, but only of the Spaniards; and as, even in my time, there was no regular money in the country, they gave her maize as alms, which was what she wanted. . . .

The Yncas, in their administration, did not forget the travellers, but along all the royal roads they ordered houses for travellers to be built, called *corpahuasi,* where they were given food and all things necessary for their journeys from the royal stores kept in each village. If they fell ill, they were attended with great care and kindness; so that they had everything as if they had been in their own houses. It is true that they did not travel for their own pleasure or amusement, nor on their own business, for no such thing was known; but by order of the King or of the Curacas, who sent them from one part to another, or by direction of captains or officials, either of war or peace. These travellers were carefully looked after, but any who travelled without just cause, were punished as vagabonds.

THE SPANISH JUSTIFICATION
FOR CONQUEST

4. *Viceroy Francisco de Toledo's Attack on Inca Rule*

LEWIS HANKE

Toledo proved to be one of the most energetic administrators Spain ever sent to America. Of all the campaigns to justify Spain's right to rule the New World, his was the most public, the most determined. His principal action was to commission one of his trusted advisers, Pedro Sarmiento de Gamboa, to compile a history that would prove that the Inca system had been tyrannical and a "rule by force, with deaths, robberies, and rapine without the will and election of the natives." Thus the Spanish conquest was eminently just, for the conquistadors had "liberated" — to use a modern term — the Indians from cruel and despotic oppressors.

Once Toledo had demolished the Inca claim to rule Peru, he proceeded to draw up a notable series of laws on practically all aspects of life in the colony that firmly established Spanish power and tightly controlled both Indians and Spaniards.

The best example of the effect produced by Fray Bartolomé de Las Casas' theoretical writings concerning the just title Spain held to America occurred in Peru during the rule of Viceroy Francisco de Toledo, wise law-giver, energetic administrator, and greatest viceroy Spain ever sent to Peru, who laid the basis for Spanish rule there during the years 1569–1582. Before his coming, Peru had had a most turbulent and bloody history, and Toledo arrived with one great aim — to establish without question in this territory the position of the King of Spain. One of his earliest acts was to execute the Inca, Lord Tupac Amaru, the Indian leader who refused to accept Spanish rule. Presently, with a view to establishing Spain's judicial title to Peru, he undertook an extensive historical investigation which attempted to demonstrate the unjust nature of the Inca regime and thus demolish the doctrines of Las Casas. . . .

The Viceroy was impelled to this task by what he considered the pernicious influence of Las Casas. Even before Toledo's arrival in Peru, in fact in the instructions given to him by the king on January 28, 1568, he had been warned against free-speaking friars. The king had understood that "the ecclesiastics who have resided and reside in those parts on the pretext of protecting the Indians have wished to busy themselves concerning the justice and the lordship of the Indies and in other matters which lead them into much scandal, particularly when they treat these subjects in pulpits and public places." Therefore, he warned Toledo to take care to prevent such occurrences by conferring with the provincials and superiors of these ecclesiastics, for in no wise should such scandals be permitted. So serious did Toledo consider this problem that early in his career as viceroy he conferred with the higher ecclesiastical authorities of Peru to determine whether the newly established Inquisition could not be utilized, not to smoke out heretics but to impose silence "on preachers and confessors in this realm who hold contrary opinions on jurisdictional matters and on security of conscience." . . .

The Viceroy took three positive steps to combat these theories. First, he inspired the composition of a treatise against Las Casas; second, he embarked upon an investigation of the justice of Inca rule by collecting the so-called *Informaciones;* and finally, he arranged for the preparation of a "true history"

From "Viceroy Francisco de Toledo and the Just Titles of Spain to the Inca Empire" by Lewis Hanke, *The Americas,* 2 (July 1946), pp. 3–19, passim. Reprinted by permission of the Academy of American Franciscan History.

of Peru's past by Pedro Sarmiento de Gamboa. This section will discuss the treatise.

The treatise is in the form of an anonymous letter dated at the Valley of Yucay on March 16, 1571, and is entitled "Defense of the Legitimacy of the Rule of the Kings of Spain in the Indies, in Opposition to Friar Bartolomé de Las Casas." The author, who appears to be rendering a formal opinion to Viceroy Toledo, has been identified by some as Polo de Ondegardo, one of Toledo's principal jurists, by others as Pedro Sármiento de Gamboa, another one of Toledo's principal officers, but perhaps was neither. For at one point, after referring to himself he mentions "many other friars" as though he were one himself and the impression that the author is a friar is strengthened when in closing he states that he was happy to give an opinion "on a matter so appropriate to my profession." If the author were an ecclesiastic, he may have been the Viceroy's chaplain, the Franciscan Pero Gutiérrez.[1]

At any rate this treatise was a frontal attack on the theories of Las Casas who, the author points out, although he was never in Peru and therefore could know nothing first hand of conditions there, has stirred up all the trouble. The author states that the Indies were given to Spain as a reward for her eight centuries of warfare against the Moslems and insists that the Incas were tyrants in Peru "which fact, Your Excellency is now making abundantly clear with great authority in the investigation you are making." . . .

Much harm will come if the just title of the king of Spain is not clarified, continues the author. Christian government and justice will be hindered, conversion will lag, and other Christian princes will use the excuse of ill treatment of the Indians to try to take over part or all of the Indies. Moreover, and this is a curious sidelight on the times, some Spaniards have married Indian women of the Inca family in order to be in line to rule by the hereditary right if the Incas should return to power, as will happen, warned the author, "if this indiscreet and mistaken Bishop has his way." Finally, Lutheran, English, and French heretics will use the beclouded title of Spain as an excuse to rob Spaniards in the Indies, to harry the land, to ascend rivers and disseminate their heresies in all the empire.

The author then proceeds to state certain basic propositions, such as, that the Incas were modern tyrants, that before Topa Inga conquered the land there was no general overlord, that the Pope made the king of Spain lord over them and that, since they had no natural or legitimate lord, the king of Spain became their ruler. The author combats the idea put forward by Las Casas that the Incas had been received voluntarily as lords, and the charge that,

---

[1] Marcel Bataillon has recently concluded that the author probably was the first Jesuit provincial in Peru, Jerónimo Ruiz del Portillo, *Études sur Bartolomé de Las Casas* (Paris: Centre de Recherches de l'Institut d'Études Hispaniques, 1966), pp. 273–274. [Ed.]

whereas the Spaniards levy taxes and send money abroad, the Incas levied none and spent what money they had in Peru.

In a final burst, the author expresses his amazement at those who "under the guise of zealousness try to give these Indians titles and things which did not belong to them, because God didn't choose to give them nor is it appropriate . . . for they are minors who must be governed. . . . It has been a most delicate subtlety of the Devil to select as his instrument an ecclesiastic and apparently a person of zeal, but deceived and ill-speaking and of little discretion, as may be seen by the publication of his books, and by the disturbances he created in Peru when Blasco Núñez came." . . .

THE "INFORMACIONES" OF VICEROY FRANCISCO DE TOLEDO

The *Informaciones* consisted of a formal inquiry, by order of the Viceroy, into the ancient history of the Incas, the conquests of Tupac Yupanqui the last Inca ruler, the institution of the *Curacas,* the Inca religious beliefs and practices, and their sacrifices, nature, and customs. Information was taken down, by means of translators, from two hundred Indians at eleven different points in Peru during the period November, 1570–March, 1572, while Viceroy Toledo was making a general inspection of Peru at the beginning of his rule there, much in the same way the Inca rulers began their administration by first formally surveying their realms. The complete record of this inquiry has only recently been made available by the Argentine historian, Roberto Levillier.

Few episodes in the colonial history of Peru have been interpreted so variously by modern historians as this inquiry. Clements Markham, José de la Riva-Agüero, Horacio Urteaga, and Philip A. Means believe that Toledo organized this as a public spectacle to present the Incas as monsters of cruelty, to falsify their history and customs in order to make certain of Spain's title. They state that senile, servile "yes-men" were chosen as witnesses, and that if a witness happened to tell an unpalatable truth his answer was changed by the interpreter from "no" to "yes," or "yes" to "no," as the occasion required. In short, that it was intended to blacken the Incas. . . .

Levillier rejects this conclusion vehemently. He points out that not one of these writers had available all the *Informaciones,* and insists that the inquiry was an honest and important investigation which constitutes one of the most trustworthy sources available for a reconstruction of the events and of the spirit of the prodigious Inca communist republic.

These inquiries make curious and interesting reading. The records tell us, for example, that on March 13, 1571, there were examined at Cuzco these witnesses: Don Francisco Antigualpa, Governor of Los Andesuyos, aged eighty years; Don Joan Llamoca, Principal of Los Lurinsoras, aged sixty years; Don Joan Caquya, Principal of Los Lurinsoras, aged fifty-five years; Don Lucas Chico, Cacique of Urcos, aged seventy years; Don Bautista Gualpuracana, Curaca of Cachec, aged seventy-five years; and Don Lope Martín Cuntimaycta, Curaca of Yucay, aged sixty years. Among the questions put to them were these:

1. Is it true that the first Inca, he who was called Mango Capac, tyrannically subjugated the Indians living around Cuzco by force of arms and despoiled them of their lands, killing them, warring against them, and otherwise maltreating them? And did all the rest of the Incas do likewise, until the fourth, called Maita Capac, who completed the conquest?

2. Is it true that the Indians never recognized voluntarily these Incas as their lords, and only obeyed them through fear of great cruelties inflicted against them?

3. Is it true that neither you nor your ancestors ever elected the Incas as your lords, but that they supported their tyrannical position by force of arms and the inculcation of fear?

Practically all the questions were of this yes-or-no character, and there were evidently more yes- than no-men in the group interrogated, for the answers all tended to establish that the whole history of the Incas, from 565 A.D. when Manco Capac founded the dynasty until 1533 when Francisco Pizarro won Peru for Spain, was but a succession of tyrannical and brutal overlords who ruled despotically. It was thereupon an easy transition for the interrogators to elicit that the Spanish invasion was thus a deliverance and greatly to the advantage of the Indians, who were now to be Christianized by the ecclesiastics and protected by the Crown. Another set of questions put to a different set of witnesses drew information that the Incas sacrificed to their gods and idols the most beautiful children to be found, that the Incas realized the laziness of their subjects and kept them at work, even if it had no real value, and that some of the Indians were cannibals.

Although Levillier has published all these *Informaciones* in a bulky volume and attacked the "campaign" theory vigorously in an extensive and detailed analysis, it is probable that we can never be quite certain that the last word has been said on this controversy. For the purposes of this present study it is enough to know Toledo's motive in instituting the inquiry. As his secretary, Alvaro Ruiz de Nabamuel, declared "he had seen how badly the rights of the King of Spain to the Indies were treated in Spain and in the Indies, and how unreasonable and dangerous it was to attribute to these Incas the true lordship of these kingdoms."

Viceroy Toledo summed up his own view on the meaning of the inquiry

when he transmitted to the King a summary of the *Informaciones* with a letter dated March 1, 1572, in which he declared:

1. Your Majesty is the legitimate ruler of this kingdom and the Incas
   are tyrannical usurpers.
2. Your Majesty may assign at will the *Cacicazgos* as you see fit, and
   this action would be one of the most important steps you could take
   for the spiritual and temporal rule of the Indians.
3. Your Majesty may therefore bestow the lands of Peru upon Spaniards and ignore the scruples of those who have claimed the Incas are
   the legitimate rulers.
4. Moreover, all mines and minerals, as well as the property of the
   Incas, belong to Your Majesty.
5. As legitimate ruler, Your Majesty rightly exercises jurisdiction over
   the Indians, and, given their weak reason and rude understanding,
   Your Majesty must devise laws for their conservation and require
   them to obey these ordinances.

Toledo closes this letter with the earnest hope that "such a variety of opinion on matters of great importance will cease," and the King, his ministers
and the inhabitants of Peru will no longer have their consciences so disturbed
and confused as in the past whenever some ignorant person dares to open his
mouth and cry to high heaven.

THE "HISTORIA INDICA" OF
PEDRO SARMIENTO DE GAMBOA

The inquiry into Inca history and Indian customs was not enough. Neither
did the treatise "Defense of the Legitimacy of the Rule of the King of Spain in
the Indies" wholly satisfy the Viceroy or the conquistadores and their descendants. What the situation really required, they felt, was a history — a true
history, which would supplant the false histories then current. . . .

The widespread and intense dissatisfaction among the Spanish rulers of
Peru with the historical accounts of Spanish deeds in the New World and with
the justification of Spanish rule in Peru is well-illustrated by the expressive
memorial drawn up by the Town Council of Cuzco and forwarded to the
Council of the Indies on October 24, 1572. These worthies wrote in an injured tone as follows:

Not only did the Greek and Roman historians have a high opinion of the
importance of writing history, but even barbarians who have no knowledge of writing still have by a natural instinct sought means to record
their past with paintings and marks, and in Peru by a system of threads

and knots and registers. Certain persons were appointed whose sole duty was to teach the meaning of it all. Such care has been taken by these Indians that they have a record for the past three hundred years of their deeds, their achievements, their edifices, their wars, and the events of their history. Truly this is to be admired and it is difficult to believe unless one has seen it with his own eyes. All the greater, then, is the fault of the discoverers, the conquistadores, and the colonizers who, having performed great feats and having labored more greatly and with more determination than any other nation in the world, permit these deeds to be forgotten.

Many of those who conquered this realm still live, and we understand that chroniclers who never were here are writing the story of our deeds without ascertaining the truth. These writers do this only to get money by publishing, and sometimes to the detriment of the estates and the honor of those whose deeds they describe. Thus there has resulted a world of conflicting opinions which have left the people disturbed and depressed. When we read the histories written about us, we think they must be describing another kind of people.

We believe ours the most justified cause of all that we know because the basis was the concession which Our Lord and His Vicar-General of our Church made to the Kings of Castile, giving them sovereign dominion and making them patrons in spiritual matters charged with the conversion and evangelical preaching, with general authority to concern themselves in everything discovered and to be discovered without any limitation whatsoever.

This spiritual obligation has been fulfilled. In Cuzco alone there are five monasteries of ecclesiastics and one convent of sisters and a hospital. In this district alone are more than one hundred and twenty priests laboring for the conversion and indoctrination of the natives, not counting the priests Your Excellency has ordered to be added whose expenses are so heavy that they amount to more than one hundred thousand *castellanos*. Moreover, there are only Spanish inhabitants here and they are poor.

Therefore, considering the expense which Your Majesty bears with five tribunals of judges, and mayors, and so many *corregimientos* and the many other salaries which are paid, which consume almost all the revenue gained in Peru, we do not know if there exists in the world a dominion possessed by such just and such reasonable titles, and from which such usefulness and benefit have resulted for the service of God and the increase of His Holy Roman Church.

Moreover, those who are curious to know the origin and basis of other dominions that are in France, Germany, and many other places will discover that most of them have their rights to possession written in the bones of men. And though they have no other reason or basis for their rule than this, they have lived and continue to live so quietly and peacefully that all they have to do is maintain their defenses. They do not have to reply to scruples because nobody raises them. We, the inhabitants of this land, have been less fortunate.

Then the Spaniards resident in Cuzco in 1572 proceeded to describe the tyranny of the Incas, to deplore their bad customs — in much the same vein as the *Informaciones* — and to approve heartily Viceroy Toledo's inquiry. They concluded with the statement that of the one thousand *encomenderos* appointed by the King in Peru, eight hundred have been killed in putting down rebellions and in defense of the realm and those who remained required assistance and favors. It was to satisfy the demands for an honesty history, and to meet the threat to Spanish rule in America that Toledo . . . commissioned Pedro Sarmiento de Gamboa to write a history to set at rest forever the doubts concerning the justice of Spain's rule in Peru.

Sarmiento was one of that group of able officials with whom the Viceroy had surrounded himself, and upon whom he leaned heavily in the administration of his far-flung realm. As a soldier, astronomer, and later explorer of the Solomon Islands and the Straits of Magellan, Sarmiento was typical of the principal Spanish administrative officers who kept the large and complicated machinery of empire in motion. For two years he had been traversing Peru, drawing out from the oldest inhabitants their recollection of the events of the past. To a considerable extent Sarmiento depended upon the *Informaciones* brought forth by Toledo's inquiry, but he had also carried on other investigations in the Valley of the Jauja, in Guamanga, but principally in Cuzco where the Incas had made their capital and where the best informants still lived.

Sarmiento officially presented his history to the Viceroy on February 29, 1572, for examination and correction. Toledo thereupon ordered the "principal and most able descendants" of the Incas to be brought together to listen to a reading of the history. Each Indian swore by the Cross to tell the truth and to indicate, by means of an interpreter, whatever corrections he considered necessary. Day after day the history was read, chapter by chapter. Now and then some name was corrected, or other minor change made, as when Doña María Cusi Guarcai objected to the prominent place accorded to certain Incas not of her own family, but all the listeners declared that they found the history good and true and according to the tales handed down by their fathers. The four living conquistadores who had entered Peru with Pizarro almost half a century before also testified that the history coincided with what they had been told by other Indians.

The corrected version was then legally certified and despatched to the king, with a covering letter from the Viceroy, a genealogical tree, and four painted cloths illustrating certain events of Inca history. These paintings had also been examined by various competent Indians and pronounced good. The Viceroy suggested in his letter to the king that such an accurate history, which would serve as the best possible justification of Spain's title to America, should be published, "in order to refute the other false and lying books that have circulated in these parts, and to explain the truth, not only to our own people but to foreign nations as well."

The *Historia Indica* of Sarmiento described in detail the history of the Incas, their cruelty, their revolting customs, and their tyranny, in a tone and in a spirit reminiscent of that in which Las Casas had denounced the conquistadores in his *Very Brief Account of the Destruction of the Indies*. Sarmiento concluded that because of the sins of the Incas against the law of nature they should be forced to obey this law, "as had been taught by the Archbishop of Florence and confirmed by Friar Francisco de Vitoria in the discussion he made concerning the title of the Indies. Therefore, Your Majesty, by this title alone holds just as sufficient and legitimate title to the Indies as any prince in the world holds to any realm whatsoever, because in all the lands thus far discovered in the two seas to the North and to the South there has been found this general violation of the law of nature." But the king never published the history so laboriously compiled by Pedro Sarmiento de Gamboa. It was allowed to remain in obscurity and not permitted to be spread abroad through Europe in opposition to the writings of Bishop Bartolomé de Las Casas; indeed, it has never been published in Spain and only saw the light of day in 1906, because of the interest of a German scholar.

Nor was Toledo able to convince all the Spaniards in Peru. The Jesuit José de Acosta, perhaps the outstanding ecclesiastic of the time, without mentioning Sarmiento by name, rejected the theory that Indians could be deprived of dominion if they persisted in error. Acosta affirmed: "We must reject those false titles of dominion which some persons are trying to propagate, unnecessary defenders of the royal authority in my opinion, not to say deceivers, who would prove their assertions by the tyranny of the Incas . . . which we do not understand and do not admit. For it is not lawful to rob a thief, nor does the crime committed by some one else add to our own justice."

Another prominent figure of the time, Juan de Matienzo, jurist and adviser of Toledo, was just as certain that the Viceroy was absolutely right. In the *Gobierno del Perú,* not published until three hundred years after it was written, Matienzo followed the same view set forth in Sarmiento's history. He first described the cruelty and tyranny of the Incas, how they killed five thousand persons at one time in one place and jerked out their hearts, how they sacrificed boys to their idols, how they burned alive the women and children of their chief men, and how the Incas governed in their own interest, and not for the welfare of their people. Then Matienzo made a rousing justification of Spanish rule, declaring:

> The Indies were justly won. By the concession of the pope, or because those kingdoms were found deserted by the Spaniards. Or because of their abominable sins against nature. Or because of their infidelity. Although this last reason alone would be sufficient, as would each of the others, the tyranny of the Indians is enough to establish the fact that the kingdom of Peru was justly gained and that His Majesty has a very just title to it. . . . Moreover, the Indians have learned to trade and thereby win profits, and to use mechanical and agricultural instruments, which is no less a just title than the others.

Curiously enough, just as certain historians today accuse the Spaniards of hypocritically seeking to justify their rule, so Polo de Ondegardo, another important adviser to Toledo, stated that the Incas, once they had determined upon a particular conquest, "looked for some title and pretext to accomplish what they wanted to do, which is only natural.". . .

Today there still exist two well-defined attitudes toward the history compiled by Sarmiento de Gamboa at the behest of Viceroy Toledo, similar to the divergence of opinion on the *Informaciones*. Markham attempted to discredit Sarmiento's work, and Means considers it "an abominably unjust and inaccurate account of a great but fallen dynasty" and the author a pliant tool who was willing to aid in the Viceroy's "nefarious literary attack." Levillier, on the other hand, stoutly defends the essential truthfulness of Sarmiento's history, lashes out at Markham for what appears to be his plain mendacity, and supports Viceroy Toledo at every point. Today, just as almost four hundred years ago, the differences of opinion on the justice of Spanish rule in Peru are deep, bitter, and apparently irreconcilable.

A MODERN INTERPRETATION

5. The Incas Combined the Most Absolute Kind of Despotism with the Greatest Tolerance Toward the Social and Political Order of Its Subject Peoples

ALFRED MÉTRAUX

The late Dr. Métraux was one of the most active anthropologists during the last quarter century in the study of South American Indians. He conducted field research as well as library investigations, which help to explain his balanced judgment on such a controversial issue as the true nature of Inca rule.

The true character of the Inca Empire is poorly set forth in works dealing with its economic and social structure. Too many historians or sociologists have attempted, in their enthusiasm, to make of it a state corresponding to a modern formula: a socialist, a totalitarian or a welfare state. From the sixteenth century on, how many arbitrary pictures have been drawn, propped up by quotations! In fact among the chronicles and reports and documents which Spain, that rummager of old papers, has handed down to us, and in the accounts of the Indians themselves, one finds enough mixed-up assertions and facts to bolster or justify the most diverse interpretations. Reality has frequently been confused with a schematic, abstract order which was the fruit of frequently gratuitous speculations.

Undoubtedly, the Indians who described their system of government to the Spaniards gave them a somewhat idealized image, exaggerating the geometrical order and rigorous discipline which it implied. The perfection attributed to this administrative machine, in its functioning as much as in its intentions, cannot but fail to arouse suspicion in our minds. The Inca Empire, as it is usually evoked, escapes history. It is a Utopian republic and not a kingdom of this world which collapsed in a few months under the aggression

From "The Inca Empire: Despotism or Socialism?" by Alfred Métraux from *Diogenes* (a journal of the International Council for Philosophy and Humanistic Studies, Paris; published by Mario Casalini, Montreal), no. 35 (Fall 1961), pp. 78–98, passim. Reprinted by permission.

of a band of adventurers. The terms used to define its institutions, constantly creating false associations, only add to the disease. Even contemporary authors often speak of the Empire of the Sun as did their colleagues of the sixteenth and seventeenth centuries who attributed the customs of its inhabitants to legislators as beneficent as they were wise and ingenious.

Professor Baudin, in a celebrated work, *The Socialist Empire of the Incas,* while admitting the traditional character of the rural communities, considers all the other institutions as a form of organization bearing the true trademark of socialism, for, as he explains, "it is an attempt at the rationalization of society." For this eminent economist, this organization would seem to respond to a preconceived plan tending "to realize a veritable absorption of the individual into the State, the well-being of the first being assured only in order to redound to the grandeur of the second. . . ." One of the aims of this article is to confront this concept of the Inca Empire with a new interpretation of the facts. . . .

The myth of the great socialist State of the Incas is based upon a rather summary notion of its institutions. The property system, especially, as well as the duties of the subjects toward the emperor, have been interpreted according to a terminology and spirit only vaguely corresponding to a civilization which was still archaic despite its complexity and subtlety.

Based on Garcilaso, a picture has been drawn of an Inca economic and social system, thus briefly summed up: the monarchs of ancient Peru, seeking to establish a reign of justice and prosperity among their people, once a province was conquered, "divided it into three parts, the first for the Sun, the second for the king and the third for the natives of the country."

The fields of the Sun were cultivated for the needs of the cult and their products served to support a numerous clergy. The domain of the Inca, exploited for the government's profit, were drawn upon as from a safety vault, when disaster struck some province. Finally, the third group of arable lands were annually divided into equal lots, then redivided among the families of each community according to their members. Each individual's private property was reduced to possession of a hut, an enclosure, some domestic animals, and household goods such as clothes and utensils. All the rest belonged to the State. The inhabitants of the Empire worked for the emperor, who, in exchange, left the free disposition of the communal lands to them and equitably redistributed a part of the fruits of their labor. If the economic structure of the Inca Empire was carried on in this manner, one would more accurately entitle it State Socialism grafted upon agrarian collectivism. Did the reality correspond to the ideal image here evoked?

As a matter of fact, the Incas combined the most absolute kind of despotism with the greatest tolerance toward the social and political order of its subject peoples. The emperor's will was primary, but this will reached the common man via the intermediary of local chiefs whose authority and privileges were maintained and reinforced. The centralizing tendencies of power harmonized with the practice of indirect government, a good and bad harmony — if such an anachronism may be permitted us.

The most original aspects of Inca civilization — the tripartite division of the land, the convents of the Virgins of the Sun, the State granaries, the system of statistics transcribed by means of knotted cords, the network of roads — reflect, in great detail, the conception of the subject's obligations toward his sovereign, and a most ingenious exploitation of resources — both in manpower and products — which a brutally imperialist political system had set up for itself in less than a century. . . .

The forced labor system which the Incas imposed within their Empire derives directly from the work-payments out of which they formerly profited when they were only chiefs of rural communities. The peasants for whom they had been, in bygone times, the *koraka* ("elders") followed them to war, cultivated their fields, and, in turn, took it upon themselves to serve them. Having become masters of a great empire the Incas organized it in such a way as to derive the same advantages from it, but on an incomparably vaster scale. . . .

The evidence of our sources is unanimous: the Incas avoided crushing their subjects under the weight of too-heavy tributes, and, as a rule, distributed personal services equitably. Despite its implacable discipline their government appears to us paternalistic by comparison with the truly ferocious régime which the Spaniards introduced into Peru. Perhaps we are baptising with the name of wisdom and political sense that which was only respect for norms of behavior and archaic traditions to which the Incas adapted themselves like the smallest community chief. Was not the structure of the imperial *ayllu* identical with that of other Andean *ayllu,* and did not their conceptions of the chief, as well as that of community rights, fit into the general ethic held by peoples of the same stock? What was at the beginning a simple confederation of agrarian communities in a Sierra valley was transformed into a hegemony over immense territories without fundamentally altering the primordial relationships between the ruling and ruled groups. In the mountainous region the relatively fertile earth derived its main value from the manpower available for its exploitation. Masters of an empire, the Incas imposed the obligations of work with much severity and made it a moral duty. Undoubtedly, the only condemnable idleness was that which harmed the state and which constituted for this reason an undisciplined act, almost a rebellion.

To read the numerous works treating of the Incas one would gather the impression that at the time of the Spanish conquest, their civilization had reached a dead point and that their empire had become inert in its rigidity and perfection. If one objectively examines the sources, devoting oneself to the exegesis of Spanish documentation without neglecting the teaching of modern ethnography, one would perceive that the Empire's institutions were in full evolution, and that in this apparently so harmonious system, the Incas had introduced innovations which would sooner or later have modified the structure of their State.

These as yet scarcely indicated tendencies, however, are sufficient to permit us to imagine an epoch in which, after repeated gifts, the nobles and high officials would have ended by carving out vast lordships for themselves. The Inca then would have been able to satisfy the ambition of his aides only by dispossessing a growing number of communities whose members would have changed status from freedom to servitude. Among these people uprooted from their *ayllu* were the specialized artisans, servants or tenants, Virgins of the Sun and the *mitima,* farmers transferred to conquered territories. They formed a new category of men whose status was not determined by blood ties, weakening, in proportion, the traditional communities.

Civic officials to whom land had been granted would have also been able to form a new class whose mentality and mode of life would no longer conform to the ideas of old Andean society. If the Empire's evolution had not been brutally interrupted by the Spanish conquest, would it have transformed itself into a kingdom with a structure similar in many ways with that of the late Roman Empire or the decadent Carolingians? With the multiplication of large domains, would not the ruling class have constituted a powerful aristocracy and would it not have been opposed to the central power? The number of *yana,* domestic servants of the great and tenant farmers on their properties, would certainly have augmented at the expense of free peasants. These, of course, are only conjectures based on limited clues but these do reveal the possibilities of transformation which would have operated in a directly opposed sense to the idea of a "Socialist State of the Sun."

Let us consider the political and economic system described here in terms of the famous definition of Socialism by Bertrand Russell. For him, socialism essentially means common ownership of land and capital under a democratic form of government. It implies production for use and not for profit and distributed, if not equally to all, at any rate according to inequalities justified only in the public interest.

The Inca Empire hardly corresponds to these qualifications. Subjected to the despotism of a caste, its aristocratic tendencies were emphasized as a result of the consecration which the authority of the petty kings and local chiefs had received from the conquerors. Besides, in addition to the traditional privileges enjoyed by the *koraka,* were added those deriving from their status as Inca officials. An increasing distance separated them from their former subjects. Agrarian collectivism existed only on the level of the rural communities (*ayllu*) and represented an ancient system whose equivalent may be found in the Old as well as the New World. Therefore, it is certainly a peculiar anachronism to apply a term applicable only to industrial societies to the collective property of archaic societies.

Production was only partially influenced according to the needs of the subjects, the entire surplus reverting to a ruling caste and to its administration. Certainly a part of the excess was redistributed under the form of provisions and material allocated to work crews and soldiers or as presents made to noblemen, clergy, and officials. Assistance to the aged and to the sick which one would be tempted to compare with our social security was an obligation of the village and not of the State. This responsibility simply expressed the old group solidarity still present today among primitive farmers of the Amazon and the peasants of modern Peru.

Socialism, as its theoreticians have emphasized, is not limited to State ownership but implies that the latter be put to the service of the collectivity. In the Inca Empire the tribute paid in personal services and wrought objects profited a caste whose riches and power were growing.

The classical tradition, extolled by the Spanish chroniclers, was imposed on modern historians and sociologists, who, vying with each other, compared the Inca Empire to ancient Rome, to modern States, and to Utopian Republics, but hardly ever dreamed of comparing it with States which existed or still exist among people characterized, for good or evil, as "primitive.". . .

The conquistadores accustomed to fight "naked and savage" Indians were dazzled by the manifestations of high civilization among peoples whom they were naturally inclined to treat as irrational barbarians. Nothing astonished them so much as the discipline ruling the Empire. Later, the old order seemed even more just and humane to the degree that the rule introduced by the Spaniards was marked by wretchedness and cruelty. By contrast with the horrors of the conquest and colonization, the Inca despotism was molded in memory into an age of gold. And so it was, to the degree that the Cuzco emperors, respecting millennary customs, managed their subjects, and under the *pax Incaica,* guaranteed their well-being and happiness.

Bartolomé de Las Casas. Spanish Dominican and Bishop of Chiapas, Mexico. Las Casas became the best-known champion of the Indians in the New World by challenging the racist and imperialist assumptions of the conquistadors. He emphasized Christian teaching about human dignity as developed by St. Thomas Acquinas, and throughout his long career, he defended Indian culture as the equal of the European. In his celebrated debate at Valladolid in 1550 with the Aristotelian scholar, Juan Ginés de Sepúlveda, Las Casas denounced Spain's war against the Indians and with ringing words proclaimed, "All the peoples of the world are men." (Reading 9)

SECTION III

Relations between Indians and Spaniards

THE STRUGGLE FOR JUSTICE

Such a large part of the history of Spanish America involves the relations between the conquering Spaniards and the conquered Indians that this whole volume might be devoted to it. So much controversy has revolved around the subject from 1492 until today that selecting representative material is a difficult task.

No great champions of the Indians came to the fore in Brazil comparable to such figures as Bartolomé de Las Casas in Spanish America except the Jesuit António Vieira, who will be presented in Section V. This fact, combined with the condition of the Indians in Brazil, who were much more primitive than the Aztecs, Mayas, and Incas, resulted in a much less dramatic cultural clash between the Portuguese and the indigenous peoples they encountered during the colonial period in Brazil. We therefore limit this section to the Spanish experience in America, although interesting parallels may be drawn by consulting such works as Dr. Mathias Kiemen's writings.[1]

The struggle for justice for the Indians began in the conquest's earliest years, although the sermons of Antonio de Montesinos marked the first sharp, public confrontation of colonists and friars on how the Indians were to be treated justly, according to Christian doctrine (Reading 1). The struggle for justice occurred because the crown, ecclesiastics, and even some soldiers wanted the conquest to be conducted justly, for one of the principal aims of

---

[1] Mathias Kiemen, "The Indian Policy of Portugal in America, with Special Reference to the Old State of Maranhão, 1500–1755," *The Americas,* 5 (1948), pp. 131–171, and *The Indian Policy of Portugal in the Amazon Region, 1614–1693* (Washington, D.C.: Catholic University of America Press, 1954).

Spain was to Christianize the Indians. What constituted justice and how it could be achieved were thorny questions; they were raised frequently during the discovery, colonization, and administration of the new dominions. One immediate problem the Spanish captains faced in the New World was how to conduct a just war against the Indians. The Requirement, drawn up in 1513 to be read before hostilities began, was the answer of Dr. Palacios Rubios (Reading 2). This document rests upon principles accepted for many years by the crown.

FUNDAMENTAL LAWS

The Requirement was only one of the many ordinances devised by Spain in its attempt to regulate relations with the Indians. The Spaniards were very legalistically minded and within twenty years after Columbus first landed in America had worked out the Laws of Burgos. In 1526 the Requirement was incorporated into the basic law governing conquests, which was first followed during the conquest of Yucatán by Francisco de Montejo. In 1542 the Council of the Indies hammered out the New Laws, after terrific disputes in Spain. The hot controversies continued between those who would protect the Indians and those who would exploit them. By 1573 the principal conquests were over, and a law on discoveries was promulgated that lasted for a long time. Each of these fundamental laws had a long and complicated history, and the controversies surrounding their interpretation reveal much of the spirit and practice peculiar to Spanish legislation. The most important question, of course, was to what extent were they actually obeyed, and no one has yet been able to answer this question in a way satisfactory to all historians.

THE SHOCK OF CONQUEST

However important the legal issues involved in the conquest, at least on the part of the Spaniards, the confrontation between the New World natives and the invading Europeans was also a great dramatic event. Both peoples expressed wonder at the actions and achievements of their adversaries. Bernal Díaz del Castillo, the foot soldier in the little band of warriors with which Cortez toppled the Aztec empire, describes in his classic *True History of the Conquest of New Spain* their first battle with the Indians, and their first view of the great City of Mexico and of Montezuma and his court in awestruck tones (Reading 3). History is usually written by the winners, and Indian records of the conquest are scanty. But a Mexican anthropologist, Miguel León Portilla, has skillfully pieced together the fragments of Indian documentation recording their reaction to the Spaniards and the conquest, which is a moving statement with true poetic power (Reading 4). But the decisive fact was the military superiority of the Spaniards, well exemplified in the analysis John Hemming gives of the final battle for Cuzco as Pizarro's men strove to complete their work by capturing the Inca stronghold (Reading 5).

INDIAN WOMEN AND THE CONQUEST

Although "the Spanish Conquest was a conquest of women" according to one authority, we know very little about this fundamental part of Latin American history. A useful generalized picture has been given (Reading 6), but this can provide only a slight understanding of the intimate drama that must have often occurred when a European married or had relations with an Indian.

A Swedish anthropologist has recently pointed out that the Aztec women lost even more than their men as a result of the triumph of Cortez, "for the women lost their social position and became servants to the new masters." Moreover, some Aztec women were economically independent through careers as weavers or midwives and even as merchants. After the conquest "the general situation of the women deteriorated, so that such activities as were formerly performed by a servant group fell to them, and this often without the social appreciation that the professional groups had enjoyed." The Catholic Church further restrained Indian women's "possibilities of extending their activities and thus their cultural participation beyond the traditional home-sphere."[2]

Though the details of the process of "the conquest of women" are far from clear, the results are obvious. Mestizaje, the mixing of the races (Indian, Negro, and White) for some qualified observers constitutes the main theme in Latin America's entire history.

THE MANY DIFFERENT INTERPRETATIONS

Interpretations of Spanish rule in America began in the sixteenth century and have continued until today. Here we see a variety of views, sometimes contradictory.

Spaniards have been sensitive to attacks upon their actions in America, particularly to the allegations—often made by their political enemies—that they mistreated the Indians, whom they considered as their wards to be protected and Christianized. One of the most reasoned defenses to be made in Spain was prepared by the eminent seventeenth-century administrator and judge, Juan de Solórzano y Pereyra (Reading 7). Contradictory interpretations still persist, especially among non-Spaniards, as will be seen by the

---

[2] Anna-Britta Hellborn, *La participación cultural de las mujeres: Indias y mestizas en el México precortesiano y postrevolucionario* (Stockholm: The Ethnographical Museum, 1967), pp. 300–301.

concluding selections by two Americans—a historian who has written an outstanding work on colonial Mexico, and another historian who has concerned himself with the struggle for justice. (Readings 8–9).

These contrasting opinions and perspectives on the essential contribution of Spain offer students an excellent opportunity to exercise critical judgment on what they read. This, after all, is one of the principal reasons we study history.

THE FIRST CRY
FOR JUSTICE IN AMERICA

1. *The Sermons of Friar Antonio de Montesinos, 1511*

It is symbolic that the struggle for justice was touched off by an almost unknown friar. No writings of Montesinos have come down to us, nor any picture of him, and of his life after his famous sermons on the Caribbean island of Hispaniola we know little, except that he spoke once at court in Spain on behalf of the Indians and met his death while protecting them in Venezuela. Millions of Americans have never heard his name or been aware of his first cry on behalf of human liberty in the New World, which Pedro Henríquez Ureña termed one of the great events in the spiritual history of mankind. Our only records of his great moment in history appear in the royal instruction ordering him to be silent and in the *History of the Indies* by Bartolomé de Las Casas, whose description, written over four hundred years ago, conveys to us vividly the passion and the force of this first dramatic blow struck for freedom in the New World.

On the Sunday before Christmas in 1511 a Dominican friar named Antonio de Montesinos preached a revolutionary sermon in a straw-thatched church on the island of Hispaniola. Speaking on the text "I am a voice crying in the wilderness," Montesinos delivered the first important and deliberate public protest against the kind of treatment being accorded the Indians by his Spanish countrymen. This first cry on behalf of human liberty in the New World was a turning point in the history of America and, as Pedro Henríquez Ureña termed it, one of the great events in the spiritual history of mankind.

The sermon, preached before the "best people" of the first Spanish town established in the New World, was designed to shock and terrify its hearers. Montesinos thundered, according to Las Casas:

> In order to make your sins against the Indians known to you I have come up on this pulpit, I who am a voice of Christ crying in the wilderness of this island, and therefore it behooves you to listen, not with care-

less attention, but with all your heart and senses, so that you may hear it; for this is going to be the strangest voice that ever you heard, the harshest and hardest and most awful and most dangerous that ever you expected to hear. . . . This voice says that you are in mortal sin, that you live and die in it, for the cruelty and tyranny you use in dealing with these innocent people. Tell me, by what right or justice do you keep these Indians in such a cruel and horrible servitude? On what authority have you waged a detestable war against these people, who dwelt quietly and peacefully on their own land? . . . Why do you keep them so oppressed and weary, not giving them enough to eat nor taking care of them in their illness? For with the excessive work you demand of them they fall ill and die, or rather you kill them with your desire to extract and acquire gold every day. And what care do you take that they should be instructed in religion? . . . Are these not men? Have they not rational souls? Are you not bound to love them as you love yourselves? . . . Be certain that, in such a state as this, you can no more be saved than the Moors or Turks.

Montesinos thereupon strode out of the church with head high, leaving a muttering crowd of colonists and officials behind him, who were astounded, but not one was converted. He had come as near to convincing his hearers of their wrongdoing as would a theological student in our day who delivered a soapbox philippic in Wall Street on the biblical text "Sell that which thou hast and give to the poor, and thou shalt have treasure in heaven."

The colonists gathered at the house of the Governor, Diego Columbus, protested against the sermon as a scandalous denial of the lordship of the king in the Indies, and delegated a group which went indignantly to the monastery to exact an apology and disavowal. The vicar, Pedro de Córdoba, unimpressed by the delegation's threat to expel the offensive friar, assured them that Montesinos had spoken for the Dominican group. He promised, however, that Montesinos would preach the next Sunday on the same topic. The colonists thereupon retired, believing they had won their point.

Word of the expected retreat spread quickly, and the following Sunday most of the leading Spaniards crowded into the church. Montesinos mounted the pulpit and announced the disquieting text "Suffer me a little, and I will show thee that I have yet to speak on God's behalf." Rather than explaining away his previous sermon with dialectic subtleties, he proceeded to belabor the colonists anew, with even more passion than before, warning them that the friars would no more receive them for confession and absolution than if they were so many highway robbers. And they might write home what they pleased, to whom they pleased.

These words were soon heard in Spain, even by the King. On March 20, 1512, Ferdinand ordered Governor Diego Columbus to reason with Montesinos. If the Dominican and his brothers persisted in their error, previously condemned by the canonists, theologians, and learned men gathered to deliberate on the problem ten years before, the Governor was instructed to send them to Spain by the first ship so that their Superior might punish them "because every hour that they remain in the islands holding such wrong ideas they will do much harm."

Three days later on March 23, 1512, the Dominican Superior in Spain, Alonso de Loaysa, reproved Montesinos in an official communication to the Dominican Provincial in Hispaniola and ordered him to prevail upon the friars to stop preaching such scandalous doctrine. The Provincial was warned that no more friars would be sent if such preaching were permitted to continue.

Thus began the first great struggle for justice in the New World.

A FUNDAMENTAL LAW

2. The Requirement, 1513, a Most Remarkable Document

One of the most dramatic and most debated documents in the history of Spanish America has been the Requirement or manifesto drawn up by jurists and theologians in Valladolid in 1513. It was designed to be read to Indians before hostilities could be legally launched, and was first employed in 1514 by the aged and vitriolic conquistador Pedrarias Dávila near Santa Marta. Later it was made part of the baggage that every conquistador carried to America, and it was used in a number of curious circumstances:

> The Requirement was read to trees and empty huts when no Indians were to be found. Captains muttered its theological phrases into their beards on the edge of sleeping Indian settlements, or even a league away before starting the formal attack, and at times some leather-lunged Spanish notary hurled its sonorous phrases after the Indians as they fled into the mountains. Once it was read in camp before the soldiers to the beat of the drum. Ship captains would sometimes have the document read from the deck as they approached an island, and at night would send out enslaving expeditions, whose leaders would shout the traditional Castilian war cry "Santiago!" rather than read the Requirement before they attacked the near-by villages.*

* Lewis Hanke, *The Spanish Struggle for Justice in the Conquest of America* (Boston: Little, Brown and Company, 1965), p. 34.

Modern historians have usually treated the Requirement in a derisive or ironical spirit. Spaniards themselves, when describing this document, have often shared the dilemma of Las Casas, who confessed on reading it that he could not decide whether to laugh or to weep. He roundly denounced it on practical as well as theoretical grounds. Even its author, the jurist Palacio Rubios, "laughed often" when he was told of how it was applied in the New World, though the learned doctor still believed that it satisfied the demands of Christian conscience when executed in the manner originally intended.

On the part of the King, don Fernando, and of doña Juana, his daughter, Queen of Castille and Leon, subduers of the barbarous nations, we their servants notify and make known to you, as best we can, that the Lord our God, Living and Eternal, created the Heaven and the Earth, and one man and one woman, of whom you and I, and all the men of the world, were and are descendants, and all those who come after us. But, on account of the multitude which has sprung from this man and woman in the five thousand years since the world was created, it was necessary that some men should go one way and some another, and that they should be divided into many kingdoms and provinces, for in one alone they could not be sustained.

Of all these nations God our Lord gave charge to one man, called St. Peter, that he should be Lord and Superior of all the men in the world, that all should obey him, and that he should be head of the whole human race, wherever men should live, and under whatever law, sect, or belief they should be; and he gave him the world for his kingdom and jurisdiction.

And he commanded him to place his seat in Rome, as the spot most fitting to rule the world from; but also he permitted him to have his seat in any other part of the world, and to judge and govern all Christians, Moors, Jews, Gentiles, and all other sects. This man was called Pope, as if to say, Admirable Great Father and Governor of men. The men who lived in that time obeyed that St. Peter, and took him for Lord, King, and Superior of the universe; so also have they regarded the others who after him have been elected to the Pontificate, and so it has been continued even until now, and will continue until the end of the world.

One of these Pontiffs, who succeeded that St. Peter as Lord of the world, in the dignity and seat which I have before mentioned, made donation of these isles and Terra-firme to the aforesaid King and Queen and to their successors, our lords, with all that there are in these territories, as is contained in certain writings which passed upon the subject as aforesaid, which you can see if you wish.

Based upon the translation given in Arthur Helps, *The Spanish Conquest in America and Its Relation to the History of Slavery and to the Government of the Colonies,* vol. 1 (London, 1900), pp. 264–267.

So their Highnesses are kings and lords of these islands and land of Terra-firme by virtue of this donation; and some islands, and indeed almost all those to whom this has been notified, have received and served their Highnesses, as lords and kings, in the way that subjects ought to do, with good will, without any resistance, immediately, without delay, when they were informed of the aforesaid facts. And also they received and obeyed the priests whom their Highnesses sent to preach to them and to teach them our Holy Faith; and all these, of their own free will, without any reward or condition, have become Christians, and are so, and their Highnesses have joyfully and benignantly received them, and also have commanded them to be treated as their subjects and vassals; and you too are held and obliged to do the same. Wherefore as best we can, we ask and require you that you consider what we have said to you, and that you take the time that shall be necessary to understand and deliberate upon it, and that you acknowledge the Church as the Ruler and Superior of the whole world and the high priest called Pope, and in his name the King and Queen doña Juana our lords, in his place, as superiors and lords and kings of these islands and this Terra-firme by virtue of the said donation, and that you consent and give place that these religious fathers should declare and preach to you the aforesaid.

If you do so, you will do well, and that which you are obliged to do to their Highnesses, and we in their name shall receive you in all love and charity, and shall leave you your wives, and your children, and your lands, free without servitude, that you may do with them and with yourselves freely that which you like and think best, and they shall not compel you to turn Christians, unless you yourselves, when informed of the truth, should wish to be converted to our Holy Catholic Faith, as almost all the inhabitants of the rest of the islands have done. And besides this, their Highnesses award you many privileges and exceptions and will grant you many benefits.

But if you do not do this, and wickedly and intentionally delay to do so, I certify to you that, with the help of God, we shall forcibly enter into your country and shall make war against you in all ways and manners that we can, and shall subject you to the yoke and obedience of the Church and of their Highnesses; we shall take you and your wives and your children, and shall make slaves of them, and as such shall sell and dispose of them as their Highnesses may command; and we shall take away your goods, and shall do all the harm and damage that we can, as to vassals who do not obey, and refuse to receive their lord, and resist and contradict him; and we protest that the deaths and losses which shall accrue from this are your fault, and not that of their Highnesses, or ours, nor of these cavaliers who come with us. And that we have said this to you and made this Requirement, we request the notary here present to give us his testimony in writing, and we ask the rest who are present that they should be witnesses of this Requirement.

THE SHOCK OF CONQUEST

3. *The True History of the Conquest of Mexico*

BERNAL DÍAZ DEL CASTILLO

One of the classics of the conquest is *The True History of the Conquest of New Spain,* written down long after the events by Bernal Díaz del Castillo, one of the small number of conquistadors who fought under Ferdinand Cortez in the conquest of Mexico. His honest and forthright account gives us a lifelike picture of how it all really happened. A more official account may be found in the letters Cortez sent back to Spain to impress the king and court of his great deeds in the New World.* The foot soldier's story is in a more familiar tone; Bernal Díaz was blunt, too, for he was responsible for that pithy explanation of why Spaniards went to America: "We came to serve God, and also to get rich."

Bernal Díaz throughout his detailed *True History* displayed a respect and admiration for many aspects of Indian culture. But like practically all Spaniards the human sacrifices practiced by the Indians revolted him from the first time he heard of them:

> Thirty of us soldiers, well armed, went in two boats to the Island [of San Juan de Ulúa] and we found there a temple where there was a very large and ugly idol which was called Tescatepuca and in charge of it were four Indians with very large black cloaks and hoods, such as the Dominicans or canons wear. . . .
>
> They had this day sacrificed two boys and cut open their chests, and offered the blood and hearts to that cursed Idol. The priests came towards us to fumigate us with the incense with which they had fumigated their Tescatepuca, for when we approached them they were burning something which had the scent of incense, but we would not allow them to fumigate us, for we felt much pity at seeing those two boys who had just been killed and at beholding such great cruelty.†

The Indian prisons also brought stern condemnation by Bernal Díaz: "In Tlaxcala we found wooden houses furnished with gratings, full of Indian men and women imprisoned in them, being fed up until they were fat enough to be sacrificed and eaten. These prisons we broke open and destroyed, and set free the prisoners who were in them, and these poor Indians did not dare to go in any direction, only to stay there with us and thus

---

* *Hernando Cortés: Five Letters, 1519–1526* (New York: Norton, 1962). The most recent and best edition is *Hernán Cortés: Letters from Mexico,* trans. and ed. A. R. Pagden (New York: Grossman, 1971).

† *The True History of the Conquest of New Spain, by Bernal Díaz de Castillo,* trans. and ed. Alfred Percival Maudslay (London: The Hakluyt Society, 1908), vol. 1, pp. 55–56.

escape with their lives. From now on, in all the towns that we entered, the first thing our Captain ordered us to do was to break open these prisons and set free the prisoners."‡

The *True History* deserves to be read in its entirety, and good paperback editions are available.§ Here are a few selections in which Bernal Díaz records their early impressions of Mexico and the Mexican Indians.

1. *How all the Caciques of Tabasco and its dependencies attacked us, and what came of it*

I have already said how we were marching along when we met all the forces of the enemy which were moving in search of us, and all of the men wore great feather crests and they carried drums and trumpets, and their faces were coloured black and white, and they were armed with large bows and arrows, lances and shields and swords shaped like our two-handed swords, and many slings and stones and fire-hardened javelins, and all wore quilted cotton armour. As they approached us their squadrons were so numerous that they covered the whole plain, and they rushed on us like mad dogs completely surrounding us, and they let fly such a cloud of arrows, javelins and stones that on the first assault they wounded over seventy of us, and fighting hand to hand they did us great damage with their lances, and one soldier fell dead at once from an arrow wound in the ear, and they kept on shooting and wounding us. With our muskets and crossbows and with good sword play we did not fail as stout fighters, and when they came to feel the edge of our swords little by little they fell back, but it was only so as to shoot at us in greater safety. Mesa, our artilleryman, killed many of them with his cannon, for they were formed in great squadrons and they did not open out so that he could fire at them as he pleased, but with all the hurts and wounds which we gave them, we could not drive them off. I said to Diego de Ordás "it seems to me that we ought to close up and charge them," for in truth they suffered greatly from the strokes and thrusts of our swords, and that was why they fell away from us,

‡ Ibid., pp. 288–289.
§ Bernal Díaz, *The Conquest of New Spain,* trans. J. M. Cohen (Baltimore: Penguin Books, 1967), and *The Discovery and Conquest of Mexico by Bernal Díaz del Castillo,* trans. with notes by A. P. Maudslay, Intro. by Irving A. Leonard (New York: Grove Press, 1958).
From *The True History of the Conquest of New Spain, by Bernal Díaz del Castillo,* trans. and ed. Alfred Percival Maudslay (London: The Hakluyt Society, 1908–1910), vol. 1, pp. 118–121; vol. 2, pp. 34–63, passim.

both from fear of these swords, and the better to shoot their arrows and hurl their javelins and the hail of stones. Ordás replied that it was not good advice, for there were three hundred Indians to every one of us, and that we could not hold out against such a multitude, — so there we stood enduring their attack. However, we did agree to get as near as we could to them, as I had advised Ordás, so as to give them a bad time with our swordsmanship, and they suffered so much from it that they retreated towards a swamp.

During all this time Cortés and his horsemen failed to appear, although we greatly longed for him, and we feared that by chance some disaster had befallen him.

I remember that when we fired shots the Indians gave great shouts and whistles and threw dust and rubbish into the air so that we should not see the damage done to them, and they sounded their trumpets and drums and shouted and whistled and cried "Alala! alala!"

Just at this time we caught sight of our horsemen, and as the great Indian host was crazed with its attack on us, it did not at once perceive them coming up behind their backs, and as the plain was level ground and the horsemen were good riders, and many of the horses were very handy and fine gallopers, they came quickly on the enemy and speared them as they chose. As soon as we saw the horsemen we fell on the Indians with such energy that with us attacking on one side and the horsemen on the other, they soon turned tail. The Indians thought that the horse and its rider was all one animal, for they had never seen horses up to this time.

The savannas and fields were crowded with Indians running to take refuge in the thick woods near by.

After we had defeated the enemy Cortés told us that he had not been able to come to us sooner as there was a swamp in the way, and he had to fight his way through another force of warriors before he could reach us, and three horsemen and five horses had been wounded.

As soon as the horsemen had dismounted under some trees and houses, we returned thanks to God for giving us so complete a victory.

As it was Lady day we gave to the town which was afterwards founded here the name of Santa Maria de la Victoria, on account of this great victory being won on Our Lady's day. This was the first battle that we fought under Cortés in New Spain.

After this we bound up the hurts of the wounded with cloths, for we had nothing else, and we doctored the horses by searing their wounds with the fat from the body of a dead Indian which we cut up to get out the fat, and we went to look at the dead lying on the plain and there were more than eight hundred of them, the greater number killed by thrusts, the others by the cannon, muskets and crossbows, and many were stretched on the ground half dead. Where the horsemen had passed, numbers of them lay dead or groaning from their wounds. The battle lasted over an hour, and the Indians fought all the time like brave warriors, until the horsemen came up.

We took five prisoners, two of them Captains. As it was late and we had had enough of fighting, and we had not eaten anything, we returned to our camp. Then we buried the two soldiers who had been killed, one by a wound in the ear, and the other by a wound in the throat, and we smeared the wounds of the others and of the horses with the fat of the Indian, and after posting sentinels and guards, we had supper and rested.

2. [*The Great City of Mexico*]

As soon as the messengers had been despatched, we set out for Mexico, and as the people of Huexotzingo and Chalco had told us that Montezuma had held consultations with his Idols and priests whether he should allow us to enter Mexico, or whether he should attack us, and all the priests had answered that his Huichilobos had said he was to allow us to enter and that then he could kill us, as I have already related in the chapter that deals with the subject, and as we are but human and feared death, we never ceased thinking about it. As that country is very thickly peopled we made short marches, and commended ourselves to God and to Our Lady his blessed Mother, and talked about how and by what means we could enter [the City], and it put courage into our hearts to think that as our Lord Jesus Christ had vouchsafed us protection through past dangers, he would likewise guard us from the power of the Mexicans.

We went to sleep at a town called Iztapalatengo where half the houses are in the water and the other half on dry land, where there is a small mountain (and now there is an Inn there) and there they gave us a good supper. . . .

The next day, in the morning, we arrived at a broad Causeway, and continued our march towards Iztapalapa, and when we saw so many cities and villages built in the water and other great towns on dry land and that straight and level causeway going towards Mexico, we were amazed and said that it was like the enchantments they tell of in the legend of Amadis, on account of the great towers and cues and buildings rising from the water, and all built of masonry. And some of our soldiers even asked whether the things that we saw were not a dream? It is not to be wondered at that I here write it down in this manner, for there is so much to think over that I do not know how to describe it, seeing things as we did that had never been heard of or seen before, not even dreamed about.

Thus, we arrived near Iztapalapa, to behold the splendour of the other Caciques who came out to meet us, who were the Lord of the town named Cuitlahuac, and the Lord of Culuacan, both of them near relations of Montezuma. And then when we entered that city of Iztapalapa, the appearance of the palaces in which they lodged us! How spacious and well built they were, of beautiful stone work and cedar wood, and the wood of other sweet scented trees, with great rooms and courts, wonderful to behold, covered with awnings of cotton cloth.

When we had looked well at all of this, we went to the orchard and garden, which was such a wonderful thing to see and walk in, that I was never tired of looking at the diversity of the trees, and noting the scent which each one had, and the paths full of roses and flowers, and the many fruit trees and native roses, and the pond of fresh water. There was another thing to observe, that great canoes were able to pass into the garden from the lake through an opening that had been made so that there was no need for their occupants to land. And all was cemented and very splendid with many kinds of stone [monuments] with pictures on them, which gave much to think about. Then the birds of many kinds and breeds which came into the pond. I say again that I stood looking at it and thought that never in the world would there be discovered other lands such as these, for at that time there was no Peru, nor any thought of it. [Of all these wonders that I then beheld] to-day all is overthrown and lost, nothing left standing. . . .

Early next day we left Iztapalapa with a large escort of those great Caciques whom I have already mentioned. We proceeded along the Causeway which is here eight paces in width and runs so straight to the City of Mexico that it does not seem to me to turn either much or little, but, broad as it is, it was so crowded with people that there was hardly room for them all, some of them going to and others returning from Mexico, besides those who had come out to see us, so that we were hardly able to pass by the crowds of them that came; and the towers and cues were full of people as well as the canoes from all parts of the lake. It was not to be wondered at, for they had never before seen horses or men such as we are.

Gazing on such wonderful sights, we did not know what to say, or whether what appeared before us was real, for on one side, on the land, there were great cities, and in the lake ever so many more, and the lake itself was crowded with canoes, and in the Causeway were many bridges at intervals, and in front of us stood the great City of Mexico, and we, — we did not even number four hundred soldiers! and we well remembered the words and warnings given us by the people of Huexotzingo and Tlaxcala and Tlamanalco, and the many other warnings that had been given that we should beware of entering Mexico, where they would kill us, as soon as they had us inside.

Let the curious readers consider whether there is not much to ponder over in this that I am writing. What men have there been in the world who have shown such daring? But let us get on, and march along the Causeway. When we arrived where another small causeway branches off (leading to Coyoacan, which is another city) where there were some buildings like towers, which are their oratories, many more chieftains and Caciques approached clad in very rich mantles, the brilliant liveries of one chieftain differing from those of another, and the causeways were crowded with them. The Great Montezuma had sent these great Caciques in advance to receive us, and when they came before Cortés they bade us welcome in their language, and as a sign of peace, they touched their hands against the ground, and kissed the ground with the hand. . . .

3. [Montezuma and His Splendid Court]

The Great Montezuma was about forty years old, of good height and well proportioned, slender, and spare of flesh, not very swarthy, but of the natural colour and shade of an Indian. He did not wear his hair long, but so as just to cover his ears, his scanty black beard was well shaped and thin. His face was somewhat long, but cheerful, and he had good eyes and showed in his appearance and manner both tenderness and, when necessary, gravity. He was very neat and clean and bathed once every day in the afternoon. He had many women as mistresses, daughters of Chieftains, and he had two great Cacicas as his legitimate wives, and when he had intercourse with them it was so secretly that no one knew anything about it, except some of his servants. He was free from unnatural offences. The clothes that he wore one day, he did not put on again until four days later. He had over two hundred chieftains in his guard, in other rooms close to his own, not that all were meant to converse with him, but only one or another, and when they went to speak to him they were obliged to take off their rich mantles and put on others of little worth, but they had to be clean, and they had to enter barefoot with their eyes lowered to the ground, and not to look up in his face. And they made him three obeisances, and said: "Lord, my Lord, my Great Lord," before they came up to him, and then they made their report and with a few words he dismissed them, and on taking leave they did not turn their backs, but kept their faces toward him with their eyes to the ground, and they did not turn their backs until they left the room. I noticed another thing, that when other great chiefs came from distant lands about disputes or business, when they reached the apartments of the Great Montezuma, they had to come barefoot and with poor mantles, and they might not enter directly into the Palace, but had to loiter about a little on one side of the Palace door, for to enter hurriedly was considered to be disrespectful.

For each meal, over thirty different dishes were prepared by his cooks according to their ways and usage, and they placed small pottery brasiers beneath the dishes so that they should not get cold. They prepared more than three hundred plates of the food that Montezuma was going to eat, and more than a thousand for the guard. When he was going to eat, Montezuma would sometimes go out with his chiefs and stewards, and they would point out to him which dish was best, and of what birds and other things it was composed, and as they advised him, so he would eat, but it was not often that he would go out to see the food, and then merely as a pastime.

I have heard it said that they were wont to cook for him the flesh of young boys, but as he had such a variety of dishes, made of so many things, we could not succeed in seeing if they were of human flesh or of other things, for they daily cooked fowls, turkeys, pheasants, native partridges, quail, tame and wild ducks, venison, wild boar, reed birds, pigeons, hares and rabbits, and many sorts of birds and other things which are bred in this country, and they are so numerous that I cannot finish naming them in a hurry; so we had no insight into it, but I know for certain that after our Captain censured the sacrifice of human beings, and the eating of their flesh, he ordered that such food should not be prepared for him thenceforth.

Let us cease speaking of this and return to the way things were served to him at meal times. It was in this way: if it was cold they made up a large fire of live coals of a firewood made from the bark of trees which did not give off any smoke, and the scent of the bark from which the fire was made was very fragrant, and so that it should not give off more heat than he required, they placed in front of it a sort of screen adorned with figures of idols worked in gold. He was seated on a low stool, soft and richly worked, and the table, which was also low, was made in the same style as the seats, and on it they placed the table cloths of white cloth and some rather long napkins of the same material. Four very beautiful cleanly women brought water for his hands in a sort of deep basin which they call "xicales," and they held others like plates below to catch the water, and they brought him towels. And two other women brought him tortilla bread, and as soon as he began to eat they placed before him a sort of wooden screen painted over with gold, so that no one should watch him eating. Then the four women stood aside, and four great chieftains who were old men came and stood beside them, and with these Montezuma now and then conversed, and asked them questions, and as a great favour he would give to each of these elders a dish of what to him tasted best. They say that these elders were his near relations, and were his counsellors and judges of law suits, and the dishes and food which Montezuma gave them they ate standing up with much reverence and without looking at his face. He was served on Cholula earthenware either red or black. While he was at his meal the men of his guard who were in the rooms near to that of Montezuma, never dreamed of making any noise or speaking aloud. They brought him fruit of all the different kinds that the land produced, but he ate very little of it. From time to time they brought him, in cup-shaped vessels of pure gold, a certain drink made from cacao which they said he took when he was going to visit his wives, and at the time he took no heed of it, but what I did see was that they brought over fifty great jugs of good cacao frothed up, and he drank of that, and the women served this drink to him with great reverence.

Sometimes at meal-times there were present some very ugly humpbacks, very small of stature and their bodies almost broken in half, who are their jesters, and other Indians, who must have been buffoons, who told him witty sayings, and others who sang and danced, for Montezuma was fond of pleasure and song, and to these he ordered to be given what was left of the food and jugs of cacao. Then the same four women removed the table cloths, and with much ceremony they brought water for his hands. And Montezuma talked with those four old chieftains about things that interested him, and they took leave of him with the great reverence in which they held him, and he remained to repose. . . .

4. The Grief of the Conquered:
"Broken Spears Lie in the Roads"

MIGUEL LEÓN PORTILLA

Spanish chronicles present only one side of the story, that of the conquerors. The Mexican anthropologist Miguel León Portilla was the first to
bring together a selection of the accounts by the Indians, some written as
early as 1528, only seven years after the fall of Mexico City. These writings
give a brief history of the dramatic confrontation of Indians and Spaniards
as told by the victims, and include reports by native priests and wise men
who managed to survive the persecution and death that took place during
the final struggle.

The selection begins with the story of how frightened Montezuma was
by the reports of the messengers he had sent to see Cortez and his soldiers.

MOTECUHZOMA GOES OUT
TO MEET CORTES

The Spaniards arrived in Xoloco, near the entrance to Tenochtitlan. That was
the end of the march, for they had reached their goal.

Motecuhzoma now arrayed himself in his finery, preparing to go out to
meet them. The other great princes also adorned their persons, as did the
nobles and their chieftains and knights. They all went out together to meet
the strangers.

They brought trays heaped with the finest flowers — the flower that resembles a shield; the flower shaped like a heart; in the center, the flower with
the sweetest aroma; and the fragrant yellow flower, the most precious of all.
They also brought garlands of flowers, and ornaments for the breast, and
necklaces of gold, necklaces hung with rich stones, necklaces fashioned in the
petatillo style.

Thus Motecuhzoma went out to meet them, there in Huitzillan. He presented many gifts to the Captain and his commanders, those who had come
to make war. He showered gifts upon them and hung flowers around their
necks; he gave them necklaces of flowers and bands of flowers to adorn their
breasts; he set garlands of flowers upon their heads. Then he hung the gold

necklaces around their necks and gave them presents of every sort as gifts of welcome. . . .

MOTECUHZOMA AWAITS WORD
FROM THE MESSENGERS

While the messengers were away, Motecuhzoma could neither sleep nor eat, and no one could speak with him. He thought that everything he did was in vain, and he sighed almost every moment. He was lost in despair, in the deepest gloom and sorrow. Nothing could comfort him, nothing could calm him, nothing could give him any pleasure.

He said: "What will happen to us? Who will outlive it? Ah, in other times I was contented, but now I have death in my heart! My heart burns and suffers, as if it were drowned in spices . . . ! But will our lord come here?"

Then he gave orders to the watchmen, to the men who guarded the palace: "Tell me, even if I am sleeping: 'The messengers have come back from the sea.'" But when they went to tell him, he immediately said: "They are not to report to me here. I will receive them in the House of the Serpent. Tell them to go there." And he gave this order: "Two captives are to be painted with chalk."

The messengers went to the House of the Serpent, and Motecuhzoma arrived. The two captives were then sacrificed before his eyes: their breasts were torn open, and the messengers were sprinkled with their blood. This was done because the messengers had completed a difficult mission: they had seen the gods, their eyes had looked on their faces. They had even conversed with the gods!

THE MESSENGERS' REPORT

When the sacrifice was finished, the messengers reported to the king. They told him how they had made the journey, and what they had seen, and what food the strangers ate. Motecuhzoma was astonished and terrified by their report, and the description of the strangers' food astonished him above all else.

He was also terrified to learn how the cannon roared, how its noise resounded, how it caused one to faint and grow deaf. The messengers told him: "A thing like a ball of stone comes out of its entrails: it comes out shooting sparks and raining fire. The smoke that comes out with it has a pestilent odor, like that of rotten mud. This odor penetrates even to the brain and causes the greatest discomfort. If the cannon is aimed against a mountain, the mountain splits and cracks open. If it is aimed against a tree, it shatters the tree into splinters. This is a most unnatural sight as if the tree had exploded from within."

The messengers also said: "Their trappings and arms are all made of iron. They dress in iron and wear iron casques on their heads. Their swords are iron; their bows are iron; their shields are iron; their spears are iron. Their deer carry them on their backs wherever they wish to go. These deer, our lord, are as tall as the roof of a house.

"The strangers' bodies are completely covered, so that only their faces can be seen. Their skin is white, as if it were made of lime. They have yellow hair, though some of them have black. Their beards are long and yellow, and their moustaches are also yellow. Their hair is curly, with very fine strands.

"As for their food, it is like human food. It is large and white, and not heavy. It is something like straw, but with the taste of a cornstalk, of the pith of a cornstalk. It is a little sweet, as if it were flavored with honey; it tastes of honey, it is sweet-tasting food.

"Their dogs are enormous, with flat ears and long, dangling tongues. The color of their eyes is a burning yellow; their eyes flash fire and shoot off sparks. Their bellies are hollow, their flanks long and narrow. They are tireless and very powerful. They bound here and there, panting, with their tongues hanging out. And they are spotted like an ocelot."

When Motecuhzoma heard this report, he was filled with terror. It was as if his heart had fainted, as if it had shriveled. It was as if he were conquered by despair. . . .

THE SPANIARDS TAKE POSSESSION OF THE CITY

When the Spaniards entered the Royal House, they placed Motecuhzoma under guard and kept him under their vigilance. They also placed a guard over Itzcuauhtzin, but the other lords were permitted to depart.

Then the Spaniards fired one of their cannons, and this caused great confusion in the city. The people scattered in every direction; they fled without rhyme or reason; they ran off as if they were being pursued. It was as if they had eaten the mushrooms that confuse the mind, or had seen some dreadful apparition. They were all overcome by terror, as if their hearts had fainted. And when night fell, the panic spread through the city and their fears would not let them sleep.

In the morning the Spaniards told Motecuhzoma what they needed in the way of supplies: tortillas, fried chickens, hens' eggs, pure water, firewood and charcoal. Also: large, clean cooking pots, water jars, pitchers, dishes and other pottery. Motecuhzoma ordered that it be sent to them. The chiefs who received this order were angry with the king and no longer revered or respected him. But they furnished the Spaniards with all the provisions they needed — food, beverages and water, and fodder for the horses.

THE SPANIARDS REVEAL THEIR GREED

When the Spaniards were installed in the palace, they asked Motecuhzoma about the city's resources and reserves and about the warriors' ensigns and shields. They questioned him closely and then demanded gold.

Motecuhzoma guided them to it. They surrounded him and crowded close with their weapons. He walked in the center, while they formed a circle around him.

When they arrived at the treasure house called Teucalco, the riches of gold and feathers were brought out to them: ornaments made of quetzal feathers, richly worked shields, disks of gold, the necklaces of the idols, gold nose plugs, gold greaves and bracelets and crowns.

The Spaniards immediately stripped the feathers from the gold shields and ensigns. They gathered all the gold into a great mound and set fire to everything else, regardless of its value. Then they melted down the gold into ingots. As for the precious green stones, they took only the best of them; the rest were snatched up by the Tlaxcaltecas. The Spaniards searched through the whole treasure house, questioning and quarreling, and seized every object they thought was beautiful.

THE SEIZURE OF MOTECUHZOMA'S TREASURES

Next they went to Motecuhzoma's storehouse, in the place called Totocalco [Place of the Palace of the Birds], where his personal treasures were kept. The Spaniards grinned like little beasts and patted each other with delight.

When they entered the hall of treasures, it was as if they had arrived in Paradise. They searched everywhere and coveted everything; they were slaves to their own greed. All of Motecuhzoma's possessions were brought out: fine bracelets, necklaces with large stones, ankle rings with little gold bells, the royal crowns and all the royal finery — everything that belonged to the king and was reserved to him only. They seized these treasures as if they were their own, as if this plunder were merely a stroke of good luck. And when they had taken all the gold, they heaped up everything else in the middle of the patio.

La Malinche called the nobles together. She climbed up to the palace roof and cried: "Mexicanos, come forward! The Spaniards need your help! Bring them food and pure water. They are tired and hungry; they are almost fainting from exhaustion! Why do you not come forward? Are you angry with them?"

The Mexicans were too frightened to approach. They were crushed by terror and would not risk coming forward. They shied away as if the Spaniards were wild beasts, as if the hour were midnight on the blackest night of the year. Yet they did not abandon the Spaniards to hunger and thirst. They brought them whatever they needed, but shook with fear as they did so. They delivered the supplies to the Spaniards with trembling hands, then turned and hurried away. . . .

THE MASSACRE IN THE MAIN TEMPLE DURING THE FIESTA OF TOXCATL

At this moment in the fiesta, when the dance was loveliest and when song was linked to song, the Spaniards were seized with an urge to kill the celebrants. They all ran forward, armed as if for battle. They closed the entrances and passageways, all the gates of the patio: the Eagle Gate in the lesser palace, the Gate of the Canestalk and the Gate of the Serpent of Mirrors. They posted guards so that no one could escape, and then rushed into the Sacred Patio to slaughter the celebrants. They came on foot, carrying their swords and their wooden or metal shields.

They ran in among the dancers, forcing their way to the place where the drums were played. They attacked the man who was drumming and cut off his arms. Then they cut off his head, and it rolled across the floor.

They attacked all the celebrants, stabbing them, spearing them, striking them with their swords. They attacked some of them from behind, and these fell instantly to the ground with their entrails hanging out. Others they beheaded: they cut off their heads, or split their heads to pieces.

They struck others in the shoulders, and their arms were torn from their bodies. They wounded some in the thigh and some in the calf. They slashed others in the abdomen, and their entrails all spilled to the ground. Some attempted to run away, but their intestines dragged as they ran; they seemed to tangle their feet in their own entrails. No matter how they tried to save themselves, they could find no escape.

Some attempted to force their way out, but the Spaniards murdered them at the gates. Others climbed the walls, but they could not save themselves. Those who ran into the communal houses were safe there for a while; so were those who lay down among the victims and pretended to be dead. But if they stood up again, the Spaniards saw them and killed them.

The blood of the warriors flowed like water and gathered into pools. The pools widened, and the stench of blood and entrails filled the air. The Spaniards ran into the communal houses to kill those who were hiding. They ran everywhere and searched everywhere; they invaded every room, hunting and killing.

THE SIEGE OF TENOCHTITLAN

Now the Spaniards began to wage war against us. They attacked us by land for ten days, and then their ships appeared. Twenty days later, they gathered all their ships together near Nonohualco, off the place called Mazatzintamalco. The allies from Tlaxcala and Huexotzinco set up camp on either side of the road.

Our warriors from Tlatelolco immediately leaped into their canoes and set out for Mazatzintamalco and the Nonohualco road. But no one set out from Tenochtitlan to assist us: only the Tlatelolcas were ready when the Spaniards arrived in their ships. On the following day, the ships sailed to Xoloco.

The fighting at Xoloco and Huitzillan lasted for two days. While the battle was under way, the warriors from Tenochtitlan began to mutiny. They said: "Where are our chiefs? They have fired scarcely a single arrow! Do they think they have fought like men?" Then they seized four of their own leaders and put them to death. The victims were two captains, Cuauhnochtli and Cuapan, and the priests of Amantlan and Tlalocan. This was the second time that the people of Tenochtitlan killed their own leaders. . . .

THE FIGHTING IS RENEWED

The Spaniards made ready to attack us, and the war broke out again. They assembled their forces in Cuepopan and Cozcacuahco. A vast number of our warriors were killed by their metal darts. Their ships sailed to Texopan, and the battle there lasted three days. When they had forced us to retreat, they entered the Sacred Patio, where there was a four-day battle. Then they reached Yacacolco.

The Tlatelolcas set up three racks of heads in three different places. The first rack was in the Sacred Patio of Tlilancalco [Black House], where we strung up the heads of our lords the Spaniards. The second was in Acacolco, where we strung up Spanish heads and the heads of two of their horses. The third was in Zacatla, in front of the temple of the earth-goddess Cihuacoatl, where we strung up the heads of Tlaxcaltecas.

The women of Tlatelolco joined in the fighting. They struck at the enemy and shot arrows at them; they tucked up their skirts and dressed in the regalia of war.

The Spaniards forced us to retreat. Then they occupied the market place. The Tlatelolcas — the Jaguar Knights, the Eagle Knights, the great warriors

— were defeated, and this was the end of the battle. It had lasted five days, and two thousand Tlatelolcas were killed in action. During the battle, the Spaniards set up a canopy for the Captain in the market place. They also mounted a catapult on the temple platform.

EPIC DESCRIPTION OF THE BESIEGED CITY

And all these misfortunes befell us. We saw them and wondered at them; we suffered this unhappy fate.

> Broken spears lie in the roads;
> we have torn our hair in our grief.
> The houses are roofless now, and their walls
> are red with blood.
>
> Worms are swarming in the streets and plazas,
> and the walls are splattered with gore.
> The water has turned red, as if it were dyed,
> and when we drink it,
> it has the taste of brine.
>
> We have pounded our hands in despair
> against the adobe walls,
> for our inheritance, our city, is lost and dead.
> The shields of our warriors were its defense,
> but they could not save it.
>
> We have chewed dry twigs and salt grasses;
> we have filled our mouths with dust and bits of adobe;
> we have eaten lizards, rats and worms. . . .

When we had meat, we ate it almost raw. It was scarcely on the fire before we snatched it and gobbled it down.

They set a price on all of us: on the young men, the priests, the boys and girls. The price of a poor man was only two handfuls of corn, or ten cakes made from mosses or twenty cakes of salty couch-grass. Gold, jade, rich cloths, quetzal feathers — everything that once was precious was now considered worthless.

The captains delivered several prisoners of war to Cuauhtemoc to be sacrificed. He performed the sacrifices in person, cutting them open with a stone knife. . . .

ELEGIES ON THE FALL OF THE CITY

INTRODUCTION. By way of conclusion, we present three "songs of sorrow," true elegies written by the post-Conquest Aztec poets. The first song, from the collection of *Cantares mexicanos* in the National Library of Mexico, was probably composed in 1523. The second is part of a whole series of poems recounting the Conquest from the arrival of the Spaniards in Tenochtitlan to the ultimate defeat of the Aztecs. We have selected only the most dramatic moments from the last section of this series. The third song, also from the *Cantares mexicanos,* recalls the traditional symbolism of "flowers and songs." It laments that only grief and suffering remain in the once proud capital.

These elegies are among the first and most poignant expressions of what Dr. Garibay has called "the trauma of the Conquest." They reveal, with greater eloquence than the other texts, the deep emotional wound inflicted on the Indians by the defeat. (Introductory note by Miguel León Portilla.)

The Fall of Tenochtitlan

Our cries of grief rise up
and our tears rain down,
for Tlatelolco is lost.
The Aztecs are fleeing across the lake;
they are running away like women.

How can we save our homes, my people?
The Aztecs are deserting the city:
the city is in flames, and all
is darkness and destruction.

Motelchiuhtzin the Huiznahuacatl,
Tlacotzin the Tlailotlacatl,
Oquitzin the Tlacatecuhtli
are greeted with tears.

Weep, my people:
know that with these disasters
we have lost the Mexican nation.
The water has turned bitter,
our food is bitter!
These are the acts of the Giver of Life. . . .

The Imprisonment of Cuauhtemoc

The Aztecs are besieged in the city;
the Tlatelolcas are besieged in the city!

The walls are black,
the air is black with smoke,
the guns flash in the darkness.
They have captured Cuauhtemoc;
they have captured the princes of Mexico.

The Aztecs are besieged in the city;
the Tlatelolcas are besieged in the city!
After nine days, they were taken to Coyoacan:
Cuauhtemoc, Coanacoch, Tetlepanquetzaltzin.
The kings are prisoners now.

Tlacotzin consoled them:
"Oh my nephews, take heart!
The kings are prisoners now;
they are bound with chains."

The king Cuauhtemoc replied:
"Oh my nephew, you are a prisoner;
they have bound you in irons.

"But who is that at the side of the Captain-General?
Ah, it is Dona Isabel, my little niece!
Ah, it is true: the kings are prisoners now!

"You will be a slave and belong to another:
the collar will be fashioned in Coyoacan,
where the quetzal feathers will be woven.

"Who is that at the side of the Captain-General?
Ah, it is Dona Isabel, my little niece!
Ah, it is true: the kings are prisoners now!"

Flowers and Songs of Sorrow

Nothing but flowers and songs of sorrow
are left in Mexico and Tlatelolco,
where once we saw warriors and wise men.

We know it is true
that we must perish,
for we are mortal men.

You, the Giver of Life,
you have ordained it.

We wander here and there
in our desolate poverty.
We are mortal men.
We have seen bloodshed and pain
where once we saw beauty and valor.

We are crushed to the ground;
we lie in ruins.
There is nothing but grief and suffering
in Mexico and Tlatelolco,
where once we saw beauty and valor.

Have you grown weary of your servants?
Are you angry with your servants,
O Giver of Life?

5. *Francisco Pizarro and His Men on the Road to Cuzco, 1533*

JOHN HEMMING

The conquest of Peru was not as sudden or dramatic as the downfall of the Aztec empire, but it was dramatic enough. John Hemming, a young British businessman, has demonstrated that the writing of history cannot be left exclusively to the professional historian, for his solid and well-written volume, *The Conquest of the Incas,* is the first satisfying and sound general work on the conquest of Peru that has appeared in a generation.

The following selection brings out clearly the military aspects of the clashes between European-trained soldiers and the Inca warriors.

The four battles on the road to Cuzco — Jauja, Vilcashuaman, Vilcaconga, and the pass above Cuzco — had demonstrated the immense superiority of mounted, armoured Spaniards over native warriors. The Inca empire did not, as is sometimes supposed, go under without a struggle. Whenever the native

From *The Conquest of the Incas,* copyright © 1970 by John Hemming. Reprinted by permission of Harcourt Brace Jovanovich, Inc. and Macmillan, London and Basingstoke. pp. 110-117.

armies were led by a determined commander they fought with fatalistic bravery. In the course of the Conquest the Incas, who were themselves formidable conquerors against other Andean tribes, tried to adapt their fighting methods to meet the extraordinary challenges of invasion by a more advanced civilisation. The mounted knight had dominated European military history since Roman times. This formidable figure could be stopped only by other horsemen using similar equipment, by archers, pikemen or elaborate defences. His domination of the battlefield ended only with the evolution of rapid-firing firearms. Whenever American natives had time to assimilate European weapons they were able to mount an effective resistance — for instance the natives of southern Chile, who acquired pikes and horses, or those of North America who adopted horses and firearms. But the Incas did not have time to make these adaptations to their fighting techniques, and their bare mountainous country did not possess suitable wood for pikes or bows.

The Inca armies were now confronting the finest soldiers in the world. Spanish tercios were considered the best in Europe throughout the sixteenth century. They had behind them the successful expulsion of the Moors from Spain, and many who now fought in Peru had participated in the defeat of Francis I at Pavia or of the Aztecs in Mexico. The men who were attracted to the American conquests were the most adventurous — as tough, brave and ruthless as the members of any gold rush. In addition to greed they possessed the religious fervour and unshakeable self-confidence of a crusading people which had been fighting the infidel for centuries and was still on the advance. Whatever one may think of their motives, it is impossible not to admire their bravery. In skirmish after skirmish their first reaction — almost a reflex — was to charge straight into the thick of the enemy. Such aggressiveness was intended as a psychological shock-tactic, and its effect was heightened by the invaders' reputation for success, invincibility, almost divinity.

Atahualpa's nephew Titu Cusi tried to describe the awe felt by his people in the face of these strangers. "They seemed like viracochas, which was our ancient name for the universal creator. [My people] gave this name to the men they had seen, partly because they were very different from us in clothing and appearance, and also because we saw that they rode on enormous animals that had feet of silver — we said 'silver' because of the shine of the horses' shoes. We also called them this because we had seen them expressing themselves on to white sheets, just as one person talks to another — this referred to their reading books and letters. We called them viracochas because of their magnificent appearance and physique; because of the great differences between them — some had black beards and others red ones; because we saw them eat off silver; and also because they possessed yllapas (our name for thunder) — we said this to describe the arquebuses which we thought to be thunder from heaven."

During the actual fighting of the Conquest, the Spaniards owed everything to their horses. On the march their horses gave them a mobility that continually took the natives by surprise. Even when the Indians had posted pickets, the Spanish cavalry could ride past them faster than the sentries could run back to warn of danger. And in battle a mounted man has an overwhelming advantage over a man on foot, using his horse as a weapon to ride down the enemy, more manoeuvrable, less exhausted, inaccessible and continually striking downwards from his greater height.

At the time of the Conquest there was a revolution in the method of riding. The pike and arquebus had made the fully armoured knight too vulnerable. He was now replaced by the trooper, jinete, on a lighter, faster horse. Instead of riding "a la brida" with legs stretched out to take the shock of jousting, the riders of the Conquest adopted a new style called "a la jineta." This method had the rider in "the position of the Moors, with short stirrups and the legs bent backwards so as to give the appearance of almost kneeling on the horse's back. . . . With the high Moorish saddle, the rider used the powerful Moorish bit, a single rein, and always rode with rather a high hand. The reason was that the horses were all bitted on the neck, that is to say they turned by pressure on the neck and not by pulling at the corners of the mouth. . . . As the bit had a high port, and often a long branch, the raising of the hand pressed the port into the palate . . . and a horse turned far more rapidly and suffered less [than under] the modern system."

Both Spaniards and Indians attached immense importance to horses, the tanks of the Conquest. To Spaniards the possession of a horse elevated a man, entitling him to a horseman's share of conquered treasure. During the months of waiting at Cajamarca, Spaniards had paid fantastic prices for the few available horses. Francisco de Xerez described these prices "even though some people may find them unbelievably high. One horse was bought for 1,500 pesos de oro and others for 3,300. The average price for horses was 2,500, but there were none to be found at this price." This was sixty times the price being paid for a sword at Cajamarca at the same time, and the inflated values of Peru of course represented small fortunes in contemporary Spain. Many deeds of sale that have survived from the period confirm them.

For the Indians, their enemies' great horses assumed a terrible value. They thought little of a Spaniard on foot, cumbersome in armour and breathless from the altitude; but the horses filled them with dread. "They thought more of killing one of these animals that persecuted them so than they did of killing ten men, and they always placed [the horses'] heads afterwards somewhere that the Christians could see them, decked in flowers and branches as a sign of victory."

The Spanish conquistadores wore armour and steel helmets. Some of the infantry wore a simple steel cap called a salade, of which the barbute type was still common at the time of the Conquest. It looked like a steel Balaclava helmet, similar to a modern steel helmet, but lower over the forehead and nape of the neck. The cabasset was another simple helmet. Its high domed crown resembled a 1920s cloche, and it often had a small apical peak like a French revolutionary liberty cap. But the most famous helmet was the morion. This was a bowl-like chapel-de-fer to which an elongated brim had been added. This brim swept along the sides in an elegant upward curve, rising to a point at the front and rear. The crown was often protected by a steel crest running from front to rear like that on the helmet of a French poilu of the 1914–18 War.

All Spanish soldiers wore armour, but this varied in elaboration. Many of the wealthy leaders wore full armour, which came in a wide variety of styles ranging from heavy gothic suits to the Maximilian suits of the 1530s and 1540s. The period of the Conquest was the high point of the art of making armour. Plates covering exposed areas of the body were brilliantly jointed with articulated lames and hinges to permit freedom of movement to every limb. Special protective plates covered the shoulders, elbows and knees; but the steel of the breastplates and leg and arm protections was as light as possible. A full suit of armour weighed only about sixty pounds, and this weight was quite tolerable, being evenly distributed over the entire body. In the latter half of the century some parts of the body were less thoroughly protected, in order to economise weight. Instead of head-to-foot armour, soldiers adopted a half-suit extending only to the jointed lames, called tassets, that formed a skirt below the breastplate, or a three-quarter suit extending to the knees. Suits of armour had their own helmets. A solid crown covered the head and extended over the neck where it joined a series of overlapping plates called a gorget. The cheeks and chin were defended by a piece called bevor, and a hinged visor covered the face. This helmet also became lighter, with the visor being replaced by a peak across the forehead and a series of protective bars across the face itself.

Although most of the rich men in the Conquest owned full armour or acquired it when they received shares of treasure, they often used lighter substitutes when fighting Indians. Some wore china mail shirts, which weighed between fourteen and thirty pounds. These varied according to the size of their links, but most could withstand a normal thrust. Some suits had thicker or flattened wire at vulnerable places to reduce the size of the holes. Other conquistadores abandoned even chain mail in favour of padded cloth armour called escaupil, which they adopted from the Aztecs. Escaupil normally consisted of canvas stuffed with cotton. Spanish soldiers also defended themselves with small shields, generally oval bucklers of wood or iron covered in leather.

The most effective Spanish weapon was a sword: either the double-edged cutting sword, or the rapier, which over the years gradually lost its cutting edge and became thinner and more rigid for thrusting. These were the weapons that slaughtered thinly protected Indians. Sword manufacture had reached perfection by the sixteenth century, and Toledo was one of the most famous centres for the craft. Strict regulations and apprenticeships ensured that high standards were maintained. A blade had to survive rigorous testing before being decorated and mounted in its hilt: it was bent in a semicircle and in an s-bend, and then struck with full force against a steel helmet before being passed. The sword was often decorated with a motto: "never unsheathed in vain"; "por mi dama y mi rey, es mi ley" ("for my lady and my King, this is my law"); or more blatant advertising such as "Toledan quality, the soldier's dream." The blade, some three feet long, light, flexible and extremely strong and sharp, was a deadly weapon in the hands of skilled swordsmen. And the Spanish conquistadores, acknowledged as the finest fighting men in Europe, made it their business to be supreme in this art. Throughout the century swords, like horses, were rigorously forbidden to Indians under any circumstances whatsoever.

In addition to his sword, and to supporting daggers and poniards, the cavalryman's favourite weapon was his lance. Along with the crouching, highly mobile jineta method of riding, came the "lanza jineta." This was ten to fourteen feet long, but light and thin, with a metal tip shaped like a diamond or olive leaf. The rider could charge with the shaft resting against his chest; he could hold it down level with his thigh, parallel to the galloping horse, with his thumb pointed forwards in the direction of the blow; or he could stab downwards with it. Each method was enough to penetrate Indian padded armour.

It has sometimes been said that the Spanish triumph was due to their firearms. This was not so. Arquebuses were sometimes fired during the Conquest, but there were very few of them, and they played no significant role beyond producing a great psychological effect when they did go off. It was not surprising that few arquebuses were used. The cavalry despised them as an ungentlemanly arm, and the Conquest was largely the work of horsemen. They were unwieldy, from three to five feet long, and often needing a support at the end of the barrel. They were difficult to load: a measured charge of powder had to be pushed down the muzzle, followed by the ball. And they were even more difficult to fire: fine powder led through a hole to the main charge, and this had to be lit by a wick. Arquebusiers carried the long rope-like wick coiled around themselves or around the weapon; they lit it by striking a flint and tinder; and they had to blow on the lighted end before applying it to the powder. Later innovations produced an s-curved piece of metal that slightly accelerated the process by pressing the wick on to the powder. But it was almost a century before the flintlock was introduced.

Crossbows were used in the Conquest, but again with limited effect. This weapon had been invented to shoot a missile with sufficient velocity to penetrate armour, but the thrust was gained at the expense of ease or speed. The steel bow had to be bent back mechanically, either by heaving on a system of pulleys or by winding back along a series of ratchets with the help of a wheel called a cranequin. All this involved a laborious process of upending the weapon, treading the head against the ground, and heaving up the bowstring. The metal bolt, once fired, killed any Indian it struck, but the natives were not impressed by this cumbersome device, which often misfired or suffered mechanical breakages.

What could Quisquis's men offer against this armoury? They were still fighting in the bronze age, and their use of metal was unimaginative. They simply copied shapes that had been developed in stone, and their bronze was sadly blunt when matched against Spanish steel. They used a variety of clubs and maces, massive, heavy clubs of some hard jungle palm, and smaller hand-axes or head-breakers called champis. These had stone or bronze heads, shaped either as simple circles or adorned with star-shaped spikes — such heads litter museums and collections of Inca artefacts. Some of the larger clubs had blades like butchers' choppers. Almost all the Spanish soldiers and horses were battered and wounded by these clubs. But it was all too rare for one of these biblical weapons actually to kill a mounted, armoured, slashing Spaniard.

The natives had more success with their missiles. A favourite among the highland tribes was the sling, a belt of wool or fibre some two to four feet long. This was doubled over the projectile, generally a stone the size of an apple, and twirled about the head before one end was released. The sling-shot then spun off to its target with deadly force and accuracy. Coastal tribes used palm throwing-sticks to fire javelins with fire-hardened points. The most effective weapon against cavalry was the long bow, but this was rarely used in Inca armies. Forest Indians used bows and arrows, just as they do today — their forests produced the necessary springy woods for their manufacture, and the dense conditions made arrows ideal weapons for shooting forest game. Whenever Inca armies fought near the Amazonian forests they could enlist jungle tribes with deadly contingents of archers, but they failed to exploit this fine weapon in the highlands.

An Inca warrior was a splendid figure. He wore the normal male dress of a knee-length tunic and resembled a Roman or Greek soldier or a medieval page. His tunic was often adorned with a patterned border and a gold or bronze disc called canipu in the centre of the chest and back. He had bright woollen fringes around his legs, below the knee and at the ankle, and often a plumed crest across the top of his helmet. The helmets themselves were thick woollen caps or were made of plaited cane or wood. Many soldiers wore quilted armour similar to the escaupil of the Aztecs. Beyond this the only protection was a round shield of hard chonta-palm slats worn on the back, and a small shield carried on the arms. These shields added further colour to the Inca battle line, for their wooden bases were covered with cloth or feather-cloth and had a hanging apron, all of which was decorated with magical patterns and devices.

After their defeat in the fierce fight above Cuzco, Quisquis's men lost heart. While the Spaniards spent an anxious night on the hill above the city, the natives left their campfires burning and slipped away in the darkness. When dawn broke Quisquis's army had vanished. "The Governor drew up the infantry and cavalry at the first light of dawn the following morning, and marched off to enter Cuzco. They were in careful battle order, and on the alert, for they were certain that the enemy would launch an attack on them along the road. But no one appeared. In this way the Governor and his men entered the great city of Cuzco, with no further resistance or fighting, at the hour of high mass, on Saturday, 15 November 1533."

INDIAN WOMEN AND SPANISH MEN

6. The Conquest of Women

MAGNUS MÖRNER

The Swedish historian Magnus Mörner has been the leader in this generation in the study of the large and complicated subject of race relations in Latin America. During the last decade he has published widely on various aspects of the problem and has stimulated other scholars to enter the field. The following selection comes from one of his recent studies, which, though brief, is the best single volume on the subject with an excellent guide to widely scattered publications.

When they went ashore, Columbus and his men found that often the Indians of the Antilles tried to hide their women from the white strangers. On other occasions the Indian women showed themselves and were even importune

From *Race Mixture in the History of Latin America* by Magnus Mörner (Boston: Little, Brown and Company, 1967), pp. 21–27, passim. Reprinted by permission.

in their admiration for the newcomers. Naturally enough, the discoverers thought that the first attitude was due to the jealousy of the Indian husbands, whereas the women, of course, were only expressing their love. Such a romantic interpretation of the first meeting of the races can also be found in the accounts of contemporary chroniclers and later historians. But in 1924 a Spanish historian made the sobering observation that the Indian attitudes would be better explained by their animist belief. At first they had to resist the alien spirits. When this was no longer possible, they had to surrender entirely. In addition, the Arawaks were not aware of any relationship between copulation and pregnancy. The latter was explained merely in an animistic way. However true this may be, perhaps the boldness of the alien spirits at last succeeded in arousing the jealousy of the Indian husbands — when Columbus returned to Hispaniola on his second voyage, he found that the men he had left there had been killed. The Indians explained, an eyewitness reports, that one of the Spaniards "had taken three women to himself, and another four; from whence we drew the inference that jealousy was the cause of the misfortune that had occurred."

From the very beginning, Spanish and Portuguese eyewitnesses and chroniclers devoted enthusiastic accounts to the beauty of the Indian girls. Also, a tough German mercenary, Ulrich Schmidel, who took part in the conquest of Río de la Plata, sounds inspired when talking about the Jarayes women: "Very handsome and great lovers, affectionate and with ardent bodies, in my opinion." I would be the last to deny that such expressions in the otherwise not overly romantic chronicles might sometimes be sincere and based on experience. In fact, the female type of the forest tribes is rather close to the feminine ideal in Europe during the Renaissance and later. But I suspect that the sixteenth-century authors sometimes dwelt on the beauty and enchantment of the Indian women in order to satisfy the literary taste of the times. Therefore there is little reason to take these accounts very seriously, or to refer to them, as some historians do, as explaining the rapidity and character of the process of race mixture. Above all it would, as I see it, be absurd to consider them an evidence of a lack of prejudice on the part of the conquistadores. The basic explanation of the rapidity with which race mixture proceeded after the first contact is undoubtedly to be found in the lack of white women at the time of the first expeditions, and the months of abstention during the passage. The satisfaction of a natural instinct should not be confused with social and esthetic attitudes. . . .

In a way, the Spanish Conquest of the Americas was a conquest of women. The Spaniards obtained the Indian girls both by force and by peaceful means. The seizure of women was simply one element in the general enslavement of Indians that took place in the New World during the first decades of the sixteenth century. Indian slavery was finally prohibited categorically in the

New Laws of 1542. It then gradually disappeared, at least in most areas of Spanish America. . . .

Bernal Díaz, that remarkable eyewitness of the conquest of Mexico, presents a lively account of the actual enslavement of women. Cortés had decided that all the slaves taken by the soldiers should be branded, so that the Royal fifth (the Crown's share) and his own share of the human booty could be taken. When the soldiers returned the following day to recover the remaining slaves, they discovered to their dismay that Cortés and his officers had "hidden and taken away the best looking slaves so that there was not a single pretty one left. The ones we received were old and ugly. There was much grumbling against Cortés on this account. . . ." Military campaigns have no doubt always been accompanied by rape and other brutalities against the defenseless. . . .

The Spaniards also obtained women in the form of gifts and as tokens of friendship from the Indian *caciques*. This kind of hospitality has existed in many other environments and ages. Bernal Díaz tells us how the Cacique Xicotenga offered Cortés his virgin daughter and four other pretty girls to his captains. Similar episodes abound in the chronicles of the times. From Paraguay, Rui Díaz de Guzmán reports that the Guaraní caciques considered the gift of women to be an excellent means of allying themselves with the Spaniards. "They called all of them brothers-in-law. This is the origin of the existing custom of calling the Indians entrusted to you *Tobayá* which means brother-in-law. And it so happened that the Spaniards had many sons and daughters with the Indian women they received." Once confirmed by the gift of women, the alliances between Spaniards and Indians were likely to be strong and lasting. This could very well be of greatest importance for the success of a small group of conquistadores. As Inca Garcilaso de la Vega puts it, "as soon as the Indians saw that a woman had been begotten by a Spaniard, all the kinsfolk rallied to pay homage to the Spaniard as their idol and to serve him because they were now related to him. Such Indians were of great help during the Conquest of the Indies.

Another way of obtaining women was provided by the *encomienda,* the famous institution by which Indians were distributed among Spaniards who were granted their tribute. In his turn, the recipient of an encomienda was supposed to protect and civilize his Indians and see to it that they were Christianized. At least until the New Laws (1542), the Indians usually paid their tributes to the *encomendero* in days of work. It is not surprising that the encomenderos often asked for female domestic servants. As Bishop Juan de Zumárraga of Mexico observed, in his well-known letter to Emperor Charles in 1529, such servants were used as concubines more often than not. Near Cuenca in present Ecuador, Cieza de León reports, the Indians sent their wives and daughters to carry the Spaniards' luggage, while they stayed at home. The chronicler remarks that these women were "beautiful, and not a little lascivious, and fond of the Spaniards." . . .

However the Spaniard and the Portuguese of the early sixteenth century had obtained them, by force, purchase, or gift, he lived surrounded by Indian women. Sometimes they were his slaves or the kind of serfs called *naborías* in the Caribbean and *yanaconas* in Peru; sometimes they were, theoretically, free servants. This way of life often produced the impression of a real harem, though some accounts of contemporary observers seem exaggerated, perhaps because they were shocked or too enthusiastic. We should not take as a statistically verified fact the report that in Paraguay, called the Paradise of Mohammed, every Spaniard had an average of twenty to thirty women.

The Church, of course, by no means approved of this situation, but it was certainly not easy to do anything about it. The Bishop of Santo Domingo wrote to the Emperor in 1529 that when his Spanish parishioners were living in sin the concubines were their own Indian servants "and nothing can be found out about it." Furthermore, the results of such unions were often born in faraway places. As another report from Santo Domingo during the same period put it: "there are a great many mestizos here, sons of Spaniards and Indian women who are usually born in *estancias* and uninhabited places." The civil authorities during the Conquest were often satisfied with having the Indian women baptized prior to coition. Thus, the commander of an expedition in Cartagena in 1538 was instructed that he should see to it that "no soldier slept with any Indian who was not a Christian." The conquistadores themselves seem to have taken the reproaches for being promiscuous very lightly, whether they were aware of fulfilling a "civilizing" mission or not. Accused by the Inquisition of a great many blasphemous utterances, the old conquistador Francisco de Aguirre, governor of Tucumán, confessed among other things to having declared that "the service rendered to God in producing mestizos is greater than the sin committed by the same act." . . .

There can be no doubt that casual intercourse and concubinage accounted for most of the crossing during the Conquest. And polygyny was more than frequent. But it should not be forgotten that marriage also brought about race mixture. Intermarriage was explicitly permitted by the monarch in 1501. Two years later Governor Ovando of Santo Domingo was instructed to see to it that "some Christians [i.e., Spaniards] marry some Indian women and some Christian women marry some Indian men, so that both parties can communicate and teach each other and the Indians become men and women of reason.". . . The colonial authorities were far from enthusiastic about it, but there were always some churchmen around who put pressure on them to permit or even promote intermarriage. Spanish-Indian couples living in concubinage should be persuaded to marry. According to a chronicler, Governor Ovando ordered the Spaniards in Santo Domingo either to marry their

Indian partners or to part company: "In order not to lose their authority over the Indian women and their services they married them.". . .

It seems fair to draw two conclusions on the basis of what we know about race mixture during the Conquest. In the first place, the color of the sexual partner was of no importance, as well stated by Juan de Carvajal, a conquistador of Venezuela. When accused of promiscuity he flatly replied: "No one in these parts who has a homestead can live without women, Spanish *or* Indian." Second, it is obvious that the Spaniards preferred to marry Spanish women, above all, probably because of their desire to provide their descendants with a good lineage.

To the Indian women, association with the conquistadores offered many advantages, even though they were not allowed to marry. But many seem to have become aware of their inferiority to their white rivals. Chronicler Gonzalo Fernández de Oviedo tells a pathetic story of how Indian girls tried to bleach their skin. The Indian women could hope that the children they had with the whites would be accepted as free "Spaniards.". . .

INTERPRETATIONS

7. A Seventeenth-Century Defense of Spanish Treatment of the Indians

JUAN DE SOLÓRZANO Y PEREYRA

Juan de Solórzano y Pereyra was one of Spain's foremost seventeenth-century administrators and jurists. After law training at the University of Salamanca he served for a number of years as judge in the important audiencia in Lima, Peru. Then he returned to Spain where he became a member of the prestigious Council of the Indies. He also wrote extensively. His *De Jure Indiarum* (1629) was a learned defense of Spain's titles to the Indies and government, while his *Política Indiana* (1648) became the most widely cited treatise on Spanish administration in America. He also played an important role in the organization of the great law code, *Recopilación de leyes de las Indias,* which finally was published in 1681. Solórzano was distinctly a member of the imperial establishment, but an intelligent and knowledgeable one.

Although heretics and other rivals of the glories of our Spanish nation have realized the validity of its titles to the New World and the great increase that the Monarchy has achieved through its conquests and conversions, they try to discredit these titles, saying in the first place that we were impelled more by greed for the gold and silver of its provinces than by zeal for the propagation of the Gospel. They also say that since all things must be judged by their intent or principal end, if this is wicked or erroneous, then it cannot produce a title or effect that can be considered constant and legitimate. . . .

Even if we concede that greed for gold and riches . . . may have prevailed among some, this blemish does not lessen the merit of the many good men who took part so sincerely and apostolically in the conversion of the New World. Nor does it lessen the merit of the zeal and concern repeatedly displayed by our Kings in their sagacious *cédulas* and instructions. . . .

The second charge of our enemies is that this greed was the cause of the slight peacefulness and benevolence which have been shown to the Indians. . . . They also say that these are the only qualities needed for the conversion

From *Política indiana* by Juan de Solórzano y Pereyra (Madrid, 1930), vol. 1, pp. 117–127, passim.

of the Indians and that gentle and pacific methods can be efficacious, as the example of our Lord Jesus Christ and His Holy Apostles shows and as is proven by many passages of Scripture. They also feel that Christians, even when they take part in just wars should always be as kind and amiable as possible. . . .

At each step they throw in our faces the fact that the Indians have been badly treated and that in many places they have completely disappeared. To prove this they have recourse to the treatise written by the Bishop of Chiapas advancing the same argument, which, to stir up greater hatred for us, has been printed in four languages. . . .

But although I do not wish to excuse completely — nor should I — the wars that must have been waged unjustifiably against the Indians in the early days of the conquest, nor the many injuries that have been and are still being done to them, . . . I still make bold to assert that these excesses cannot wipe out all the good that has been accomplished in the conversion and instruction of these non-believers by clerics who were disinterested and punctual in the fulfillment of their mission of preaching the Gospel. Even less can they wipe out the piety and ardent zeal of our Kings, nor the justice of their titles. With great solicitude and care and without taking costs or difficulties of any kind into account, our Kings have tried to provide for the conversion of the Indians in a kind, religious, and Christian manner and have sought the services of persons of all estates, laymen as well as ecclesiastics, in order to repress bad treatment and offenses against the Indians and to carry out the obligations imposed on them by the Holy See. . . .

Thus the principles and regulations governing the conquests and conversions were always laid down with all the vigilance and Christian and human prudence that their high ends demanded, though it is understood that in their execution there may have been some excesses and Indian deaths, as our rivals, heretics, and rumor-mongers charge. However, these flaws cannot prejudice the titles and rights of our Kings, nor diminish the glory and repute of what has been achieved in those remote and extensive provinces by means of their expenditures and conscientious attention in converting so many savage infidels and in reducing them to civil life. This is a fact acknowledged by all the serious and Christian authors, both foreign and Spanish, who have dealt with this matter and have endlessly praised the way in which our conquests were organized and conducted. . . .

Although Nicetas audaciously declared that there is nothing that kings and emperors cannot correct, nor that surpasses their power and authority, much truer is the aphorism of Tacitus that wherever there are human beings there are bound to be vices and sin, especially in provinces so distant from their Kings, where royal commands tend to be ignored or diluted and the residents or governors can regard as licit anything that occurs to them. The temerity of human beings easily leads them to scorn what is very remote. And just as doctors considered the cure of diseased lungs to be extremely difficult because medicaments must reach them through the stomach, following a long and narrow route, so the distance of the Supreme Power makes it unlikely that appropriate remedies can succeed in alleviating the ailments of these provinces.

This state of affairs was even less to be wondered at in the early days of the conquest of the New World, when governors and magistrates were not yet able to protect the Indians nor rigorously execute the laws enacted for this purpose. At that time everything was ruled by captains, soldiers, and sailors — people driven by ferocity and greed who did not hesitate to violate the laws of men and, as Lucan, Seneca, Sallust and many other authors point out, were not likely to refrain from transgressing divine laws as well. People of this type regard as just only what fills the depths of their greed; they do not know how to return their swords to their sheathes without shedding blood nor to restrain themselves from despoiling the vanquished.

For this reason the Marquis of Pescara, Don Fernando Davalos, used to say that nothing is more difficult in war than to respect Christ and Mars with equal discipline. We will not pause to consider this point at present . . . nor the question of when and how the misdeeds of servants cast a reflection on their masters, a matter that various authors have discussed at great length. All agree that when kings do not order these misdeeds nor know of them nor fail to punish them when they are discovered nor are guilty of negligence in appointing their servants, they are absolved of all blame. And this is precisely the position of our glorious and Catholic Kings, as we have shown. . . .

In addition, if this question is considered dispassionately, in many places the Indians gave cause for their mistreatment or for war to be made against them, either because of their bestial and savage customs or because of the excesses and treason that they attempted or committed against our people. . . .

Moreover, it is not the Spaniards who have exterminated them, but their own vices and drunkenness or the earthquakes and repeated epidemics of smallpox and other diseases with which God in His mysterious wisdom has seen fit to reduce their numbers, as Acosta and other eye-witness writers testify.

Everywhere they seem destined to undergo these hardships, for . . . nothing is ordered or legislated for their health, usefulness, and preservation that does not turn out to cause greater harm to them, according to what the same authors affirm. All of this, therefore, should be attributed to the wrath and punishments of God rather than to the oppression and other offenses that we are said to commit against them. Perhaps God has acted in this fashion because of their grave sins and persistent and abominable idolatry, as some historians observe with respect to similar calamities that befell the cities of Rome and Jerusalem.

In any event, I would like those persons who calumniate us to state frankly whether they would not have been guilty of greater excesses if it had been their lot to make our conquests. This is a point made by one of the very authors [Theodorus de Bry] who has depicted our cruelties in print.

Indeed, we have already seen the destruction of the islands and other lands which they have unjustly occupied and sacked with great cruelty and insatiable greed. Nor have they shown that they took any pains to instruct the natives in religion but instead have tried to pervert them with their execrable errors, without establishing bishoprics or building churches, which we have erected in large numbers.

But to put an end to this chapter, I again repeat what I said at the outset: I do not wish to extoll past excesses against the Indians and even less those that may occur in the future because the principal wealth we ought to seek from them is their conversion, instruction, and preservation, since it was for this purpose that they were commended to us, and it can be accomplished more effectively with gentleness and piety than with bad treatment and atrocities. . . .

8. *Spanish Exploitation of Indians in Central Mexico.*

CHARLES GIBSON

Every student of Latin American history must at some time tackle the problem of how to handle the Black Legend of Spanish cruelty and oppression in America. The literature on the subject is enormous, and the emotions involved are sometimes considerable. Here we see how one of the veteran scholars in the field judges Spain's work in Mexico. Professor Gibson's meticulous research, published in *The Aztecs under Spanish Rule,* has given him an excellent background for the task.

The Black Legend provides a gross but essentially accurate interpretation of relations between Spaniards and Indians. The Legend builds upon the record of deliberate sadism. It flourishes in an atmosphere of indignation, which removes the issue from the category of objective understanding. It is insufficient in its awareness of the institutions of colonial history. But the substantive content of the Black Legend asserts that Indians were exploited by Spaniards, and in empirical fact they were.

We have not commented in detail on the conquest itself, a separate subject, already much studied. The conquest has a bearing here not for its military events but for its consequences, and the over-all consequence of conquest was the condition of Spanish domination and Indian subjugation. Aztec peoples could not confront Spaniards as a unified nation, with diplomacy and negotiation. Conquest destroyed Aztec nationalism and fixed adjustments at a local level. Nearly everything that could be called imperial in Aztec affairs came to an end. If Aztec society be thought of as a graduated complex of progressively more inclusive units, from the family and calpulli at one end to the total empire at the other, it becomes evident that conquest eliminated all the more comprehensive structures while it permitted the local and less comprehensive ones to survive.

The demarcation or cut-off point was the jurisdiction of the tlatoani. This became the cabecera, the essential unit of the early colonial period, on which encomienda, the missionary church, cacicazgo, and tribute and labor exactions directly depended. The cabecera won out over alternative organizing principles of greater or lesser range. One may suppose that this followed in part from the role of the tlatoani in Indian society, a role that was repeatedly affirmed in the events of pre-conquest history. But it was the consequence also of relations between Spaniards and Indians. Conceivably a differently ordered Spanish rule might have made the tribe rather than the cabecera the essential colonial unit. An opposite type of Spanish power might have settled on the calpulli. We can glimpse some such alternative forces at work in the various readjustments and modifications made upon the standard cabecera, as when repartimiento reinvoked the tribal groups or when nontlatoani towns were granted in encomienda and allowed to become cabeceras.

The most evident changes in Indian society occurred during the first forty or fifty years. This was the time when Indian peoples, or some of them, met the Spanish influence part way and reached positive degrees of cultural accord. The mid-sixteenth century has a special interest in the history of humanistic tutelage, with the community of Santa Fe, the Gante school, and above all the Colegio of Santa Cruz in Tlatelolco. One can speak here of a cultural florescence for upper-class Indians, and we may cite again the remarkable Badianus Herbal, a systematic catalogue of plants, classified in a European tradition, painted in an Indian style, its glosses written in Nahuatl by one learned native commentator and translated into Latin by another. The herbal was composed in 1552, and it seemed to give promise, thirty years after the conquest, of a combined culture, with enduring Indian values enriched by a European admixture.

The total possible range of Indian reaction at this time was relatively extensive. Because two complicated societies were intermeshing, opportunities for new combinations continually arose. It is in the sixteenth century that we find the most diverse individual incidents and the most unsettled conditions in both societies. But the long-term tendencies were toward the solutions of the seventeenth and eighteenth centuries, and the scope of Indian response became more limited. As the Indian population was reduced in size, Spanish controls became fixed and the traditional leaders lost power. Colonial law only partially reacted to what occurred, and local customs acquired a greater force than law. After the sixteenth century few individuals stand out in either society, and the history becomes one of localized groups. The seventeenth and eighteenth centuries have a peculiarly leaderless quality, as if all alternative solutions had been discarded.

Neither society was at first unified in its response to the conditions proffered by the other. Indians were at first divided between those who cooperated and those who resisted, and between the upper class and the maceguales. Both lines of division tended to disappear. But the geographical divisions in Indian society remained. The patterns of subordination, however uniform in their abstract characteristics, were locally bounded. Cabecera jurisdictions, encomiendas, and haciendas were discrete manifestations of localism effectively preventing a consolidation of Indian interests. All native conduct was so confined. No two towns were ever capable of uniting in organized resistance. The common qualities of Indian towns were insufficient bases for concerted action.

In Spanish society friars and encomenderos were the main conflicting parties of the early period. The friars, almost alone among Spaniards, were guided by principles of Christian humanitarianism. It could be argued that even they exploited native peoples in their coercive indoctrination and their extirpation of pagan practices. Yet their effort as a whole may be distinguished from that of other Spaniards. What happened was that the spiritual component of Hispanic imperialism disappeared or concentrated its energies elsewhere. Its effect for Indians was confined to the early period. The church ceased to be active in Indian defense as ecclesiastics adopted the methods and attitudes of civilian colonists. Churchmen could oppose encomienda in part because they were prohibited from becoming encomenderos, but ecclesiastical condemnation of latifundium would have meant condemnation of an institution that was essential to ecclesiastical wealth and power. There were many other divisions, of course, within Spanish society, but none of them bore directly upon Indian life or livelihood. Thus the creoles despised the peninsulares, but the issue between them was not native welfare, and in some degree what they were disputing over was Indian spoils.

Tribute, labor, and land were the most clearly defined categories of Spanish demand. The three were differentiated in the colonial period, and the legal instruments were different in each case. Tribute and labor were state-controlled after the mid-sixteenth century, and their consequences for Indian society, however serious, were less severe than in the case of land. Tribute and labor were periodically adjusted to population changes, and the extreme Spanish requirements were confined to the earliest times. Moreover, tribute and labor were already familiar types of pre-conquest exaction, and the degree of change between the one period and the other has often been overstated by critics of the Spanish regime.

Spanish usurpation of land has received less attention, probably because it followed the conquest by some years and did not occupy a major position among the Las Casas accusations. It occurred gradually, through many individual events over a long period, and phenomena that take place in this way lack the dramatic appeal of cataclysms like conquest. So deficient is the Black Legend with regard to land that until recently historians were interpreting hacienda as a direct outgrowth of encomienda. Only in our own time has this fundamental error been corrected, most effectively through the work of Silvio Zavala.

It is often said, with an implication of significance, that the lands of America were the property of the crown of Castile. But the point is at best legalistic, and for Indian history it is immaterial. The crown played an insignificant role either in fostering or in inhibiting latifundia. Legal possession of land by the crown did not mean that land usurpation, too, was a state-controlled enterprise. It was private and frequently illegal, though the state came to tolerate it and to profit from it through the devices of denuncia and composición. That it did not occur immediately is probably less the result of legal restriction than of sheer numbers of Indian people and the universality of Indian occupation of land. A prerequisite was available land, and this was not present when the Spaniards first came. Encomienda was therefore an appropriate institution for the early years. But with Indian depopulation, land became accessible, and when it became accessible, it was usurped.

One consequence of the historical concern with selected Black Legend themes is a weakness in our knowledge of hacienda history. The sections of this book that deal with hacienda make some contribution to the subject, but they suffer from inadequate information and lack a secure conceptual frame. Hacienda, perhaps more than any other single colonial topic, still needs systematic investigation, not alone in the Valley of Mexico but in all areas. We cannot now confidently compare our documented examples of Valley of Mexico hacienda with the institution in other regions, and until we can the Valley conditions will remain imperfectly defined. . . . My own feeling is that the hacienda is a crucial institution, that for various reasons its study has been slighted, and that we would be well advised to make a concerted effort toward solving the historical problems that it raises.

With respect to land there can be no doubt that the hacienda came to be the dominant mode of control. In the tempo of its history it contrasts with tribute and labor. The extreme Spanish demands for tribute and labor occurred early, before much land was transferred to Spanish possession. This transfer, on the other hand, took place on a large scale only in the late sixteenth century and after, when private exploitation of tribute and labor had already been brought under state control. In a sense, land represented a new avenue of exploitation for Spaniards, after other avenues were blocked. But the hacienda combined its essential control of land with secondary controls over labor and tribute, and the result was the most comprehensive institution yet devised for Spanish mastery and Indian subordination. If there appeared, as we have thought, some benign features of hacienda, these are explicable in terms of the total matrix within which hacienda developed. Human character tends toward benevolence as well as toward cruelty, and the hacienda could afford certain kinds of benevolence that would have been incongruous with the harsher, more superficial, less subtle coercions of encomienda. Thus the hacendado could appear as the protector and advocate of his Indians against outside pressures. The encomendero was intended by law to play this same role, but he never did.

That land was important to Indians is obvious. Some of the most intimate and revealing documents of all Indian history are the native títulos for community land possession. The títulos were an Indian response to Spanish usurpation and Spanish legalism. Their purpose was to integrate community opposition against alienation. They speak only sparingly, or not at all, of conquest, tribute, and labor. They see the essential threat to community existence where in fact it lay, in Spanish seizures of land.

There had been seizures of land before the conquest, as in the "lands of Montezuma," but these had been accommodated within Indian practices of land disposition. The difference is one of degree. Moreover, the pre-conquest period, so far as we know, offers no comparable situation of population change. When Indian society seemed headed for extinction, in the late sixteenth and early seventeenth centuries, its practical need for land likewise diminished, and Indian gobernadores and others became the accomplices of Spaniards in the transfer of titles. When the population began to increase in the late seventeenth and eighteenth centuries the need for land correspondingly increased. But by then it was too late. Land transfer was cumulative in a way that tribute and labor exactions were not. Every increase in Indian population in the late colonial period meant an additional number that could not be incorporated in the traditional calpulli tenure, or could be incorporated only with a corresponding strain on other community institutions. The available land was hacienda land, and the new population could now be incorporated within colonial society only through the mediation of hacienda. When the hacendado authorized the towns to rent some of his lands or gave permission to individuals to occupy huts on the hacienda properties, both the hacendado and the Indian beneficiaries could regard the act as one of benevolence. All surrounding conditions were accepted as normal. An aristocracy had been created through innumerable acts over generations of time. Even if there had been an inclination to assign blame, there was no one to accuse, for no one was responsible. The institution and the ethos of the institution dominated all its members. A conquistador who killed or an encomendero who overcharged could be convincingly criticized on moral grounds, but similar criticism appeared excessive when turned against the hacendado, who had inherited most of his lands and played a paternalistic role in a society he had not created. . . .

The Indian community was further beset by a series of demands not comprehended in the three classifications of tribute, labor, and land. Most of these were designed to extract from its economy the increment remaining beyond minimum subsistence. Ecclesiastical fees fall in this category, as do the forced sales in corregimiento and the usurpations of produce. The political officials' handbook of 1777 openly declared the corregimiento of Chalco to be worth thirty times the corregidor's salary, a statement that suggests the extent of precedented extra-legal exploitation by officials appointed to uphold the law.

Variations occurred from area to area in the timing and intensity of these processes. Tacuba was an early victim. Xaltocan prospered for a time and yielded in the seventeenth century. Tepetlaoztoc made a late recovery based not on land but on a pack-train commerce. Chalco province attracted powerful hacendados and became an area of extreme land pressures. By contrast, Xochimilco lacked the kind of land that attracted hacendados and by a coincidence of circumstances maintained its craft economy and chinampa agriculture throughout the colonial period. Tenochtitlan and Tlatelolco, which lacked land from the start, remained virtually immune from the struggle against the hacienda. But Tenochtitlan made a more viable economic adjustment than Tlatelolco, which suffered progressively from drought, emigration, and neglect.

What we have studied is the deterioration of a native empire and civilization. The empire collapsed first, and the civilization was fragmented in individual communities. Some creativity appeared in the early stages of change, but the process as a whole could not be called a creative one for Indians. The community proved to be the largest Indian social unit capable of survival, and it survived in spite of manifold and severe stresses. The cofradía and the fiesta were enlisted to support it. Indians in general yielded to Spanish demands, protesting only in rare instances of community resistance. The civilization became infused with Hispanic traits at many points, but it retained an essential Indian character, partly through the conviction of its members, partly because it was depressed to a social status so low that it was given no opportunities for change. One of the earliest and most persistent individual reponses was drink. If our sources may be believed, few people in the whole of history were more prone to drunkenness than the Indians of the Spanish colony.

9. The Dawn of Conscience in America

LEWIS HANKE

Generalizations are often dangerous because it is almost always difficult or even impossible to summarize in a few words a complicated historical event. Yet most of us concerned with the history of Spain in America sometimes indulge in generalizations, as they stimulate us to think about our work in large terms. Here are mine!

The image many English-speaking people have of Spanish action in America is one of almost unrelieved cruelty to the Indians, and many unfavorable judgments have been made on Spanish action in the New World in comparison with English colonization. Spaniards naturally resented these judgments, and a "war of the myths" has resulted. One myth makes the Spaniards the heroes, the English the villains, and the Indians the victims and the opposing myth makes the Spaniards into villains, the English into heroes, but still casts the Indians in the role of victims. My aim is to present some relatively little-known aspects of Spanish-Indian relations, not to present a well-rounded comparison of European colonial practices, and certainly not to engage in the war of the myths.

All European explorers and colonists who came to the New World encountered native peoples. But only the Spaniards met so many millions of natives, whom they called Indians, in the vast stretches of their empire which eventually reached from California to Patagonia. The very fact of large numbers of natives settled under the control of the Aztec, Inca, and Maya empires required the Spaniards to devise a different method of treating them from that worked out by the English, French, and Portuguese for the largely nomadic and much smaller number of natives they found sparsely scattered in their territories. . . .

In the effort to govern the mass of Indians in their great empire the Spaniards adapted some institutions from their own medieval experience of long

From "The Dawn of Conscience in America: Spanish Experiments and Experiences with Indians in the New World" by Lewis Hanke, *Proceedings of the American Philosophical Society*, 107, no. 2 (April 1963), pp. 83–92, passim. Reprinted by permission of the American Philosophical Society.

fighting against the Moslems and created others to meet the needs of New World conditions. The determination of the Crown and the Church to Christianize the Indians, the imperious demand of Spaniards for labor forces to exploit the new lands for revenue for the Crown and for themselves, and the attempts of some Spaniards to protect the Indians resulted in a very remarkable complex of relations, laws, and institutions which even today leads historians to contradictory conclusions on the reality of Spanish rule in America. The encomienda system, by which groups of Indians were assigned to Spaniards, a device to provide both labor and goods to the Spaniard and protection and religious instruction for the Indians, was both stoutly defended as necessary and bitterly attacked as un-Christian throughout the sixteenth century by Spaniards themselves. The Spanish imperial policy of attempting to civilize the Indians by urbanizing them led to many curious experiments and experiences, and in the end was fatal for large numbers of natives. George Kubler has pointed out in his substantial work on Mexican architecture:

> no building could be achieved without the prior urbanization of the participants. To urbanize the Indian populations was to dislocate and destroy the patterns of indigenous culture. Such cultural extirpation brought about, in turn, the biological decrease of the Indian race. . . . Each building, and each colonial artifact, was nourished by the destruction of of a culture and the decline of a race.

Spain made many efforts to mitigate the lot of the Indians by appointing official "Protectors," setting up special courts to try cases involving them, and sending out numerous investigating groups to discover what might be done to help them. She tried many stratagems in the sixteenth century particularly to ensure that Indians would be brought under Spanish rule by peaceful means alone, and be persuaded to accept Christianity by reason instead of by force. To achieve this end the Dominican Bartolomé de Las Casas and his brother Dominicans attempted to preach the faith without the backing of the sword in Chiapas, and Vasco de Quiroga established his Utopian communities in Michoacán. In many places a system of Indian segregation was worked out by friars and royal officials to protect them from other Spaniards who would exploit them, and this practice was followed throughout the colonial period, culminating in the famous Jesuit missions in eighteenth-century Paraguay. The difficult, indeed impossible, double purpose of the Crown to secure revenue and also to Christianize the Indians inevitably led in fact to a series of angry disputes, evil compromises, and some glorious episodes throughout the more than three centuries of Spanish rule in America.

Today, in looking back on the total encounter of Spaniards and Indians, two developments hold special interest for us, living as we do in a world society whose multiplicity and variety of cultures become daily more evident and more significant. For the first time in history one people — the Spaniards

— paid serious attention to the nature of the culture of the peoples they met; and, perhaps most striking of all, the controversies which developed in sixteenth-century Spain and America over the just method of treating the Indians led to a fundamental consideration of the nature of man himself. This "dawn of conscience in America" was only a faint daybreak; indeed, who can say that in the twentieth century we have reached high noon? The fact that we are still struggling ourselves to discover how to live justly in a world of many races and many cultures give the Spanish struggles of the sixteenth century a poignant and familiar ring. . . . .

It was the friars, looking for souls to win, rather than the conquistadores, who first began to study Indian customs, history, and religion. The missionaries needed to know the names and attributes of Indian gods, the sacrifices made to them, and as accurately as possible the mentality of the Indians in order to lead them away from their pagan rites toward Christianity. The founder of American anthropology was Friar Ramón Pané, who accompanied Columbus on his second voyage for the express purpose of observing the natives and reporting on their ways and who was the first European to learn an Indian language.

The Crown encouraged ecclesiastics throughout the sixteenth century to study the Indians, and numerous volumes on their cultures were in fact prepared. Administration officials such as Alonso de Zurita also compiled reports, and the questionnaires sent out regularly to all Spanish governors in the New World by the Council of the Indies included a number of items on Indians. The result of all this enquiry is a magnificent body of linguistic, archaeological, and ethnographical material which is both contradictory at times and difficult to assess because so much remains in manuscript and even the printed editions available are often poor, lacking indexes and proper notes. . . .

Closely linked with these anthropological studies and with Spain's struggle to work out a just Indian policy was the much disputed question of the nature of the Indians. The first twinge of official conscience was expressed by Ferdinand and Isabella in 1495 when they learned that a shipload of Indians Columbus had sent back from Hispaniola had been sold as slaves because they had been taken in rebellion. The monarchs thereupon instructed Bishop Fonseca, who managed Indian affairs, that the money from this sale should not be accepted until their Highnesses could inform themselves from men learned in law whether these Indians could be sold with good conscience. No document that I know of has recorded the answer the sovereigns requested. A dramatic public protest in America against Indian slavery was made by a Dominican friar named Antonio de Montesinos, who in a revolutionary sermon preached in 1511 on the island of Hispaniola thundered:

Tell me, by what right or justice do you keep these Indians in cruel servitude? On what authority have you waged a detestable war against these people, who dwelt quietly and peacefully on their own land? . . . Are these not men? Have they not rational souls?

This sermon led to serious disputes and discussions in Spain, out of which came the 1512 Laws of Burgos to govern relations between Spaniards and Indians as well as juridical treatises on the basis for Spanish dominion in the New World.

The legalistic and religious nature of the Spaniards led both to their intense preoccupation with the just basis for their newly discovered overseas territory and with the nature of the Indians whom they were attempting to draw into the Christian world. Francisco de Vitoria, a Dominican professor at the University of Salamanca, discussed these matters with great vision and clarity in his lectures and many of his students later went to America with their attitudes determined by his teachings. Vitoria remarked in one treatise, *De Indis:* "The Indians are stupid only because they are uneducated and, if they live like beasts, so for the same reason do many Spanish peasants." He also asserted that discovery alone gave Spaniards no more right to American territory than the Indians would have acquired had they "discovered" Spain. Vitoria and other Spanish political theorists of the time addressed themselves to the fundamental legal questions raised when Europe invaded America and, long before Grotius, laid down an enduring basis for international law.

Most significant of all, the Spanish inquiry into the nature of the Indians and their capacity for entering into the Christian commonwealth led Spaniards to grapple with that ultimate problem — the nature of man himself. Of all the ideas churned up during the early tumultuous years of American history, none had more dramatic implications than the attempts made to apply to the natives there the Aristotelian doctrine of natural slavery: that one part of mankind is set aside by nature to be slaves in the service of masters born for a life of virtue free of manual labor. Learned authorities such as the Spanish scholar Sepúlveda not only sustained this view with great tenacity and erudition but also concluded, without having visited America, that the Indians were in fact such rude and brutal beings that war against them to make possible their forcible Christianization was not only expedient but lawful. Many ecclesiastics, especially Las Casas, opposed this idea scornfully, with appeals to divine and natural laws as well as to their own experience in America. The controversy became so heated and the emperor's conscience so troubled over the question of how to carry on the conquest of the Indies in a Christian way that Charles V actually ordered the suspension of all expeditions to America while a junta of foremost theologians, jurists, and officials was convoked in the royal capital of Valladolid to listen to the arguments of Las Casas and Sepúlveda. All this occurred in 1550, after Cortez had conquered Mexico, Francisco Pizarro had shattered the Inca empire, and many other lesser-known captains had carried the Spanish banners to far corners of the New World.

Las Casas and Sepúlveda duly fought their great battle of ideas before the junta in Valladolid. The details of their arguments cannot be indicated here. The foundation on which Las Casas based his argument was that the Indians were truly men capable of becoming Christians. Drawing upon the information he had brought together in his massive anthropological work the *Apologetic History,* he documented his contention that the Indians had many skills and accomplishments and in fact possessed a culture worthy of respect. He cited their agricultural methods as well as their irrigation systems; illustrated their ingenuity by the way they derived twenty-two products from the maguey tree, contrived delicate ornamental collars of fish bones, and created remarkable gold jewelry. He drew special attention to their extraordinary capacity to learn the Old World crafts which the Spaniards had brought with them, giving a careful account of the way the Indians made knives and rubber balls. He also described the cleverness of their painters, their feather work, their silver making with few tools, and, after little training, their competence in fashioning musical instruments, their work as carpenters, and their hand lettering so fine that it could sometimes not be distinguished from printing. The only thing he found an Indian could not do as well as a Spaniard was to shoe a horse. He described the Indian mining methods and included an account of their ball games. Above all, however, he claimed, the Indians excelled in the dramatic arts and demonstrated this with various illustrations. He described the military organization of both the Mexican Indians and the Incas of Peru, a topic on which relatively few data are provided by other works, and gave much information on their coca chewing and tobacco smoking, together with an excellent description of the great teeming market in Mexico City.

He devoted many pages to the religion of the Indians, and the most striking aspect of this section is his attitude toward Indian sacrifices. He considered that the most religious peoples were those which offered to God the most magnificent sacrifice, and those who offered human beings had — in his opinion — a very noble concept indeed of their God. The Indian fasts, mortifications of the body, sacrifices of animals and men, were clearly superior to the sacrifices of the ancient peoples. Under the horrible and bloody aspects of these rites Las Çasas discerned a commendable spirit of religious devotion which could be directed to higher ends and enlisted in the service of the only true God.

Las Casas was deeply convinced of the importance of education and therefore was particularly impressed by the meticulous attention paid by the Mexican Indians to the education of their children in the ways of chastity, honesty, fortitude, obedience, and sobriety. He cried:

Did Plato, Socrates, Pythagoras, or even Aristotle leave us better or more natural or more necessary exhortations to the virtuous life than these barbarians delivered to their children? Does the Christian religion teach us more, save the faith and what it teaches us of invisible and supernatural matters? Therefore, no one may deny that these people are fully capable of governing themselves and of living like men of good intelligence and that they are more than others well ordered, sensible, prudent, and rational.

Las Casas believed firmly in the capacity of all people for civilization; he emphatically rejected a static and hopeless barbarism. "All the peoples of the world are men," he insisted, and declared that God would not allow any nation to exist, "no matter how barbarous, fierce, or depraved its customs" which might not be "persuaded and brought to a good order and way of life" provided the persuasion was peaceful. To practical conquistadores and administrators, men aiming at immediate worldly goals and faced with different kinds of Indians, and perhaps to the Crown as well, jealous of all royal prerogatives, Las Casas' reiteration that the only justification for the presence of Spaniards in the New World was the Christianization of Indians by peaceful means alone must have seemed dangerous nonsense. One can imagine with what contempt and horror his announcement was received that Spain ought to abandon America, with all its Indians un-Christianized, rather than to bring them into the fold by forcible and — to him — profoundly un-Christian methods. The important fact to us today is that Sepúlveda's doctrine did not triumph at Valladolid in 1550 and that his treatise was not approved for publication until late in the eighteenth century.

Since the Valladolid debate the problem of how to treat peoples unlike ourselves in color, race, religion, or customs has given rise in every century to the most diverse and inflammatory opinions. In general the idea of the inferiority of natives to Europeans appeared in whatever far corners of the world Europeans reached. In the English colonies, for example, only Roger Williams had any respect for Indian culture and small attention was given the theories about Indians.

The battle waged by Las Casas and all the other Spaniards of his opinion to win recognition of the humanity of the Indians and to understand their culture is far from won. But today those who believe that "all the peoples of the world are men" have powerful allies. Anthropologists have gone on record that "the basic principles of opportunity and equality before the law are compatible with all that is known of human biology. All races possess the abilities needed to participate fully in the democratic way of life and in modern technological civilization." The United Nations Universal Declaration of Human Rights, adopted four centuries after the Valladolid controversy, announced: "All human beings are born free and equal in dignity and rights. They are endowed with reason and conscience and should act towards one another in a spirit of brotherhood." The Ecumenical Council, now in session at the Vatican, with members "from every nation under heaven" expressed the thought even more succinctly in its Message to Humanity: "We proclaim that all men are brothers, irrespective of the race or nation to which they belong."

Only a partisan in the "war of the myths" would dare to claim that the ideals announced by the Spanish crown were generally followed in the American territory under Spanish rule. Nor should anyone claim that the Spaniards fully accomplished their purpose: to incorporate the mass of New World Indians into a Christian and a European world.

For we know in the twentieth century that the Spaniards faced impossible problems: the clash of cultures complicated by the great area in which they operated, the tremendous diversity of the Indians encountered, and the small number of Spaniards available for conversion and education of the millions of Indians. One important doctrinal question remains. Why did Negroes never receive the same solicitous attention as Indians, and why did the conscience of Spaniards twinge so much more easily for Indians than for Negroes?

The Jesuit Alonso de Sandoval did indeed write a treatise in the seventeenth century on the culture of the different tribes of Negroes brought to Cartagena and may therefore be called the first Africanist in America. But neither Sandoval nor his disciple Pedro Claver ever denounced Negro slavery as an unChristian institution, and the moral conscience of Europe was first roused in modern times by the plight of the Indians of America. The difference between the Spanish attitude toward Indians and Negroes has not yet been satisfactorily explained, and remains an important problem for investigation.

Is it not remarkable enough, however, that some sixteenth-century Spaniards studied Indian cultures and that a whole school of powerful and articulate members of this intensely nationalistic people fought stoutly for the rights of the Indians? During the early years of expansion which eventually carried European ideas and goods to almost every corner of the earth, Spain produced, it is true, an aggressive advocate of Aristotle's doctrine of natural slavery. But she also produced the powerful champion of Indians as men, whose voice along with many other Spanish voices proclaimed the dawn of conscience in America. No matter how far rockets may reach into outer space, will any more significant problems be discovered than those which agitated many Spaniards during the conquest of America? When the story is told of man's attempts in history to grapple with this most difficult problem — how to relate to other men of unfamiliar cultures — will not this become clear: that when the Spanish Crown and Council of the Indies refrained from stigmatizing the natives of the New World as natural slaves they placed an important milestone on the long road, still under construction, which winds all too slowly toward civilizations which respect the dignity of man, that is to say of all men?

The Acolman Convent in Mexico. This large and imposing convent was one of the many religious structures built in Mexico during the first generation or so after Cortez defeated Montezuma. Its enormous walls and artistic facade are eloquent testimony of the great contribution by Indians and Spaniards alike to the architecture of sixteenth-century Mexico which George Kubler has described so well (Reading 2).

SECTION IV

Population Questions

HOW MANY INDIANS?

A lively controversy has been under way for a long time on how many Indians inhabited America in 1492 and how many were in Mexico in 1519 on the eve of the Spanish conquest.[1] These are important questions, but difficult to handle in brief selections. Bailey W. Diffie and Ángel Rosenblat have tended to discount the early very high estimates, while Woodrow W. Borah and Sherburne F. Cook have concluded that central Mexico at least had a very dense population with perhaps as many as 25 million in 1519, and that about only 1 million survived by 1600.[2] Rosenblat estimates that the aboriginal population of both Mexico and Peru in 1492 was only about 13 million, while Borah conjectures that there may have been about 100 million Indians in the New World. Another scholar has arrived at a figure even higher than that of Borah. Doubtless further research will resolve some of the present doubts, but no matter what the figure arrived at it is clear that the demographic disaster that

---

[1] For excellent treatments of the enormous and complicated literature, see Henry F. Dobyns, "Estimating Aboriginal American Population: An Appraisal of Techniques with a New Hemispheric Estimate," *Current Anthropology*, 7 (1966), pp. 395–416; Woodrow W. Borah, *The Historical Demography of "Aboriginal and Colonial Latin America: An Attempt at Perspective"* (a paper delivered at the XXXVII International Congress of Americanists, Mar del Plata, 1966); and "The Historical Demography of Latin America: Sources, Techniques, Controversies, Yields," in *Population and Economics. Proceedings of Section V of the Fourth Congress of the International Economic History Association, 1968,* ed. Paul Deprez (Winnipeg, Canada: University of Manitoba Press, 1969[?]).

[2] Woodrow Borah and Sherburne F. Cook, *The Aboriginal Population of Central Mexico on the Eve of the Spanish Conquest* (Berkeley and Los Angeles: University of California Press, 1963), p. 89, and Woodrow W. Borah, "La despoblación del México Central en el siglo XVI," *Historia Mexicana*, 12 (1962), p. 179. Ángel Rosenblat presents his latest views in *La población de América en 1492 — viejos y nuevos cálculos* (Mexico: El Colegio de México, 1967).

took place in Mexico after 1492 was one of the most severe known to history. This demographic revolution varied in intensity from region to region of the Spanish empire, and the decline appears to have been generally less in South America than in Mexico. For example, "the remarkable fact about the Indians of the Ecuadoran highlands during the three centuries of colonial rule was that their numbers did not diminish appreciably." [3]

THE DISASTROUS EFFECTS OF DISEASE

On the causes for the startling decline of the Indian population, no one doubts that disease was a decisive influence (Reading 1). Closely allied to disease and overwork was the traumatic shock of conquest on the Indians, which Professor George Kubler expertly explores (Reading 2). Though Professor Kubler's interests are largely in the field of art history, he is at home in a number of social science disciplines and has read widely in the copious literature on the conquest. Thus his writing reflects an unusual sensitivity to the complex problems involved in a study of the demographic disaster in Mexico. Notice his analysis of the astonishing development of large-scale ecclesiastical building campaigns at the same time as the periods of severe population loss. Notice also that Kubler cites the *Relaciones geográficas* to show that Indian informants, responding to this official query on why the Indian population declined, testified that their diet, clothing, and living conditions were better before the Spaniards came. This point has previously been emphasized by the anthropologist Zelia Nuttall.[4]

Nor was disease limited to the sixteenth century. In one of the few monographs on the history of medicine in Latin America, Professor Donald B. Cooper of Ohio State University shows how epidemics troubled Spanish administrators in Mexico during the later part of the colonial period.[5] And the veteran scholar Sherburne F. Cook gives an interesting description of the round-the-world voyage of Dr. Francisco Xavier Balmis to vaccinate the

---

[3] John L. Phelan, *The Kingdom of Quito in the Seventeenth Century* (Madison: University of Wisconsin Press, 1967), p. 44.

[4] Zelia Nuttall, "The Causes of the Physical Degeneracy of Mexican Indians after the Spanish Conquest as Set Forth by Mexican Informants in 1580," *Journal of Hygiene,* 27 (1927), pp. 40–43. This was reported from the pueblo of Ocelotepec: "In olden times the natives lived a hundred years or more and now they die young and what they say and explain and communicate to each other on the subject is that the reason for this is: that anciently the children were put to work at the age of six or seven. As there were so many wars there was no time to cultivate much and so they ate little, slept in the open and were fitted to live in constant labour. After the Spaniards came they wore clothes, slept in houses, ate and drank and indulged themselves much. In those days an Indian married at forty and now at twelve or fifteen. . . ."

[5] Donald B. Cooper, *Epidemic Disease in Mexico City, 1761–1813* (Austin: University of Texas Press, 1965).

Spanish colonial population against smallpox. "Seldom, perhaps never," wrote Professor Cook, "in the history of medicine has there embarked an expedition so grandly conceived, so well executed, so uniformly successful as that of Balmis. . . . Through this one act on the part of the corrupt and decadent government of Spain more lives probably were saved than were lost in all the battles of Napoleon." (Reading 3)

THE EFFECTS OF THE DEMOGRAPHIC DISASTER

Grave economic and social consequences resulted from the immense loss of Indian life, though the precise figures are still in doubt. Professor Borah has been a pioneer here, too, and has presented a challenging hypothesis of a century-long depression in Mexico beginning in the 1570s, with significant results:

> The sharp and long-continued decrease of Mexico's Indians from the Conquest until the beginning of the eighteenth century must be accounted one of the most important factors in Mexican history. Had the aboriginal populations of central Mexico borne the impact of Conquest with little demographic loss, there would have been scant room for their conquerors except as administrators and receivers of tribute. Mexico today would be an Indian area from which, in the process of achieving independence from Spain, a white upper stratum holding itself apart, like the British in India, could easily have been expelled. In Haiti, expulsion and massacre at the time of the great slave uprisings disposed rather easily of a similar group of owners and administrators. . . . At the end of the seventeenth century, the distinctively Mexican economy was already organized on the basis of latifundia and debt peonage, the twin aspects of Mexican life which continued nearly to our day and which helped provoke the Revolution of 1910–1917.[6]

The "Berkeley School" has produced many detailed and technical studies to make known their research findings. Here is a recent overview by Borah and Cook, giving a résumé of the more important conclusions in their population studies for the economic and social history of Mexico. (Reading 4)

SPECIAL PROBLEMS

Much new material has been made known in recent years on the history of the Negro in the New World, as Professor Frederick P. Bowser has recently dem-

---

[6] Woodrow W. Borah, *New Spain's Century of Depression* (Berkeley and Los Angeles: University of California Press, 1951), p. 44.

onstrated in a valuable survey article.[7] Relatively little has been published on the population of Brazil, but Professor Dauril Alden of the University of Washington has recently revealed that there is much to be learned. [8]

The coming generation of students will benefit from the increasing interest and competence of historians in population questions. Problems of interpretation will still remain. For example, disease certainly helped Cortez win over Montezuma, but other elements were involved such as the assistance of Indian allies who had long opposed the Aztecs. The army that captured Tenochtitlán was really an army of Indians captained by a few Spaniards.

And despite the growing interest in medical history much remains to be done. The situation has not greatly changed from the description made by John Tate Lanning some years ago:

> In the history of the transition from medico-astrological texts and such drugs as crawfish eyes, tapir claws, livers of the pelican, gallbladder, calcined frogs, spirit of earthworms, and lizard oil to modern chemistry and pharmacy there is ample latitude for work. . . . From the quacks and midwives to the experimenting Dr. Hipólito Unánue; from the time that a disguised obstetrician was executed for practicing his art to the establishment of obstetrical hospitals; for the search for symptoms in the stars to their location in the patient, is also a long, uncharted course. As late as the eighteenth century, the primary medical question about a two-headed child was: Do such creatures have souls, and if so, one or two? As late as 1785, patients' blood was taken alternately from the right and left arms to maintain the equilibrium of the patient.[9]

One further thought. Unless the Latin American statistical sources upon which historians depend greatly improve, calculations are bound to be tentative and subject to revision. In France, for example, such detailed information is extant that historians know that in a given small community "there was a marked increase in the numbers of both illegitimate births and pregnant brides, and that from 1789 to 1839 the latter represented 24 percent of all brides." [10] It is doubtful that sources will be available to this extent for any period of Latin American history.

---

[7] Frederick P. Bowser, "The African in Colonial Spanish America: Reflections on Research Achievements and Priorities," *Latin American Research Review*, 7 (1972), pp. 77–94.

[8] Dauril Alden, "The Population of Brazil in the Late Eighteenth Century: A Preliminary Survey," *Hispanic American Historical Review*, 43 (May 1963), pp. 173–201.

[9] John Tate Lanning, "Research Possibilities in the Cultural History of Spain in America," *Hispanic American Historical Review*, 16 (1936), p. 156.

[10] *Times Literary Supplement* (London), March 3, 1972, p. 243. The book reviewed was Marcel Lachiver, *La Population de Meulan du XVIIᵉ au XIXᵉ Siècle* (Paris: Sevpen, 1971).

WHY THE INDIAN POPULATION DECLINED

1. The Disastrous Effects of Disease

ALFRED W. CROSBY

Historians have been very slow to recognize how formidable an ally the Spaniards had in disease, which goes far to explain some of the stunning victories of the conquistadors. Much remains to be discovered about the medical history of Latin America, but at least we have here one detailed statement on the ravages of various diseases during the conquest, by Professor Alfred W. Crosby of Washington State University.

The most sensational military conquests in all history are probably those of the Spanish conquistadores over the Aztec and Incan empires. Cortés and Pizarro toppled the highest civilizations of the New World in a few months each. A few hundred Spaniards defeated populations containing thousands of dedicated warriors, armed with a wide assembly of weapons from the stone and early metal ages. Societies which had created huge empires through generations of fierce fighting collapsed at the touch of the Castilian.

After four hundred years the Spanish feat still seems incredible. Many explanations suggest themselves: the advantage of steel over stone, of cannon and firearms over bows and arrows and slings; the terrorizing effect of horses on foot-soldiers who had never seen such beasts before; the lack of unity in the Aztec and Incan empires; the prophecies in Indian mythology about the arrival of white gods. . . .

For all of that, one might have expected the highly organized, militaristic societies of Mexico and the Andean highlands to survive at least the initial contact with European societies. Thousands of Indian warriors, even if confused and frightened and wielding only obsidian-studded war clubs, should have been able to repel at least the first few hundred Spaniards to arrive.

The Spaniard had a formidable ally to which neither he nor the historian has given sufficient credit — disease. The arrival of Columbus in the New

From "Conquistador y Pestilencia: The First New World Pandemic and the Fall of the Great Indian Empires" by Alfred W. Crosby, *Hispanic American Historical Review*, 47 (1967), pp. 321–337, passim. Reprinted by permission of Duke University press.

World brought about one of the greatest population disasters in history. After the Spanish conquest an Indian of Yucatán wrote of his people in the happier days before the advent of the Spaniard:

> There was then no sickness; they had no aching bones; they had then no high fever; they had then no smallpox; they had then no burning chest; they had then no abdominal pain; they had then no consumption; they had then no headache. At that time the course of humanity was orderly. The foreigners made it otherwise when they arrived here.

It would be easy to attribute this lamentation to the nostalgia that the conquered always feel for the time before the conqueror appeared, but the statement is probably in part true. During the millennia before the European brought together the compass and the three-masted vessel to revolutionize world history, men at sea moved slowly, seldom over long distances, and across the great oceans hardly at all. Men lived at least in the same continents where their greatgrandfathers had lived and rarely caused violent and rapid changes in the delicate balance between themselves and their environments. Diseases tended to be endemic rather than epidemic. . . .

Migration of man and his maladies is the chief cause of epidemics. And when migration takes place, those creatures who have been longest in isolation suffer most, for their genetic material has been least tempered by the variety of world diseases. Among the major subdivisions of the species *homo sapiens* the American Indian probably had the dangerous privilege of longest isolation from the rest of mankind. The Indians appear to have lived, died, and bred without extra-American contacts for generation after generation, developing unique cultures and working out tolerances for a limited, native American selection of pathological micro-life. Medical historians guess that few of the first rank killers among the diseases are native to the Americas. (A possible exception is syphilis. It may be true, as Gonzalo Fernández Oviedo maintained four hundred years ago, that syphilis should not be called *mal francés* or *mal de Nápoles,* but *mal de las Indias.*)

When the isolation of the Americas was broken, and Columbus brought the two halves of this planet together, the American Indian met for the first time his most hideous enemy — not the white man or his black servant, but the invisible killers which these men brought in their blood and breath. The fatal diseases of the Old World killed more effectively in the New, and comparatively benign diseases of the Old World turned killers in the New. There is little exaggeration in the statement of a German missionary in 1699 that "the Indians die so easily that the bare look and smell of a Spaniard causes them to give up the ghost." The process is still going on in the twentieth century, as the last jungle tribes of South America lose their shield of isolation.

The most spectacular period of mortality among the American Indians occurred during the first century of contact with the Europeans and Africans. Almost all contemporary historians of the early settlements from Bartolomé de las Casas to William Bradford of Plymouth Plantation were awed by the ravages of epidemic disease among the native populations of America. We know that the most deadly of the early epidemics in the New World were those of the eruptive fevers — smallpox, measles, plague, typhus, etc. The first to arrive and the deadliest, said contemporaries, was smallpox.

At this point the reader should be forewarned against too easy credulity. Even today smallpox is occasionally misdiagnosed as influenza, pneumonia, measles, scarlet fever, syphilis, or chicken pox, for example. Four hundred years ago such mistakes were even more common, and writers of the accounts upon which we must base our examination of the early history of smallpox in America did not have any special interest in accurate diagnosis. The early historians were much more likely to cast their eyes skywards and comment on the sinfulness that had called down such obvious evidences of God's wrath as epidemics than to describe in any detail the diseases involved. It should also be noted that conditions which facilitate the spread of one disease will usually encourage the spread of others, and that "very rarely is there a pure epidemic of a single malady." Pneumonia and pleurisy, for instance, often follow after smallpox, smothering those whom it has weakened. . . .

Smallpox has been so successfully controlled by vaccination and quarantine in the industrialized nations of the twentieth century that few North Americans or Europeans have ever seen it. But it is an old companion of humanity, and for most of the last millennium it was among the commonest diseases in Europe. With reason it was long thought one of the most infectious of maladies. Smallpox is usually communicated through the air by means of droplets or dust particles, and its virus enters the new host through the respiratory tract. There are many cases of hospital visitors who have contracted the disease simply by breathing for a moment the air of a room in which someone lies ill with the pox. . . .

Where smallpox has been endemic, it has been a steady, dependable killer, taking every year from three to ten percent of those who die. Where it has struck isolated groups, the death rate has been awesome. Analysis of figures for some twenty outbreaks shows that the case mortality among an unvaccinated population is about thirty percent. Presumably, in people who have had no contact whatever with smallpox, the disease will infect nearly every single individual it touches. When in 1707 smallpox first appeared in Iceland, it is said that in two years 18,000 out of the island's 50,000 inhabitants died of it.

The first people of the New World to meet the white and black races and their diseases were Indians of the Taino culture who spoke the Arawak language and lived on the islands of the Greater Antilles and the Bahamas. On the very first day of landfall in 1492 Columbus noted that the Tainos "are very unskilled with arms . . ." and "could all be subjected and made to do all that one wished." These Tainos lived long enough to provide the Spaniard with his first generation of slaves in America, and Old World disease with its first beachhead in the New World.

Oviedo, one of the earliest historians of the Americas, estimated that a million Indians lived on Santo Domingo when the European arrived to plant his first permanent colony in the New World. "Of all those," Oviedo wrote, "and of all those born afterwards, there are not now believed to be at the present time in this year of 1548 five hundred persons, children and adults, who are natives and are the progeny or lineage of those first."

The destruction of the Tainos has been largely blamed on the Spanish cruelty, not only by the later Protestant historians of the "Black Legend" school but also by such contemporary Spanish writers as Oviedo and Bartolomé de las Casas. Without doubt the early Spaniard brutally exploited the Indians. But it was obviously not in order to kill them off, for the early colonist had to deal with a chronic labor shortage and needed the Indians. Disease would seem to be a more logical explanation for the disappearance of the Tainos, because they, like other Indians, had little immunity to Old World diseases. At the same time, one may concede that the effects of Spanish exploitation undoubtedly weakened their resistance to disease.

Yet it is interesting to note that there is no record of any massive smallpox epidemic among the Indians of the Antilles for a quarter of a century after the first voyage of Columbus. Indians apparently suffered a steady decline in numbers, which was probably due to extreme overwork, other diseases, and a general lack of will to live after their whole culture had been shattered by alien invasion. How can the evident absence of smallpox be explained, if the American Indian was so susceptible, and if ships carrying Europeans and Africans from the pestilential Old World were constantly arriving in Santo Domingo? The answer lies in the nature of the disease. It is a deadly malady, but it lasts only a brief time in each patient. After an incubation period of twelve days or so, the patient suffers from high fever and vomiting followed three or four days later by the characteristic skin eruptions. For those who do not die, these pustules dry up in a week or ten days and form scabs which soon fall off, leaving the disfiguring pocks that give the disease its name. The whole process takes a month or less, and after that time the patient is either dead or immune, at least for a period of years. Also there is no non-human carrier of smallpox, such as the flea of typhus or the mosquito of malaria; it must pass from man to man. Nor are there any long-term human carriers of smallpox, as, for instance, with typhoid and syphilis. It is not an over-simplification to say that one either has smallpox and can transmit it, or one has not and cannot transmit it.

Consider that, except for children, most Europeans and their slaves had

had smallpox and were at least partially immune, and that few but adults sailed from Europe to America in the first decades after discovery. Consider that the voyage was one of several weeks, so that, even if an immigrant or sailor contracted smallpox on the day of embarkation, he would most likely be dead or rid of its virus before he arrived in Santo Domingo. Consider that moist heat and strong sunlight, characteristic of a tropical sea voyage, are particularly deadly to the smallpox virus. The lack of any rapid means of crossing the Atlantic in the sixteenth century delayed the delivery of the Old World's worst gift to the New.

It was delayed; that was all. An especially fast passage from Spain to the New World; the presence on a vessel of several nonimmune persons who could transmit the disease from one to the other until arrival in the Indies; the presence of smallpox scabs, in which the virus can live for weeks, accidentally packed into a bale of textiles — by any of these means smallpox could have been brought to Spanish America.

In December 1518 or January 1516 a disease identified as smallpox appeared among the Indians of Santo Domingo, brought, said Las Casas, from Castile. It touched few Spaniards, and none of them died, but it devasted the Indians. The Spaniards reported that it killed one-third to one-half of the Indians. Las Casas, never one to understate the appalling, said that it left no more than one thousand alive "of that immensity of people that was on this island and which we have seen with our own eyes." . . .

Thus began the first recorded pandemic in the New World, which was "in all likelihood the most severe single loss of aboriginal population that ever occurred." In a matter of days after smallpox appeared in Santo Domingo, it leaped the channel to Puerto Rico. Before long, Tainos were dying a hideous and unfamiliar death in all the islands of the Greater Antilles. Crushed by a quarter-century of exploitation, they now performed their last function on earth: to act as a reserve of pestilence in the New World from which the conquistador drew invisible biological allies for his assault on the mainland. . . .

The melodrama of Cortés and the conquest of Mexico need no retelling. After occupying Tenochtitlán and defeating the army of his rival, Narváez, he and his troops had to fight their way out of the city to sanctuary in Tlaxcala. Even as the Spanish withdrew, an ally more formidable than Tlaxcala appeared. Years later Francisco de Aguilar, once a follower of Cortés and now a Dominican friar, recalled the terrible retreat of the *Noche Triste*. "When the Christians were exhausted from war," he wrote, "God saw fit to send the Indians smallpox, and there was a great pestilence in the city. . . ."

With the men of Narváez had come a Negro sick with the smallpox, "and he infected the household in Cempoala where he was quartered; and it spread from one Indian to another, and they, being so numerous and eating and sleeping together, quickly infected the whole country." The Mexicans had never seen smallpox before and did not have even the European's meager knowledge of how to deal with it. The old soldier-chronicler, Bernal Díaz del Castillo, called the Negro "a very black dose" for Mexico, "for it was because of him that the whole country was stricken, with a great many deaths."

Probably, several diseases were at work. Shortly after the retreat from Tenochtitlán Bernal Díaz, immune to smallpox like most of the Spaniards, "was very sick with fever and was vomiting blood." The Aztec sources mention the racking cough of those who had smallpox, which suggests a respiratory complication such as pneumonia or a streptococcal infection, both common among smallpox victims. Great numbers of the Cakchiquel people of Guatemala were felled by a devastating epidemic in 1520 and 1521, having as its most prominent symptom fearsome nosebleeds. Whatever this disease was, it may have been present in central Mexico along with the pox.

The triumphant Aztecs had not expected the Spaniards to return after their expulsion from Tenochtitlán. The sixty days during which the epidemic lasted in the city, however, gave Cortés and his troops a desperately needed respite to reorganize and prepare a counterattack. When the epidemic subsided, the siege of the Aztec capital began. Had there been no epidemic, the Aztecs, their war-making potential unimpaired and their warriors fired with victory, could have pursued the Spaniards, and Cortés might have ended his life spread-eagled beneath the obsidian blade of a priest of Huitzilopochtli. Clearly the epidemic sapped the endurance of Tenochtitlán to survive the Spanish assault. As it was, the siege went on for seventy-five days, until the deaths within the city from combat, starvation, and disease — probably not smallpox now — numbered many thousands. When the city fell "the streets, squares, houses, and courts were filled with bodies, so that it was almost impossible to pass. Even Cortés was sick from the stench in his nostrils." . . .

If we attempt to describe the first coming of Old World disease to the areas south of Panama, we shall have to deal with ambiguity, equivocation, and simple guesswork, for eruptive fever, now operating from continental bases, apparently outstripped the Spaniards and sped south from the isthmus into the Incan Empire before Pizarro's invasion. Long before the invasion, the Inca Huayna Capac was aware that the Spaniards — "monstrous marine animals, bearded men who moved upon the sea in large houses — were pushing down the coast from Panama. Such is the communicability of smallpox and the other eruptive fevers that any Indian who received news of the Spaniards could also have easily received the infection of the European diseases. The biologically defenseless Indians made vastly more efficient carriers of such pestilence than the Spaniards.

Our evidence for the first post-Columbian epidemic in Incan lands is entirely hearsay, because the Incan people had no system of writing. Therefore, we must depend on secondary accounts by Spaniards and by mestizos or Indians born after the conquest, accounts based on Indian memory and written years and even decades after the epidemic of the 1520s. The few accounts we have of the great epidemic are associated with the death of Huayna Capac. He spent the last years of his life campaigning against the people of what is today northern Peru and Ecuador. There, in the province of Quito, he first received news of an epidemic raging in his empire, and there he himself was stricken. Huayna Capac and his captains died with shocking rapidity, "their faces being covered with scabs."

Of what did the Inca and his captains die? One of the most generally reliable of our sources, that of Garcilaso de la Vega, describes Huayna Capac's death as the result of "a trembling chill . . . , which the Indians call *chucchu,* and a fever, called by the Indians *rupu.* . . ." We dare not, four hundred years later, unequivocally state that the disease was not one native to the Americas. Most accounts call it smallpox, or suggest that it was either smallpox or measles. Smallpox seems the best guess because the epidemic struck in that period when the Spaniards, operating from bases where smallpox was killing multitudes, were first coasting along the shores of Incan lands.

The impact of the smallpox pandemic on the Aztec and Incan Empires is easy for us of the twentieth century to underestimate. We have so long been hypnotized by the derring-do of the conquistador that we have overlooked the importance of his biological allies. Because of the achievements of medical science in our day we find it hard to accept statements from the conquest period that the pandemic killed one-third to one-half of the populations struck by it. Toribio Motolinía claimed that in most provinces of Mexico "more than one half of the population died; in others the proportion was little less." "They died in heaps," he said, "like bedbugs."

The proportion may be exaggerated, but perhaps not as much as we might think. The Mexicans had no natural resistance to the disease at all. Other diseases were probably operating quietly and efficiently behind the screen of smallpox. Add too the factors of food shortage and the lack of even minimal care for the sick. Motolinía wrote: "Many others died of starvation, because as they were all taken sick at once, they could not care for each other, nor was there anyone to give them bread or anything else." We shall never be certain what the death rate was, but, from all evidence, it must have been immense. . . .

In Peru the epidemic of the 1520s was a stunning blow to the very nerve center of Incan society, throwing that society into a self-destructive convulsion. The government of the Incan Empire was an absolute autocracy with a demigod, the Child of the Sun, as its emperor. The loss of the emperor could do enormous damage to the whole society, as Pizarro proved by his capture of Atahualpa. Presumably the damage was greater if the Inca were much esteemed, as was Huayna Capac. When he died, said Cieza de León, the mourning "was such that the lamentation and shrieks rose to the skies, causing the birds to fall to the ground. The news traveled far and wide, and nowhere did it not evoke great sorrow." Pedro Pizarro, one of the first to record what the Indians told of the last days before the conquest, judged that had "this Huayna Capac been alive when we Spaniards entered this land, it would have been impossible for us to win it, for he was much beloved by all his vassals."

Not only the Inca but many others in key positions in Incan society died in the epidemic. The general Mihcnaca Mayta and many other military leaders, the governors Apu Hilaquito and Auqui Tupac (uncle and brother to the Inca), the Inca's sister, Mama Coca, and many others of the royal family all perished of the disease. The deaths of these important persons must have robbed the empire of much resiliency. Most ominous loss of all was the Inca's son and heir Ninan Cuyoche.

In an autocracy no problem is more dangerous or more chronic than that of succession. One crude but workable solution is to have the autocrat, himself, choose his successor. The Inca named one of his sons, Ninan Cuyoche, as next wearer of "the fringe" or crown, on the condition that the *calpa,* a ceremony of divination, show this to be an auspicious choice. The first *calpa* indicated that the gods did not favor Ninan Cuyoche, the second that Huascar was no better candidate. The high nobles returned to the Inca for another choice, and found him dead. Suddenly a terrible gap had opened in Incan society: the autocrat had died, and there was no one to take his place. One of the nobles moved to close the gap. "Take care of the body," he said, "for I go to Tumipampa to give the fringe to Ninan Cuyoche." But it was too late. When he arrived at Tumipampa, he found that Ninan Cuyoche had also succumbed to smallpox pestilence.

Among the several varying accounts of the Inca's death the one just related best fits the thesis of this paper. And while these accounts may differ on many points, they all agree that confusion over the succession followed the unexpected death of Huayna Capac. War broke out between Huascar and Atahualpa, a war which devastated the empire and prepared the way for a quick Spanish conquest. "Had the land not been divided between Huascar and Atahualpa," Pedro Pizarro wrote, "we would not have been able to enter or win the land unless we could gather a thousand Spaniards for the task, and at that time it was impossible to get together even five hundred Spaniards. . . ."

The psychological effect of epidemic disease is enormous, especially of an unknown disfiguring disease which strikes swiftly. Within a few days smallpox can transform a healthy man into a pustuled, oozing horror, whom his closest relatives can barely recognize. The impact can be sensed in the following terse, stoic account, drawn from Indian testimony, of Tenochtitlán during the epidemic.

It was [the month of] Tepeilhuitl when it began, and it spread over the people as great destruction. Some it quite covered [with pustules] on all parts — their faces, their heads, their breasts, etc. There was a great havoc. Very many died of it. They could not walk; they only lay in their resting places and beds. They could not move; they could not stir; they could not change position, nor lie on one side; nor face down, nor on their backs. And if they stirred, much did they cry out. Great was its [smallpox'] destruction. Covered, mantled with pustles, very many people died of them.

. . . For those who survived, the horror was only diminished, for smallpox is a disease which marks its victims for the rest of their lives. The Spanish recalled that the Indians who survived, having scratched themselves, "were left in such a condition that they frightened the others with the many deep pits on their faces, hands, and bodies." "And on some," an Indian said, "the pustules were widely separated; they suffered not greatly, neither did many [of them] die. Yet many people were marred by them on their faces; one's face or nose was pitted." Some lost their sight — a fairly common aftereffect of smallpox.

The contrast between the Indians' extreme susceptibility to the new disease and the Spaniards' almost universal immunity, acquired in Spain and reinforced in pestilential Cuba, must have deeply impressed the native Americans. The Indian, of course, soon realized that there was little relationship between Cortés and Quetzalcóatl, and that the Spaniards had all the vices and weaknesses of ordinary men, but he must have kept a lingering suspicion that the Spaniards were some kind of supermen. Their steel swords and arquebuses, their marvelously agile galleys, and, above all, their horses could only be the tools and servants of supermen. And their invulnerability to the pox — surely this was a shield of the gods themselves!

One can only imagine the psychological impact of smallpox on the Incan peoples. It must have been less than in Mexico, because the disease and the Spaniards did not arrive simultaneously, but epidemic disease is terrifying under any circumstances and must have shaken the confidence of the Incan people that they still enjoyed the esteem of their gods. Then came the long, ferocious civil war, confusing a people accustomed to the autocracy of the true Child of the Sun. And then the final disaster, the coming of the Spaniards.

The Mayan peoples, probably the most sensitive and brilliant of all American aborigines, expressed more poignantly than any other Indians the overwhelming effect of epidemic. Some disease struck into Guatemala in 1520 and 1521, clearing the way for the invasion shortly thereafter by Pedro de

Alvarado, one of Cortés' captains. It was apparently not smallpox, for the accounts do not mention pustules but emphasize nosebleeds, cough, and illness of the bladder as the prominent symptoms. It may have been influenza; whatever it was, the Cakchiquel Mayas who kept a chronicle of the tragedy for their posterity, were helpless to deal with it. Their words speak for all the Indians touched by Old World disease in the sixteenth century:

> Great was the stench of the dead. After our fathers and grandfathers succumbed, half of the people fled to the fields. The dogs and vultures devoured the bodies. The mortality was terrible. Your grandfathers died, and with them died the son of the king and his brothers and kinsmen. So it was that we became orphans, oh, my sons! So we became when we were young. All of us were thus. We were born to die!

2. Why So Many Indians Died in Mexico and What Effects This Had Upon Their Life and Upon the Building of Churches

GEORGE KUBLER

The two-volume contribution by Professor George Kubler of Yale, *Mexican Architecture in the Sixteenth Century,* is impressive not merely because of the splendidly detailed description of the great burst of Spanish building activity but also because of his broad approach to the problems involved. His is no narrowly technical architectural work but includes valuable information and insights into labor questions, religious influences, and culture shock that make these volumes one of the outstanding cross-disciplinary studies in Latin American studies.

An appalling mortality among the Indians marked the first century of Spanish colonization. The sources are unanimous about the fact. Even the hyperbolic statements of interested parties could only suggest a reality that defied any exhaustive statistical approach. Measurement and tabulation were incapable of keeping pace with the successive population disasters that struck New Spain, New Galicia, and the other territories of what is today the repub-

From *Mexican Architecture of the Sixteenth Century* by George Kubler, 2 vols. (New Haven: Yale University Press, 1948), vol. 1, pp. 30–67, passim; vol. 2, pp. 417–418. Reprinted by permission of the author.

lic of Mexico. The diction of the historians of the time is replete with allusions to calamity; Motolinía, for instance, enlarged upon the ten various "plagues" that had beset the affairs of the colony, Mendieta dedicated an entire chapter to the problem of depopulation, and Domingo de Betanzos, the eminent Dominican missionary, prophesied the total extinction of the Indian race if the disasters were to continue without abatement.

On the other hand, during these troubled years of the sixteenth century, a great colonial state was brought into being, with its administrative and spiritual center in Mexico. The foundation of hundreds of new urban settlements took place. A stable and highly productive colonial economy was established. Many specialized institutions came into being, and the tangible economic returns from the colony soared to a peak at the end of the century. In other words, more and more of the equipment of civilization was being produced among a race that simultaneously underwent a diminution of numbers rarely equalled in the history of mankind. . . .

The nearly constant presence of disease naturally perturbed the white colonists, although epidemic was no novelty for Europeans of the sixteenth century. . . . A nation, such as Spain or England, suddenly fell ill, agonized, and recovered, but meanwhile the disease had swept communities bare, sometimes taking the children, sometimes the old people, or only the women, but more generally leaving an exhausted fraction of the population to bury the dead and renew the life of the community. The phenomenon was therefore not unfamiliar to the colonists, and they accepted it as an ineradicable condition of communal existence. Many remedial measures were taken to abate the severity of disaster, but on the whole, the colonists were far more agitated about the social causes of loss than about disease itself.

The other great primary cause of elimination has evoked much controversy. In brief, it may be designated as the "homicidal theory" of loss, and its best-known publicist was the Dominican Bishop of Chiapas, fray Bartolomé de las Casas. The title of Las Casas' famous tract, *Breve relación de la destrucción de las Indias occidentales,* is an epitome of the homicidal theory, which attempts to assign all losses of population to direct action — to the bestial cruelty of the Spanish colonists, and their systematic slaughter of enormous masses of the Indian population. Torture and overwork and massacre were the chief instruments of mass homicide, with the result that the *Breve relación* is a catalogue of horrors, containing no mention of disease. Las Casas' attention was devoted mainly to conditions in the Antilles, where, in his opinion, in 1552, of three million Indians on Española at the time of the Discovery, only two hundred remained alive. Las Casas felt that the situation was less incriminating in Mexico, but he insisted that between 1518 and 1530, four millions had been slaughtered there, and in 1519, thirty thousands were massacred in Cholula alone. Two facts should be kept in mind.

Las Casas never experienced the fury of any of the great epidemics. In 1520–21, he was engaged in the foundation of the ill-starred colony of the Knights of the Golden Spur on the Pearl Coast of Venezuela, while in 1531, he resided in Española and in Nicaragua. . . .

The homicidal theory nevertheless bears some relation to a reality that we may reconstruct from other sources. As we have seen, torture, overwork, and murder were the means employed by the Spaniards, in Las Casas' theory, to destroy the Indian populations. In this form, it was a massive and undifferentiated theory, which assigned effects of an unknown magnitude to direct, malevolent action. The encomendero lashed his Indians to death, buried them alive, loaded their bodies to the breaking point, or else he murdered them with knife and gun. Las Casas admitted no indirect causes that might lie beyond the control of the indicted party. Later in the century, however, it is of the greatest interest to behold this blunt doctrine analyzed, refined, and made accurately descriptive in the hands of civil servants, whose commissions probably derived in part from the agitation aroused in Spain by Las Casas' writings.

The treatment of the question by the learned and intelligent Auditor, Alonso de Zorita, is worth close attention. In general, Zorita interpreted excessive mortality as a function of economic extortion. For the concept of direct homicide, he substituted a far richer social interpretation. Thus he catalogued the examples of extravagant forced labor conducive to a high death rate. Among these were the great public works; an excessive rate of tribute; heavy labor in the mines, in personal services, in the cultivation of certain crops, such as cacao and sugar-cane; and in military duty. Zorita even assigned pestilence to these various causes, and he was perhaps not far from the mark. For instance, reform legislation upon forced labor (the Nuevas Leyes) preceded the longest recess from epidemic during the century, from 1546 to 1573. . . .

In addition to the obvious check or hindrance to increase — a high incidence of epidemic disease that is possibly related to homicidal forms of economic exploitation — other determinants worked towards depopulation. Such causes are of two distinct kinds; those deriving from the dislocation of Indian culture, with attendant cultural shock, and those deriving from the reorientation of Indian culture — into the channels of a Christian society, an absolute State, and a mercantile economy. Both were powerful agents for depopulation, acting in rather different ways.

The effects of reorientation are fairly obvious. It should be emphasized that such effects occurred, not directly because of the greed and ill-will of the colonists, but as part of the price of any cultural reorganization, however benevolent in intention.

We must look to the Indians themselves for some account of the effects of reorientation. About 1580, after the great epidemic losses, the Crown was sufficiently concerned to inquire through its agents what interpretation the natives themselves placed upon the fact of their decline. The answers are recorded in the *Relaciones geográficas,* and although the full series has not been published, the available documents of this class yield most interesting clues to the problem. In these cosmographic questionnaires, it was asked of the natives in each community why the Indian race displayed greater longevity in antiquity. The answers came from many regions, and they display surprising acuity. Their general drift pertains to the superiority of indigenous culture over that of the Europeans. The ancient ways are always portrayed as more austere and less luxurious. Nearly all the declarants who pronounced upon the matter asserted that the Indians took less food in antiquity, and therefore enjoyed better health. The taking of much salt and hot food were particularly blamed. Only one settlement claimed that the diet did not differ as to quantity. The ancient restrictions upon alcoholic beverages, the practice of ceremonial warfare with its limited mortality, and the observance of the ancient pieties are also very frequently catalogued among the reasons for the superior health of the Indians before the Conquest. In many communities it was significantly reported that general hygiene and medication were much better in antiquity. The Indians especially approved the pre-Conquest costume, which involved fewer clothes and greater immunity to weather. They also noted that their ancestors had been more addicted to bathing; that they slept upon hard beds; that their herb-doctors were better than the colonial practitioners; and that the European custom of bloodletting was harmful. Finally, the ancient cleanly method of disposing of the dead by cremation was preferred to the Christian burial enforced by the whites. An allusion to the deleterious effects of a mercantile economy dependent upon transportation by human carriers is contained in the numerous assertions that the Indians were formerly more healthy and long-lived because they travelled less. Finally, direct reference to the central problems of fertility and the sex-ratio between males and females is carried by the many protests against the abolition of polygamy and against the practice of youthful marriages enforced by the Christians. Here the Indians touched upon the heart of the problem: the most delicate mechanisms of the culture, its rituals and customs of procreation, had been tampered with by the whites. The complaints are registered from all the main areas of New Spain, and they are among the few verbal expressions from Indian sources attesting to the essential lesions effected by the reorientation of Indian life into a colonial pattern.

As to losses deriving from the dislocation of Indian culture, no quantitative measure of any kind is suggested by the texts. But one set of replies from Indian informants, contained in the *Relaciones geográficas* cited above, bears upon the question, and it yields an important clue. It was supposed by the

Indians that their reduced longevity was partly to be explained by the amount of work they were doing. A peculiar difference of opinion was expressed: in some communities, the view was advanced that the Indians did *less* work in antiquity than in colonial life, and in others, it was stated that the Indians did *more* work in antiquity and therefore lived longer. The number of communities in which the latter view was voiced is double the number of those in which the Indians were represented as doing less work before the Conquest. The prevalent opinion in 1580 was therefore that the Indians were not working so hard as before the Conquest.

A sixteenth-century text explicitly mentions this situation. In 1545, a colonist writing to the Emperor said that great orderliness had prevailed in Motecuzoma's time: "Each man followed his calling. . . . There were inspectors . . . and now all are vagabonds and idlers." The white settlers naturally shared this official opinion. But it may be pointed out that their allegations did not always benefit their interests. To assever that the Indians were not working hard enough was needed to undermine the pro-Indian, humanitarian legislation on forced labor. The tax-collector, however, took it to signify that the tribute-burden was inadequate. The encomendero, in turn, knew that increase in the tribute-burden entailed some decrease in his own profit from Indian labor.

The most articulate opinion upon this question came from the pen of the learned and experienced Alonso de Zorita. He pointed out, after 1565, that the Europeans were mistaken in believing that the Indians were not working hard. But most of their work was being done for Europeans, and very little work was being done by the Indians for themselves. Hence it was perfectly true that the work of self-sustenance done by Indians was less in colonial times and more in antiquity; in the total labor-burden, however, the Indians were giving most of their time to the service of the whites.

To return to the Indians' own views upon the matter, it is to be emphasized that any proper interpretation of the proposition that the Indians worked harder in antiquity depends upon the meaning of the term, "work," to Indians. Their allegations make sense only when "work" is interpreted as "occupation," that is, as the entire routine of a ritual life that includes subsistence activities. To the pre-Conquest highland Indians, few differences were apparent between the work of producing ceremonial, and the ceremonial of doing work. All communal activities were ritual in character, and the year was filled with an intricate succession of ceremonial occasions, among which subsistence activities played a cardinal role. But in colonial life, when physical labor without ceremonial adornment was forced on the Indians, they became, so to speak, psychologically unemployed. In the absence of ceremonial, a dissipated indolence between moments of forced economic labor was inevitable. What would have been "leisure" to a modern community was complete absence of "occupation" to the Indians, only partly filled by the ritual and service of the church. Thus an extravagant economic exploitation may quite rightly have been regarded by the Indians as insufficient "work." An unoccupied leisure, filled with idling, drunkenness, and a minor ritual obligation to the church, would also be regarded as insufficient. In brief, the European secularization of all labor was antithetic to the Indian concept of "work." For the pre-Conquest Indian, all work was ultimately a ritual: for the European, work was almost exclusively a profane necessity, and to the Indians, the metamorphosis of work from ritual into an unadorned necessity must have been among the most disturbing and revolutionary aspects of their contact with Europeans.

Now the ritual life of Indian culture, with its rich and intricate form of esthetic experience, may have been far from ideal. It was punctuated by human sacrifice and by rites of great cruelty. Yet its psychic values must have been more satisfying to Indians than the drab and incomprehensible life of partial labor for economic ends imposed by the Spaniards. The Mendicant missionaries realized these deficiencies in colonial life, and sought to compensate for them with an abundant ceremonial which was unusual even by contemporary European standards. In an admirable chapter, Robert Ricard commented upon the extraordinary frequency and complexity of the ceremonial instituted by Mendicants. Sumptuous decorations filled the churches for the many important festivals; each community prepared musical offerings of voices and instruments; pilgrimages were encouraged to holy sites; each week processions, public dances, and theatrical performances of religious character were arranged; the needs of organized sociability were supplied by the intricate system of the sodalities, or *cofradías,* in each settlement. All these ceremonial activities, Ricard implies, were continuous, occupying the various groups and classes during the entire year, replacing the elaborate pre-Conquest calendar, and bringing Christianity a little closer to the Indians. Yet all this could be true only for the great Mendicant communities, in which friars were constantly resident, always available to supervise and encourage the new festivities. Where there were no friars, and where the secular clergy held control, little of the substitute or surrogate ceremonial could be supplied. In effect, a majority of the Indian population of Mexico was not provided with such relief from labor.

Hence it is reasonable to suggest that the Indians of Mexico were psychologically unemployed during the first century following the Conquest. Their situation in the sixteenth century is closely comparable to that of the natives of Polynesia and Melanesia and other island groups of the Pacific during the nineteenth century. The dislocation and reorientation of an antecedent culture entail a decrease in the rate of replacement among the bearers of that culture. An observable depopulation of the area is apparent. As the reorientation and dislocation of Indian life went on, numerous symptoms of a state of shock among the affected peoples became evident. These symptoms usually took the form either of violently destructive action, or of a lowered vitality and will to survive.

Systematic abortion and infanticide, as well as mass suicides, were reported from several areas. In Michoacan, for instance, a certain sorcerer was said to have induced crowds of bewitched Indians to kill themselves. Alonso de Zorita knew of many cases of Indian suicide to escape the payment of an impossible tribute, and he also cited the numerous abortions and the general refusal to procreate among the Mixe and Chontal Indians. In western Mexico as well, Lebrón de Quiñones found that the Indian women had been ordered not to conceive, that many refrained from intercourse, and that abortion was regularly practised, to ensure the rapid disappearance of the tribe. These are perhaps no more than isolated and sporadic instances, but they bespeak a general disintegration of the vital forces of the Indian race that also took much less radical forms. Drunkenness, for example, became alarmingly common, as reported by the Indian informants of 1579–81, and it appears to have been the drunkenness of despair and frustration.

The history of the many Indian revolts during the century may also be construed as a phenomenon of cultural shock. Such revolts were severely punished, and the rate of elimination in certain areas may reasonably be attributed to Spanish reprisals. The uprisings were especially common at the periphery of the colony. . . .

Hence all approaches to the problem appear to yield the same answer: increased elimination and decreased replacement are the results of colonization, constantly reducing the spread and density of the native populations. . . . At every point the two processes of increased elimination and decreased replacement are closely related. It is hard to believe that great epidemic losses are not registered in some decreases of the birth-rate, for an epidemic reducing the numbers of young women involves losses in fecundity which cannot immediately be recovered. . . .

Every available line of evidence returns us to the correlation between decline and the building activity of the religious orders. This activity does not mean simply the building of churches; it signifies the layout and construction of entire settlements according to rudimentary concepts of regional planning. The greatest number of urban projects was in progress at the time of the most severe losses of population. Was such activity a cause, or an effect of decline in number? The correct answer depends upon how we assess the intentions of the building friars. It is certain that the friars regarded a well regulated community life as essential to the health of the inhabitants. Such a community life could develop only in well planned, well built towns.

The urbanizing work of the Mendicants was both cause and effect, disease and cure, reason and consequence, at least in part, for the high mortality suffered by the Indians. The heavy burden of labor, and the unhygienic conditions of work in new and improperly equipped settlements gave epidemic disease a rich harvest. And yet the same work, continued through and beyond the epoch of contagion, helped to protect and shelter the town-dwellers from new incursions.

As with other significant fragments of colonial life, the construction of any one of the buildings studied in this book is a process enmeshed in most intricate relationships. It has been demonstrated that no building could be achieved in Mexico without prior urbanization of the participants. To urbanize the Indian populations was to dislocate and destroy the patterns of indigenous culture. Such cultural extirpation, in turn, brought about the biological decrease of the Indian race. Hence the architecture that is the subject of this study was built at the expense of one of the great historical configurations of human society. Each building, and each colonial artifact was nourished by the destruction of a culture, and the decline of a race. . . .

The amount and quality of building in Mexico between the Conquest and 1600 may now be evaluated. In terms of quantity alone it probably exceeded by many times the total volume of monumental building in all Mexico during Aztec history (1250–1520). The Mexican landscape was basically altered by urban reconcentration, by hydrostatic works, by the profiles of the immense churches rearing high above the Indian pyramids. Not only was volume of construction increased, but the demands upon human skill were vastly greater than in pre-Conquest building.

How can we explain so much activity? How did it happen that three and a half million Indians accepted the material culture of so few colonists? Why is this architecture so various in structure and style, and so excellent in form? Why did so few pre-Conquest traits of technique, iconography, and style survive in early colonial art? In general, why did the Indians of Mexico, unlike the Pueblos of New Mexico, accept and reduplicate nearly the entire range of European building techniques, without essential loss or deformation?

The form of the questions, as they are written here, suggests a preliminary answer. The conventional interpretation, that the Indian peoples were coerced and exploited to these ends, against their will, and under conditions of slavery, is unsatisfactory in face of the evidence of texts and buildings. It is as if we were to say that the growth of a prize crop of corn results only from the farmer's bellicose design against nature; his merciless exploitation of water, sun, and soil; his ruthless tyranny in depriving the seed of the natural conditions of growth. But anyone will agree that the seed is essential, and that without it, the farmer's pains are for nothing. The conventional view appears in another form of statement: had the Indian peoples been left to their own devices, their cultural achievement would have been far richer and more valuable. This again amounts to saying that the farmer is at fault for subjecting plants to any kind of cultivation, good or bad, or that the finest fruits will grow from the least tended plants. However these things may be, such conventional views either overestimate or underestimate the rôle of an autonomous response to colonization from indigenous peoples.

The simple empirical fact is that the Indians were not exterminated by colonization in Mexico, and that their labor produced an intricate, abundant, and qualitative material culture. That their absolute productive capacity increased during the sixteenth century cannot be questioned, in spite of the loss of numbers through epidemic disease. The phenomenon of reduced populations attaining a more complex civilization in the span of fifty years suggests intimate participation and eager acquiescence by those numbers in the work at hand. The occasional withdrawals or resistances to colonization have already been noted; they were sporadic and peripheral: events in the metropolitan regions indicate the avidity of the Indians for European ceremonial and technology. No one will deny that the initial conquest meant coercion of Indians by Europeans. No one will deny that coercion continued throughout the sixteenth century. But the kind and degree of coercion changed between the conquest and the early stages of colonization: from military coercion to the forms of social compulsion without which society cannot persist. There is good reason to believe that sixteenth-century colonial compulsions upon Indian society were less onerous and less destructive of human resources than those applied by the Aztec confederacy during the fifteenth century. . . .

3. The Introduction of Vaccination Against Smallpox to Spanish America

SHERBURNE F. COOK

The prevention of disease involves political and social as well as medical matters, as Dr. Francisco Xavier Balmis discovered when he embarked on the Royal Expedition to introduce the newly discovered vaccination to the Spanish empire. It was a remarkable effort, as Professor Sherburne F. Cook explains in another of his well-wrought historical essays on Spanish American history.

On November 30, 1803 Francisco Xavier Balmis sailed from Coruña, Spain for the purpose of carrying the newly discovered vaccination to the wide dominions of the Spanish Empire. Seldom, perhaps never, in the history of medicine has there embarked an expedition so grandly conceived, so well executed, so uniformly successful as that of Balmis. Certainly no new therapeutic procedure of similar magnitude has ever been made available by a single agency to such a wide segment of the world's population. By it the discovery of Jenner was made available to the populations of the West Indies, Mexico, Central America, much of South America, the Philippine Islands, the East Indies and China. Through this one act on the part of the corrupt and decadent government of Spain more lives probably were saved than were lost in all the battles of Napoleon. Yet this magnificent experiment in social welfare and public health has gone substantially unnoticed and unrecorded by both medical and political historians. . . .

The plans involved three principal items: the administrative personnel, the mode of conservation of the vaccine, and the route to be followed. With respect to personnel, Balmis was named Director. His salary was set at 2,000 pesos annually to run from his departure from Madrid to the return of the expedition. Thereafter, until he secured a position appropriate to his standing he was to receive half pay, and in addition he was granted a subsidy of 200 doubloons wherewith to purchase an outfit. As principal lieutenants his majesty appointed the following four physicians: Don Joseph Salvani, Don Ramon Fernandez Ochoa, Don Manuel Julian Grajales, and Don Antonio Gutierrez y Robredo. Each of these was to be paid just one half that assigned to Balmis. . . .

The problem of vaccine transport was serious. The voyage was certainly to be of long duration, involving a minimum of several weeks passage from the Canary Islands to the West Indies. Several rather different methods were in vogue at the time. The first was to prepare the virus by placing active matter from a pustule of a cow between two small plates of glass or otherwise sealing it in glass out of contact with the air. Another was to impregnate cloth, or silk threads with the virus and allow it to dry. Both these procedures suffered from lack of aseptic precautions and moreover the virus was very likely to deteriorate. Since these and similar devices were notoriously unreliable, it was determined to utilize another safer although much more cumbersome and expensive method. The latter consisted of transporting the vaccine fluid

"Francisco Xavier Balmis and the Introduction of Vaccine to Latin America" by S. F. Cook from *Bulletin of the History of Medicine* (© The Johns Hopkins Press, Baltimore), vol. 11, pp. 543–557, vol. 12, pp. 70–89 (1941–1942), passim. Reprinted by permission of the Johns Hopkins Press.

in human reservoirs. At the outset of the voyage a small, non-immune boy was to be vaccinated with a potent preparation of cow pox virus. At the point when the reaction was at its peak, matter was to be transferred from this individual to the arm of another boy who would preserve the active principle until it was transferred to the next. This chain vaccination was to be continued until the New World was reached, at which time any number of new patients would be available. The royal orders specified simply a "sufficient number" of children. The boys were to be selected from various orphan asylums, with permission of relatives if known, and were to be well cared for. They were to be retained in the colonies after arrival, and of course after their usefulness had ceased. Nevertheless they were to be given every consideration and were to be educated at the expense of the state until they were able to enter some regular employment. Actually twenty-two sailed from Spain. Unfortunately since their names were not recorded they must forever remain anonymous contributors to the cause of medical progress. . . .

The expedition arrived in Havana in early June. On the 8th of that month the Royal Patriotic Society convened to consider the vaccination question. They informed themselves "in minute detail" of the matter, ordering two copies of the instructions to be placed in the library of the Society, and elected Balmis to an honorary membership. At the same time a central vaccination board was formed for the dissemination of the fluid among the inhabitants of of the Island of Cuba. However, Balmis was anxious to continue his journey for he wrote the Viceroy on June 10 that he intended to depart on or about June 17 for Yucatan whence he would proceed to Vera Cruz, arriving there toward the end of July. Since the original royal instructions directed the expedition to go directly to Vera Cruz from Havana, the decision to make a detour to Yucatan seems to have been reached by Balmis while on the voyage. Whether any extraordinary motives prompted him to take this course is doubtful, but it may perhaps have been more than coincidence that when he arrived he found vaccine already introduced both on the peninsula and the region of Vera Cruz. . . .

It is quite clear that vaccine was in the Caribbean colonies prior to the arrival of the Royal Expedition, although its ultimate origin is obscure. Two introductions seem to have occurred, probably independently, one in Vera Cruz, the other in Yucatan. . . .

[In Yucatán there developed an unpleasant controversy between Balmis and the other introducing the vaccine.]

This entire episode might be regarded as too trivial for serious consideration did it not possess significance as an illustration of the difficulties attending even great undertakings. But for the timely intervention of the Governor of Vera Cruz, the vaccine might have been lost and the entire scheme might have failed in its object. It is quite clear that the fault lay on both sides. When the vaccinated sailors arrived in Vera Cruz, the Ayuntamiento of that city, knowing of the royal expedition, doubtless saw an opportunity to anticipate Balmis and achieve publicity and merit in the eyes of the Viceroy. . . . In support of this point of view may be noted the obsequious care with which they notified the Viceroy of their every action and on the other hand the carelessness with which they permitted the smallpox virus to disappear from their own town as soon as it had served its purpose. Entirely in line with such policy was the rude treatment they accorded Balmis and their utter indifference to the welfare of the king's expedition.

At the other end of the controversy the behavior of Balmis was, to say the least, undiplomatic. Instead of being in any way gratified that the great humanitarian object of his visit was being accomplished by private individuals in advance of his arrival he obviously became subject to strong irritation. Judging by his actions in Yucatan, and his letters from Vera Cruz he regarded any efforts by others toward introduction of vaccine as a personal affront and a presumption upon his own prerogatives as the king's emissary. In short, all parties concerned behaved as if the propagation of vaccine in the interest of the public welfare were wholly secondary to considerations of personal aggrandizement and royal or viceregal favor.

Tarrying only a few days in the inhospitable atmosphere of Vera Cruz, Balmis, Gutierrez and 22 boys departed on July 28 for Mexico. Passing by the old road through Jalapa and Perote, the group arrived at the suburb of Guadalupe on August 8. . . .

The introduction of vaccine into Mexico City was the most vital single necessity confronting the Balmis expedition. The capital of New Spain exercised an enormous influence upon the entire stretch of the continent from San Francisco Bay to Panama. That capital was the physical or spiritual home of the entire ruling class, the group which moulded and determined public opinion. It was absolutely essential for the success of the new therapy to establish its desirability in the minds of the Mexican upper class. Hence Balmis made a particularly strong effort in this direction.

For some reason every attempt to perform vaccinations in Mexico City met with remarkable lack of success. Indeed, the amazing reluctance on the part of the inhabitants lends weight to the theory that certain persons in high places, perhaps the Viceroy himself, were engaged in secret sabotage. It will be remembered that in Vera Cruz, despite numerous previous vaccinations at the hands of local authorities, Balmis was unable to find a single individual upon whom to perform the operation. In Mexico City much the same situation presented itself. Some months previously Don Alexandro Garcia Arboleya had been commissioned by the Viceroy himself to propagate vaccine in the suburbs of Coyoacan and Tacuba where he had encountered little difficulty and had performed several hundred operations. The consistent support of the

Viceroy in favor of pre-expedition introduction of vaccine argues a definite policy which manifested itself not only in Mexico City but in Vera Cruz, Yucatan and various other regions. It is very probable that colonial politics and ambitions were involved although there is no concrete documentary evidence bearing on the point. If so, this will not have been the first occasion on which a protagonist of some form of public health improvement met with reverses at the hands of ignorant and selfish political appointees.

Apart from the motivation, however, Balmis found that when he issued a call for volunteers to be vaccinated at a free public clinic on August 19 and 20 not a single soul responded. What occurred at that clinic is most vividly told by Balmis himself:

> Another proof of this (popular resistance) is seen in the fact that no person whatever has presented himself in order to participate in this immense benefaction, . . . the *Alcalde,* commissioned by your Excellency, having to resort to force to obtain 12 children to be vaccinated for the purpose of insuring continuance of the precious vaccine brought from Madrid. . . . On the 19th and 20th of this month I might have lost the fluid . . . had it not been for the zealous *Alcalde.* He dragged in as many as twenty Indian mothers, whose children we finally vaccinated after much persuasion on our part and after loud vociferation and exclaiming that they were not under obligation to anybody. Some admitted that it was right but that they could not pay, and every single one went to the apothecary, demanding an antidote against the venom that had just been introduced into the arm of her child. . . .

Since the primary purpose of the Royal Expedition was to introduce vaccination to the inhabitants of the territories visited, it was necessary for the Director or selected assistants to make personal contact with the officials and leading citizens of as many towns as possible. Mere regulations and orders promulgated by the viceregal government or even the clerical hierarchy were likely to be received with indifference. Haphazard introduction depending upon local initiative or the exigency of epidemics likewise would be too uncertain and risky. To depend upon the nearly non-existent national medical profession or the caprice of municipal politicians was manifestly out of the question since the former were too ignorant and the latter too selfish and corrupt to ensure proper handling of the treatment. For these reasons it was desirable for competent and disinterested persons to go as emissaries or missionaries and make the people themselves acquainted with the procedure and merits of vaccination. . . .

In the space of approximately six months the director, or his assistants, visited every important city, and many of the small towns of Mexico. The medical profession was given such complete training in the practice of the new method that numerous persons remained after the departure of Balmis who were qualified to continue the work. At all key points an adequate supply existed both of preserved vaccine and living carriers. The administration of smallpox prevention was vested in a series of local vaccination boards which in turn were under the direct authority of the colonial government. A system of free public clinics was established. Finally, a great many thousand inhabitants were actually vaccinated and, perhaps more important, caused to lose their initial fear and suspicion of the strange procedure.

Concerning the actual number of vaccinations performed from July, 1804 to January, 1806, we have only the scattered estimates cited previously. From these data it is evident that the numbers varied enormously from district to district. Moreover, it is probable that many vaccinations were never recorded officially. If a specific figure were demanded I should be inclined to feel that 100,000 might not be an overestimate. This would represent roughly two per cent of the entire population. If this is regarded as, after all a rather insignificant total, it should be remembered that not only were large sections of the country skipped by the expedition (such as Sinaloa, Sonora, Chihuahua, Coahuila, Tamaulipas and Nuevo Leon) but also vaccinations were confined to children. This was due to the fact that in 1804 practically every individual over twenty had already been exposed to smallpox in the sweeping epidemics of 1779 and 1797. If we make the fairly safe assumptions that the expedition reached only half the population by area and that only 20 per cent of the inhabitants were non-immune, then we may conclude that Balmis and his helpers reached twenty per cent of those who might have benefited by their ministrations. Such a record on the part of an introductory and propagandising expedition by strangers rather than on the part of a long-term public health program sponsored by the local government represents a real achievement.

POPULATION ESTIMATES

4. Why Population Estimates Are Important in the Interpretation of Mexican History

WOODROW BORAH and SHERBURNE F. COOK

For some twenty years Professors Borah and Cook have been studying the records of population in Mexico, and have produced a literature which is remarkable for its scope and depth. The methods they have developed are somewhat complicated and require more mathematical knowledge than most historians possess. Their conclusions on the meaning of their calculations for the interpretation of Mexican history are clearly of importance, even though they have not been universally accepted. Here is one of their most recent condensed statements on their findings.

A long series of questions comes to focus on the debate over the size of the population of central Mexico on the eve of the Spanish conquest, say A.D. 1518. Scholars who hold to the view that there was a dense aboriginal population also find that there was a complex society with very extensive division of labor, highly elaborate social stratification even to hereditary rulers and nobility, and that a numerous peasantry very much like that of pharaonic Egypt supported the elaborate superstructure. . . .

Scholars who hold to the opposing view that there was a relatively sparse population would find that pre-Conquest Meso-American society consisted of a series of chiefdoms somewhat more elaborate than those of the Iroquois. . . . The positions have remained strangely fixed since the eighteenth century and even earlier. Additional questions are (1) whether the Spanish conquest brought about a drastic decrease in Indian numbers, and (2) whether over the course of millennia since the beginnings of the Classical (Teotihuacán) Period in the first centuries of the Christian Era, Indian population has shown fairly steady increase until the explosion of our century or whether population in central Mexico has been characterized by an essentially cyclical movement. If this last interpretation is correct, after the nadir of the early seventeenth century Mexican numbers may now be nearing the climax of another upswing.

The debate has been able to continue for centuries because so much of the information available consisted of reports and chronicles of an essentially qualitative character. The relatively few statements of number could be declared moot or discredited by resort to techniques of literary and textual criticism. The discussion itself was essentially literary, characterized by the well-turned phrase heaping scorn upon opponents.

An essentially new approach to the debate has become possible in recent years through the uncovering in archives of substantial masses of quantitative data. Most materials are fiscal, but can be used for estimating population. . . .

Our results . . . strongly support the view that there was in central Mexico when Cortés landed on the coast of Veracruz a very dense popula-

From "Conquest and Population: A Demographic Approach to Mexican History" by Woodrow Borah and Sherburne F. Cook, *Proceedings of the American Philosophical Society,* 113, no. 2 (April 1969), pp. 177–183, passim. Reprinted by permission.

tion. The two hundred thousand square miles of central Mexico had an average population density of one hundred twenty-five persons per square mile. A peasantry, using digging stick methods of cultivation, with stone and wooden implements, with no large domesticated animals for power or food, but profiting from the highly productive maize-beans-squash complex, provided support for a superstructure of artisans, merchants, priesthood, nobility, and rulers. The surplus from each family was small but the peasantry was enormous and the superstructure accordingly elaborate. It was most elaborate in the seats of empire on the Mexican plateau, which drew huge stocks of foodstuffs and other products as tribute and levied on the lowlands for prized cotton, cacao, and feathers. Around the lakes of the Valley of Mexico and Lake Pátzcuaro, where canoe traffic meant a considerable advantage over transportation by human bearer, there grew up substantial metropolitan concentrations.

The vast population of early sixteenth-century central Mexico developed because of an unusually productive agriculture and relative isolation which shielded it from the epidemics of the Old World. Population density probably had passed the long-term carrying power of the land at the then level of technology as is evident from the widespread erosion that was taking place even under relatively benign cultivation by digging stick. The vast extension of human sacrifice in the middle of the fifteenth century looks remarkably like a response to population pressure. To an already overextended population the Spanish conquest came as catastrophe. Destruction of war and the dislocation of productive and distributive systems were greatly compounded by the unwitting introduction within a few years and in rapid succession of the temperate and tropical diseases of the Old World. Within less than a century the population of central Mexico shrank from approximately twenty-five millions to under two millions; the tropical coasts became the disease-ridden wastes that they have remained until recent decades.

Had the Spanish conquest taken place without catastrophic shrinkage of population, the history of Mexico might have been more nearly parallel to that of Indian or China, the superimposition of a numerically small ruling stratum that at a later date could be expelled by a reorganized native society. As events actually occurred in Mexico, the disappearance of the Indians made room for the addition of substantial contingents of Europeans and Negroes, who contributed the increasingly important and now numerically predominant group of mixed-bloods, mostly the Indian-European mixture known as mestizos. Culturally, the shrinkage of the Indian population permitted the entrance of European elements on a scale and with a thoroughness that would otherwise have been difficult, if not impossible.

The reorganization of social and political structures paralleled the decline in native numbers. In the first decades after the conquest, the Spaniards tended to preserve native forms and systems, except for the replacement of native religion by Christianity, the Europeans entering as a small uppermost class that attempted to draw support through tribute and other forms of taxation with the minimum of change needed to adjust native forms to European wants. The Spaniards, for example, wanted gold but had little use for the prized featherwork that was an important component of Aztec levies. By the middle of the sixteenth century, the native population shrank to a point at which it could no longer support both native and Spanish superstructures. At the mid-century the growing arrears in payments and complaints of too harsh levy led to a prolonged series of investigations by the royal government, and the investigations in turn into a struggle among the recipients of support to preserve their shares. In the end, the native rulers, nobility, and community governments and the Christian church lost very substantially whereas the Crown and the small group of Spanish who received tributes as its surrogates (the encomenderos) actually increased their shares. The native nobility and native officials were held to tribute; all exemption of their servants and serfs was ended; and a moderate, uniform tribute based on a uniform classification was instituted. In the same years, the burden on the Indian peasantry through levy by nobility and church for community expenditures was severely limited, and the exaction of labor put under a system of viceregal license (in effect, a kind of rationing). By the closing decades of the sixteenth century, although the reformed tribute system continued to function well, the native population shrank to so low a level that it could not furnish labor and goods to the Europeans under the existing forms of levy. A more radical solution was slowly put into effect, namely, that much of food for the Europeans, especially wheat and meat, was raised on their own estates, that the Europeans carried on much of their own production, and that labor was provided increasingly by Indians working for wages but tied to the Spaniard by debt. The system had the vast advantage for the Spaniards that the debt peons were available for all or substantial portions of their time. It had the further effect of withdrawing large numbers of Indians from their towns and placing them in Spanish towns, mines, and on Spanish estates, where tribal and community linkage was lost and the Indians merged into the new mixed-blood, Hispanized population. The Indian communities, beyond the losses through deaths, lost members further through recruitment of debt peons, migration to the economically more active Spanish settlements, and interbreeding. Accordingly, demographic recovery, when it began in the early and middle seventeenth century, was marked by the slower rate of increase of the Indians relative to the Europeans and Hispanized segments. Today the population of central Mexico is larger than it was in the reign of Montezuma the Younger, but Mexico is essentially a European state, with European language and European culture.

We may look at Mexican history in yet another way. Professor Cook has found in the Teotlalpan, the region northwest of Mexico City that was once the seat of the Toltec Empire (ninth to twelve centuries A.D.), a series of cyclical movements of population, the cycles covering from four to five centuries each. The upward movements within the cycles coincided with the dominance of the societies of Teotihuacán, the Toltecs, and the Aztecs. The downward movements have coincided with the breakdown of political systems. That breakdown has been marked by the successful invasion of central Mexico by invaders from outside the region. In all cycles before the coming of the Spaniards, the invaders were nomads from the arid regions to the north (Chichemecs) who became the dominant stratum in a reorganized society. One may hold that the coming of the Spaniards ended such cyclical movements, or that it has continued the movements save for the fact that the invaders came from across the ocean. Concomitantly with the coming of the Spaniards there has taken place the decline of population that in other cycles either preceded or accompanied invasion. The Spaniards more thoroughly reorganized society and technology than previous invaders. The state that they established eventually covered a far larger territory that included much of the old Chichemec domain. During their domination, as in other cycles, the population reached a low point and began an upswing that has continued with little interruption for over three centuries, the change from Spanish colony to independent but Europeanized state in 1821 having little effect. Today Mexico has the largest human population it has ever had. The Teotlalpan is again heavily populated. Whether or not Mexico has freed itself from a cyclical pattern may be tested in the coming century.

Spaniards Mistreating their Black Slaves in Peru (Reading 4). Despite humanitarian laws and the efforts of the Catholic Church, slavery in Spanish America was inherently cruel. The caption on this drawing from an early seventeenth century manuscript states, "Consider how the masters mistreat their male and female black slaves and the good slaves bear it with patience for the love of God and they do not give them anything to wear or to eat and do not think about the fact that God made them and died for them as well as the Spanish." The illustration is one of many that accompanied a 1,200 page report sent by an acculturated Peruvian Indian, Felipe Guaman Poma de Ayala, to the King of Spain to expose the abuses of the colonial regime. The complete manuscript, first published in Paris in 1936 under the title Nueva Corónica y buen gobierno, *is one of the most valuable indigenous sources from colonial Peru.*

The Introduction of African Slavery in Spanish America

THE INFLUENCE OF AFRICA

Africans were present from the earliest days of the "discovery" of America. Two of the men in Columbus's crew are thought to have been black. Africans accompanied Vasco Núñez de Balboa in Panama, the Pizarro brothers in Peru, and, as Peter Gerhard's study of Juan Garrido reveals, they took part in the conquest of Mexico (Reading 3). But the overwhelming majority of those who arrived in the New World were brought as unwilling migrants from their African homelands to labor in the colonies of Spain, Portugal, England, and France. Philip Curtin, a historian at Johns Hopkins University, has estimated that from 1518, when Charles I granted an *asiento,* or license, to ship slaves from Africa directly to America, until 1850, when the trade was finally abolished, more than 9.6 million men and women had been seized against their will in Africa and transported across the Atlantic. Of this total, approximately 1.5 million went to Spanish America and 3.6 million to Brazil.[1] Black slavery undergirded nearly every economic activity performed in the New World, but as Ann Pescatello points out in the introduction to *The African in Latin America,* along with the tradition of servitude, Africans brought with them "a rich heritage of art and religion, advanced cultural methods, technology and sophisticated political and social organization. . . .

---

[1] Philip D. Curtin, *The Atlantic Slave Trade. A Census* (Madison: University of Wisconsin Press, 1969), p. 268. The British and French Caribbean took in over 3.2 million while 399,000 went to British North America.

The story of black men and women in an alien environment is one of both human endurance and the survival of cultures."[2]

THE ATLANTIC SLAVE TRADE

The Atlantic slave trade persisted for nearly three hundred and fifty years, and involved all the great powers in Europe. The Portuguese were the first to sail along the African coast, seeking commerce and a route to Asia, and the papal bull of 1493 ratified by the Treaty of Tordesillas a year later ensured their access to that continent. As a result, the Spanish were purchasers rather than suppliers of slaves. First the Portuguese and later the Dutch, French, and English vied with one another to win the *asiento*, which, along with the exclusive right to transport slaves to the Spanish colonies, offered unparalleled opportunities to smuggle in contraband goods as well. As Reading 1 suggests, the impact of this trade on Africa was far-reaching, and regardless of the nations involved in slave trafficking, the horrors of the Middle Passage were constant: "A classic example of man's inhumanity to man, of commercial transactions based entirely on the estimated value of a pound of flesh."[3]

Why didn't the Spanish clergy denounce African slavery when they so vigorously defended the Indians? For one reason, black slavery already existed in Spain; it was tolerated by the Catholic Church and regulated according to civil law. Secondly, the Indians had owned the New World before the Spanish came, and after the conquest were regarded as vassals of the King; the blacks had no such claim, being citizens of African nations who had been sold into slavery by their own rulers. Thirdly, Spanish humanitarians were moved by the plight of the Indians when their numbers were decimated by epidemic disease, while the blacks who survived the Atlantic voyage seemed stronger, having previously acquired resistance to diseases brought by the whites to America. Finally, since all slaves were baptized in Africa before beginning their journey, the clergy could rationalize their bondage by affirming that no matter how difficult their lives were in the present world, their souls would find salvation in the world that was to come.

Nevertheless, some voices were raised. Las Casas himself, who once recommended African slavery in the hope of saving his beloved Indians, later recanted and declared that it was as unjust to enslave blacks as Indians, "and for the same reasons." Another Dominican, Tomás de Mercado, condemned the West African slave trade in his *Tratos y Contratos* (1569), and a Portuguese Jesuit argued in 1608 that the law against Amerindian slavery

---

[2]Ann M. Pescatello, ed., *The African in Latin America* (New York: Alfred A. Knopf, 1975), p. 3.
[3]Ibid., p. 33.

should be extended to include blacks; yet nothing changed. The most informed critic was the Spanish Jesuit, Alonso de Sandoval, who denounced the slave trade in his treatise *De instaurande Aethiopum* (Seville, 1627) (Reading 2). As Professor Charles R. Boxer states:

> Sandoval, though with obvious reluctance, admitted the validity of Negro slavery under the conditions stipulated by canon and civil law. He also admitted that the Amerindian in his natural state was born free, and consequently felt himself to be such, whereas the Negro was used to servitude in his native habitat. Having said this, he then proceeded to denounce the Negro slave-trade even more violently than had Tomás de Mercado. He argued that Negros were just as human as were any of the other races of mankind, although they were more shamefully abused than any, and that in the eyes of God a Negro's soul was worth just as much as that of a white man. Far from finding them bestial and unruly savages, as many slave-owners and dealers claimed that they were, he praises their candid and tractable character, providing his points with a wealth of anecdote from his own experience as rector of the Jesuit college at Cartagena de Indias.
>
> Sandoval denounced the sophistries and abuses of the slave traders, even going so far as to advise that they should be refused the sacraments, if they do not mend their ways. He points out that internecine tribal wars in Africa had greatly increased as a result of the European demand for slaves, and that the slaves obtained in this way could not be regarded as having been taken in a "just war." Contrary to what many modern apologists for the slave system assert, he states emphatically that most slave-owners made no efforts to look after their slaves, or to treat them as valuable property which was difficult to replace; but on the contrary the owners and planters treated their Negroes with callous and calculated brutality, careless if they died as a result of it.[4]

SLAVERY IN SPANISH AMERICA

Since the publication of Frank Tannenbaum's provocative little book, *Slave and Citizen: The Negro in the Americas* in 1947, scholars have hotly debated the character of slavery in Spanish America. The first case studies based on archival sources appeared to support Tannenbaum's thesis that slavery was less harsh in Latin America, because of such factors as medieval Iberian law, which recognized the unnaturalness of slavery, the efforts of the Catholic Church to protect the slave family, and the elaborate body of Spanish law

---

[4]Charles R. Boxer, *Salvador de Sá and the Struggle for Brazil and Angola, 1602–1686* (London: The Athlone Press, University of London, 1952), pp. 237–238.

defining the rights of slaves.[5] More recently, historians have tended to reject this interpretation as wishful thinking, by pointing out that the protective legislation was often ignored and that "economic rather than cultural factors determined the specific differences between slave societies."[6] One of the most comprehensive investigations into the lives of black slaves in sixteenth-century Peru forms a chapter in James Lockhart's important book, *Spanish Peru 1532–1560: A Colonial Society* (Madison: University of Wisconsin Press, 1968) (Reading 4). Although plantations had yet to be formed in Peru, Lockhart shows that already by the second generation blacks were "an organic part of the enterprise of occupying Peru," and were "in a hundred ways the agents and auxiliaries of the Spaniards."

SLAVE RESISTANCE

African resistance to slavery took many forms. On occasion spontaneous reactions to cruel treatment or excessive work escalated into open rebellion. Slave unrest in Panama by the mid-sixteenth century was so serious that the crown temporarily banned further importation of blacks. In Mexico, between 1569 and 1580, slave insurrections covered nearly the entire settled area of the colony outside Mexico City (Reading 5). Venezuela was the scene of two unsuccessful revolts in the eighteenth century: one plot was foiled in 1749 when a conspirator was captured and forced to confess the plans under torture; another rebellion actually broke out in Coro in 1795 but was quickly suppressed. Though greatly feared by slave-owners everywhere, such massive revolts were rare.

A more common method of protest has been called "passive resistance." Slaves routinely pretended to be too stupid to follow orders, broke tools, deliberately killed livestock, and in other ways sought to sabotage the plantations. As Frederick Bowser has commented, in these ways slaves could vent their frustrations "without quite crossing the thin line between perceived indolence and insolence. The former was grudgingly tolerated by the white

---

[5]See for example Herbert Klein, *Slavery in the Americas: A Comparative Study of Virginia and Cuba* (Chicago: University of Chicago Press, 1967); Stanley M. Elkins, *Slavery: A Problem in American Institutional and Intellectual Life* (Chicago: University of Chicago Press, 1959).

[6]Benjamin Keen, *A History of Latin America*, 4th ed. (Boston: Houghton Mifflin, 1992), p. 114. One of the first to reject the Tannenbaum thesis was Marvin Harris, *Patterns of Race in the Americas* (New York: Walker and Company, 1964). Other major works on Spanish American slavery include Colin A. Palmer, *Slaves of the White God, Blacks in Mexico, 1570–1650* (Cambridge: Harvard University Press, 1976); Frederick P. Bowser, *The African Slave in Colonial Peru 1524–1650* (Stanford: Stanford University Press, 1974); and William F. Sharp, *Slavery on the Spanish Frontier: The Colombian Chocó, 1680–1810* (Norman: University of Oklahoma Press, 1976).

master as a racial characteristic impossible, or difficult, to correct; but the latter received the tender mercies of the whip or worse."[7]

Perhaps the most successful ploy was simply to run away. Over the centuries, thousands of slaves fled to remote areas beyond the reach of Spanish authorities. Known as *cimarrones*, or maroons, they formed free communities called *palenques* in Spanish America and *quilombos* in Brazil. An account of Palmares, the largest *quilombo* in Brazil, can be found in Section VI. In Spanish America, one of the most successful *palenques* began in 1570 in Esmeraldas, Ecuador, when a cargo of West African slaves en route from Panama to Peru was wrecked off the northern coast. The newly freed slaves took possession of the wilderness, killing the local Indian men and taking the women as wives. Isolated from Spanish authorities in Quito by high mountains, the *zambo* society flourished, blending Indian and African traits into a unique culture. The population had reached five thousand in 1597 when the *audiencia* decided to negotiate a peace treaty with its leaders, rather than to send an expedition to try to subdue them. In 1599 three *caciques* came to Quito. They agreed to swear allegiance to the Spanish King as long as the Spanish made no attempt to enforce their overlordship, to collect tribute, or to demand labor. The *caciques* did permit Catholic missionaries to enter their region, but the Dominicans never arrived in sufficient numbers to carry out intensive indoctrination. Taking pains not to antagonize the Spaniards, the *palenque* at Esmeraldas preserved its independence into the nineteenth century. Even today the region remains one in which African influence predominates.[8]

---

[7]Frederick P. Bowser, "Africans in Spanish American Colonial Society," *Cambridge History of Latin America,* ed. by Leslie Bethell (7 vols., Cambridge: Cambridge University Press, 1984–91), 2: p. 374.

[8]John L. Phelan, *The Kingdom of Quito* (Madison: University of Wisconsin Press, 1967), pp. 8–10.

THE ATLANTIC SLAVE TRADE

1. "The Greatest Involuntary Migration in Western History"

ANN M. PESCATELLO

Ann M. Pescatello received her Ph.D. from the University of California, Los Angeles, specializing in social history. As a professor at Florida International University, she was one of the first scholars to publish anthologies on women and blacks in Latin American history. Her book *Female and Male in Latin America* (Pittsburgh: University of Pittsburgh Press, 1973) is still an important source of information, as is *The African in Latin America* (New York: Knopf, 1975), from which the following selections discussing aspects of the Atlantic slave trade have been taken.

AN AFRICAN HERITAGE

Early African history is the record of small groups of state-forming conquerors merging with more numerous conquered populations. With the formation of states from the eleventh century on, slavery and slave trading had developed to meet the demands of an expanding foreign trade. A "slave economy" was established by at least the fourteenth century in western and central Sudan, and by the fifteenth century it had spread to the Senegal and Lower Guinea coasts. Once Europeans entered the trading arena, West Africa rulers and merchants "reacted to the demand with economic reasoning and used it to strengthen streams of economic and political development that were already current before the Atlantic slave trade began."

The area from Senegal to Sierra Leone was the dominant slave-exporting region during the fifteenth century. An area of small states, its population was divided into groups with differing degrees of power and wealth, a significant fact in light of increasing warfare there and the consequent despoilation of the masses. In the sixteenth century Europeans acquired labor supplies from the Senegambia-Guinea-Bissau-Sierra Leone areas and from regions south of the mouth of the Congo River. The Wolof Empire, which

From *The African in Latin America*, ed. with intro. by Ann M. Pescatello (New York: Knopf, 1975), pp. 3–10; 49–57, *passim*. Reprinted by permission.

had dominated the region between Senegal and Gambia, eventually disintegrated into several separate kingdoms. This resulted in protracted warfare, which provided an abundance of prisoners of war for sale as slaves.

In the areas around the Congo, African political feuds and penetration by the Portuguese also influenced the course of slavery. Under Portuguese influence São Tomé became the slave entrepôt for the entire Lower Guinea coast and also for the Congo, where struggles between African chiefs for political succession and economic control had provided another supply of prisoners of war. By the last quarter of the sixteenth century, the "kingdom of Kongo" was little more than a giant slave warehouse. Mulatto offspring of Africans and Portuguese served as agents in its slave trade, establishing a pattern that endured until the 1640s. During this period the Portuguese province of Angola also increased in importance as a source of human labor. The first three centuries of Angolan history (ca. 1550–1850) were, in fact, a patchwork of small wars, expeditions, and commerce in human beings.

Coeval with increasing European involvement in African commercial activities were the massive political, technological, and social changes occurring within West Africa, all of which had a profound impact on slavery in America. By the early seventeenth century West Africa was an organization of highly developed states and empires. Professional armies guarded its lucrative trade routes, causing frequent and destructive wars and thus swelling markets with prisoners of war. Troubles with political and commercial alliances along long-distance trade routes and in the western Sudan also affected trade, as did new commercial links forged between West African and European polities. With the arrival of European ships, Africans, particularly along the Guinea coast, could now purchase commodities from traders directly at shore. The source of supply for goods was thereby shifted from North Africa to West Africa, eliminating costly middlemen along the land routes.

This new local economic partnership changed throughout the seventeenth century from one of transactions in raw materials and manufactures to overseas trade in prisoners of war. From the 1450s until the 1650s African slaves either "were persons who had lost their civic rights, in the state that sold them, by sentence of the courts, or they were citizens of another state who had lost their rights through capture in war," a situation similar to that of medieval Europe. The shift to reliance on slaves as the chief commodity for trade occurred partly because of the disintegration of old empires in Africa and partly because European-African commercial opportunities increased with the extension southward to the coast of old trade routes.

THE SOUTH ATLANTIC SYSTEM

The Atlantic slave trade, already underway, changed and acquired momentum during the second quarter of the seventeenth century. Old patterns of servitude and traditional sources of supply persisted in Africa, on the one hand because of the changes that had occurred in Afro-European relations, on the other because plantation systems had already taken root in America. European colonists succeeded in obtaining millions of African workers because "in the master-servant organization which operated in many states and societies . . . Western African chiefs and kings regularly turned war captives and certain classes of law breakers into slaves." This servitude is best characterized as one in which certain peoples had fewer rights and more obligations relative to the general populace.

By the late seventeenth century expanding trade had engendered new coastal markets and power centers, controlled by Africans acting as middlemen between European sea merchants and African inland merchants. Prosperous city-states developed in the Niger Delta and along the Dahomey coast, while in the Guinea-Gold Coast-Senegal-Gambia area commerce underwent tremendous expansion. The eighteenth century also witnessed the proliferation of slaving along the western coast of Senegambia to Angola, and from central Africa around the Cape of Good Hope to Mozambique. The acquisition of firearms, the reinforcement of slavery as an institution in Africa itself, European encouragement of hostilities between African peoples, and the development of slave-trading organizations among Africans and Europeans, all assured the continued growth of slavery. Some states, such as Ashanti and Dahomey, emerged solely in response to demand for slaves. These states depended on European guns to maintain armies for continuous warfare and slave raiding. This important chapter in African history is one of almost continuous warfare, of the growth of complex states that depended on war and indigenous socioreligious institutions (such as the Ibo oracle) to support their slave-based economy.

The South Atlantic system, established by the beginning of the seventeenth century, was based on a plantation system of export agriculture. Its primary commercial crop was sugar. This required massive supplies of labor that the Africans were called upon to provide. Slave-trading operations had three phases: the slave was captured in Africa, he or she was transported to an African coastal trading point and attractively displayed to European buyers, and then he or she was shipped to America. The growth of plantation slavery in the Americas had coincided with a revolution in European maritime technology, which gave Europe a naval hegemony almost everywhere in the world. With this also came a sharp change in transport costs: ships could carry more cargo, more swiftly and over longer distances, for less money.

American planters generally preferred male workers to female; the feeling was that the economic value of women slaves was greatly reduced by the eventuality of motherhood. Curtin states that slavers normally imported two men for each woman. Since birth rates depend directly on the number of women of child-bearing age in a population, this meant an automatic reduction of 30 percent in potential birth rate among slaves. Also, since planters regarded female slaves essentially as labor units, they did not encourage their female slaves to bear children, and the women themselves used abortive and contraceptive techniques. The key, then, to the continuation of the Atlantic slave trade was the failure on the part of American slave owners to foster a self-sustaining slave population.

The Atlantic slave trade represented the greatest involuntary migration in Western history. Not only was it of demographic importance to Africa and the Americas, but it also was at the core of an economic system in which Africa supplied the labor, Europe the entrepreneurial expertise, North America the food and transport, and South America the precious metals and other raw materials. . . .

THE MIDDLE PASSAGE

The "middle passage" was a euphemism for the horrors endured by the captured African before he ever set a chained foot on American soil. To transport slaves, small ships of 40 to 400 tons were often used. During the eighteenth century the most common slave ship in use was a square-sterned 140 tonner, 57 feet long, with 9-foot holds and only 5 feet of space between decks. The larger frigates (200 to 400 tons) were 77 feet long and 10 feet wide, with separate quarters for men, women, and children. The hands and feet of male slaves were usually shackled during their voyage. There was little fresh air in the holds, which were often intolerably hot. Sanitary conditions were primitive, water was a scarce commodity, and the food was barely edible. The passage from West Africa to America lasted from six to ten weeks, while that from East Africa often took up to four months. Under such conditions disease was rampant and mortality rates were high, even among the ships' crews. Ships' doctors on these voyages often reported finding dead cargo chained to the living!

Without qualifying the misery of the slaves in transit, it should be noted that extreme hardships were borne by almost all workers, slave or free, in this capitalistic and exploitative enterprise. Such miserable conditions could be expected to exist given European attitudes, class relationships, and travel facilities at the time. Philip Curtin demonstrates that the death rate per voyage among ships' crews was even higher than that among slaves. The reading of novels, memoirs, and other accounts of sixteenth- to nineteenth-century naval life and ship travel—for example, Mutiny on the Bounty, Two Years Before the Mast, and Damn the Defiant—will put the horrors of a transoceanic crossing into better perspective.

The main narrative that follows is by an Ibo, Olaudah Equiano, who was kidnapped as a boy from his home in Benin, Nigeria. Olaudah worked first *as a slave for other Africans; eventually, he was taken to America, where he was sold as a slave in the United States and then in the West Indies. He later served with Quakers, earned his freedom, and became involved in the antislavery movement. His memoirs, published in 1789, represent a unique account by an African of the process into and out of enslavement.*

EQUIANO: A SLAVE NARRATIVE

. . . When I was carried on board I was immediately handled, and tossed up, to see if I were sound, by some of the crew; and I was now persuaded that I had got into a world of bad spirits, and that they were going to kill me. . . . When I looked round the ship too, and saw a large furnace or copper boiling, and a multitude of black people of every description chained together, every one of their countenances expressing dejection and sorrow, I no longer doubted of my fate; and, quite overpowered with horror and anguish, I fell motionless on the deck and fainted. When I recovered a little, I found some black people about me, who I believed were some of those who brought me on board and had been receiving their pay; they talked to me in order to cheer me, but all in vain. I asked them if we were not to be eaten by those white men with horrible looks, red faces, and long hair. They told me I was not; and one of the crew brought me a small portion of spirituous liquor in a wine-glass; but, being afraid of him, I would not take it out of his hand. One of the blacks therefore took it from him, and gave it to me, and I took a little down my palate, which, instead of reviving me, as they thought it would, threw me into the greatest consternation at the strange feeling it produced having never tasted any such liquor before. Soon after this, the blacks who brought me on board went off, and left me abandoned to despair. I now saw myself deprived of all chance of returning to my native country, or even the least glimpse of hope of gaining the shore, which I now considered as friendly; and I even wished for my former slavery, in preference to my present situation, was filled with horrors of every kind, still heightened by my ignorance of what I was to undergo. I was not long suffered to indulge my grief; I was soon put down under the decks, and there I received such a salutation in my nostrils as I had never experienced in my life; so that, with the loathsomeness of the stench, and crying together, I became so sick and low that I was not able to eat, nor had I the least desire to taste any thing. I now wished for the last friend, death, to relieve me; but soon, to my grief, two of the white men offered me eatables; and, on my refusing to eat, one of them held me fast by the hands, and laid me across,

The narrative sequence "Equiano" is from Robert I. Rotberg, *A Political History of Tropical Africa* (New York: Harcourt, Brace & World, 1965), pp. 143–153, *passim.* Reprinted by permission.

I think, the windlass, and tied my feet while the other flogged me severely. I had never experienced any thing of this kind before; and, although not being used to the water, I naturally feared that element the first time I saw it; yet, nevertheless, could I have got over the nettings, I would have jumped over the side; but I could not; and, besides, the crew used to watch us very closely who were not chained down to the decks, lest we should leap into the water: and I have seen some of these poor African prisoners most severely cut for attempting to do so, and hourly whipped for not eating. This indeed was often the case with myself. In a little time after, amongst the poor chained men, I found some of my own nation, which in a small degree gave ease to my mind. I inquired of them what was to be done with us? They gave me to understand we were to be carried to these white people's country to work for them. I then was a little revived, and thought, if it were no worse than working, my situation was not so desperate: but still I feared I should be put to death, the white people looked and acted, as I thought, in so savage a manner; for I had never seen among any people such instances of brutal cruelty; and this was not only shown towards us blacks, but also to some of the whites themselves. One white man in particular I saw, when we were permitted to be on deck, flogged so unmercifully with a large rope near the foremast, that he died in consequence of it; and they tossed him over the side as they would have done a brute. This made me fear these people the more. . . .

. . . The stench of the hold while we were on the coast was so intolerably loathsome, that it was dangerous to remain there for any time, and some of us had been permitted to stay on the deck for the fresh air; but now that the whole ship's cargo were confined together, it became absolutely pestilential. The closeness of the place, and the heat of the climate, added to the number in the ship, which was so crowded that each had scarcely room to turn himself, almost suffocated us. This produced copious perspirations, so that the air soon became unfit for respiration, from a variety of loathsome smells, and brought on a sickness amongst the slaves, of which many died, thus falling victims to the improvident avarice, as I may call it, of their purchasers. This wretched situation was again aggravated by the galling of the chains, now become insupportable; and the filth of the necessary tubs, into which the children often fell, and were almost suffocated. The shrieks of the women, and the groans of the dying, rendered the whole a scene of horror almost inconceivable. Happily perhaps for myself I was soon reduced so low here that it was thought necessary to keep me almost always on deck; and from my extreme youth I was not put in fetters. In this situation I expected every hour to share the fate of my companions, some of whom were almost daily brought upon deck at the point of death, which I began to hope would soon put an end to my miseries. Often did I think many of the inhabitants of the deep much more happy than myself; I envied them the freedom they enjoyed, and as often wished I could change my condition for theirs. Every circumstance I met with served only to render my state more painful, and heighten my apprehensions and my opinion of the cruelty of the whites. One day they had taken a number of fishes; and when they had killed and satisfied themselves with as many as they thought fit, to our astonishment who were on the deck, rather than give any of them to us to eat, as we expected, they tossed the remaining fish into the sea again, although we begged and prayed for some as well as we could, but in vain; and some of my countrymen, being pressed by hunger, took an opportunity, when they thought no one saw them, of trying to get a little privately; but they were discovered, and the attempt procured them some very severe floggings.

One day, when we had a smooth sea, and moderate wind, two of my wearied countrymen, who were chained together (I was near them at the time), preferring death to such a life of misery, somehow made through the nettings, and jumped into the sea; immediately another quite dejected fellow, who, on account of his illness, was suffered to be out of irons, also followed their example; and I believe many more would very soon have done the same, if they had not been prevented by the ship's crew, who were instantly alarmed. Those of us that were the most active were in a moment put down under the deck; and there was such a noise and confusion amongst the people of the ship as I never heard before, to stop her, and get the boat out to go after the slaves. However, two of the wretches were drowned, but they got the other, and afterwards flogged him unmercifully, for this attempting to prefer death to slavery. In this manner we continued to undergo more hardships than I can now relate; hardships which are inseparable from this accursed trade. Many a time we were near suffocation, from the want of fresh air, which we were often without for whole days together. This, and the stench of the necessary tubs, carried off many. . . .

[Once in the Americas they were again oiled and shaved and displayed for sale.]

It was the practice . . . to open the sale on shipboard, the males being arranged in one part of the ship, and the females in another. . . . [C]rowds of people went on board, and began so disgraceful a scramble . . .

[In other parts of the New World slaves were sold on shore.]

. . . [O]n a given signal . . . the buyers rush at once into the yard where the slaves are confined, and make choice of that parcel they like best. . . . In this manner, without scruple, are relations and friends separated, most of them never to see each other again. . . . O, ye nominal Christians! Might not an African ask you, learned you this from your God? . . . Surely this is a new refinement in cruelty, which, . . . adds fresh horrors to the wretchedness of slavery.

2. Alonso de Sandoval, the First Advocate of Black Studies in America

NORMAN MEIKLEJOHN

Reverend Norman Meiklejohn, A.A., of Assumption College in Worcester, Massachusetts, prepared his doctoral dissertation at Columbia University on Negro slavery in Nueva Granada. The following selection comes from this dissertation. Some day we should have an English translation of Sandoval's notable treatise. It is full of unusual detail; Professor Boxer states: "Sandoval gives a very interesting description of the tribal markings of the Guinea and Angola slaves, so that the tribes and districts from which they came could be better identified. I believe this to be the first time that such a classification was attempted, or at any rate printed."* But enough is known now to salute Sandoval for his recognition of the cultural diversity of the Negroes and the need to study their languages and customs so as better to evangelize them.

Later on, another Spanish Jesuit in Peru, Diego de Avendaño, became convinced that Negro slavery was just as wrong as Indian slavery and in his two-volume *Thesaurus Indicus* (Amberes, 1668) called for another royal investigation similar to that which provoked the disputation in 1550 between Sepúlveda and Las Casas, whose doctrine Avendaño largely was following. Nothing happened. The Spanish crown did establish in Spain in 1683 a royal commission to examine the legitimacy of African Negro enslavements and of the slave trade. The commission, on the basis of age-old custom, the toleration of these practices by the papacy and the clergy, and the economic advantage to the crown from Negro slavery, concluded that the king should entertain no scruples concerning legitimacy.

Alonso de Sandoval, the remarkable apostle to the Negroes, was born in 1576 in Seville, while his parents were en route to the Indies. Educated by the Jesuits in Lima, Peru, he entered the Jesuit Order in 1593 and was ordained a priest circa 1600. In 1604, he volunteered for service in the newly established Jesuit vice-province of Nueva Granada, and in 1605 he began to work in the Jesuit college in Cartagena. His duties there, like those of the other members of the college community, were wide-ranging. They included teaching, ministering to the spiritual needs of the white, Negro, and Indian populations, and making missionary field trips to outlying settlements along the Caribbean coast and inland. For a number of years, Sandoval served as procurator of the Cartagena community, and from 1624 to 1627 he held the

*Charles R. Boxer, *Salvador de Sá and the Struggle for Brazil and Angola, 1602–1686* (London: The Athlone Press, University of London, 1952) p. 238, note 35.
From "The Observance of Negro Slave Legislation in Colonial Nueva Granada," by Norman Meiklejohn (Ph.D. dissertation, Columbia University, 1968), pp. 264–284, *passim*. Printed by permission of the author.

post of rector of the college. Dynamic, energetic, and aggressive, Sandoval could be sharp in tongue and harsh in manner. As an administrator, his unorthodox methods earned him a rebuke from his Superior General and made him ineligible to receive the highest honors which the Order bestowed upon its most outstanding members.

Like his fellow Jesuits on the staff of the college, Sandoval ministered to the Negro slaves. But unlike them, he experienced a strong sense of mission to Christianize them. A possible explanation for this sense of mission to the Negro may be Sandoval's background in Lima.

In 1607, Martín de Funes, Procurator of the Jesuits in Nueva Granada, presented a report on the Negro slaves to the Superior General, Father Aquaviva. In this report, the physical and spiritual situation of the Negro slaves in Nueva Granada was described as utterly miserable, and the Jesuits there requested permission to assume the responsibility of serving as their *doctrineros*. Shortly afterward, the General entrusted the major responsibility for the Negro ministry of Cartagena to Sandoval. On the strength of this assignment, Sandoval later took pride in calling himself the Father of the Slaves.

Already, in 1610, the Negro slave population of Cartagena numbered in the thousands. There were more than 5,000 residing on the surrounding estancias alone. To these numbers must be added the yearly transient population of 2,000 to 4,000 slaves who arrived fresh from Africa and who remained in Cartagena while waiting to be sold locally or to be shipped to other ports. If the spiritual destitution of the Negro slaves of Cartagena had sparked the zeal of Sandoval, the utter misery of the Negro slave cargoes set him ablaze. Many were ill with contagious diseases; some were on the point of death. All were hungry, thirsty, exhausted, and practically naked. Many entertained fantastic fears as to the dire fate which awaited them.

Sandoval made it a practice, on receiving news of the arrival of a slave ship, to hasten to the port and board the ship. There he proffered drinking water (especially to the infants), and then sought out the dying to prepare them for their final journey. Once the slave cargo had been unloaded and deposited in warehouses, Sandoval went among the slaves offering them a measure of relief and consolation, and trying to identify them as to language and tribe. Then, having called those of his Cartagena slave acquaintances who had knowledge of the languages of the newly arrived slaves to serve as interpreters, he set about examining the new arrivals in order to verify their baptism. Those who had been baptized he helped to prepare to receive the sacraments. Those who had not been baptized, or whose baptism seemed doubtfully valid, he catechized and then baptized. To all he gave words of encouragement regarding their future as slaves.

The preoccupation of Sandoval with the baptism of slaves was not merely juridicial; i.e., seeing to it that all African immigrants had been baptized in accordance with the law. Rather it was apostolic. As a minister of the gospel, he considered baptism a matter of paramount importance. On their baptism depended the slaves' eternal salvation or their eternal perdition. Until Sandoval began to look into the matter of slave baptisms, the presumption had been that all Negro slaves arriving in Cartagena had been baptized in Africa. No one in Cartagena had checked into the matter, any more than had any of the priests and masters in various parts of Spanish America among whom the slaves spent the remainder of their days.

What was Sandoval's dismay when his inquiries began to reveal that many of the slaves had never been baptized, and that the baptism of an even greater number had been invalidly performed? This meant that many slaves were going through life being treated as Catholics and receiving the sacraments when in reality they were pagan. Those slaves who had to continue their voyage by land or sea were in danger of loss of life. If by chance they had not been baptized, or their baptism was invalid, those who died were, in the mind of the sixteenth-century Catholic, doomed to hell fire.

Proceeding cautiously and methodically, Sandoval looked more closely into the matter. He continued to question arriving slaves concerning the details of their baptism. He questioned the masters of slave ships, asking them what they knew of baptismal procedures at the African ports; he also wrote to priests stationed in African slave ports. His most pessimistic suspicions were verified. He found that, although some efforts had been made to correct abuses in Luanda, many baptisms were invalidly performed there, and even more so at Cabo Verde and the river ports in Guinea. The sacrament was being given mechanically and without concern for those circumstances necessary for an adult baptism to be valid. That is, the receiver of the sacrament had to know what the sacrament meant. He had to want to receive it. And the water had to touch his scalp. Sandoval learned that before sailing to America the slaves were assembled on the docks to hear a priest give a short harangue in Portuguese. Then, without making any further attempt to explain to the slaves the significance of what he was about to do, or to ask them if they wished to receive baptism, the priest sprinkled them with water and pronounced the words of baptism. . . .

Deeply concerned over this neglect in such an important matter as baptism, Sandoval submitted his findings to the Archbishop of Seville. Seville was the only Spanish port trading with both Africa and America, and many slave traders and investors resided there. It was also the port of entry for African slaves into Spain and contained a large Negro population. The prelate had his Negro faithful examined by a committee of theologians. Their conclusions agreed with those of Sandoval. Thereupon, besides sending a report to the Holy See, which apparently took no action, the Archbishop decreed that in his diocese the entire Negro population of 30,000 should be assiduously examined with regard to the validity of their baptism. The procedure which he ordered for this examination was the one proposed by Sandoval.

The work undertaken by Sandoval to examine the baptismal credentials of every slave who arrived in Cartagena was monumental. It meant that Sandoval and his assistants would have to examine the entire slave and free Negro population of Cartagena and its surroundings, as well as the many Indians whose baptism had been equally invalid because of lack of understanding and consent on their part. It meant that they would have to examine individually the thousands of Negro slaves arriving in Cartagena annually. Since, in Sandoval's estimation, any one of seventy different languages and dialects were apt to be spoken by the incoming slaves, he had to secure interpreters for all those languages. This entailed first of all identifying the slave's tribe according to his physical appearance, traits, scarifications. Then he had to identify a slave's language. After this had been done, he had to check his list of interpreters, find the proper ones, and obtain the loan of their services from their masters. It also meant working for hours on end through interpreters who were often tired, and who found the work distasteful because many of the slaves were diseased. Some time after the publication of his treatise, Sandoval's superiors were persuaded to buy seven slaves whose principal role was to serve as interpreters for Father Sandoval and his principal assistant, Father Peter Claver.

Once the interpreter was on hand, Sandoval proceeded to pose all sorts of technical questions regarding their baptism to men and women who were of an entirely different culture and at a very different level of sophistication. All this was done in the tropical heat of Cartagena, amid the human stench of the slave ships or slave depots. Once the unbaptized, the doubtfully baptized, and the invalidly baptized had been identified and set apart, there followed a lengthy instruction on the basic teachings of the Church and on the meaning of baptism. . . .

In spite of his noble intentions, and the correctness of his methods, Sandoval met with criticism and resistance. Some clerics resented the intervention of a friar into what they considered their exclusive preserve. This of course was only one of many instances of clashes in the colonies between order priests and the diocesan clergy. The latter had official jurisdiction over the faithful, whereas order priests could minister to them only as a result of privileges extended to them by the Holy See and approved by the Crown. The diocesan clergy were scandalized that Sandoval should baptize slaves in a warehouse; they insisted that, according to regulations, the ceremony should be performed in church with all the customary solemnity. To this objection, Sandoval responded that there was no way of knowing who among the slaves would stay long enough in Cartagena to be able to receive baptism in the church. Rather than risk the possibility of their departure before being baptized, it was safer to perform the rite as quickly as possible. Besides, he added, clergymen did not permit the invasion of their churches by filthy naked slaves. On the contrary, they considered it an affront to the house of God and to the dignity of the sacrament being administered. The objection regarding jurisdiction was more serious since it was made by the Bishop's Council and added the further charge that the Jesuits were deriving financial profit from their endeavor. The matter was taken to court and a legal suit followed between the Jesuits on the one hand and the Archbishop of Cartagena and his Council on the other. The Jesuits not only won their case in court; they also won the administration of the plaintiffs as well. They did this by having the clerics accompany them for a routine day of work among the shipboard and warehouse slaves.

A further source of resistance was the slaves themselves. Many had been living as Catholics; to admit that they might have been pagans all along was a humiliation they could not bear. Thus, some of them did not cooperate with the examining priests who sought to ascertain if their baptism had been valid or not. Others suspected that their baptism had not been valid, but postponed admitting it to the priests out of shame. Another difficulty arose when the slaves who had been baptized on the ships and in the warehouses discovered that there was a more solemn form of baptism. Envious of those slaves who had been solemnly baptized in the church, they tended to conclude that their original baptism had not been valid and they sought to be baptized anew in a church ceremony.

For Sandoval it was not enough that the Negro slaves were baptized. He also wanted them to share fully with their masters the privileges of the Christian life. To this end he strove to persuade them to confess their sins and receive Holy Communion a few times a year. . . .

Success in his undertaking to have slaves share in the fullness of the Church's sacramental life depended to a great extent on the master's cooperation in facilitating the slave's recourse to the confessional and to Communion. While admitting that some masters cooperated in this, Sandoval complained gloomily that others took all sorts of devious means to impede the further catechesis of their slaves and especially their reception of the sacraments other than baptism.

Some motives for this reticence were mentioned at the beginning of this chapter. An additional motive, which might have been a pretext on the part of some, was the contention that Negroes, like Indians, were incapable of comprehending the Christian religion. As we have seen, many priests completely neglected their spiritual ministry to the Negroes, allegedly for that reason. No arguments, nor papal bulls could eradicate their prejudices. The priests, even the missionaries, tended to attribute to the stupidity of the Negroes what was really poor pedagogy on their part. Besides entertaining the notion that they could evangelize Indians or Negroes in a language that these latter could barely understand, if at all, they explained Christian doctrine in scholastic terms. They made little or no effort to adapt their teaching to the native capacity, the culture, and the language patterns of the Negroes. Furthermore, the priests were more comfortable with their prejudices, for the serious and thorough Christianization of the slaves would have required considerable work. The conviction that the Negroes were incapable of anything beyond baptism freed them from any obligation to further ministry.

If this reluctance was true of confessions and Communion, it was even more true of the sacrament of Extreme Unction, the ministering of which would often have entailed going about at night, bringing the viaticum and the holy oils to dying slaves in squalid and repugnant surroundings. In the same spirit, masters who were convinced of their slaves' limited capacity for Christian living did not bother to call the priest when their slaves were dying. Even if the priest came, Sandoval tells us, some masters pretended that none of their slaves was ill. Sandoval was forced to rely on doctors to inform him when slaves were in serious danger of death.

It is no wonder that, faced with the monumental task we have just described, Sandoval required assistance. Apparently he was never given more than one assistant at a time; the one who assisted him longest was Peter Claver. Less dynamic than Sandoval, Peter Claver was a humble lover and servant of the poor. Sandoval exhausted himself for the spiritual profit of the slaves. Yet he was never able to forget the slaves' crudeness, their ignorance, their dirtiness, and their smell. Throughout his treatise his disdain for the Negro slaves shows through. In his later years he even admitted to Claver that news of an arriving slave ship made him break into a cold sweat, so revolting to his nature were the conditions under which he would once against exercise his apostolic ministry. At opposite poles was Claver, who had the advantage of a mild temperament, a profound humility, an authentic affection and love for the poor, and an acquired indifference to filth and stench and festering sores. Different as they were, these two Jesuits, in a period of fifty years, affected the lives of 300,000 Negro slaves who either passed through the port of Cartagena or lived in that city, its surroundings, and in settlements along the coast and inland. There is no calculating the untold thousands of Negro slaves who received better treatment as a result of the heroic example of Sandoval and Claver.

But Sandoval was not content with the work he was doing directly with the bozales in the Port of Cartagena. He dreamed of making authentic Christians of all the Negro slaves in the Spanish empire. This he would do by writing a treatise on the subject and addressing it to the members of the Company of Ignatius Loyola. His treatise would be both a clarion call to all Jesuits to bring Christ to the most abandoned of God's children, the Negro slaves, and a handbook on methods appropriate to that end. The treatise, which was finished by 1620, represented the fruit of fifteen years of experience as well as of extensive research. Though Sandoval was successful in having it published in 1627, he continued to improve it and the first volume of an expanded second edition was published in 1647. The second volume of the expanded edition never appeared.

One finds in Sandoval's treatise much material of considerable interest, not only on the subject of Negro slaves and the Church, but on the seventeenth-century mind and on the state of knowledge of geography, anthropology, and natural science in that century. Sandoval's geography is imperfect; his anthropology is a compendium of information on Africans and Asians that could be found in contemporary sources, enriched by first-hand observation of Negroes in Cartagena. The treatise also speculates on the causes of monsters, of Negroid characteristics, and of the incidence of albinos.

In Part One of his treatise Sandoval examined Negro peoples and their customs, and various aspects of the slave trade. He considered the various groups of Negroid peoples and described their location, social organization, religion, customs, and practices. Because the Negroes living in the area between Cabo Verde and Angola constituted the bulk of the Negro population brought to Nueva Granada, Sandoval described their coloring, physical characteristics, tatoos and scarifications, natural disposition, and religious attitudes.

On the basis of a study of contemporary theologians and his own investigations, Sandoval was convinced that much of the slave trade was immoral, but he accepted the opinion of the Jesuit school that purchasers in America could buy slaves in perfect good faith. The important thing for Sandoval, however, was not to complain of slavery but rather to labor to improve the lot of the slaves. He described the slaves' departure from Africa, the "middle passage," their condition as they arrived in Cartagena, and the treatment they received in the depots and slave market.

Part Two of the treatise contains descriptions of the life of slaves in Nueva Granada and of the ministry to Negro slaves. The Negro slaves suffered greatly at the hands of their masters. Indeed, some masters treated their animals better than they treated their slaves. Nevertheless, Sandoval conceded, some masters did treat their slaves well. Slaves were also made to suffer spiritually as their masters neglected their spiritual needs and opposed their full participation in church life. As a result, Sandoval claimed, slaves lived like brutes and appeared incapable of living like civilized Christians, Sandoval further accused masters of favoring concubinage and prostitution, and of seeking to prevent marriages, of making the conjugal state undesirable by restricting a married slave's movements and by separating children from their parents. Nonetheless, Sandoval encouraged the slaves to obey their masters in the spirit of the gospels. He also encouraged masters to treat their slaves with paternal care, giving them what they needed, correcting them with charity, and bearing with them patiently.

In concluding Part Two Sandoval told his Jesuit readers that the Negro ministry was an excellent school for the acquisition of holiness through the practice of all the virtues. It offered numberless occasions for exercising the corporal and spiritual works of mercy.

In the third part of his treatise, Sandoval presented his method for evangelizing the Negro slaves. This method, which we considered earlier, can be summarized in a few phrases. The missioner should always take the initiative in seeking out slaves. He should prepare and use wisely his own corps of interpreters, and use simple language in teaching Christian doctrine. He should always check the validity of the baptism of the slaves he attends, foster frequent reception of sacraments, and the observance of the Church's precepts. . . .

SLAVERY IN SPANISH AMERICA

3. A Black Conquistador in Mexico

PETER GERHARD

Even in the early years of the conquest not all blacks were slaves as Peter Gerhard shows in this intriguing biographical sketch of Juan Garrido, a free black who took part in the defeat of Technochtitlán and became "the first wheat farmer on the American continent." Mr. Gerhard abandoned a career as an accountant with an American oil firm to become a specialist in the historical geography of colonial Mexico.

While the role played by the people of equatorial Africa in the colonization of Latin America is relatively well-known, it is for the most part an impersonal history that emerges from the contemporary documents: the establishment of a Negro slave trade as a result of the demand for labor to replace a devastated native population; the employment of these black slaves in the more arduous tasks throughout the colonies; and, in most areas, their gradual assimilation through miscegenation with natives (and to a far lesser extent with Europeans). Information about individual blacks is usually confined to a brief statement of age, physical characteristics, and degree of acculturation at the moment of sale or the taking of estate inventories; less frequently, the place of origin of a slave is indicated. Only rarely do we hear about a Negro slave who achieved distinction in some way. Two examples that come to mind are Juan Valiente, the conquistador of Chile, and Yanga, the famed maroon leader in Veracruz.

Although most blacks who came to America in [the] early years were slaves, records of the Casa de Contratación show that a good many black freedmen from Seville and elsewhere found passage on westward-bound ships. Some of them settled in the Caribbean region, and others followed the tide of conquest to Mexico and Peru, identifying themselves no doubt as Catholc subjects of a Spanish king, with much the same privileges and ambitions as white Spaniards. "Benito el Negro" and "Juan el Negro" (the latter's real name seems to have been Juan de Villanueva) were encomenderos in the province of Pánuco and thus they should not have been slaves, but we cannot be sure of their origin. Spaniards might call anyone with a very dark skin "negro," and indeed the fact that Villanueva was from Granada makes it seem likely that he was a morisco. On the other hand there is record of an African who apparently crossed the Atlantic as a freeman, participated in the siege of Tenochtitlán and, in subsequent conquests and explorations, tried his hand as an entrepreneur (with both Negro and Indian slaves of his own) in the early search for gold, and took his place as a citizen in the Spanish quarter of Mexico City. His name was Juan Garrido, and he was still alive in the late 1540s when he wrote or dictated a short resume of his services to the crown:

> Juan Garrido, black in color . . . says that he, of his own free will, became a Christian in Lisbon, [then] was in Castile for seven years, and crossed to Santo Domingo where he remained an equal length of time. From there he visited other islands, and then went to San Juan de Puerto Rico, where he spent much time, after which he came to New Spain. He was present at the taking of this city of Mexico and in other conquests, and later [went] to the island with the marquis. He was the first to plant and harvest wheat in this land, the source of all that there now is, and he brought many vegetable seeds to New Spain. He is married and has three children, and is very poor with nothing to maintain himself. . . .

The early chronology of this statement is vague, but working backwards from the fall of Tenochtitlán (1521), one can assume that Garrido arrived in America about 1510. It is perhaps more than a coincidence that a Spaniard called Pedro Garrido landed in Santo Domingo with his family and entourage in 1510, and later accompanied Cortés to Mexico. Slaves were often given

From "A Black Conquistador in Mexico," by Peter Gerhard, *Hispanic American Historical Review,* 58 (1978), pp. 451–459, *passim.* Reprinted by permission of Duke University Press.

the surnames of their masters, and while we do not know whether Juan Garrido was ever a slave it seems most probable that he was at least a protégé of a Spaniard at one time. However, this is pure conjecture, and we might also consider the possibility that the subject of this essay was named for his physical appearance (Juan Garrido can be roughly translated as "Handsome John"). In fact, the matter of how and when Garrido got to Mexico, and what part he played in the conquest, are something of a mystery. The *Diccionario Porrúa,* perhaps relying on an inconclusive passage in Bernal Díaz, says that he arrived with Juan Núñez Sedeño, who accompanied Cortés' 1519 expedition in his own ship with a large retinue that included "un negro"; Manuel Orozco y Berra has him crossing a year later with the army of Pánfilo de Narváez. Magnus Mörner, after claiming that "many" hispanicized and Spanish-speaking blacks took part in the conquest, leaves us without any details, nor does one find any mention of Garrido by name in the various contemporary accounts of the siege and surrender of Tenochtitlán (indeed the same might be said of many Spaniards who were there). His name appears for the first time in the proceedings of Mexico City's cabildo on March 8, 1524, when that body granted a piece of land for the establishment of a smithy on the Tacuba causeway "going out of this city, just past the chapel [hermita] of Juan Garrido." Lucas Alamán identifies this as the church subsequently rebuilt and dedicated to San Hipólito de los Mártires, occupying the site where so many of Cortés' men died as they fled from Tenochtitlán on the Noche Triste. It may have been the brief statement in Alamán that gave rise to a somewhat embellished and much repeated version of which the following is an example:

> *San Hipólito . . .* Historically and sentimentally this is one of the most interesting churches in the city. In front of the spot where it now stands there existed in the year 1520 the second line of defenses on the causeway (now the street occupied by the horse railway to Tacuba) that connected the Aztec city with the main-land westward. At this point was the greatest slaughter of the Spaniards during the retreat of the memorable Noche Triste (July 1, 1520). After the final conquest of the city, one of the survivors of that dismal night, Juan Garrido, having freshly in mind its bloody horrors, built of adobe at this place a little commemorative chapel.

Terry's guide, drawing on the story as told by Orozco y Berra, identifies Garrido as "one of the Conquistadores [who] undertook to recover the bodies of his slaughtered countrymen and to erect a chapel wherein they could be buried with religious rites."

While his role in the Tenochtitlán episode remains obscure, Garrido took part in at least one of the expeditions sent out by Cortés after the conquest of the Triple Alliance to secure control and investigate the economic potential of outlying areas. According to a *relación geográfica* of 1580, "A Negro ... who called himself Juan Garrido" accompanied Antonio de Caravajal and three other Spaniards to the hot country of Michoacán and the coast of Zacatula, most likely in 1523–1524. This little group was received hospitably by the Tarascans of Zirándaro, after which it proceeded across the Sierra Madre del Sur "on a deserted trail through a cold rugged area with lions and tigers and snakes and other animals." Zirándaro belonged to the Tarascan empire which in 1522 had accepted Spanish rule practically without resistance, while the more truculent Indians of the coast had recently surrendered to the army of Gonzalo de Sandoval, which may explain how a small force could emerge unscathed from such an expedition. In fact, Caravajal's mission was to introduce Christianity to the natives (although there was no priest in his party) and to make a careful census of the communities visited, noting the mineral wealth and the tribute-paying capacity of each, for the guidance of Cortés in the first distribution of encomiendas. We do not know whether Garrido stayed with Caravajal throughout the visitation of Michoacán, which lasted about a year; in any event, we find him once again in Mexico City early in August 1524.

It must have been before he went off with the Caravajal party that Garrido became the first wheat farmer on the American continent. The importance to the expatriate Spaniards, both as a matter of taste and as a measure of social status, of having wheat bread rather than cassava or maize tortillas, can hardly be overstressed. According to the conquistador Andrés de Tapia, "after Mexico was taken, and while [Cortés] was in Coyoacán, they brought him a small amount of rice, and in it were three grains of wheat; he ordered a free Negro [*un negro horro*] to plant them." The Negro referred to by Tapia is identified in a parallel account by the seventeenth-century chronicle Gil González Dávila as "Juan Garrido, a servant [*criado*] of Hernando Cortés." Both sources agree that the tiny crop harvested by Garrido at this time was the first in New Spain, and that all wheat subsequently grown came from its seed. . . .

4. Africans in Sixteenth-Century Peru

JAMES LOCKHART

Professor James Lockhart of the University of California, Los Angeles, created a social history of early Peru by mining systematically the rich notarial records there. His monograph on *Spanish Peru, 1532–1560* was a pioneering volume that revealed how promptly and how strongly Spaniards developed a stable society in Peru. In the following section he discusses the roles of Africans and Afro-Peruvians in a Spanish colonial society and their influence on Peruvian culture.

Planned or accidental, ethnic diversity was an element of prime importance in determining the Africans' role in Peru. It meant that Africans lived and acted almost entirely within the Spanish context. Most Africans must have had to speak Spanish to each other. Separated from the Indians by race, culture, and mutual hostility, cut off from one another by their diversity, Africans counted in the conquest and occupation of Peru mainly as so many more Spaniards, so many more spreaders of Spanish language and European ways.

The only African traits that could at all assert themselves were the very general patterns that were more universal than language. African-type dancing was one of these, and appeared wherever Africans could congregate. Kingship was another. The few independent communities of renegade Negroes which managed to exist in certain parts of Peru for a few years operated under that African political institution. It would be of great interest to know what language the renegades spoke. Probably it was Spanish. Or possibly these communities enjoyed some degree of success because they had been able to concentrate enough people from one or another of the ethnic groups to form a strong nucleus. In any case, ethnic diversity was one effective deterrent to slave rebellions. . . .

For years the Spanish Negroes were the only significant group of non-African Negroes in Peru. Though much is hidden behind the all-inclusive term "creole," it appears that very few Negroes born in other parts of the Indies ever reached Peru. Only isolated examples occur, mainly from the Isthmus and the Antilles. The first major addition to the Negroes born outside Africa came in the mid-1550's, when a generation of Peruvian-born Negroes reached saleable age, according to the criterion of the time. . . .

"Ladino" and "bozal" were two words that did heavy duty in the description of slaves. Buyers wanted to know two things, whether or not a slave was experienced, used to life outside Africa and among Europeans, and whether or not he spoke Spanish. Two sets of terms were really needed to express all this, but, in the peculiar conditions of slavery in the Indies at the time, experience and Spanish speaking so nearly coincided that one set of terms sufficed. "Bozal" basically meant just an inexperienced new arrival from Africa, and "ladino" merely meant Spanish-speaking, but they were

From *Spanish Peru, 1532–1560*, by James Lockhart (Madison: University of Wisconsin, Press, © 1968 by the Regents of the University of Wisconsin), pp. 174–198, *passim*.

used as opposite poles, "bozal" to mean a new slave who therefore knew no Spanish, and "ladino" to mean a Spanish-speaking slave who was therefore experienced. . . .

To express all kinds and degrees of mixtures of Negroes with other races, only one word, "mulatto," was in common use. Mulattoes were not generally thought of as a group distinct from Negroes; a mulatto was a type of a Negro. . . .

Most Negro slaves went through life with no more than a simple Christian name like Pedro, Antón, or Catalina, often qualified by the word Negro. Generally Negroes assumed surnames only when they were freed, . . .

. . . [I]n the period of 1530–60 Negro slaves did not yet ordinarily arrive in Peru by whole boatloads, as they did in the Caribbean. Negroes got to Peru by miscellaneous and various means, as the Spaniards themselves did. Many Negroes came with their permanent owners, or with Spaniards who, as a sideline, were speculating on the sale of two or three slaves. Small private activity may have accounted for as many Negroes as the more or less official trade carried on by large merchants. . . .

The vast majority of Negro slaves changed hands in small transactions, mostly sales of one slave, less often of two or three. Many of these sales can be called primary; that is, they represented the sale of a newly arrived Negro, by the merchant or speculator who imported him, to the person who was going to own him permanently. But many other transactions were part of a constant, disturbingly prevalent process of resale. Among various reasons for the frequency of resale, the most basic was the peculiarly insistent demand for Negro slaves. In a general market situation where most prices, despite violent short-term fluctuations, were remarkably stable over the years, and prices of livestock and food staples actually fell, the price of Negro slaves rose steadily, giving owners a constant opportunity to make a profit by reselling. It was very common for a slave to have had two or three previous owners at time of sale . . .

. . . When, as often happened, Negro slaves were sold along with the land they cultivated, the livestock they cared for, or the tools they worked with, the slave was an element of continuity while the masters changed. At times this became a conscious process of capital formation. A Spanish artisan could acquire untrained Negroes, equip and train them, and sell them as a highly valuable independent unit. Some of the largest sales recorded were of gradually accumulated, trained teams of Negro slaves sold together with the other assets of the company that owned them. In these cases the lives of the Negroes and the operations of the companies remained largely unaffected by a changeover at the top.

After an initial period of instability, the price of Negro slaves was constantly on the rise during the period from 1530 to 1560. . . .

Negro slave owning was very widespread in Peru; not every Spaniard owned Negro slaves, but it can be said that there was no stratum of Spanish Peruvian society which did not include owners of slaves. A complete list of slave owners would include artisans of many kinds, priests, lawyers, notaries, merchants, sailors, and free Negroes, as well as captains and encomenderos. Negro slaves were never the monopoly of the great captains. . . .

. . . With practically all encomenderos and artisans owning several slaves, and many other Spaniards, from rich to poor, at least owning personal servants, or slaves to care for land and stock, it is apparent that Negroes were present in very substantial numbers. All in all, it seems probable that on the coast at least, there were as many Negroes as Spaniards. In the first coastal censuses, around 1570, Negroes had overtaken Spaniards, and may have already done so by 1560. . . . Negroes were present in the highlands in substantial numbers, but less numerous than on the coast.

While there is no sure way of knowing who owned the most Negroes, something can be said about the type of ownership represented by the two most prominent groups of owners, encomenderos and artisans. The encomenderos were purely consumers. The artisans were partly consumers, and partly trainers of slaves, and therefore speculators and sellers. When, in 1560, officials attempted to fix the prices of Negro slaves, forty residents of Lima protested. Of the forty, twenty-one are identifiable as artisans, while not a single encomendero joined the protest.

Whatever else they may have been, most Negro slaves in Peru were personal servants. Though the proportion of full-time personal servants to agricultural workers and artisan slaves is not known, slaves in the latter two categories also performed as servants, and certainly were thought of as such. Personal service was the role most closely associated with Negroes in the minds of the Spaniards. Only those slaves who spent or lost their lives in the migrant gangs organized for gold mining completely escaped the category, and such slaves do not seem to have been really numerous except during the Carabaya gold rush in the Cuzco area in 1542 and 1543. Large encomenderos might own a whole houseful of Negro servants. A notary, priest, or merchant would often have only one, preferably female, as general housekeeper.

Negro slaves were in great demand as servants for two main reasons. The first had to do with their utter foreignness. [It was felt that] foreign slaves who were isolated from the populace at large . . . cannot melt into it. . . .

The second reason why Negroes were desired as servants was that they were one essential part of the general pattern of Spanish ambitions. No encomendero felt happy until he owned a large house, land, livestock and . . . Negro servants. Most Spaniards could not hope to achieve this goal in its entirety, but they aimed at least for two essentials, a house (which could be rented) and Negroes. One of the most important yardsticks for a Spaniard's contribution to any of the various war efforts was the number of Negro servants he brought to the battle with him. . . .

Negro artisan slaves were at the top of the ladder in the slave world, the most highly skilled and the highest priced, with a certain measure of intrinsic freedom. Doubtless they were less numerous than ordinary personal servants and field workers, but there were enough to form the backbone of the skilled labor force working in the shops of Peruvian Spanish artisans. . . .

The category of artisan slaves merged imperceptibly into the category of slaves with less valuable skills who were employed in large teams or gangs. On the borderline between these two types were the Negro muleteers. Of the three main carriers of goods in the highlands—Indian porters, llamas, and mules—trains of mules were the fastest and most reliable, and the most valuable goods were generally entrusted to them. A pack train consisted of a Spanish muleteer, several mules, and some Negroes who cared for and loaded the mules; Negro slaves had a practical monopoly of the function of accompanying pack trains. Most trains were of moderate size, with ten to twenty mules and, ideally, one Negro for every three mules. The merchants who were the chief owners of pack trains often sold them as a unit, mules, tackle, Negroes, and all.

Certain types of Spanish enterprises employed semiskilled Negroes in relatively large teams of ten to twenty. They were, principally, the carting companies of Lima, the coastal fisheries, and some incipient large cattle owners. The teams were overwhelmingly male, with only one or two Negro women cooks. . . .

Large-scale use of unskilled Negro slaves on plantations was not yet a factor of importance in Peru by 1560. Only one such operation is known to have existed in Nazca, on the southern coast, where a royal official and encomendero ran a sugar plantation and also carried on stock-raising and general agriculture, with the labor of Negro slaves. . . .

The most frequent use of groups of unskilled Negroes was in mining, particularly gold mining. Even this was not of really basic importance; the great silver mines of highland Peru were always worked by Indians, with an exception or two. Gold mining was thought to be appropriate for Negroes because gold mines were mainly in hot, low-lying river areas. Even so, gold mining was far from a Negro monopoly. There were two major gold rushes in Peru within our period, one in Carabaya, a low-altitude area in the jurisdiction of Cuzco, in 1542 and 1543, and the other in the Quito area in 1545 and 1546. . . . In Carabaya, . . . Spaniards brought in numbers of Negro slave gangs. Less intensive gold mining with Negroes took place intermittently in various parts of Peru. . . .

Small-scale agriculture was one of the main areas of endeavor of Negro slaves, comparable in importance to personal service and artisanry. In Lima as in other towns, the surrounding agricultural land was divided out to encomenderos and others, in quite small parcels, at the city's founding, in this case in 1535. By the early 1540's at latest, the environs of Lima had become an impressive garden spot, full of closely spaced small holdings where Spanish agriculture was practiced, with irrigation, to supply Lima's markets. Almost every one of thse holdings, called chácaras or estancias indiscriminately, had one or more Negroes working on it. In Arequipa the situation was much the same, and apparently in Trujillo as well. It is doubtful that nearly as many Negroes did agricultural work in Cuzco and Upper Peru, but the pattern did extend that far, . . .

Outside the immediate environs of the cities, small landholdings devoted mainly to intensive agriculture gave way to larger, more loosely defined properties where stock raising took precedence over agriculture, and, in distant plains, superseded it entirely. . . . Whatever they were called, they had Negro slaves working on them. . . .

As large-scale ranching began to develop in the 1550's, whole teams of Negroes worked at cattle herding. Even in the 1540's, there were some good-sized establishments, like the six Negro slave men and women who cared for a herd of cattle and goats in the Lima area in 1547. But most characteristic were the lone Negroes living deep in the country, far from the Spaniards, in charge of several cows, goats, or pigs. Herdsmen were more closely attached to the stock than to the land; whereas field Negroes were sold along with the land they worked, herdsmen were sold together with the herds. . . .

Despite occasional disappointments, Spaniards placed extraordinary trust in their Negro slaves. Agricultural slaves had infinite opportunities to run away. Negro herdsmen not only could run away, but were in complete charge of easily movable property that had an especially high value in a country only in the process of being stocked with European varieties. The degree of independence of Negro master artisan slaves has also already been seen.

Some slaves were allowed to lend and borrow money, and it was common for Negro slaves to be entrusted with merchandise to sell. . . .

When Spaniards knew individual slaves really well, they gave them the kind of absolute confidence they otherwise extended only to close blood relatives. In 1553 a Spanish muleteer fell ill while taking his pack train, loaded with merchandise, from Arequipa to Potosí. He returned to Arequipa for treatment, leaving the senior Negro slave muleteer in charge of the merchandise, the mules, and the other Negroes, with 30 pesos in silver to spend on food and maintenance. The pack train and the merchandise, worth several thousand pesos, represented the Spanish muleteer's life savings and more.

Why Negro slaves in Peru, presented with such multiple opportunity, did not all run away, may seem a mystery. Part of the explanation is the lack of a place of refuge. Most Spanish settlements were far away from such dense tropical forests as protected runaway slaves in Panama and the Antilles. Runaway Negroes could not hope to be received among the Indians, to whom Negroes were merely another type of intruder. In any case, hiding among the Indians was impossible for Negroes because their distinctive physical appearance made them readily identifiable. In effect, runaways had only one place to go, some other Spanish settlement than the one they were in. Slaves who had a specific fear or grievance could at times find temporary refuge in the Spanish monasteries, but this was hardly running away.

In conditions like these, the recovery of runaway Negro slaves was a relatively easy, even a predictable process. The Spaniards were so confident of recovering runaways that it was not at all uncommon for a runaway slave, while still absent, to be sold without conditions, at a good price, to a new owner. . . .

Since runaway Negroes could not live among the Indians and were quickly detected in the cities, the only way they could hope to maintain themselves was by organizing bands of cimarrons or renegades in the countryside. Geography kept Peru from becoming a land of cimarrons like Panama, but there were usually a few small bands in operation in some part of the country. . . .

The Spaniards felt little or no reluctance to liberate individual Negro slaves. Negroes in Peru started obtaining their freedom very early, by 1536 at the latest, and the movement continued with increasing momentum right through 1560. Most of the Negroes freed had to buy their liberty in one way or another. Charity played an important role, even when freedom was bought, but it came into full operation only when the owner no longer needed the slave, or the slave was not in the prime of life. Spaniards made true grants of freedom in their testaments, or when they left for Spain; also to aged slaves and to infant children of slaves. Such grants were in their sum effect a significant factor, but they cannot be said to represent the ordinary avenue to freedom.

Slaves somehow managed to accumulate the money to free themselves. If there was any legal obligation on the part of masters to liberate slaves for their just price, the masters did not recognize it. Some owners let their slaves go cheaply as an act of charity, others for a good price. Others held out for exorbitant amounts; . . . Either slaves were allowed to earn money on the side, or they received some sort of pay or allowance from their masters. However they did it, it was a difficult process. . . . Many slaves could not get the money together, and relied on loans, or worked out the equivalent of the price. The loans came from various sources, often from other Negroes who were already free and solvent. Loans might take the form of an advance in pay from the new freedman's employer.

Along with the flood of the newly freed was a trickle of Negroes who arrived in Peru already free.

Free Negroes were an important class of people. Though it is impossible to estimate their absolute numbers, . . . they were numerous indeed. In Lima they were already considered a problem as early as 1538. As was true of Negro slaves, more free Negroes lived on the coast than in the highlands, but they were to be found in the highlands too.

The freedom that Negroes bought was far from absolute. In all kinds of legal records, Spaniards were careful to see that freedmen were specifically called free Negroes, the only ordinary exceptions being some light mulattoes. Spanish legal authorities, often calling free Negroes simply slaves, continued to claim farreaching jurisdiction over them. Freedmen were periodically ordered to register and to take positions with Spanish masters. Once authorities issued a peremptory order for all free Negroes to leave the country; another time all freedmen were to join an unpaid, involuntary street-cleaning force. All such orders and schemes failed partially or completely, because of the social reality. Though Spaniards as a group were disturbed to see the rise of a class of independent Negroes (whose contribution to slave delinquency is undeniable), Spaniards as individuals tolerated them and found them useful. Not a single free Negro left Peru; . . .

Legislation requiring former slaves to take Spanish masters was more serious. First, it had a strong nuisance value, forcing the freedmen into at least ostensible and sporadic compliance. More basically, such ordinances had a certain shaping effect on the lives of free Negroes; they were the legal precipitation of the Spaniards' determination not to let Negroes take over positions and functions that they desired for themselves. Artisans' shops run independently by free Negroes, for example, were in constant jeopardy. With this upper limit, freedom enjoyed the legal privileges of Spaniards (and it should be remembered that even Spaniards were subject to orders to find a job or leave town). A freedman could own and bequeath any kind of property, marry, and carry on litigation. . . .

Since practically all free Negroes had been slaves, there was a close relationship between the occupations of the two groups. The activities of freedmen can be described summarily by saying that they merely did all the same things slaves did, except that they did them as independent operators or as wage earners. Personal service, agriculture, and artisanry were the primary occupations for Negroes, whether free or slave. As in other ages and countries, many freedmen maintained a close relationship with their former masters. Slaves ordinarily took their master's surname at the time of freedom; many either continued to work for their masters, or stayed dependent on them indirectly, living on or near the master's properties. The very word "freedman" *(horro)* could be synonymous with servant. Free Negro servants got a yearly wage . . . which was not much less than the wage of an unskilled Spaniard. . . .

Africans, or Negroes as we must call them, since some of them were born in Spain or the Indies, were a factor of absolutely first importance in Peru in the conquest period. They were an organic part of the enterprise of occupying Peru from its inception. The dominance of Spanish language and culture was never threatened, but in terms of ethnic or racial groups, the conquest of Peru was carried out by an equal partnership. Negroes were in a hundred ways the agents and auxiliaries of the Spaniards, in effect, doubling their numbers, making the Spanish occupation a much more thorough affair than it could have been without them. Far from their own roots, apart from the Indians, the Negroes assimilated Spanish culture with amazing speed, and were for the main part the Spaniards' willing allies, in spite of the cimarrons. And this willingness is understandable. Though Negroes were subordinated to Spaniards, they were not exploited in the plantation manner; except for mining gangs, Negroes in Peru counted as individuals.

SLAVE RESISTANCE

5. Negro Slave Control and Resistance in Colonial Mexico

DAVID M. DAVIDSON

In recent years historians have been investigating patterns of slave resistance, flight and rebellion in different parts of Spanish America and the Caribbean. In this essay David M. Davidson shows that slave control was a persistant problem for authorities in sixteenth and seventeenth-century Mexico.

Negro resistance to enslavement was an integral feature of the history of African slavery in the Americas. Studies in the past few decades in the United States and Latin America have successfully refuted if not entirely erased the once accepted notions of Negro docility and acquiescence in slavery. These works have provided a most convincing panorama of slave mutinies, insurrections, clandestine conspiracies, and individual escapes. Repeated evidence of more subtle forms of resistance—for example, suicide and voluntary abortion and infanticide—reveals further the determined refusal of many slaves to accept their position, and their reluctance to bear children in slavery. Such resistance occurred in varying degrees wherever

From "Negro Slave Control and Resistance in Colonial Mexico, 1519–1650," by David M. Davidson, *Hispanic American Historical Review,* 46 (1966), pp. 235–253, *passim.* Reprinted by permission.

Europeans established Negro slavery in the New World, primarily in the southern United States, the Antilles, the Pacific and Caribbean coasts of Central and South America, and northeastern Brazil. Although most studies have been restricted to these regions, there is a considerable body of evidence to indicate that Negro slave resistance was also present in colonial Mexico.

Recently, and primarily through the efforts of Gonzalo Aguirre Beltrán, we have gained substantial information concerning the number and role of Africans in Mexico. It is now fairly certain that in the period 1519–1650 the area received at least 120,000 slaves, or two-thirds of all the Africans imported into the Spanish possessions in America. The early development of Negro slavery in colonial Mexico was a direct response to the serious labor shortage resulting from the startling decline of the Indian population. Demographic studies suggest that the indigenous population of central Mexico alone, which may have been as high as 25,000,000 in 1519, had decreased to around 1,075,000 by 1605. The spread of European diseases, wars, relocations, and the ecological changes wrought by Spanish settlement and control all contributed to the decline. The advance of Spanish mining and, particularly, ranching and agriculture (which spread quickly in the sixteenth century to provision Mexico when decreasing indigenous food production threatened starvation) produced a demand for labor which the declining Indian population could not fulfill.

Although the crown soon made concessions to the colonists' demands for workers by sanctioning forced wage labor (the *repartimiento*), and by failing or refusing to thwart the spread of debt peonage, it hoped to fill the need with African slaves. Royal decrees throughout the late sixteenth century prohibited the use of Indians in certain industries considered detrimental to their health, especially sugar processing and cloth production, and ordered their replacement by Negro slaves. African labor was also encouraged for the mines.

The response to these conditions was a constant demand for Negroes, a flourishing slave trade, and a rising Negro population throughout the sixteenth and early seventeenth centuries. As a result, by 1570 Mexico contained over 20,000 Negroes, and by 1650 there were more than 35,000 Negroes and over 100,000 Afromestizos (mulattoes and zambos). Slaves were found throughout the colony, serving in the mines, plantations and ranches, as well as in the urban areas as peddlers, muleteers, craftsman, day laborers, and domestics. . . .

Spanish officials sought to incorporate this large, culturally distinct labor force into the neo-medieval structure of the American colonies. Legislation spanning the 1530s to 1550s, intended for the most part for general application to the Indies, stipulated the privileges and limitations pertaining to the slaves' place within society. Royal intentions derived in general from the profound Hispano-Catholic faith in the organic structure of a divinely imposed social unity, in which each person or group found its privileges and limitations defined according to its role in the hierarchy of inequality. More specifically, as Frank Tannenbaum has noted, this policy was rooted in the Iberian heritage which had long allowed slaves a legal and moral personality.

Yet the current of realism which accompanied and at times contradicted much of Spain's early idealism in America emerged forcefully in the regulation of slavery. The royal concern for slaves as Spanish subjects and Catholic souls was tempered by the need to create a stable and dependable labor force, maintained by consent in a situation where physical control was difficult. Much of the legislation concerning slavery assumed a conciliatory tone, in which certain privileges granted to slaves were intended to reduce or eliminate causes of slave discontent.

Thus royal decrees and Church proclamations provided legal release from bondage by allowing slaves to purchase their freedom and by encouraging voluntary manumission. Such declarations served equally to give substance to the Spanish belief in the essentially transitory nature of slavery and in the humanity of the slave. Some of them, such as the royal cédula of 1536 to Mexico, also suggested that slaves would work with more spirit and be less inclined to revolt. In seeking to make slave life more palatable by guaranteeing family solidarity and marital privileges, the king observed that a protected marital life was not only a Christian obligation, but also an essential means of insuring slave tranquility and stability. Both Church and crown were adamant in restricting the disciplinary authority of masters and in encouraging good treatment, for, as Juan de Solórzano commented, such conditions would protect the slaves as well as preserve an important labor base. Finally there was the desire to hispanize Africans in order to bring them into a community of spiritual and cultural brotherhood with their masters. Slaves would receive the benefits of Hispanic culture and religion, and their masters might rest assured that such fraternal bonds would temper resentment. In these respects the dictates of self-interest and religion went hand in hand.

The conciliatory measures appear to have had only a limited effect. Slaves did not achieve much success in purchasing their freedom or in being manumitted, if the few recorded instances of these are true indications. Such extralegal channels to freedom as intermarriage and miscegenation were relatively more successful. . . .

Slaves also tried to gain freedom by marrying into the free Indian population. Bartolomé de Zarate complained to the emperor in 1537 that Negroes were marrying Indians and declaring themselves freed. Although the *Siete Partidas,* Spain's ancient legal code, had granted liberty to some slaves who married free persons, Charles V nullified this provision, thus emphasizing that if the authorities would condone a trickle of free Negroes, they would not tolerate a substantial loss of their slave labor. Despite the royal desires slaves continued to marry Indians in order that their children might be free. "Indian women are very weak and succumb to Negroes," wrote Viceroy Martín Enríquez in 1574. "Thus Indian women would rather marry Negroes than Indians; and neither more nor less, Negroes prefer to marry Indian women rather than Negresses, so that their children will be born free." Spanish law and custom respected these marriages, which, with common law unions, produced the free zambo population of Mexico.

Legislation which sought to cure some of the worst abuses in slave life provided only minimal protection. Whereas both crown and Church hoped to protect the familial stability of slave life, many masters seemed bent on its disruption. Juan de la Peña informed Philip II in 1569 that masters were separating slave families by selling male slaves, "from which results great harm to their wives and children, because they remain in this land with no aid." The Archivo General de la Nación has many examples of masters forcing slaves to marry against their will, separating slave families, and violating wives and daughters. Both crown and Church did on occasion protect slave families, but in general Aguirre Beltrán seems accurate in stating that slave family life was highly unstable and vulnerable to the masters' whims.

The regulation of slave treatment and discipline did not fare much better. . . . Furthermore, neither crown nor Church intervened in situations which modern opinion would consider brutal. . . . Repeated evidence reveals that cruelty and mistreatment were as much a part of slavery in colonial Mexico as they were in most slave regimes in the New World. As the king frankly stated on more than one occasion, slaves in Mexico and the Spanish Indies in general were subject to "scandalous abuses," and mistreated "to such an extreme that some die without confession." "The poor slaves are molested and badly cared for."

The hispanization of Mexico's African population sought to ease the transition into slavery. While conversion was certainly one facet of the broader evangelical mission of Spanish expansion, in regard to slave control the policy served three possible functions: it would influence the development of a society where shared religious and cultural values produced a slave regime based on consent; it would provide certain outlets for slave tensions and discontent through religious ritual and social activities; and it sought to offer slaves spiritual equality in the City of God in return for deference and obedience to their masters in this world. Iberian Catholicism was ideally suited to these ends with its many saint's days and fiestas, auxiliary social organizations, and ingrained sense of hierarchy.

Hispanization of Africans was relatively successful, judging from the countless references to creole Negroes in the archives. True religious conversion was somewhat more difficult, although missionaries apparently made notable gains. Evidence of Negro brotherhoods (*cofradías*) in the urban and mining districts suggests that some slaves benefited from the social outlets and religious balm of Christianity. The Church also established hospitals to serve the Negro population, although the charitable intentions and social functions of these institutions probably outweighed their medical efficacy.

That many slaves did adopt the forms and receive the benefits of Hispanic culture and religion, did not make them contented with their servile life. Christian slaves were just as likely to resist or revolt as any others. In fact, in 1523, the first slaves to revolt in the colony erected crosses to celebrate their freedom "and to let it be known that they were Christians."

Unfortunately conciliatory legislation and hispanization failed to eliminate the general causes of slave resistance in Mexico. Unstable familial and marital life, mistreatment, overwork, and the scarcity of effective channels to freedom undoubtedly contributed heavily to slave discontent. Although these conditions certainly varied from one region, master, and economic activity to another, the worst treatment and the most brutal revolts occurred in the mines and sugar plantations of the colony. . . .

Although individual Negroes fled in the early years, the first alleged effort by slaves to organize a large-scale uprising occurred in 1537. On December 10, 1537, Viceroy Antonio de Mendoza informed the emperor of a plot intended to free the slave population of the young colony. "On the twenty-fourth of the month of November past," wrote Mendoza, "I was warned that the Negroes had chosen a king, and had agreed amongst themselves to kill all the Spaniards and rise up to take the land, and that the Indians were also with them." Mendoza sent an agent to corroborate the rumor and soon received the reply that a plot existed which included the capital city and the outlying mines. He swiftly arrested the "king" and his principal lieutenants, and, after eliciting confessions, had the leading conspirators drawn and quartered. There is a good possibility that the alleged plot, although it never materialized, was not a figment of the viceroy's imagination, since an independent sixteenth-century source also records the plot and subsequent events. . . .

Continued tension in Mexico City and the occurrence of at least two more revolts in the 1540s prompted Spanish officials to issue a number of decrees restricting Mexico's Negro population. Mendoza's ordinances of 1548 prohibited the sale of arms to Negroes and forbade public gatherings of three or more Negroes when not with their masters. The viceroy also declared a night curfew on Negroes in the capital city. Mendoza's warnings to Luis de Velasco apparently alarmed the new viceroy, for he repeated Mendoza's restrictions in 1551 and wrote in 1553: "This land is so full of Negroes and mestizos who exceed the Spaniards in great quantity, and all desire to purchase their liberty with the lives of their masters." In the same year Velasco also established a civil militia (the *Santa Hermandad*) in the colony, in part to cope with slave uprisings.

With restrictive measures barely under way, Mexico experienced its first widespread wave of slave insurrections in the period 1560–1580 as a result of the increased use of Negroes in mines and estates. By the 1560s fugitive slaves from the mines of the north were terrorizing the regions from Guadalajara to Zacatecas, allying with the Indians and raiding ranches. . . . The insurrections continued into the 1570s as Martín Enríquez attempted to implement the royal ordinances. Yet neither the code of 1571–1574 nor the issuance of restrictive legislation in the 1570s and 1580s was of any avail. A viceregal order of 1579 revealed that the contagion of revolt nearly covered the entire settled area of the colony outside of Mexico City, in particular the provinces of Veracruz and Pánuco, the area between Oaxaca and Gualtuco on the Pacific coast, and almost the whole of the *Gran Chichimeca*. Only emergency repressive measures and the continued importation of Africans maintained Mexico's slave labor supply.

During the last decades of the sixteenth century the focus of slave revolts shifted to the eastern sugar regions of the viceroyalty. Isolated uprisings had occurred there since the 1560s, but by the turn of the century the slopes and lowlands between Mt. Orizaba and Veracruz teemed with small maroon settlements and roaming bands of slaves who raided the many plantations and towns in the area.

The geography of the region so favored maroon guerrilla activities that local authorities proved incapable of thwarting their raids or pursuing them to the palenques. [In one famous incident, a Negro leader named Yanga was able in 1609 to negotiate an agreement with Spanish authorities on favorable terms.]

Yanga's maroon movement is a notable example in the history of Negroes in Mexico—the only known example of a fully successful attempt by slaves to secure their freedom *en masse* by revolt and negotiation and to have it sanctioned and guaranteed in law. This experience demonstrates that, under capable leadership, slaves could maintain an active guerrilla campaign, negotiate a truce, and win recognition of their freedom. In view of the tenacity displayed by other maroons as well, it is likely that similar incidents occurred which have not been recorded.

The violence of slave insurrections in the eastern slopes and northern mining regions kept Mexico City in a prolonged state of anxiety. By the first decade of the seventeenth century the Negro population of the capital had grown enormously, and there was a general fear that the urban slaves would unite to take the city. The tensions in the metropolis exploded in 1609 and 1612 when rumors circulated that the Negroes had chosen leaders and planned massive uprisings. In both cases elaborate defensive preparations followed brief periods of panic and confusion. Negroes were apprehended and punished, and the plots, if indeed they existed at all, never materialized. Yet whether or not these conspiracies actually existed, the terror which they caused was a reflection of the tensions inherent in multiracial Mexico where insecurity plagued the Spanish and creole population well into the seventeenth century. . . .

It is apparent that officials and slaveowners found it extremely difficult to prevent or contain slave resistance. Few in numbers, they were forced to rely on the scarce royal troops in Mexico aided by untrained and undisciplined bands of mestizos and Indians. These haphazard military operations faced serious strategic and tactical problems, especially in campaigns against distant hideaways in the frontier regions. Mexico's rugged terrain compounded the difficulties, for fugitives could establish settlements in the mountains and isolated barrancas which afforded excellent defensive sites. Moreover, Indian cooperation seems to have been instrumental to the success of various revolts and made the job of repression all the more difficult. With such a weak system of control, the flight and insurrection of slaves continued into the eighteenth century, and it was only the abolition of slavery in the early nineteenth century that put an end to slave resistance in Mexico.

In conclusion, some implications of slave control and resistance in colonial Mexico are evident. In the first place, it appears that flight and revolt constituted the most effective avenue to liberty for the slave population, despite the existence of an elaborate (if often ineffective) machinery of control and conciliation. Thus a major consequence of resistance was the development of the free Negro and Afromestizo population of the colony. Second, slave resistance, real or imagined, had a notably disturbing effect on the society of the conquerors. In this respect the anxiety of colonial society differed more in degree than in kind from that of the fear-ridden slavocracies of the Caribbean and southern United States. The same restrictive and precautionary measures, the same false alarms, and similar bands of roaming vigilantes characterized Mexico as well. Moreover, preventive legislation and Spanish fears extended to the free Negro population, and the status of freedom in the colony suffered regardless of their role in slave resistance. Finally, the study of Negro slave activity reveals an area of social life barely perceived by many students of colonial Mexico—the relations within the nonwhite and mixed peoples in the multracial societies that developed throughout tropical America. Of particular importance here are Indian-Negro relations, where miscegenation, marital and common-law unions, cooperation in resistance and also mutual antagonisms provide a rewarding field of study of social history. Slave resistance in Mexico is more than just another chapter in the Negroes' long struggle for freedom and justice. In the context of Mexican social history it illustrates the interplay of diverse races and cultures which make that history one of the most complex and fascinating in the New World.

*António Vieira. This Jesuit missionary, man of letters, economist, orator,
and diplomat was "one of the most remarkable Portuguese who ever lived."
He played a large part in most of the affairs of seventeenth-century Brazil,
especially in the effort to protect the Indians.*

The Crises of Seventeenth-Century Brazil

A PERIOD OF CRISIS AND CHANGE

Seventeenth-century Spanish America has been characterized as "the forgotten century" or as a period when no spectacular events occurred as in the previous century of conquest or the succeeding century of reform and impending revolution. This may be true, or it may reflect our ignorance of these years when the basic institutions and ways of life were implanted throughout the Spanish empire in America. But it is certain that the seventeenth century in Brazil was a period of crisis and change.

Yet Portuguese and Spanish-speaking historians alike have usually neglected those significant years from 1580 until 1640, when Portugal and Spain were jointly ruled by the Spanish Hapsburgs. It has remained for a young American scholar, Professor Stuart B. Schwartz, to analyze this union from the standpoint of the influence of reforms and policies initiated by the Hapsburgs on Brazilian administration and affairs (Reading 1). Though the Spanish yoke was thrown off in 1640, the so-called "Babylonian Captivity" proved a significant period for the development of Portuguese America.

THE DUTCH IN BRAZIL

Another crisis occurred in 1654 when the Brazilians evicted the Dutch from their sugar colony in the northeastern province of Pernambuco. The economic and political importance of the Dutch period in Brazilian history has long been studied and debated by historians. A Brazilian revisionist historian argues that the sugar economy began to decline even before the Dutch arrived, and their invasion was a crippling blow that brought no compensating economic advantages.[1] One remarkable contribution by the Dutch was the appointment of Governor-General Johan Maurits, whose cultural activities and enlightened rule put Brazil on the map in a way never before accomplished. That indefatigable English historian Charles R. Boxer has well described his beneficent work (Reading 2).

THE "NEGRO REPUBLIC" IN PALMARES

The effect of Africa on Brazil and the role of the blacks in Brazilian history are well known and are subjects of an extensive literature. The sugar-based economy could not have been developed in Brazil without the African laborer, and the Portuguese could not have held Brazil without the African soldier. One powerful manifestation of the strength of African politics and culture in Brazil was the "Negro Republic" of Palmares in Pernambuco that lasted throughout most of the seventeenth century despite determined efforts of both the Dutch and the Portuguese to destroy it. When Palmares finally fell in 1694, "the greatest threat to the future evolution of the Brazilian people and civilization" was removed (Reading 3).

VIEIRA AND THE INDIANS

Some crises last for decades and never are resolved in any decisive or permanent way. Such was the struggle to abolish Indian slavery, which in Brazil was largely the work of the Jesuits. The first significant struggle on behalf of the Indians in seventeenth-century Brazil took place in Rio de Janeiro in 1640 when the Jesuit Francisco Díaz Taño arrived with the brief *Commissum nobis* of Pope Urban VIII that had been promulgated the year before in Rome. This brief "vigorously reaffirmed the validity of Pope Paul III's brief of 1537, proclaiming the liberty of the Amerindians, and forbidding their enslavement on any pretext whatsoever." It was not received well by either the colonists or some of the clergy in southern Brazil who were openly hostile to Jesuit support for the freedom of the Indians. Father Taño arranged for the formal promulgation of the brief, which so infuriated an angry crowd in Rio that they "rushed to the Jesuit college, and finding the doors barred, broke them open with axes and swarmed into the building shouting 'kill them, kill them,' and 'kick them out, kick them out.' High words passed between the two parties, and a Jesuit is alleged to have told some of the mob that they should be grateful for the brief since it made free women of their wives and

---

[1] Mírcea Buescu, "Invasão holandesa: perdas da economia açucareira," *Verbum* (Rio de Janeiro), 25 (1968), pp. 397–408.

mothers — a caustic if not very tactful allusion to the high proportion of Indian blood in the infuriated aggressors." [2]

The outstanding Jesuit in Brazil was António Vieira, the famous preacher whom Charles Boxer acclaims as "the most remarkable man in the seventeenth-century Luso-Brazilian world." Because Vieira's efforts to abolish Indian slavery were most important to understanding his role in Brazilian history, Dr. Mathias C. Kiemen's exposition of the general Indian policy of Portugal is given as a background (Reading 5).

One of the reasons why Vieira is usually neglected in our courses is that his sermons, letters, and state papers, which are considered "the best collective source for our understanding of the climate of opinion in seventeenth-century Brazil and Portugal," have never been translated into English. A one-volume selection is badly needed. Fortunately Professor Gregory Rabassa of Queens College has in preparation such a work for the Borzoi Books on Latin America series. Meanwhile, here are samples of his fire and eloquence in his "Sermon Condemning Indian Slavery" and his "Report on the Conversion of the Nheengaíbas" in the Amazon (Reading 4).

BANDEIRANTES

Another great theme in the history of the seventeenth-century Brazil was the movement westward of the pioneers known as the *bandeirantes,* or "pathfinders." It was an exciting development, which resulted in an enormous extension of Brazil's boundaries and the growth of a boom spirit that has had a marked influence in the strengthening of Brazilian national feeling. But the subject is too vast for brief treatment, and merits the attention given in the volume edited by Richard Morse.[3]

---

[2] Charles R. Boxer, *Salvador de Sá and the Struggle for Brazil and Angola, 1602–1686* (London: The Athlone Press, University of London, 1952), pp. 131–132.

[3] *The Bandeirantes: The Historical Role of the Brazilian Pathfinders,* Borzoi Books on Latin America (New York: Knopf, 1965).

THE "BABYLONIAN CAPTIVITY"

1. *Brazil Under Spanish Rule, 1580–1640*

STUART B. SCHWARTZ

Neither Spanish nor Portuguese historians have devoted much attention to the influences Brazil received during the sixty years when it was ruled along with Portugal itself by the Spanish Hapsburgs. It was a period of important and varied development, as Professor Stuart B. Schwartz explains in this informative and interpretive article.

Few epochs in the history of the Portuguese colonial empire have received less attention from historians than the sixty years from 1580–1640 when Portugal and Spain were jointly ruled by the Spanish Hapsburgs, Philip II, III, IV (or I, II, III by Portuguese reckoning). The union of the crowns in 1580 brought together the two greatest maritime empires of the sixteenth century, yet, curiously, this phenomenon has remained relatively unstudied. Portuguese neglect is based on the premise that the union with Spain was a "Babylonian Captivity" during which the Spanish rulers and their policies destroyed in a half century what had taken the Portuguese two hundred years to build. Nationalism has prompted Portuguese scholars to concentrate on the loss of independence in 1580 or its triumphant restitution in 1640, but although this motivation is still present, a new generation of Portuguese historians has begun to turn from the shibboleths of their nineteenth-century predecessors. Spanish historiography, on the other hand, disdains the topic; hardly surprising since even today to many Spaniards "a Portuguese is a Galician who speaks poorly." Moreover, there is the embarrassing fact that the Portuguese were able to wrest their independence from Spanish rule.

Brazilian historians have also neglected this period of their history and with the exception of a few outstanding monographs and some suggestive essays our knowledge of Hapsburg Brazil remains characterized by hoary and often unfounded generalizations or by crude attempts at revision. The usual claims

From "Luso-Brazilian Relations in Hapsburg Brazil, 1580–1640" by Stuart B. Schwartz, *The Americas,* 25 (1968), pp. 33–48, passim. Reprinted by permission.

that the period had no distinctive effects on Brazil, that Brazilians were indifferent about the union, and that Spanish neglect ruined the colony are often repeated. I hope to present some alternative to this line of thought. Considerations of scope and space limit my remarks to Brazil but I wish to emphasize at the outset that Brazil was only one area of a vast imperial structure, and in 1580 far from the most important region. Linked to the metropolis and the empire of the South Atlantic, Brazilian developments were often determined or influenced by events in other lands.

In the Cortes of Tomar (April, 1581), at which Philip II negotiated the final settlement of his acquisition of the Portuguese throne, no mention was made of Brazil. This fact reflected not only Portuguese lack of interest, but also the motivation of Spanish action. The decision by Philip II to contest the Portuguese succession was primarily influenced by Spanish desires to become an Atlantic power and the need for a base in the coming struggle with England. If in 1580 the Portuguese colonies influenced Spanish actions, it was the spice of India and the slaves of West Africa that attracted Philip II. Although showing signs of growth after 1570, Brazil in 1580 was still the tail end of empire. Its European population lived precariously in the shadow of attack from hostile Indians and European rivals. Scattered along the littoral and concentrated at a few urban nodules the total population of colonists, officials, and clergy was probably around 20,000. Unlike Spanish America, Brazil could boast of no printing press, no universities, few noble edifices and little apparent mineral wealth. Within the next fifty years, however, Brazil because of its sugar agro-industry and because of Portuguese losses in Asia became the focal point of empire. The change in dynasty in the metropolis was accepted without difficulty in the colony and without dissent. No sympathy was given to Dom Antônio, the Portuguese Pretender, or to his French allies. The Spanish Hapsburgs, kings of Spain and now of Portugal, easily became rulers of Brazil.

The presence of Spaniards in Brazil during the union is a matter that need not detain us long. There always had been Spaniards in the Brazilian enterprise just as Portuguese had participated in Spain's colonization of America. Hence, Spaniards resident in Brazil from 1580 to 1640 should not be surprising although there was a considerable increase in their numbers during this period. The Portuguese Crown was traditionally lenient about the settlement of foreigners in Brazil and the original grants to the proprietors (*donatarios*) in the 1530's required only that the lands be distributed to Catholics. Italians, Frenchmen, Flemings, and Englishmen were along with Spaniards among the foreigners who settled in Brazil. Inquisition records of 1591–93 for northern Brazil, however, indicate that Spaniards constituted 37.8%–55% of the foreign community, by far the largest non-Portuguese group. In São Paulo and the south the percentage was probably even higher, and Spaniards were active members of the Paulista expeditions.

The long-standing and well-documented sentiments of distrust and rivalry between Spaniards and Portuguese did arise in Brazil, and colonists there considered the epithet "dirty Galician" a sufficient cause for drawn swords. Most complaints, however, were directed against specific policies and abuses committed by groups of Spaniards rather than against the individual settler. For example, the Spanish contingent in the joint armada that recaptured Bahia from the Dutch in 1625 looted as well as liberated the city, and the local residents complained that the Castilians had left "neither door nor lock unbroken." There was also a steady stream of complaint against the garrisons of Spanish soldiers stationed in Brazil occasioned by the unruly nature of these troops and the taxes levied to support them. There were some in Brazil who considered Bahia an occupied not a defended city.

Despite these colonial reflections of peninsular prejudices, the Spaniards in Brazil seem to have been well-integrated into society and Luso-Spanish personal relations were amiable. This was especially true of the nobility which in both countries shared similar attitudes and aspirations and were often directly linked by kinship or marriage to noble families across the frontier. We need go no further than Salvador de Sá, governor of Rio de Janeiro, who was the brother-in-law of Luís de Cespedes, governor of Paraguay. Just how friendly these relations could be was indicated by Fernando de Vargas, a Spanish noble who visited Bahia in 1594. He stated:

> There is in this city of Bahia a gentleman, Governor Francisco de Sousa, who did me such favors that I know not how to exaggerate them, giving me money with as much willingness as if I were his heir. . . . I found many other Portuguese hidalgos who . . . I must praise for they answered my every need; providing whatever I asked and offering me much more. . . ."

Similarities of religion, culture, and attitudes added to the rigors of colonial existence created a condition in Brazil that allowed for the integration of resident Spaniards into the community.

The common acceptance of the individual Spaniard, however, should not obscure determined Portuguese opposition to any concerted Spanish political or economic penetration of the imperial structure. Sevillian merchants were at first more interested in profiting from the West African slave trade than in participating in the Brazilian sugar and dye-wood commerce, but Spanish mercantile interests soon found it convenient to lease monopoly rights to Portuguese contractors in order to secure Negroes for the Spanish American colonies. Portuguese maritime and commercial groups including those in

Brazil derived great profit from this arrangement. Subsequent attempts by Seville and the Casa de Contratación to impose strict regulations on the contractors, to wrest control of the slave trade, or to enter the Brazilian trade were met with bitter and determined resistance by the Portuguese. Not only did the Portuguese profit from their connections with Buenos Aires, Cartagena de Indias, and Cuba, but despite Spanish regulations a considerable contraband trade developed between Brazil and Spain itself. Some of the Brazilian products passed into southern Spain, but a well-developed network arose in northern Spain where Brazilian sugar was traded for Vizcayan iron.

In Brazil, the most significant economic penetration effected by the Spaniards was the contract ceded to a coalition of Vizcayan merchants in 1602 for the hunting of whales in the Bay of All Saints. The project had been suggested by the Portuguese themselves as a means of providing the colony with oil, but the Vizcayans found it more profitable to reship some of the oil to Spain and thus maintain inflated prices for this commodity in Brazil. This situation and the development of a skilled labor force of Negroes and mulattos eventually moved enterprising Portuguese to break the monopoly, and by 1608 the Vizcayans had competitors. The price of oil in that year fell 40% as a result of the increased supply. A lawsuit developed in 1609 and the High Court of Bahia, staffed by Portuguese magistrates, ruled against the Spanish monopoly. The decision of the court was that "it should not be denied to natives . . . that which is conceded to foreigners."

Reforms and policies initiated by the Hapsburgs in Portugal had a direct effect in Brazil, especially in terms of organization and administration. The creation in Portugal of institutions for colonial control such as the merchant guild or *Consulado* in 1591, and the India Council (Conselho da India) in 1604 placed Brazil in a new administrative relationship to the Crown. Most important, the Spanish reform of Portuguese justice begun in 1582 resulted in the publication of the *Philippine Ordinances* (1603) which remained the basic law of Brazil until the nineteenth century. It was also as a result of this reform that the first High Court of Appeal (Relação) was established in Bahia in 1609. Moreover, during the Hapsburg period the first visits of the Inquisition were made to Brazil (1591–93, 1618), but despite ardent research no direct Spanish influence has been discovered.

Brazil under Hapsburg control was subject in the early years of the seventeenth century to two territorial divisions. The captaincies of the south — Espirito Santo, Rio de Janeiro, and São Vicente — were placed under a separate governor in 1609 and the vast region of Maranhão was created an independent unit in 1621. We know in both cases the ostensible reasons for these divisions; administrative independence to facilitate mining in the former, and difficulties of communication with Bahia in the latter, but whether any Spanish plan for territorial or economic aggrandizement was involved has never been investigated. Certainly, there was some Spanish interest in occupying the Amazon basin after 1640, and even during the union Viceroy Montesclaros of Peru had suggested the incorporation of São Paulo in the Spanish Indies. It may be more than coincidence that the first man chosen to be governor of Maranhão was Diego de Carcamo, a Spaniard, and that the only region of Brazil to display pro-Hapsburg sentiment in 1640 was the town of São Paulo.

Portuguese colonists in Brazil not only realized that they were under Spanish kings, but they sought to derive some benefit from this fact. Spanish forms or policies that suited the colonists and served local interests were often petitioned for by them. A common tactic was pointing to usage in Spanish America and then appealing for similar solutions in Brazil.

The encomienda and Indian slavery provide a case in point. In Spanish America the encomienda as a system for the control and exploitation of groups of Indians had gradually withered in the face of royal control and the opposition of Spanish moralists. By the beginning of the seventeenth century it was quite clear that the Crown had little intention of expanding this institution. Nevertheless, colonists in Brazil, faced with high prices for Negro slaves and royal legislation against enslavement of the Indian, saw the encomienda as an alternate solution to the chronic problem of labor. Thus in 1605 Governor Diogo Botelho petitioned for the establishment of the encomienda in Brazil. A more constant advocate of the encomienda was Bento Maciel Parente, Indian fighter and later Captain-major of Maranhão. In a number of memorials to the Crown, usually penned in Spanish, he suggested a division of the Indians of Maranhão in encomiendas "as is done in the Indies of Castile."

When, however, Hapsburg legislation for Brazil was unpopular the argument was turned about. The Spanish Hapsburgs had continued in Brazil the policy initiated by the dynasty of Aviz against enslavement of the Indian. Protective laws of 1587, 1595, and 1605 should have indicated to the colonists the thrust of royal intent. When, however, in 1609 a new and more stringent law was issued for Brazil local reaction was virulent. There were threats of rioting in Rio de Janeiro and in Bahia rioting actually erupted. Most interesting is a letter from the municipal council of Parahiba to Philip IV complaining that the law of 1609 "was made and formulated in the kingdom of Castile and it has little applicability in Brazil." The colonists in this case were able to force a withdrawal of the unpopular legislation.

Brazilian colonists were aware of the desire of the Spanish Hapsburgs to increase the flow of precious metals into the royal coffers. American silver had become the main support of imperial policy and as the production of Potosí crested in the late years of the sixteenth century the Crown became increasingly concerned with discovering new sources of supply. Portuguese in Brazil were no less anxious to find these riches and here again the example of Peru and Mexico was constantly before them. There is a Peruvian fixation readily discernible in many of the chroniclers of the period and this "edenic complex" stimulated both rumor and expeditions. But the residents of Brazil not only hoped to get rich from the discovery of mines, they desired other benefits in return for their service to the Crown.

Gabriel Soares de Sousa obtained wide-reaching powers from Madrid in return for his promise to exploit mines near the São Francisco River in the late 1580's. It is worth recalling that his famous chronicle was written as a promotional brochure to gain support at the Spanish court. Others followed his example. Dom Francisco de Sousa, Governor of Brazil when Soares de Sousa made his petition, agitated in Madrid for similar privileges. His proposal to exploit mines in southern Brazil was approved, and Francisco de Sousa was made Governor of the Captaincies of the South which were separated to aid his project. Francisco de Sousa placed a great deal of emphasis on Spanish example and Spanish participation in the mines he hoped to exploit. He urged the Crown to send goldminers from Chile, a silver specialist from Potosí, and an iron mining expert from Vizcaya to act as advisors. From Buenos Aires he wished to receive foodstuffs and even llamas (*carneiros de carga*) to carry out the minerals. To regulate the mines he asked for the mining code of Peru, the *Nuevo Caderno* and taxation according to the system used in New Spain. The labor force would be provided by Indians once again under the laws of Peru, or in other words, institution of the *mita* method of corvee labor. Francisco de Sousa wished the Indians brought to service by persuasion or coercion but the Crown ruled out the second method. It was suggested by the Crown, however, that Jesuits go into the bush to coax Indians to the mines and both Dom Francisco and his successors used this expedient.

What, in fact, we may have here is Portuguese use of Hapsburg cupidity to circumvent Hapsburg Indian legislation. Certainly, this was the case in a similar project in Bahia also considered in 1609. The India Council saw through the ruse and warned the king that the petitioners were rich men who wished to "bring Indians in from the sertão and serve themselves of them for personal ends more than to discover mines." The Hapsburg period was an important era in the search for mineral wealth and Brazilians hoped for a variety of benefits from the mineral aspirations of the Spanish Hapsburgs.

Even while the search for the elusive mines continued, sugar was providing Brazil with a basis for wealth and development. The colony was fast becoming the keystone in the economy of the Portuguese empire, an empire that had always been a commercial enterprise above all else. At the same time Brazil was becoming increasingly important to Spain but for very different reasons. This divergence between Spain and Portugal over the role of Brazil in imperial theory bespoke a growing difference in imperial concerns which became a major factor in the revolt of Portugal in 1640.

Luso-Spanish relations from 1580 to 1640 fall into two periods. The first from 1580 to 1622 is characterized by considerable Portuguese profit as a result of the union. . . . The year 1622 marks the beginning of a period of loss and disillusionment. . . .

Both Spaniards and Portuguese had long recognized the strategic importance of Brazil, a consideration of which the Dutch were also aware. Spaniards feared that with a Brazilian port as a base, the Dutch or English could make forays into the Caribbean against the silver fleets, interdict the homeward bound Indiamen, sail into the seas off Chile and Peru, interrupt the slave trade, and most important, attack Peru and its mines by way of the Rio de la Plata. This fear increasingly determined Hapsburg policy toward Brazil and the colony became crucial in Spanish geopolitics. Brazil was to be the first line of defense for Peru and a rampart for the Spanish Indies. Philip IV and the Count-Duke of Olivares considered Peru and its silver, not Brazil and its sugar, as the heart of empire, and all means had to be taken to defend the arteries to and from that heart. For this end Philip IV was willing to violate the agreements of Tomar, sacrifice Brazilian development, and alienate the Portuguese.

After 1630 Dutch capture of Pernambuco brought forth more extreme responses from Spain which in turn increased Portuguese bitterness. In 1631 Philip IV attempted to populate Brazil with Italians and other foreigners as an effective means of securing the coast. Here was an obvious violation of the Tomar agreements. It is wrong, however, to assume that Spain was unwilling to make sacrifices of her own for the Brazilian line of defense. In 1632 Spain offered diplomatically to surrender hard-won Breda to the Dutch along with 200,000 to 300,000 florins in return for their evacuation of Pernambuco.

Spain, however, expected Portugal to bear the costs for the defense of its empire. This had been the justification of the "Union of Arms" sponsored by Olivares in 1626 and was the cause of increased taxation in the 1630's. Each new measure, each new tax produced Portuguese resistance. Spanish councillors could not perceive the cause of this discontent. Why should the Portuguese grumble, they asked, about paying for the defense of Portuguese colonies? After all, had not Spain equipped fleets, provided funds, and sent troops to defend Brazil? Yet, the Portuguese were recalcitrant.

Attempts were made to force all members of the Portuguese military orders to serve in Brazil under the excuse that the war was a religious matter. The Crown set legal experts to the task of finding some clause in the grants to the *donatarios* that would require them to personally defend their areas. In both cases the Portuguese successfully resisted. In Brazil the High Court was abolished and its salaries applied to the garrison in Bahia. Taxes were imposed on the colonists and after 1633 on all the municipalities of Portugal to pay for the war in Brazil. The first major anti-Hapsburg revolt occurred in Evora, a city with little interest in Brazil, because of a new tax to support the conflict in the colony.

Rather than driving the Dutch from Brazil by force and turning Brazil into a bulwark of empire, colonial and continental Portuguese wished to open the old lines of commerce, lines that included trade with Holland. In 1626, the Governors of Portugal put the matter succinctly. They asked the Crown, "if the utility of closing commerce to enemies is worth more than the lack of commerce." Within this commercial definition of empire, Brazil now exercised a dominant influence and its trade was the motive force of the imperial structure. Spanish interest in Brazil was real but defined in strategic terms. The divergence of these two concepts of the role of Brazil was a major factor for the dissatisfaction with Hapsburg rule in both Brazil and Portugal. Brazil, disregarded in 1580, had become by 1640 a determinant of Spanish policy and a reason for rebellion in Portugal.

THE DUTCH IN BRAZIL

2. The Humanist Prince Johan Maurits in Recife, 1637–1644

C. R. BOXER

Some Brazilian historians are inclined to play down the Dutch period as a time when no substantial results were achieved because of the ever-present commercial spirit of the invaders. They emphasize rather the importance of the local Brazilian effort that successfully expelled the Dutch in 1654, and the consequences of that action. The Dutch moved their tools, slaves, and techniques for raising sugar to the West Indies, which, along with their command of shipping, enabled them to maintain a decisive lead in the world's sugar markets. Some Jews fled from Pernambuco to Manhattan and established the first synagogue there. These years also saw the beginning of a deliberate shift in Portuguese imperial policy, during which Portugal became convinced that Brazil was more valuable than were other parts of the far-flung empire such as Ceylon and decided to let it go.*

But one important result of the rule of one Dutch governor, "the humanist prince" Johan Maurits, was that Europe became aware of Brazil through paintings and books made possible by his imaginative support for a group of artists and scholars as described by Professor Boxer.

Johan Maurits has been called "the most remarkable man ever connected with the sugar industry," and an outline of his record as governor-general of Netherlands Brazil shows that this estimate is not an exaggerated one. He was not only a capable general and a first-class administrator, but a ruler who was in many respects far in advance of his time. . . .

During the seven years of his rule he spared neither his own energy nor the Company's money in his efforts to develop the colony. He improved and enlarged the existing city of Recife with new (and paved) streets, roads, and bridges. He laid out a new town named Mauritia, or Mauritsstad, on the adjoining island of Antonio Vaz, the site of which forms the heart of the modern city of Recife. Here he built two spacious country-seats, one of them complete with a well-stocked aviary and zoological and botanical gardens, where he indulged his taste for growing exotic fruits and transplanting tropical trees on a lavish scale. He also erected the first astronomical observatory and meteorological station in the New World where regular wind and rainfall records were kept. He even envisaged the foundation of a university which would be frequented by Protestant Dutch and Catholic Portuguese, although this particular project never got beyond the paper stage.

During his stay in Brazil Johan Maurits gathered around him a carefully selected entourage of forty-six scholars, scientists, artists, and craftsmen from the Netherlands, all of whom had their own special functions and assignments. Piso studied tropical diseases and their remedies, Marcgraf made scientific collections of the fauna, flora, and geography of Brazil and Angola, in addition to astronomical and meteorological observations; while half a dozen painters, including Frans Post and Albert Eckhout (the latter possibly a pupil of Rembrandt), filled their portfolios with sketches of every aspect of local life and culture. Only a part of the material amassed by these men was published in Johan Maurits's lifetime; but the sumptuous folio volumes of Barlaeus, Marcgraf, and Piso, printed at the count's expense after his return to Holland, are among the finest examples of seventeenth-century book production. For

* See George D. Winius, *The Fatal History of Portuguese Ceylon* (Cambridge, Mass.: Harvard University Press, 1971).
From *The Dutch in Brazil, 1624–1654* by C. R. Boxer (Oxford: The Clarendon Press, 1957), pp. 112–155, passim. Reprinted by permission of the Clarendon Press, Oxford.

over 150 years they remained the standard works on Brazil in any language. . . .

"La belle, très belle et bellissime maison" of the Mauritshuis at The Hague, well known to all art-lovers and visitors to the Netherlands, was originally built for Johan Maurits to the design (or at least under the supervision) of his friend, the celebrated architect Pieter Post, whose brother Frans had accompanied him to Brazil. This "sugar-house," as the disgruntled directors of the West India Company sarcastically called the new palace, was largely furnished with Brazil-wood sent home by Johan Maurits during his tenure of office, and it was no wonder that his countrymen nicknamed him "Maurits the Brazilian." The museums of Berlin, Copenhagen, and Paris still contain valuable ethnographical and artistic collections which form only a fraction of those which he and his helpers methodically amassed in Brazil. No such systematic and intelligently directed scientific work by white men in the tropics was seen again until the great expeditions of Captain Cook and his successors. With every justification did Johan Maurits choose for his motto the Latin phrase *Qua patet orbis,* "As wide as the world's bounds."

Nor was Johan Maurits less enlightened in his treatment of the local Portuguese. He fully understood the importance of reconciling the planters and the *moradores* to Dutch rule, and his efforts met with a considerable degree of success, at any rate outwardly. A staunch Protestant himself, and in an age when Calvinists and Catholics regarded each other as inevitably doomed to hell-fire, he deliberately tolerated the local Roman Catholic priests and friars (the Jesuits alone excepted), despite the opposition of the colonial Calvinist ministers and their supporters at home. In an endeavour to avoid the evils of monoculture and to make the colony self-supporting in foodstuffs, he fostered the cultivation of manioc and other crops besides sugar. He reduced taxation and allowed liberal credit-terms to the planters to help them rebuild their ruined *engenhos* and to buy Angola slaves. He gave them a form of representative local government, through the creation of municipal and rural councils on which both Portuguese and Dutch colonists could serve, although his efforts to induce the two races to co-operate whole-heartedly met with no lasting success.

On leaving the colony in 1644 he observed that the secret of ruling Pernambuco was to remember that the Dutch merchants attached more importance to their money and goods than to their lives, whereas the Portuguese inhabitants valued courtesy and politeness more than property or pelf. . . .

He stressed the unreliability of evidence extorted under torture, even when this was duly sanctioned by law; and he emphasized the importance of maintaining strict discipline among the garrison, while paying them punctually and feeding them well. All in all, it is not surprising to learn from Fr. Manuel Calado, who was a frequent and welcome guest at government-house, that the Pernambuco Portuguese called Johan Maurits their "Santo Antonio" after the most popular saint in their calendar. His departure was sincerely mourned by the whole colony, Calvinist Netherlands, Catholic Portuguese, and cannibal Tapuyas alike. The total production of sugar during his tenure of office was estimated at 218,220 chests valued at 28 million florins, and the sugar industry was well on the way to complete recovery when he left. It was also during his rule that improved methods of cultivating sugar and tobacco were introduced from Pernambuco into the Antilles, thus giving a great impetus to the economic development of the English and French possessions in the Caribbean. . . .

John Maurits was, as a Brazilian historian recently observed, a true *grand seigneur* who only felt at home in a spacious palace or on an extensive estate. He constructed two country-seats on the island of Antonio Vaz, where he laid out the new city of Mauritsstad, one being called by a Dutch name, "Vrijburg," and the other by a Portuguese, "Boa Vista." Fr. Manuel Calado gives us an entertaining account of John Maurits and his princely tastes in the graphic pages of the *Valeroso Lucideno*.

"The Prince-Count of Nassau was so preoccupied with the construction of his new city, that to induce the *moradores* to build houses, he himself went about very carefully plotting the measurements and laying out the streets, so that the town should look more beautiful. And by means of a dike or levee through the middle of it, he brought the water of the river Capivaribe from the entrance of the bar. Canoes, boats and barges entered by this dike for the use of the *moradores,* underneath wooden bridges which crossed over this dike in some places, as in Holland, so that the island was completely surrounded by water. He also made there a country-seat which cost him many *cruzados,* and in the midst of that sandy and barren waste he planted a garden stocked with every kind of fruit-tree which grows in Brazil, as well as with many others brought from different parts; and by bringing in much other fruitful earth from outside in lighters, together with a great quantity of manure, he made the site as fertile as the most fruitful soil. He planted in this garden two thousand coconut-trees bringing them there from other places, because he asked the *moradores* for them and they sent them to him in carts. He made some long and beautiful avenues of them, like the Alameda of Aranjues, and in other places many trellised vine-arbours and garden-beds of vegetables and flowers, with some summer-houses for gambling and entertainment. Hither came the ladies and his friends to pass the summer holidays, and to enjoy their convivial gatherings, picnics and drinking parties, as is the custom in Holland, to the sound of musical instruments. The Prince liked everyone to come and see his rarities, and he himself delighted in showing and explaining them. And in order to live more at his ease, he left the buildings where he stayed originally, and moved to this country-seat with the greater part of his household.

"He also brought thither every kind of bird and animal that he could find; and since the local *moradores* knew his taste and inclination, each one brought him whatever rare bird or beast he could find in the back-lands. There he brought parrots, macaws, *jacijs, canindes,* wading-birds, pheasants, guinea-fowl, ducks, swans, peacocks, turkeys, a great quantity of barnyard-fowls, and so many doves that they could not be counted. There he kept tigers, ounces, *cissuarana,* ant-bears, apes, *quati,* squirrel-monkeys, Indian boars, goats from Cape Verde, sheep from Angola, *cutia, pagua,* tapirs, wild boars, a great multitude of rabbits — and in short there was not a curious thing in Brazil which he did not have, for the *moradores* sent him these with a good will, since they saw that he was kindly and well-disposed towards them. And thus they also helped him to build these two establishments, both the country-seat Vrijburg where he lived, as well as Boa Vista on the bank of the Capivaribe, where he spent many days strolling around and enjoying himself. For some sent him wood, others tiles and bricks, others lime, and in short they all helped him in what they could." . . .

Fr. Manuel Calado did not exaggerate the popularity of Johan Maurits with the Portuguese of Pernambuco, and not for nothing did they term the heretic but humane and humanist prince their Santo Antonio. As indicated above, Johan Maurits's guiding principle in dealing with the *moradores* was his conviction that if they were treated with courtesy and consideration, they would be more amenable and obedient to the Company's rule than were the Dutch colonists themselves. . . .

Johan Maurits naturally had an uphill task in defending the Catholics against the zeal of the *predikants,* who continually tried to whittle down the amount of religious freedom which the *moradores* had been formally granted. The consistory could not very well refuse to allow liberty of conscience, since this much was guaranteed by the terms of the Company's charter and was enjoyed by Roman Catholics in the United Netherlands; but liberty of public worship was something which they were ill disposed to tolerate. In 1638, for example, the consistory complained of "the great liberty allowed the Papists, even in places which had surrendered unconditionally." The *predikants* pointed out that monks and friars were "allowed to live in their cloisters, draw their incomes and revenues unhindered, and officiate at the marriages of Netherlanders," &c. They petitioned Johan Maurits to stop these practices, as no such liberties were allowed to the Roman Catholics in the Seven Provinces.

Johan Maurits adopted a policy of masterly inactivity towards all these complaints, as he explained in his 'political testimony' of 1644. He gave the *predikants* fair words, and promised to see that all unauthorized Roman Catholic activities were duly curbed; but in fact he deliberately refrained from doing so, and continued to give aid and comfort more or less secretly to Calado and the Capuchins. . . .

Johan Mauritis's religious toleration was even extended to include the Jews, although hatred, ridicule, and contempt for Jewry was the one point on which the *predikants* and the friars were united. Fr. Manuel Calado asserts that the Jews publicly congregated for worship in two synagogues at Recife; and the Calvinist consistory remonstrated against the toleration of Jewish religious practices almost as frequently as they did against "Popish idolatry." The preachers complained that the local Jews were allowed to marry with Christians, convert Christians to Judaism, circumcise Christians, employ Christian servants in their houses, and keep Christian women as their concubines. The consistory considered it the bounden duty of Johan Maurits and his council to stop these unauthorized activities which gave great scandal to Protestants and Catholics alike. Only in Pernambuco, they complained, did the Jews enjoy unlimited freedom; being subjected to some sort of restrictions in every other country in the world. Johan Maurits ignored both these and subsequent protests; although when individual Jews occasionally overstepped the mark by publicly criticizing the Christian religion, such offenders were severely dealt with. Jewish appreciation of Johan Maurits's attitude was convincingly expressed in 1642, when their representative informed the Heeren XIX "that if His Excellency could be paid to stay in this land by the purchase of anything in the world, that they would find no price too great to pay, even if it were their own blood, if only they might retain him."

Since the religious beliefs of the Negroes and the Amerindians (such as they were) was likewise left virtually undisturbed by the authorities, it can be asserted that a greater degree of religious freedom was allowed in Netherlands Brazil during the years of Johan Maurits's rule than anywhere else in the Western world. For this alone his name and fame are deserving of lasting remembrance. Unfortunately, he was too far in advance of his time; and although he kept the peace between the warring factions of Christianity for seven years, even he could not permanently heal the breach made by the Reformation between Catholic and Protestant. . . .

Another barrier between Portuguese and Dutch was formed by their widely differing social habits and customs. Take, for example, their respective attitudes to wine and women. Although Portugal was a wine-producing country, the Portuguese were (and still are) noted for their abstemiousness. The chaplain to the English factory at Lisbon in the last quarter of the seventeenth century just observed: "I believe there is no people in Europe less addicted to that most inexcusable vice of drunkenness than they are, . . . the people of this country, persons of quality more especially, and indeed all who have the least regard to their credit, being very shy of drinking wine." Holland, on the contrary, produced no vines, but wine was cheaper, more plentiful, and better appreciated there than in many wine-drinking countries. A famous Dutch colonial governor wrote of his countrymen in the East, "our nation must drink or die"; and a much-travelled contemporary of his observed that most of the officials of the West India Company "knew nothing but how to drink themselves drunk." We have seen how Fr. Manuel Calado watched with fascinated horror the drinking-bouts over which Johan Maurits jovially presided, although prowess with the bottle was not the only art which was cultivated in Netherlands Brazil.

As for women, the attitude of the Portuguese towards the fair sex was thought to be unduly jealous and restrictive even by the Spaniards, who, like their neighbours, had perhaps inherited their ideas about the seclusion of women from the centuries of Moorish occupation. On the other hand, women in the United Provinces probably enjoyed more freedom than anywhere else in contemporary Europe. Foreign observers frequently noted that most Dutchmen not only discussed matters of business and of state with their wives in private, but drank freely with them in public. This was, of course, the strongest possible contrast to Portuguese practice. The chronicler Duarte Nunes de Leão assures us in his *Descrição do reino de Portugal* (Lisbon, 1610) that women who drank wine were regarded as being in the same category as those who committed adultery. Johan Maurits and his council wrote in 1638 that the local *moradores* jealously secluded their womenfolk, "thus recognizing that the men of their own race are prone to covet their neighbours' wives." . . .

The fact that Recife was one of the most expensive places in the world naturally made the Heeren XIX resentful of Johan Maurits's lavish expenditure. The "Prince of Nassau" had incontestable merits as a governor, statesman, and general, but none as an economist or a financier. He was a free spender of his own and the Company's money, but he never bothered about casting accounts, and he ostentatiously ignored the members of his financial council with whom he seldom deigned to speak. A princely patron of the arts, a keen amateur architect and landscape-gardener, he gave his inclinations full rein, whether in the erection of his costly seat at Vrijburg, in building the bridge between Recife and Mauritsstad, in sending home valuable timber for the Mauritshuis, and in maintaining a galaxy for artists and scientists around him in Brazil. It is true that part of this expenditure came from his own pocket, but most of it was a charge on the Company in one form or another.

The outstanding name among Johan Maurits's entourage is that of the young German scientist, Georg Marcgraf of Liebstadt (1610–44), who was educated at Rostok and Leiden, and who died from fever in Angola at the age of thirty-four and the height of his powers. A modern American scientist has remarked that if he had lived to publish more of his work he might well have become the greatest naturalist since Aristotle. Much of his work has been lost, but what survives is impressive enough. Apart from the botanical and zoological collections which he sent to Europe in 1644, and which continued to be studied down to the nineteenth century, some of the copious notes on natural history which he left were edited and published by his friend Johannes de Laet in the *Historia Naturalis Brasiliae* (Amsterdam and Leiden, 1648). This work contains the first truly scientific study of the fauna and flora of Brazil, a description of the geography and meteorology of Pernambuco, including daily wind and rainfall records, and an ethnographical survey of the local Amerindian races. The illustrations include 200 woodcuts of plants and 222 of animals, birds, insects, and fishes, most of which had never been described before.

Another version of this work appeared in 1658, in which Marcgraf's contributions were mostly embodied with the observations of his colleague, Dr. Piso, and suffered somewhat in the process. In compensation, this edition contains a few of Marcgraf's pioneer astronomical observations in the southern hemisphere, including the eclipse of the sun in 1640. It may be added that Johan Maurits helped Marcgraf by building an observatory for him in one of the towers of Vrijburg, and by ordering all ships' captains to take careful observations of solar and lunar eclipses as well as other celestial phenomena. In addition to being a naturalist and astronomer, Marcgraf was also an accomplished mathematician, surveyor, and cartographer, many of the maps in Barlaeus's truly monumental work being based on his own. He was not the only cartographer on Johan Maurits's staff, and the remarkably accurate charts and maps drawn by these men were not wholly displaced until within living memory.

Even more celebrated, although not so outstanding a scientist, was Marcgraf's Dutch medical colleague, Dr. Willem Piso of Leiden (1611–78). A year younger than Marcgraf and educated at Caen, he followed Johan Maurits to Brazil as his personal physician, returning to Holland with him in 1644. Fr. Manuel Calado declares that the two men quarrelled and became irreconcilable enemies, but he must be exaggerating if he is not entirely mistaken. At any rate, Piso continued to be the count's physician after his return home, and the doctor's studies were published with Johan Maurits's approval and financial support, as Marcgraf's had been ten years before. Piso contributed a lengthy section "De Medicina Brasiliensi" to the *Historia Naturalis Brasiliae* of 1648, which remained an authoritative work on tropical medicine and hygiene until well into the nineteenth century. We owe to Piso, among other things, the first knowledge of ipecacuanha as a cure for dysentery. Piso's interests were not purely scientific. He was a member of the celebrated "Muidencircle," which comprised the cream of Dutch literary and intellectual society, as well as twice dean of the Collegium Medicum at Amsterdam.

Many of the woodcuts which illustrate the works of Barlaeus, Marcgraf, and Piso are derived from the paintings and sketches of Frans Post and Albert Eckhout. These were two of the six artists whom Johan Maurits maintained in Brazil, as he explained to Louis XIV in 1678, when offering the Roi Soleil some specimens of their work. . . . Albert Eckhout (*fl.* 1637–64) specialized in depicting men and animals, and the quality of his work can be judged from the sketches reproduced by Thomsen, and from his lifelike (and life-size) portraits in oils which are preserved in the National Museum at Copenhagen. Better known than Eckhout is his colleague, the landscape-painter

Frans Post of Leiden (1612–80), examples of whose charming paintings of the Brazilian rural scene are to be found in several public and private collections. Both these artists have been the subjects of intensive study within recent years, but nothing has yet been discovered about their four colleagues mentioned in Johan Maurits's letter to Louis XIV.

Johan Maurits was not content with bringing six painters from the Netherlands, but encouraged local talent when he found it. Noticing that a German soldier from Dresden named Zacharias Wagener was a clever draughtsman, he made him his steward and gave him the opportunity of developing his talents. Wagener evidently worked closely with Eckhout, as many of the lively sketches in his *Thierbuch,* or album depicting Brazilian men and beasts, are miniature copies or adaptations of Eckhout's work. Wagener later entered the service of the Dutch East India Company, where he rose to be successively envoy to Canton, chief of the Dutch factory at Nagasaki in Japan, and governor of Cape Colony before his death at Amsterdam in 1668.

It is a thousand pities that Johan Maurits dispersed his magnificent Brazilian collections before his death in 1679. Always a lavish spender and, it must be admitted, avid for titles and other marks of regal or princely favour, he began to dispose of his treasures in 1652, when he handed over a large section to the elector of Brandenburg in exchange for some lands along the Rhine. Two years later he presented several of Eckhout's great pictures and other "curiosities" to the king of Denmark, who acknowledged this gift with the bestowal of the coveted Order of the White Elephant. Finally, a twelvemonth before his death, he offered a large number of pictures to Louis XIV, with the suggestion that they would make excellent designs for a series of Gobelin tapestries. The subjects of these *peintures des Indes,* as they came to be known, included Chilean and Peruvian themes, as well as Brazilian and Angolan. The tapestries, although long in the making, were so successful when finished that they were repeated at intervals on the same looms for the next 120 years. In addition to the surviving pictures of Post and Eckhout, Johan Maurits originated many other paintings and frescoes inspired by the Brazilian scene, some of which survived until lately in Saxony. Unfortunately, most of them have become war casualties, or were accidentally destroyed by fire, such as those at Christiansborg in Denmark and the interior decorations of the Mauritshuis at The Hague. Perhaps the most interesting picture which perished in this way was Eckhout's life-size portrait of Johan Maurits in the midst of a group of Tapuyas.

Johan Maurits's lasting monument remains the sumptuous folio volumes of Barlaeus, Marcgraf, and Piso, which were published under his auspices and which opened a new world to the European ken. This is not to say that they had no precursors, or that the works of the earlier Spanish savants, such as Hernández de Oviedo, Joseph de Acosta, S.J., and Fr. Francisco Ximenez, O.P., were not in themselves extremely valuable. They were, and the same can be said of some Portuguese contributions, such as Brandão's *Diálogos,* and Fr. Christovão de Lisboa's work on the natural history of the Maranhão, both of which, however, remained unpublished for centuries. But the work of Johan Maurits's scientific and artistic team, conducted and co-ordinated under his personal supervision, was less hampered by Aristotelian preconceptions and was inspired by a more rigorous idea of scientific exactitude. This was expressed by Marcgraf when he wrote, "I will not write about anything which I have not actually seen and observed."

Naturally enough, these books had a great and lasting success. We find King John IV writing to his envoy in Holland for a copy of Barlaeus's work within a few weeks of its publication. On the other side of the Atlantic, the Jesuit chronicler Simão de Vasconcellos, writing at Bahia in 1659, refers repeatedly to the books of Marcgraf and Piso which he calls "hua cousa grande." Two centuries later, Lichtenstein, Maximilian prince of Neuwied, Spix, Martius, and many other savants who made South America their field of study frequently drew attention to the accuracy and importance of the pioneer labours of Marcgraf and Piso. In 1912 the American scientist, Dr. E. W. Gudger, observed that the *Historia Naturalis Brasiliae* of 1648 was "probably the most important work on natural history after the revival of learning, and, until the explorations of the prince of Neuwied were made known, certainly the most important work on Brazil." Nor are modern Brazilian historians and scientists backward in their acknowledgements of the debt which their country owes to Johan Maurits and his collaborators in the first purely scientific researches carried out in the New World. . . .

THE AFRICAN THREAT

3. *Palmares: An African Threat in Brazil*

R. K. KENT

Throughout the colonial period Brazil suffered from the chronic instability of its slave society and the threat of slave resistance. Often this resistance took the form of flight from their masters and "the establishment of runaway communities called *ladeiras, mocambos,* or *quilambos.*" Professor Schwartz has made a study of these relatively small but numerous escapee communities in the captaincy of Bahia, which demonstrates their significance

for the understanding of the social and economic history of colonial Brazil.*
The most important single example was the "Black Republic" of Palmares, a community of over five thousand escaped slaves in Alagoas (1630–
1697). The following article shows that Palmares had a significance for
African history as well as for Brazil.

. . . Nothing . . . compares in the annals of Brazilian history with the "Negro Republic" of Palmares in Pernambuco. It spanned almost the entire seventeenth century. Between 1672–94, it withstood on the average one Portuguese expedition every fifteen months. In the last *entrada* against Palmares, a
force of 6,000 took part in 42 days of siege. The Portuguese Crown sustained
a cumulative loss of 400,000 cruzados, or roughly three times the total revenue
lease of eight Brazilian Captaincies in 1612. As Brazil's classic *quilombo,*
Palmares gained two more distinctions. It opened the study of Negro history
in modern Brazil. Minutes of the Brazilian Historical Institute reveal that
Palmares caused lively discussions in 1840, and that search for written materials relative to it began in 1851. Important gaps in knowledge persist, but
enough primary sources have been found and published to trace the development of Palmares, to examine it as a society and government, and to suggest
its significance to both Brazilian and African history.

Early writers attributed the birth of Palmares to Portuguese-Dutch struggles
for Pernambuco, from which slaves profited by escaping in groups. They made
no reference to Palmares as a quilombo. Southey came across the term in a
Minas Gerais decree of 1722. An official letter, sent from Pernambuco to Lisbon in 1692, contains the first and only definition of Palmares as a quilombo
in primary sources. The point is worth stressing. The accepted definition of a
quilombo as a fugitive slave settlement has been continuously applied to Palmares since the turn of this century, and the problem of interpretation has
been more difficult as a result. An early nineteenth-century historian, for example, could easily classify Palmares as the "unusual exception, a real government of escaped Blacks on Brazilian soil." But subsequent identification of the
state which was a major historical event with a mere colony of escaped slaves
could not provide a framework to fit the problem. . . .

Clearly, quilombo does not appear in the vocabulary of early seventeenth-
century Brazil. Instead, the fugitive slave settlement is known as *mocambo,*
an appropriate description since *mu-kambo* in Ambundu means a hideout.
Around 1603, *palmares* was simply any area covered by palm trees. There

* Stuart B. Schwartz, "The Mocambo: Slave Resistance in Colonial Bahia," *Journal
of Social History,* 3 (1970), pp. 313–333.
From "Palmares: An African State in Brazil" by R. K. Kent, *Journal of African History,*
6 (Cambridge University Press, 1965), pp. 161–175, passim. Reprinted by permission.

was no connexion between the Itapicuru mocambo south of Sergipe and the Palmares of Pernambuco. Palmares was not regarded as an ordinary mocambo. By 1612, it had a considerable reputation. It was an organization with which the *moradores* could not cope alone. The foundation of Palmares thus appears to have taken place in 1605/06, possibly earlier, but certainly not later. . . .

All of this leads to the only plausible hypothesis about the founders of Palmares. They must have been Bantu-speaking and could not have belonged exclusively to any sub-group. Palmares was a reaction to a slave-holding society entirely out of step with forms of bondage familiar to Africa. As such, it had to cut across ethnic lines and draw upon all those who managed to escape from various plantations and at different times. The Palmares which emerged out of this amalgam may be glimpsed in a little more detail during the second half of the seventeenth century. . . .

Dutch activities concerning Palmares, from 1640 until the Reijmbach expedition of 1645, are known mainly through Barleus and Nieuhof. They begin with a reconnaissance mission by Bartholomeus Lintz, a Dutch scout who brought back the first rudimentary information about Palmares. Lintz discovered that Palmares was not a single enclave, but a combination of many *kleine* and two *groote* units. The smaller ones were clustered on the left bank of the Gurungumba, six leagues from its confluence with the larger Paraiba and twenty leagues from Alagoas. They contained "about 6,000 Negroes living in numerous huts." The two large *palamars* were deeper inland, thirty leagues from Santo Amaro, in the mountain region of Barriga, and "harboured some 5,000 Negroes." In January 1643, the West India Company sent its Amerindian interpreter, Roelox Baro, with a force of Tapuyas and several Dutch regulars to "put the large Palmares through 'fire and sword,' devastate and plunder the small Palmares." Baro seems to have returned without his men to report that "100 Negroes of Palmares were killed as against one killed and four wounded Dutchmen, our force having captured 31 defenders, including 7 Indians and some mulatto children." The four Dutchmen and a handful of Tapuyas were found two months later. There was no one with them.

A second Dutch expedition left Selgado for Palmares on 26 February 1645. It was headed by Jürgens Reijmbach, an army lieutenant who kept a diary for thirty-six consecutive days. His task was to destroy the two *groote* Palmares. On 18 March Reijmbach reached the first and found that it had been abandoned months earlier. "When we arrived the bush growth was so thick that it took much doing to cut a path through." Three days later, his men located the second one. "Our Brasilenses managed to kill two or three Negroes in the bush but most of the people had vanished." Their king — the few captives told Reijmbach — "knew of the expedition for some time because he had been forewarned from Alagoas." This Palmares, reads the entry of 21 March, is equally half a mile long, its street six feet wide and running along a large swamp, tall trees alongside. . . . There are 220 *casas,* amid them a church, four smithies and a huge *casa de consello;* all kinds of artifacts are to be seen. . . . (The) king rules . . . with iron justice, without permitting any *feticeiros* among the inhabitants; when some Negroes attempt to flee, he sends *crioulos* after them and once retaken their death is swift and of the kind to instill fear, especially among the Angolan Negroes; the king also has another *casa,* some two miles away, with its own rich fields. . . . We asked the Negroes how many of them live (here) and were told some 500, and from what we saw around us as well we presumed that there were 1,500 inhabitants all told. . . . This is the Palmares *grandes* of which so much is heard in Brazil, with its well-kept lands, all kinds of cereals, beautifully irrigated with streamlets.

In military terms, Reijmbach fared no better than his two predecessors, Bartolomeu Bezzerra and Roelox Baro. An undestroyed Palmares, of which "so much is heard in Brazil," remained free of further interference by Pernambucan authorities until 1672. The ensuing two decades can best be described as a period of sustained war which ended in the complete destruction of Palmares in 1694. As is often the case, warfare and more intimate knowledge of the enemy went together, and the growing information about Palmares in the 1670s threw light on its evolution during the twenty-seven years of relative peace. . . .

There was no doubt . . . that Palmares maintained its "real strength" by providing "food as well as security" for the inhabitants — largely tillers of land who planted "every kind of vegetables" and knew how to store them against "wartime and winter." All the inhabitants of Palmares considered themselves:

> subjects of a king who is called *Ganga-Zumba,* which means Great Lord, and he is recognized as such both by those born in Palmares and by those who join them from outside; he has a palatial residence, *casas* for members of his family, and is assisted by guards and officials who have, by custom, *casas* which approach those of royalty. He is treated with all respect due a Monarch and all the honours due a Lord. Those who are in his presence kneel on the ground and strike palm leaves with their hands as sign of appreciation of His excellence. They address him as Majesty and obey him with reverence. He lives in the royal enclave, called *Macoco,* a name which was begotten from the death of an animal on the site. This is the capital of Palmares; it is fortified with parapets full of caltrops, a big danger even when detected. The enclave itself consists of some 1,500 *casas.* There are keepers of law (and) their office

is duplicated elsewhere. And although these barbarians have all but forgotten their subjugation, they have not completely lost allegiance to the Church. There is a *capela,* to which they flock whenever time allows, and *imagens* to which they direct their worship. . . . One of the most crafty, whom they venerate as *paroco,* baptizes and marries them. Baptismals are, however, not identical with the form determined by the Church and the marriage is singularly close to laws of nature. . . . The king has three (women), a *mulata* and two *crioulas.* The first has given him many sons, the other two none. All the foregoing applies to the *cidade principal* of Palmares and it is the king who rules it directly; other *cidades* are in the charge of potentates and major chiefs who govern in his name. The second *cidade* in importance is called *Subupuira* and is ruled by king's brother (Gana) *Zona.* . . . It has 800 *casas* and occupies a site one square league in size, right along the river *Cachingi.* It is here that Negroes are trained to fight our assaults (and weapons are forged there).

Nearly three decades of peace had a number of important results in the internal evolution of Palmares.

Instead of the two major *palmars* of 1645, there were now ten. There was a very substantial element in the Macoco of those native to Palmares, people unfamiliar with *engenho* slavery. Afro-Brazilians continued to enjoy preferential status, but the distinction between *crioulos* and Angolas does not appear to have been as sharp as it was in 1645. There was a greater degree of religious acculturation. The reference to a population composed mainly of those born in Palmares and those who joined from outside suggests that slaves had become less numerous than free commoners. According to Pitta, the only slaves in Palmares were those captured in razzias. But they had the option of going out on raids to secure freedom by returning with a substitute. This is confirmed by Nieuhof, who wrote that the main "business" of *palmaristas* "is to rob the Portuguese of their slaves, who remain in slavery among them, until they have redeemed themselves by stealing another; but such slaves as run over to them, are as free as the rest.". . .

Palmares did not spring from a single social structure. It was, rather, an African political system which came to govern a plural society and thus give continuity to what could have been at best a group of scattered hideouts.

The almost equally long years of peace and war between 1645–94 point to Palmares as a fluctuating "peril." While not necessarily unfair to the merits of a particular event, the Portuguese took it for an article of faith that Palmares was an aggressor state. No written document originating within Palmares has come to light. . . .

Pernambucan authorities did not view Palmares from the perspective of the *moradores* who were in contact with it. They were too far removed from the general area of Palmares. Reijmbach, for example, had to march at a fast clip for twenty days to reach it from the coast, which the Pernambucan governors — Dutch or Portuguese — seldom left. The governors did, however, respond to *morador* pressure. *"Moradores* of this Captaincy, Your Majesty, are not capable of doing much by themselves in this war. . . . At all hours they complain to me of tyrannies they must suffer from [the Negroes of Palmares]." Among the complaints most frequently heard were loss of field hands and domestic servants, loss of settler lives, kidnapping and rape of white women. Two of the common grievances do not stand up too well. Women were a rarity in Palmares and were actively sought during razzias. But female relatives of the *morador* did not constitute the main target, and those occasionally taken were returned unmolested for ransom. Checking the "rape of Sabines" tales, Edison Carneiro discovered one exception to the ransom rule, reported by a Pernambucan soldier in 1682. Equally, close examination of documents in the Ennes and Camara de Alagoas collections — 117 in all — failed to reveal a single substantiated case of a *morador* killed in *palmarista* raids. Settler lives appear to have been lost in the numerous and forever unrecorded "little" *entradas* into Palmares. They were carried out by small private armies of plantation owners who sought to recapture lost hands or to acquire new ones without paying for them. Some of the *moradores* had secret commercial compacts with Palmares, usually exchanging firearms for gold and silver taken in the razzias. Evidence of this is not lacking. A gubernatorial proclamation of 26 November 1670 bitterly denounced "those who possess firearms" and pass them on to *palmaristas* "in disregard of God and local laws." In 1687, the state of Pernambuco empowered a Paulista Colonel-of-Foot to imprison *moradores* merely suspected of relations with Palmares, "irrespective of their station." Town merchants are also known to have carried on an active trade with Palmares, bartering utensils for agricultural produce. More than that, they "were most useful to the Negroes . . . by supplying advance information on expeditions prepared against them (and) for which the Negroes paid dearly." And Reijmbach's entry of 21 March 1645 makes it clear that this relationship was an old one.

Loss of plantation slaves, through raids as well as escape, emerges as the one solid reason behind the *morador-palmarista* conflict. The price of slaves is known to have increased considerably by the late 1660s. The very growth of Palmares served to increase its fame among the plantation slaves. . . .

Six expeditions went into Palmares between 1680–6. Their total cost must have been large. In 1694, the Overseas Council in Lisbon was advised that Palmares caused a cumulative loss of not less than 1,000,000 cruzados to the "people of Pernambuco." The estimate appears exaggerated unless the 400,000 cruzados contributed directly by the Crown was included. A single municipality did, however, spend 3,000 cruzados (109,800 reis) in the fiscal year 1679/80 to cover the running cost of Palmares wars, and a tenfold figure for the local and state treasuries would seem modest for the six years. Casualties aside, the results did not justify the cost. Palmares stood undefeated at the end of 1686. It was apparent that the state of Pernambuco could not deal with Palmares out of its own resources. In March 1687, the new governor, Sotto-Maior, informed Lisbon that he had accepted the services of *bandeirantes* from São Paulo, "at small expense to the treasury of Your Majesty." The Paulistas of the time were Portuguese-Amerindian *metis* and transfrontiersmen, renowned in Brazil for special skills in jungle warfare. Their leader, Domingos Jorge Velho, had written to Sotto-Maior in 1685 asking "for commissions as commander-in-chief and captains in order to subdue . . . (Palmares)." Largely because Lisbon could not be convinced that their services would come cheap, the Paulistas did not reach Pernambuco until 1692. In crossing so great a distance, 192 lives were lost in the backlands of Brazil, and 200 men deserted the Paulista ranks, unable to face "hunger, thirst and agony."

The story of Palmares' final destruction has been told in great detail. Two-thirds of the secondary works discuss the Paulistas and the 1690s, some sixty of the ninety-five documents in the Ennes collection refer to little else, and Ennes has published a useful summary in English. The Paulistas had to fight for two years to reduce Palmares to a single fortified site. After twenty days of siege by the Paulistas, the state of Pernambuco had to provide an additional 3,000 men to keep it going for another twenty-two days. The breakthrough occurred during the night of 5–6 February 1694. Some 200 *palmaristas* fell or hurled themselves — the point has been long debated — "from a rock so high that they were broken to pieces." Hand-to-hand combat took another 200 *palmarista* lives and over 500 "of both sexes and all ages" were captured and sold outside Pernambuco. Zambi, taken alive and wounded, was decapitated on 20 November 1695. The head was exhibited in public "to kill the legend of his immortality." . . .

The service rendered by the destruction of Palmares, wrote one of Brazil's early Africanists, is beyond discussion. It removed the "greatest threat to future evolution of the Brazilian people and civilization — a threat which this new Haiti, if victorious, would have planted (forever) in the heart of Brazil." Indeed, Palmares came quite close to altering the subsequent history of Brazil. Had they not experienced the threat of Palmares in the seventeenth century, the Portuguese might well have found themselves hugging the littoral and facing not one, but a number of independent African states dominating the backlands of eighteenth-century Brazil. In spite of hundreds of *mocambos* which tried to come together, Palmares was never duplicated on Brazilian soil. This is ample testimony of its impact on the Portuguese settler and official.

They organized special units, under *capitães-do-mato* or bush-captains, to hunt for *mocambos* and nip them in the bud. And they sought to prevent, at ports of entry, an over-concentration of African slaves from the same ethnic group or ship. This policy was abandoned in the wake of the Napoleonic wars, and the immediate repercussion came by way of the nine Bahian revolts after 1807. The well-established thesis that uninhibited miscegenation and the corporate nature of the Portuguese society in Brazil produced a successful example of social engineering must also take into account the historical role of Palmares.

Palmares was a centralized kingdom with an elected ruler. Ganga-Zumba delegated territorial power and appointed to office. The most important ones went to his relatives. His nephew, Zambi, was the war chief. Ganga-Zona, the king's brother, was in charge of the arsenal. Interregnum problems do not seem to have troubled Palmares, the history of which spans about five generations of rulers. Zambi's palace revolt did not displace the ruling family. Assuming that Loanda was the main embarkation point for Pernambucan slaves, which is confirmed by the linguistic evidence, the model for Palmares could have come from nowhere else but central Africa. Can it be pinpointed? Internal attitude toward slavery, prostrations before the king, site initiation with animal blood, the placing of the *casa de conselho* in the "main square," or the use of a high rock as part of man-made fortress lead in no particular direction. The names of *mocambo* chiefs suggest a number of possible candidates. The most likely answer is that the political system did not derive from a particular central African model, but from several. Only a far more detailed study of Palmares through additional sources in the archives of Angola and Torre do Tombo could refine the answer. None the less, the most apparent significance of Palmares to African history is that an African political system could be transferred to a different continent; that it could come to govern not only individuals from a variety of ethnic groups in Africa but also those born in Brazil, pitch black or almost white, latinized or close to Amerindian roots; and that it could endure for almost a full century against two European powers, Holland and Portugal. And this is no small tribute to the vitality of traditional African art in governing men.

INDIAN PROBLEMS

4. Sermon Condemning Indian Slavery, 1653: Report on the Conversion of the Nheengaíbas, Letter to Alfonso VI, 1659

ANTÓNIO VIEIRA

António Vieira was born at Lisbon in 1608 of working-class parents, who took him to Brazil at an early age. There he entered the Jesuit order and quickly distinguished himself as a powerful preacher, skillful diplomat, and independent thinker on economic and political problems. His lifespan roughly coincided with the seventeenth century, and he took a leading part in the great events of his day, as Professor Charles R. Boxer shows in his interesting biographic sketch.*

Vieira's missionary efforts on behalf of the Brazilian Indians were both strenuous and continuous throughout his long life. His attempts to curb the colonists as they strove to enslave the Indians in their fields and homes made him extremely unpopular with most of his fellow countrymen in Brazil, including the friars of the Mendicant Order, whom he accused of disregard for the welfare of the Indians. As Professor Boxer concluded:

> Vieira was nothing if not a bonny fighter, but he had the defects of his pugnacious temperament. He did not suffer fools — or friars — gladly, although he remarked resignedly on more than one occasion that even Our Lord with all his miracles had never cured anyone of folly. . . . Above all, in an age when anti-Semitism raged with a virulence only surpassed in our own day and generation, Vieira's fearless championship of the New Christians marks him out as a truly admirable man. António Vieira may not have been what King John IV called him, "the greatest man in the world," but he is entitled to an honoured place not only in the history of Brazil and Portugal but in the story of Western civilization.†

Father Vieira preached this vigorous sermon at a time when many colonists in Brazil were clamoring for royal laws permitting the enslavement of the Indians. The *Report* affords a glimpse of one of the great missionary triumphs in the Amazon area.

* C. R. Boxer, *A Great Luso-Brazilian Figure: Padre António Vieira, S. J., 1608–1697* (London: The Hispanic and Luso-Brazilian Councils, 1957).
† Ibid., p. 32.

Sermon Condemning Indian Slavery, 1653

At what a different price the devil today buys souls compared to what he offered for them previously! There is no market in the world where the devil can get them more cheaply than right here in our own land. In the Gospel, he offered all the kingdoms of the world for one soul; in Maranhão the devil does not need to offer one-tenth as much for all the souls. It is not necessary to offer worlds, nor kingdoms; it is not necessary to offer cities, nor towns, nor villages. All he has to do is offer a couple of Tapuya Indians and at once he is adored on both knees. What a cheap market! An Indian for a soul! That Indian will be your slave for the few days that he lives; and your soul will be a slave for eternity, as long as God is God. This is the contract that the devil makes with you. Not only do you accept it but you pay him money on top of it. . . .

Christians, nobles, and people of Maranhão, do you know what God wants of you during this Lent? That you break the chains of injustice and let free those whom you have captive and oppressed. These are the sins of Maranhão; these are what God commanded me to denounce to you. Christians, God commanded me to clarify these matters to you and so I do it. All of you are in mortal sin; all of you live in a state of condemnation; and all of you are going directly to Hell. Indeed, many are there now and you will soon join them if you do not change your life.

Is it possible that an entire people live in sin, that an entire people will go to hell? Who questions thus does not understand the evil of unjust captivity. The sons of Israel went down into Egypt, and after the death of Joseph, the Pharaoh seized them and made slaves of them. God wanted to liberate those miserable people, and He sent Moses there with no other escort than a rod. God knew that in order to free the captives a rod was sufficient, even though He was dealing with a ruler as tyrannical as Pharaoh and with a people as cruel as the Egyptians. When Pharaoh refused to free the captives, the plagues rained down upon him. The land was covered with frogs and the air clouded with mosquitos; the rivers flowed with blood; the clouds poured forth thunder and lightning. All Egypt was dumbfounded and threatened with death. Do you know what brought those plagues to the earth? Unjust captivity. Who brought to Maranhão the plague of the Dutch? Who brought the smallpox? Who brought hunger and drought? These captives. Moses insisted and pressed the Pharaoh to free the people, and what did Pharaoh respond? He said one thing and he did another. What he said was, I do not know God and

From *A Documentary History of Brazil*, ed. E. Bradford Burns, pp. 82–89. Copyright © 1966 by E. Bradford Burns. Reprinted by permission of Alfred A. Knopf, Inc.

I do not have to free the captives. However, it appears to me proper and I do declare them free. Do you know why you do not give freedom to your illicitly gotten slaves? Because you do not know God. Lack of Faith is the cause of everything. If you possessed true faith, if you believed that there was an eternal Hell, then you would not take so lightly the captivity of a single Tapuya. With what confidence can the devil today say to you: *Si cadens adoraveris me?* With all the confidence of having offered you the world. The devil made this speech: I offer to this man everything; if he is greedy and covetous, he must accept. If he accepts, then, he worships me because greed and covetousness are a form of idolatry. It is an idea expressed by St. Paul. Such was the greed of Pharaoh in wanting to keep and not to free the captive sons of Israel, confessing at the same time that he did not know God. This is what he said.

What he did was to take out after the fleeing Israelites with all the power of his kingdom in order to recapture them. And what happened? The Red Sea opened so that the captives could pass on dry land (because God knows how to make miracles in order to free captives). It did not matter that the Hebrews did not merit this. They were worse than the Tapuyas. A few days later they worshiped a golden calf and of all the six hundred thousand men only two entered into the promised land, but God is so favorable to the cause of liberty that he grants it even to those who do not deserve it. When the Hebrews had reached the other side, Pharaoh entered between the walls of water which were still open, and as he crossed, the waters fell over his army and drowned them all. What impresses me is the way Moses tells this: that the waters enveloped them and the sea drowned them and the earth swallowed them up. Now, if the sea drowned them how could the earth swallow them? Those men, like his, had both a body and a soul. The waters drowned the bodies because they were at the bottom of the sea; the earth swallowed the souls because they descended to Hell. All went to Hell, without a single exception, because where all pursue and all capture, all are condemned. This is an excellent example. Now, let us look at the reasoning.

Any man who deprives others of their freedom and being able to restore that freedom does not do so is condemned. All or nearly all are therefore condemned. You will say to me that even if this were true they did not think about it or know it and that their good faith will save them. I deny that. They did think about it and know it just as you think of it and know it. If they did not think of it nor know it, they ought to have thought of it and to have known it. Some are condemned by their knowledge, others by their doubt, and still others by their ignorance. . . . If only the graves would open and some who died in that unhappy state could appear before you, and in the fire of their misery you could clearly read this truth. Do you know why God does not permit them to appear before you? It is exactly as Abraham said to the rich miser when he asked him to send Lazarus to this world:

Habent Moysen et Prophetas (Luc. 16.29). It is not necessary for one to appear on earth from Hell to tell you the truth because you already have Moses and the Law, you have the prophets and learned men. My brothers, if there are any among you who doubt this, here are the laws, here are the learned men, question them. There are in this State, three religious orders which have members of great virtue and learning. Ask them. Study the matter and inform yourselves. But it is not necessary to question the religious: go to Turkey, go to Hell, because there is no Turk so Turkish in Turkey nor no devil so devilish in Hell who will tell you that a free man can be a slave. Is there one among you with natural intelligence who can deny it? What do you doubt?

I know what you are going to tell me . . . our people, our country, our government cannot be sustained without Indians. Who will fetch a pail of water for us or carry a load of wood? Who will grind our manioc? Will our wives have to do it? Will our sons? In the first place, this is not the state into which I am placing you as you soon will see. But when necessity and conscience require such a thing, I answer yes and repeat again yes. You, your wives, your sons, all of us are able to sustain ourselves with our own labor. It is better to live from your own sweat than from the blood of others! . . .

You will tell me that your slaves are your very feet and hands. Also, you will say how much you love them because you raised them like children and took care of them as you would your very own. It may be so, but Christ said to this land: *Si oculus tuus scandalizat te, erue eum et si manus, vel pes tuus scandalizat te, amputa eum* (Math. 5.29; Marc. 9.42.44). Christ did not mean to say that we should pull out our eyes nor that we ought to cut off our hands and feet. What he meant was that if that which we loved as our eyes harmed us, or that which was as necessary as our hands and feet harmed us, we should cast away from us that source of harm even if it hurts us as if we had cut it off from us. Who amongst you does not love his arm or his hand but should it become gangrenous would not permit its amputation in order to save his life. . . . If, in order to quiet your conscience or save your soul, it is necessary to lose everything and remain as miserable as Job, lose everything.

But take heart, my friends, it is not necessary at such a state, far from it. I have studied the matter carefully and in accordance with the most lenient and favorable opinions and have come to a conclusion by which, with only minor worldy losses, all the inhabitants of this state can ease their consciences and build a better future. Give me your attention.

All the Indians of this State are either those who serve as slaves or those who live as free inhabitants in the King's villages, or those who live in the hinterlands in their natural or free condition. These latter are the ones you go upriver to buy or "to rescue" (as they say), giving the pious verb "to rescue" to a sale so involuntary and violent that at times it is made at pistol point.

These are held, owned, and bequeathed in bad faith: therefore they will be doing no small task if they forgive you for their past treatment. However, if after you have set them free, they, particularly those domestics whom you raised in your house and treated as your children, spontaneously and voluntarily wish to continue to serve you and remain in your home, no one will or can separate them from your service. And what will happen to those who do not wish to remain in your service? These will be obliged to live in the King's villages where they also will serve you in the manner which I shall mention. Each year you will be able to make your expeditions into the interior during which time you can really rescue those who are prisoners ready to be eaten. Those justly saved from death will remain your slaves. Also, all those captured in just wars will be made slaves. Upon this matter the proper judges will be the Governor of the State, the Chief Justice of the State, the Vicars of Maranhão or of Pará, and the Prelates of the four orders: Carmelite, Franciscan, Mercedarian, and the Company of Jesus. All of these who after judgment are qualified to be true captives, will be returned to the inhabitants. And what will happen to those captured in a war not classified as just? And of them will be placed in new villages or divided among the villages which exist today. There, along with the other village Indians they will be hired out to the inhabitants of this State to work for them for six months of every year alternating two months of hired work with two months devoted to their own labors and families. Thus, in this manner, all the Indians of this State will serve the Portuguese either as legitimate slaves, that is those rescued from death or captured in a just war, or those former slaves who freely and voluntarily wish to serve their old masters, or those from the King's villages who will work half the year for the good and growth of the State. It only remains to set the wages of those village Indians for their labor and service. It is a subject which would make any other nation of the world laugh and only in this land is not appreciated. The money of this land is cloth and cotton, and the ordinary price for which the Indians work and will work each month is seven feet of this cloth which has a market value of about twenty cents. An Indian will work for less than a penny a day. It is an insignificant amount and it is unworthy of a man of reason and of Christian faith not to pay such a slight price to save his soul and to avoid Hell.

Could there by anything more moderate? Could there be anything more reasonable than this? Whoever is dissatisfied or discontent with this proposal either is not a Christian or has no understanding. To conclude this point, let us look at the advantages and disadvantages of this proposal.

The single disadvantage is that some of you will lose a few Indians. I promise you they will be very few. But to you who question this, I ask: Do not some of your Indians die or flee? Many do. Will death do what reason will not? Will chance do what a good conscience will not? If smallpox strikes and carries off your Indians, what will you do? You will have to show patience. Well, is it not better to lose the Indians to the service of God than to lose them by a punishment of God? The answer is obvious.

Let us look at the advantages of which there are four principal ones. The first is that you will have a clear conscience. You will no longer live in a state of mortal sin. You will live like Christians, you will be confessed as Christians, you will die like Christians, you will bequeath your goods as Christians. In short, you will go to Heaven and not to Hell, which would certainly be a tragic ending.

The second advantage is that you will remove this curse from your homes. There is no greater curse on a home or a family than to be unjustly supported by the sweat and blood of others. . . .

The third advantage is that in this way more Indians will be rescued from cannibal practices. . . . It is important to invade the forest to save Indians from being killed and eaten.

The fourth and last advantage is that henceforth your proposals on the labor problem will be worthy of submission to His Majesty, and worthy of His Majesty's approval and confirmation. Whoever asks for the illegal and unjust deserves to have the legal and just denied him, and whoever petitions with justice, reason, and good conscience deserves the fulfillment of his request. You know the proposal which you made? It was a proposal which vassals could not make in good conscience, nor could ministers consult it in good conscience. And even if the King might have permitted it, what good would it have done you? If the King permits me to swear falsely, will it mean that the false oath is no sin? If the King permits me to steal, will the theft be any less a sin? The same thing applies to the Indians. The King can command the slaves to be free, but his jurisdiction does not extend to the power to order the free to become slaves. If such a request went to Lisbon, the stones of the street would have to rise up against the men of Maranhão. On the other hand, if you submit a just, legal, and Christian request, those very same stones would take your part. . . .

Report on the Conversion of the Nheengaíbas, Letter to Alfonso VI, November 28, 1659

. . . The great mouth of the Amazon River is obstructed by an island which is larger than the entire kingdom of Portugal and which is inhabited by many tribes of Indians, who are generally called Nheengaíbas because of the many

From *Cartas do Padre António Vieira*, ed. J. Lúcio D'Azevedo (Coimbra: Imprensa da Universidade, 1925), vol. 1, pp. 549–571, passim.

different and incomprehensible languages they speak. At first these tribes received our conquerors with friendship, but after long experience had shown them that the false words of peace with which the conquerors arrived turned into declarations of captivity, they took up arms in defense of their liberty and began to make war on the Portuguese everywhere. . . .

Past governors, and most recently André Vidal de Negreiros, often tried to rid the State of this very troublesome problem, employing all their forces, both Indian and Portuguese, and their most experienced captains in their campaigns. But the only effect of these wars was to strengthen the conviction that the Nheengaíbas were unconquerable because of their audacity, astuteness, and constancy but most of all because of the impregnable position with which nature itself defended them. . . .

Finally, last year, 1658, Governor D. Pedro de Melo arrived with news of the war declared against the Dutch, with whom some of the Nheengaíba nations had long traded because of the nearness of their ports to those of the Northern Cape, where each year they loaded twenty Dutch ships with manatees. The government of Pará realized that if the Nheengaíbas allied themselves with the Dutch, they would become masters of these captaincies, for the State lacked the power to resist them. Accordingly, a private citizen was sent to the Governor to ask for help and for permission to invade the territory of the Nheengaíbas with as large a force as possible before their alliance with the Dutch could render this precaution ineffective and cause the loss of the entire State.

After the justification and necessity for the war had been settled by the vote of all the secular and ecclesiastical dignitaries whose consultation Your Majesty requires, Father António Vieira expressed the opinion that, since the war was being prepared in secret and in order to give it additional justification, peace should first be offered to the Nheengaíbas, but without the soldiers and clash of arms that aroused their suspicions, as had occurred in the time of André Vidal. And since this proposal of peace seemed as hazardous as war because of the ferocity which was ascribed to these people, the same Father volunteered to act as an intermediary. Everyone believed, however, that not only would the Nheengaíbas refuse to consider the peace overtures but that they would reply with arrows to those who bore such a proposal, just as they had done for the twenty years since the outbreak of the war.

On Christmas Day of the same year, 1658, Father Vieira sent two Indian nobles with a letter to all the Nheengaíba tribes in which he assured them that by virtue of Your Majesty's new law, which he had gone to Portugal to seek, unjust captures and all the other injuries done to them by the Portuguese had ended forever. He also said that he would await a message from them so that he might go to their territory and that they were to believe whatever the bearers of the letter said in his name.

The ambassadors, who were themselves of the Nheengaíba nation, set out like persons going to their sacrifice (so great was the horror of the fierceness of these tribes even among those of their own blood). Thus they took their leave, stating that if they had not returned by the end of the next moon, we should conclude that they had been killed or captured. . . .

On Ash Wednesday, when they were no longer expected, the two ambassadors returned, alive and very happy, bringing with them seven Nheengaíba nobles and many other Indians of the same tribes, who were received with the acclamation and demonstrations of joy that were due to such guests. They made a lengthy defense of their conduct, in which they blamed the past war entirely on the Portuguese, as was true, and concluded as follows: "But we gave full credence to the letter of the 'Great Father,' of which we had already heard and who for love of us and of other people of our skin had risked the waves of the sea and had obtained from the King good things for us. Therefore, having forgotten all the injuries of the Portuguese, we have come here to put ourselves in your hands and in the mouths of your firearms. We are certain, however, that with the protection of the priests, of which we will henceforth call ourselves sons, no one will do us harm.". . .

The Father wished to leave with them for their territory at once, but they replied with surprising courtesy that they had hitherto lived like animals under the trees and asked for permission to move one of the Indian settlements down to the edge of the river. They said that after they had built a house and a church in which to receive the Father, they would return in large numbers so that he would be suitably escorted, stating that this would be at the time of St. John, the expression they use to distinguish between winter and summer. Although the Nheengaíbas were still hardly believed, they fulfilled exactly what they promised. Five days before the feast of St. John they arrived at the settlements of Pará with seventeen canoes, which, with thirteen of the Combocas tribe, who also inhabit the same island, brought the number to thirty. In the canoes there were as many nobles, accompanied by so many people that the fortress and city secretly armed itself.

The Father was unable to leave at this time because he was gravely ill. But it was God's will that on August 16 he was able to leave . . . in twelve large canoes, accompanied by nobles from all the Christian tribes and by only six Portuguese, including the master-sergeant of the garrison, in order to indicate our trust. On the fifth day of the journey they entered the river of the Mapuaezes, the Nheengaíba tribe that had promised to build a settlement outside the bush in which to receive the priests. Two leagues from the harbor the nobles came out to meet us in a large and well-equipped canoe which was decorated with plumes of various colors. They were playing horns and shouting *procêmas,* which are cries of happiness and praise that they utter in unison at intervals and are considered the greatest demonstration of joy among them. All of us responded in the same manner. . . .

After they had finally reached the settlement, the priests disembarked, together with the Portuguese and the Christian nobles, and the Nheengaíbas took them to the church, which they had made of palms, according to the custom of the country, and was very clean and well built. It was then dedicated with the name of the Church of the Holy Christ, and a *Te Deum laudamus* was said in thanksgiving. . . .

Messages were then sent to the various tribes. But since the tribes that lived closest to the settlement did not appear in five days, the devil was not idle, introducing into the minds of the Christian Indians and also of the Portuguese such distrust, suspicion, and fear that they almost abandoned the enterprise, which would have been lost forever. Father António Vieira settled the matter by saying to them that he thought their reasons well founded and that they should all leave; he would stay behind with his colleague, for it was they whom the Nheengaíbas were expecting and with whom they would deal.

But on the following day the Mamaianázes, of whom there was the greatest distrust because of their fierceness, began to arrive in their canoes. And so great were their demonstrations of festivity, trust, and true peace that the suspicions and fears of our people gradually disappeared, and soon their faces and minds and even their speech took on a different aspect.

After a large number of nobles had arrived and the new state of affairs had been explained to them at length both by the priests and by the Indian converts, an order was given for the oath of obedience and fidelity to be taken; and so that it might be done with due solemnity and outward ceremony (which is very important for these people, who are ruled by their senses), it was arranged in the following manner. On the right side of the church were the nobles of the Christian tribes, wearing their best clothes but without any weapons other than their swords. On the other side were the pagan nobles, naked and adorned with feathers in the manner of savages, with bows and arrows in their hands. The Portuguese were scattered among them. Father António Vieira then said the mass of the Adoration of the Kings before a richly decorated altar. The Indians heard the mass on bended knee, and it was a great source of consolation to those present to see them beat their breasts and adore the host and chalice with such strong devotion to that very precious blood, which, having been shed for all men, had a more powerful influence on them than on their grandfathers.

After the mass, the Father, still dressed in his sacerdotal vestments, preached a sermon in which he told them through interpreters of the dignity of the place in which they were standing and of their obligation to answer truthfully to all the questions that they would be asked and to faithfully carry out what they promised. Then each of the nobles was asked if he wished to receive the faith of the true God and to be a vassal of the king of Portugal, as were the Portuguese and the Indians of the Christian tribes whose nobles were present. They were also told that vassals were obliged to obey the orders of Your Majesty in everything and to keep perpetual and inviolable peace with all his vassals, being friends to his friends and enemies to his enemies. If they did this, they would enjoy with freedom and security all the possessions and privileges that had been granted to the Indians of this State by Your Majesty in the law of 1655.

They all responded in the affirmative. Only one noble, who was called Piyé and was the most intelligent of all, said that he did not want to make these promises. And since the onlookers were struck by this unexpected reply, he went on to say that "the questions and sermons of the Father should be addressed to the Portuguese and not to the Indians, for they had always been faithful to the King and had always recognized him as their lord from the beginning of the conquest. They had always been friends and servitors of the Portuguese, and if this friendship had been broken, it was the fault of the Portuguese. Therefore, it was the Portuguese who now had to make promises since they had violated them many times, while the Indians had always kept their word."

The reasoning of this savage was greeted with delight, as were the terms which which he qualified his fealty. Then the leading noble came to the altar where the Father was standing and, throwing his bow and arrows to the ground, fell to his knees. With his hands in those of the Father, he swore as follows: "I promise to God and the King of Portugal in my name and in that of all my subjects to have faith in our Lord Jesus Christ and to be the vassal of His Majesty. I also promise to keep perpetual peace with the Portuguese, to be a friend to their friends and an enemy to their enemies, and to fulfill these obligations forever." After this had been said, he kissed the hands of the Father, who gave him his blessing. Then the other nobles did the same in turn.

After the oath-taking had ended, all of them came to embrace the Father, then the Portuguese, and finally the nobles of the Christian tribes, with whom they had also been at war. And it was an occasion for great thanksgiving to God to see the happiness and true friendship with which these embraces were given and received and to hear the things that were said among them in their fashion.

Finally, they all got to their knees and the priests said a *Te Deum laudamus*. After they had left the church, the Christian nobles picked up their bows and arrows, which had been left outside. In order to make a public demonstration of what had been done in the church, the Portuguese removed the balls from their harquebuses, threw them into the river, and fired without them. Then all the nobles broke their arrows and also threw them into the river, thereby fulfilling the statement: *Arcum conteret et confringet arma*. All this was done to the accompaniment of trumpets, horns, drums, and other instruments and of the continuous shouting with which the crowd declared its happiness. . . .

The triumph of the faith was sealed with the erection on the same spot of a very handsome cross, which the fathers did not allow to be touched by any Indian of low rank. Accordingly, fifty-three nobles carried it on their shoulders to the great joy of the Christians and of the tribes, all of whom adored it. The tribes of different languages who came here were the Mamaianás, the Aruans and the Anajás, among whom are included Mapuás, Paucacás, Guajarás, Pixipixis, and others. The number of souls cannot be counted with certainty; some say that it is 40,000. Among those who came was a noble of the Tucujús, which is a province on the mainland of the Amazon, opposite the island of the Nheengaíbas, and it is reported that they greatly exceed the latter in number, both groups totalling more than 100,000 souls. . . .

5. The Indian Policy of Portugal in America

MATHIAS C. KIEMEN

Portuguese and Spanish policies in the New World afford an excellent opportunity for the exercise of the critical and comparative spirit. This is especially true with respect to the treatment of the Indians. Section III brought together much information on Spaniards and Indians. In this selection Dr. Mathias C. Kiemen, of the staff of the American Academy of American Franciscan History, provides the background on Portuguese policy needed for an understanding of the missionary campaigns of António Vieira.

The story of Indian labor legislation in Portuguese America from 1500 to 1755 is a story of the conflict between the European or Europeanized colonists, who wished to enslave the Indian for economic reasons, and the missionaries, who were determined to prevent such a practice. For this purpose the missionaries of the various religious Orders established missions where the Indians under their control were protected from the colonists, civilized according to European standards, and taught the Catholic faith. The two protagonists, in our story, which has never been adequately told, endeavored at various times to influence the course of royal legislation to achieve their respective aims. . . . [p. 131]

Consideration of Indian legislation in the first century of Brazilian coloniza-

From "The Indian Policy of Portugal in America, with Special Reference to the Old State of Maranhão, 1500–1755" by Mathias C. Kiemen, *The Americas*, 5 (1948), pp. 131–171, passim. Reprinted without documentary and explanatory footnotes, by permission of the author and the Academy of American Franciscan History.

tion has shown the development of an ever-increasing interest in slave labor among the colonists. This interest was probably due in part to the essentially *rural* or *plantation* character of Portuguese colonization in America. Gold and silver were not found until the eighteenth century; by force of necessity the early colonists turned for a livelihood first to brazilwood, and then to sugar. For both of these occupations much labor was needed. Where were the laborers to be found? Not in Portugal: the Far East was already draining far too much of that tiny country's manpower; not in the other countries of Europe: they were occupied with religious or economic troubles of their own. In the mind of the Portuguese in Brazil, the answer to the labor problem was twofold: use of the African Negro and use of the native Indian.

The Negro was utilized quite early in Brazil, his hardy physique and greater knowledge of agriculture making him preferable to the weaker native Indian, unused to regular labor. By 1600 there were about 20,000 Africans in the colony. But the supply was uncertain, and the prices were exorbitant. The price of one Negro slave ranged from 50 to 300 *milreis,* a sum equivalent in modern money to from 20 to 100 pounds sterling or about $100 to $500. This alone would limit the importation of a sufficient number to provide adequate labor.

The utilization of the native Indian was the other alternative. And it was to this labor supply, near at hand, that the colonists generally turned. They relied upon the Indian to supply them with food by hunting and fishing, to transport building materials, to row boats up the jungle rivers, to guide them through the forests, to perform domestic work, to labor on sugar plantations and in sugar mills, — in a word, to do almost all the manual labor necessary in a primitive tropical colony.

The nomadic Indian of Brazil was unused to such constant labor and his physical constitution could not long endure it; hence he proved unwilling to work freely for the white colonists. Therefore in mind of the settlers, the only solution was forced labor and slavery of the natives. Against this slavery and its abuses was directed [this] legislation. In these few laws we can see the first moves of the royal government to curb this cruel enslavement-policy of the colonists. Later legislation, to be presently considered, regulated still more exactly the relations between Indian and colonist. The home government experimented during the seventeenth century with different methods of control, until, finally, at the end of the century, the Crown gave control of the Indian definitively to the missionaries of the religious Orders, who in turn, contracted with the colonists for the labor of their mission Indians. . . . [pp. 148–9]

In the struggle for the emancipation of the Indian of Maranhão, the name of Fr. Antônio Vieira of the Society of Jesus looms large. By his influence at the court of Lisbon he introduced many far-reaching reforms in the treatment of the Indians. Fr. Vieira arrived in Maranhão in 1653, armed with a royal letter giving him a free hand to organize the missions and Indian labor. But conditions were very bad in the State of Maranhão when he arrived. In 1652 Baltasar de Sousa Pereira had been sent as *Capitão-Mór* (Military Chief) of Maranhão. In one of the chapters of his *Regimento* he was ordered to free all Indians that had been enslaved up to that time. Unfortunately, this royal order was promulgated a few days after Fr. Vieira arrived in Maranhão. As a result a grave tumult arose, directed against the government, but mainly against the Jesuits, and this provision of the *Regimento* had to be suspended for the time being.

It was in the midst of such tumultuous events that Fr. Vieira arrived with the royal letter of October 21, 1652, giving him full authority to erect churches, establish missions, bring Indians from the backlands, settle them in *aldeias,* etc., as he saw fit. The letter also empowered him to requisition any Indian help, canoes, etc., he might need in his work from the governor or other authorities, who were required to comply on the pain of incurring royal displeasure.

The colonists of Maranhão felt very bitter over the course of events, and they complained to Lisbon in 1653.

> . . . It was deplorable [they said] to compare the situation of this captaincy (Maranhão) with that of the State of Brazil, where every month large numbers of Negro slaves enter. Here the only help is the Indian; and the new settlements, placed on islands and on the shores of rivers, at great distances, cannot dispense with the services of this people [the Indians] for rowers on voyages.

In the face of the complaints, the King passed a new law on October 17, 1653, which in effect was a compromise intended to placate the angry colonists. Under it the captivity of the Indians was to be permitted in the following cases:

1. During a just war. Warfare against the Indians was just when they impeded the preaching of the Gospel and refused to defend the lives and property of the King's vassals.
2. When Indians allied themselves with enemies of Portugal and gave aid against the vassals of the King.
3. When Indians robbed by sea or land, or infested the roads, impeding commerce, etc.
4. When the Indians subject to the King failed in their obligations agreed upon at the beginning of the conquest, by refusing to pay the tributes and not obeying when called upon to work in the King's service or to fight the enemies of the King.
5. When subject Indians ate human flesh.

For any of these reasons, the Indians might justly be captured. *Entradas* or expeditions into the wilderness were authorized for the purpose of ransoming "Indians of the cord," or of securing the possession of Indians who were the legitimate slaves of Indian chiefs, provided that religious accompanied these expeditions to convert the natives. The law of 1653 was obviously a step in a backward direction. There was no time limit on the captivity of the Indians taken. In effect it permitted slavery, although the word is never mentioned.

Vieira, who had been absent in the interior when the latest law was promulgated, left for Portugal in 1654, to endeavor to change the King's mind on the matter of Indian slavery, for Vieira realized that all missionary work would be in vain unless the law were changed. He succeeded partially in his effort. A *Junta* of the principal theologians and lawyers of the kingdom was called at which the question of Indian servitude was discussed. The Archbishop of Braga presided, and the prelates of the religious Orders working in Maranhão were also present, together with Vieira, who represented the Jesuits, the procurators of Maranhão and Grão Pará who had been sent by the colonists to Portugal, and André Vidal de Negreiros, who was to be the new governor of the State of Maranhão. After the deliberations were over, the King passed the compromise law of April 9, 1655. In substance, it decreed that

1. A *Junta das Missões e Propagação da Fé* (Committee on Missions and Propagation of the Faith) be established, as a kind of consultive tribunal, with its authority restricted to matters dealing with missionary problems and Indian slavery.

2. The *aldeias* and the Indians of the whole state be governed and be under the discipline of the Jesuits alone. Antônio Vieira, as superior of all the missions, was authorized to determine the sites of the missions, to grant or refuse permission for *entradas* to the backlands, and to dispose of the converted Indians as he should judge it most convenient.

3. The governors must give all help and favor to the missionaries, so that they may be enabled to convert the Indians and avoid the tyranny of the past.

4. The missionaries were to have a vote in the destination of the captured slaves, in order to prevent violence to the Indians of the *Sertão*. The person selected to head the *entradas* was to be approved by the same missionaries, and the location of the new missions was to be at the same choice of the Father Superior of the missions.

5. The Christian Indians and inhabitants of the *aldeias* were not to be forced to serve more than six months of each year for the colonists. Such Indians were to be paid two *varas* or yards of cloth for each month of labor.

The law was a disappointment in that it did nothing regarding the principle of enslavement, nor did it define what constituted a just war. Perpetual captivity was still allowed in four cases, i.e., when the Indians were taken in a just war; when they impeded the preaching of the Gospel; when they were "Indians of the cord" and were ransomed by the Portuguese; and finally, when they were sold to the Portuguese by other Indians, who had taken them in a war of their own. The great innovation in the law of 1655 consisted in the turning over of all power over the Indians to the Jesuit Fathers, or rather, to Fr. Vieira. As regards the economic life the State of Maranhão, this made the colonists more or less subject to the Society of Jesus, since slaves were necessary for the development of the country.

To safeguard the Jesuit control over the Indians, the King on April 14, 1655, issued a *Regimento* to the new governor of the State of Maranhão, André Vidal de Negreiros, ordering him to place his authority solidly behind the Jesuits. The *Regimento* provided that the division of the captured Indians was to be made by two judges, one from the *Câmara* or city council, and the other from among the missionaries. It further provided that a record be kept of the Indians farmed out to work, and for whom, so that the colonists, rich and poor, might best be served. The Father Superior of the missions was ordered to determine the time of the *entradas;* the governor, to furnish an armed guard where this was necessary. The number of Indian villages was to be reduced, but the population of each was to be increased. Wherever possible, each village was to contain at least 150 houses, so that the Indians might be better taught the Catholic religion. Again, the governor was urged to make vassals out of as many Indian tribes as were willing to submit; no harm, however, would be done to those who refused.

When this latest piece of legislation was made known in the State of Maranhão, it provoked general discontent, both among the settlers and the other religious. The people saw themselves stopped in their efforts to obtain as many slaves as they desired; the other religious looked with displeasure on the monopoly of Vieira and the Jesuits. Both people and religious felt that Vieira had gone too far in his demands. So strong, in fact, was the opposition that only the firm hand of Governor Negreiros kept the people from revolting against the law. Fr. Vieira was aware of the opposition. On December 8, 1655, he wrote to King John IV:

> We have against us the people, the religious Orders, the donataries of the major captaincies, and also all those who in that Kingdom and State are interested in the blood and sweat of the Indians, who minority we alone defend.

Despite the temper of the colonists and the repeated protests that were made at the Court of Lisbon, the law was sullenly complied with at the insistence of Vieira. During the next five years (1655–1660) the reduction of Indians in *aldeias* was carried out unmolestedly. By the end of the year 1655, the Jesuits controlled 54 such *aldeias* in the State of Maranhão. Vieira, meanwhile, realizing their needs, tried to placate the colonists by organizing large *entradas* into the interior. Of the Indians brought back on these raids, the larger number went to the Jesuit missions, but many were enslaved, according to the precepts of the law.

Such raids, however, were apparently nothing more than palliatives. On January 15, 1661, the *Senado,* or town council, of São Luiz sent a strong representation to Fr. Vieira, setting forth the misery of the people who, as the *Senado* alleged, because of the lack of Indian labor could not make enough money to pay their taxes or support the army. In his reply, couched in moderate terms, Vieira observed that the suffering of the Portuguese also proceeded from causes other than the one alleged, and promised more slaves for the use of the people, as the result of the *entradas* then in progress or planned. Vieira's answer did not satisfy the members of the *Senado,* who sent a more sharply-worded letter to the priest on February 15. The second letter accused the Jesuits, among other things, of entirely overstepping legal bounds in taking complete temporal control of the converted Indians; to which Fr. Vieira replied that he could do nothing more than he had already promised.

The storm that arose between the settlers and the Jesuits broke in 1661. The colonists rose up against the Jesuits in São Luiz, and the revolt spread north. Before long the Jesuits were imprisoned in their colleges, and finally were put on board ships and sent to Lisbon. A few Jesuits in the backlands managed to escape the fury for a few months, but by the beginning of 1662 all members of the Company were either detained or on their way to Portugal [pp. 158–63].

Father Vieira was among the Jesuits expelled from Maranhão by the enraged colonists. As soon as he arrived in Portugal he went to the Queen Regent, Luiza de Gusmão, and told her what had occurred. So cogent, apparently, were his arguments that within a year the Jesuits had royal permission to go back to their missions in Maranhão, with the same extensive powers which they had formerly enjoyed. Vieira's triumph, however, was short-lived. In 1662 a palace-revolution deprived Queen Luiza of power, and the crown prince became king as Afonso VI. The new king was definitely not as friendly to Father Vieira as the Queen Mother was. He banished the Jesuit from Court, and gave a ready ear to Vieira's enemies. Out of this about-face in court circles came the law of September 12, 1663.

This law, in effect, was a return to the legislation of 1653. . . [p. 164]. The Jesuits, therefore, were allowed to continue in their missions, although their power over mission activity generally was curtailed. An exception, however, was made in the case of Father Vieira, whose services were not reputed advantageous to the King.

Father Vieira, in fact, was in grace difficulty in Portugal. He was haled before the Inquisition for alleged errors of faith contained in his preachings and in an unpublished book called *History of the Future*. Accused of Judaism and other errors, Vieira, according to Leite, was condemned to the privation of the right of preaching and of his active and passive voice forever, and to confinement for an indefinite period in a house of the Society. But his defeat was not permanent. When Dom Pedro II came into power on November 23, 1667, he freed Vieira and restored all the prestige formerly his under King John IV.

Despite the rebuff of the Jesuits and the passage of the law of 1663, which, from the point of view of the settlers, was in many ways an improvement over previous legislation, the colonists were not satisfied, and received the new law very coldly. They were displeased with the provisions limiting the forays into the interior to official *entradas*. So violent was the reaction that in São Luiz it was impossible to execute the law. In Belém an attempt was made by the *câmara* to carry out the prescripts of the law, but without much success. The temper of the people was such that governmental interference was not immediately possible. Only in 1673 was the law observed in all its rigor in the captaincy of Maranhão; in Pará it was never observed at all.

It was not until 1680 that the administrative anarchy in the State of Maranhão over the Indian question was ended. One of the factors in the return to normality was the law of April 1, 1680, inspired by Father Vieira. The Jesuit missionary, now bowed with age, had returned to royal favor in 1667 when Pedro II ascended the throne. Until his death in 1697 he was to keep within the good graces of the king.

The law of April 1, 1680, is one of the best known pieces of Portuguese legislation on Indian labor, and the most often quoted in any discussion of Portugal's Indian policy. After a long preamble, in which the laws of 1570, 1587, 1595, 1653, and 1655 were acknowledged as failures, the law decrees:

1. That, renewing the disposition of the law of 1609, *no Indian shall henceforth be enslaved in any capacity,* not even in cases permitted in the earlier laws.
2. That if any person of whatever quality or condition, captures or orders the capture of Indians, under any title or pretext, he shall be arrested by the *ouvidor geral* of the State and sent on the first ship to Portugal.
3. That the *ouvidor* shall immediately place at liberty the Indians already captured and send them to *aldeias* if they are Catholic Indians.
4. That the governor, the bishop [Dom Gregorio dos Anjos, Bishop of Maranhão], and the prelates of religious Orders in the State shall take care to inform the king of any infractions of the law, so that the proper measures may be taken.
5. That Indians taken in an authorized defensive or offensive war shall

be treated not as slaves but as prisoners of war, as the term was understood in Europe.

6. That the governor alone shall have the power to apportion the Indians among the *aldeias* of free Indians, where they may be converted to the Faith, be treated properly, and serve the State, while yet retaining their liberty.

7. That those who inflict any harm on the Indians shall be severely chastized, and those who do so during the time the Indians are working for them shall be even more severely punished.

On the day that the law was put into effect, a series of royal orders was promulgated for the purpose of clarifying certain details. These royal orders, among other things, ordained the following:

1. That every year five or six hundred Negroes shall be offered for sale in the State of Maranhão at moderate prices to take the place of Indian slaves.

2. That the Indians capable of working shall be divided into three groups: one third shall remain at the *aldeias* for the purpose of working for themselves and families; one third shall serve the colonists; and one third shall be used to accompany the missionaries to the interior missions. The division of these Indians shall be made by the bishop together with the Superior of the Franciscan Province of Santo Antônio, in Maranhão, and with one other person elected by the *câmara,* on the basis of lists furnished them by the pastors of the *aldeias.*

3. That missions to the interior shall be made only by the religious of the Society of Jesus.

4. That the *aldeias* of Christianized Indians shall be controlled by their pastors and their own chiefs, and not by captains or administrators of any kind.

5. That the Jesuits shall control all *aldeias* of Christianized Indians, except those which other religious may have had before the coming of the bishop to the state of Maranhão.

6. That all the other *aldeias* along the Gurupá and Amazon Rivers and those without pastors of their own shall be turned over to the Jesuits.

7. That the Jesuits shall be pastors of all Indians brought from the interior and of the *aldeias* and churches that may be newly established.

8. That no Indian shall be allowed to serve the colonists until his wages shall have first been deposited by them.

9. That the Jesuits shall be in charge of missions set up in the interior

for the more remote Indians who cannot or will not live among the Portuguese.

The most significant point in the legislation of 1680 is the proposal to use Negro in place of Indian slaves. If it is true, as all authors say, that Father Vieira is the sponsor of the legislation of 1680, he must be held responsible for the clause on the introduction of Negroes. This is further proof of the fact that at least some ecclesiastics of the time did not condemn slavery as such, but rather the horrors of enslavement as it was then practiced. One other point is significant; the Jesuits were endeavoring once more to obtain a monopoly over the Indian missions at the expense of the other religious Orders, notably the Franciscans. Furthermore, the clause permitting the Jesuits to establish missions far in the interior, from which the Indians could bring their products to the coast settlements for trade, carried the seeds of future discord. In the eighteenth century the enemies of the Jesuits were to charge them with using their Indian wards for commercial gain. . . [pp. 165–9].

In February, 1684, a few malcontents, led by Manuel Beckman or Bequimão, a rich proprietor, seized the governor and the missionaries. Beckman won the support of his followers by promising them slaves. The revolt, however, was purely local; it never spread beyond the borders of the captaincy of Maranhão. Pará, for example, because of its dislike of Maranhão, never took part in the uprising.

As a result of the uprising, the Jesuits were expelled once more from Maranhão. But this time the home government did not side with their enemies. Insofar as the Crown was concerned, the question was not merely one of Indian slavery; the very principle of authority had been impugned. General Gomes Freire de Andrade was therefore given extraordinary powers to put down the revolt, which he did in 1685, and by September 23 of that year, the Jesuits were back.

The events of 1684–1685 mark a turning point in the Jesuit attitude towards the missions of Maranhão. A dilemma was now posed to the Fathers of the Society. Should they forsake the mission field and retire to other work, or should they adapt themselves to local conditions and give up their idea of monopolizing the control of the Indians? Both possibilities were discussed by the Order in Maranhão. The Jesuits finally compromised. They would no longer oppose the admittance of other religious Orders to the government of the Indians, and they would be more generous in answering the demands of the colonists for Indian laborers. With this compromise the Jesuits were able to remain comparatively unmolested in Maranhão until 1755 [pp. 170–1].

Juana Inés de la Cruz, Poet and Scholar in Seventeenth-Century Mexico. This famous nun and outstanding poet of the Hispanic world in the seventeenth century is portrayed, quietly seated, in the only painting that has come down to us. But she was an independent thinker, too, whose life was one great struggle to develop her immense talent in the conservative society of her time (Reading 3). She did not disdain manual labor and found inspiration in everyday concerns, for she once remarked that if Aristotle had been a cook and had observed what went on in a kitchen he would have had many more ideas.

SECTION VII

The Development of Society

THE POSITION OF WOMEN

The history of the women of Latin America has not yet been written or even attempted, though there is rich documentation on the subject. Apparently historians have considered women scarcely worth writing about. They were convinced that very few Iberian women went to the New World, the conquistadors mated with the Indian women to produce a mixed race, so what more was there to say? Then Richard Konetzke, the distinguished German historian who revived Latin American studies at the University of Cologne after World War II, demonstrated that there was a great deal more that could and should be said. Though few women went to America in the early, rough days of conquest, the Crown steadfastly encouraged women to migrate in order to establish a sound Spanish society. A permanent society would not develop without women to establish stable homes, and matrimony was favored in every way the Crown could think of.[1]

Professor James Lockhart has illustrated how sound were these views by publishing a pioneer work on the social history of Peru that is bound to have a powerful influence in turning the attention of students to the rich possibilities of the field. The selection on the second generation of women in Peru shows his methods and their exciting results (Reading 1). Brazilian women are even less known, but Dr. A. J. R. Russell-Wood turned up in his researches on the Misericórdia (Brotherhood) of Bahia much valuable information on dowries for women, which also reveals much of their position in colonial society (Reading 2).

[1] Richard Konetzke, "La emigración de mujeres españolas a América durante la época colonial," *Revista Internacional de Sociología* (Madrid), 3 (1945), pp. 123–150.

257

BIOGRAPHICAL SOURCES

One of the noticeable deficiencies of our present documentation is that so much of it is limited to official or legal sources. Some material on the life of merchants is coming to light, which should greatly enlarge our understanding because business played such a large role.[2] And at long last, private letters on family affairs are being printed to reveal more intimate aspects of colonial life.[3] But much more can and should be done to widen the documentary base.

Another important initiative has been the demonstration by Professor Lockhart of the value of biographical sources; indeed, he has stimulated the present experiment in this section to provide a variety of sources on the lives of Spaniards in America that constitute the raw material for social history. Some of these sources are statements drawn up by individuals to convince the government that they merited preferment or position, while others are remarkable vignettes carved by Professor Lockhart out of the solid rock of archival collections to tell the story of the "Men of Cajamarca," that blue-ribbon group of men who captured Atahualpa in Cajamarca on November 16, 1532. Sometime we may have an adequate biographical dictionary, whose need was recognized long ago by Marcos Jiménez de la Espada. He planned to produce such a work, but never achieved it.[4]

TENSIONS IN COLONIAL LIFE

The colonial centuries have often been presented as a quiet, even dull time when nothing much happened. This was largely due to the ignorance of his-

---

[2] Guillermo Lohmann Villena, *Les Espinosa: Une famille d'hommes d'affaires en Espagne et aux Indies à l'époque de la colonisation* (Paris: École Pratiques des Hautes Études, 1968); Enrique Otte, "Mercaderes burgaleses en los indicios del comercio con México," *Historia Mexicana*, 18 (1968), pp. 108–144, 258–285; "Los mercaderes vascos y los Pizarro: cartas inéditas de Gonzalo y Hernando Pizarro y su mayordomo Diego Martín," *Travaux de l'Institut d'Études Latino-Américaines de l'Université de Strasbourg*, 6 (1966), pp. 25–42; and "Mercaderes vascos en Tierra Firme a raiz del descubrimiento del Perú," *Mercurio Peruano*, nos. 443–444 (1964) (Libro Jubilar de Víctor Andrés Belaúnde), pp. 81–89.

[3] Professor Enrique Otte of the Free University of Berlin has started to publish family letters that he discovered during his long experience in the Archive of the Indies. As samples, see his "Nueve cartas de Diego de Ordás," *Historia Mexicana*, 14 (1964), pp. 102–129, 321–338; "Cartas privadas de Puebla del siglo XVI," *Jahrbuch für Geschichte von Staat Wirtschaft und Gesellschaft lateinamerikas*, 3 (Cologne, 1960), pp. 10–87; "Semblanza espiritual del poblador de Indias (siglos XVI y XVII)," *Verhandlungen des XXXVIII: Internationalen Amerikanistenkongresses*, 3 (Munich, 1970), pp. 441–449; and "La Nueva España en 1529," *Historia y sociedad en el mundo de habla española: Homenaje a José Miranda* (Mexico: El Colegio de México, 1971), pp. 95–111.

[4] Marcos Jiménez de la Espada, *Relaciones Geográficas de Indias: Peru*, 1 (Madrid, 1965), p. xxxix.

torians, for we now know that it was a time of tensions. In Brazil, there was civil war in the mining camps, while in Mexico the relatively small number of Negro slaves nevertheless caused much concern because of their revolts. Riots resulting from economic problems sometimes occurred in Mexico City (Reading 4). Moreover, in Mexico the native-born Spaniards lost out to the men from the mother country, which led to widespread frustration, and in Peru rivalry between friars from Spain and those born in Peru led to bloodshed and a continuing bitterness (Reading 5). The loud cries of anguish by the *criollos* on discrimination against them may have been somewhat exaggerated, at least in Peru. A recent study shows that the judges of the Audiencia of Lima were predominantly creoles: "The creole aristocrats in Peru were no powerless political ingenues. Rather they had built up an extremely strong position combining local wealth and social prominence with high administrative and judicial position." [5] Tensions existed among all sections of society in the booming mining camp, at the Villa Imperial de Potosí, for this mountain of silver in the high Andes exemplified in gaudy colors the passion for wealth that drew many Spaniards to the New World (Reading 6).

INDIAN MOBILITY

Another element in the varied pattern of emerging society was the Indians. Some few were able to enter Spanish society, at least to some extent, while others were able to increase their wealth and power by taking advantage of the opportunities offered by the economic and administrative structure introduced by the Spaniards. So there was some mobility, at least for the men.

COLONIAL SOCIETY NOT MONOLITHIC

All of these readings tend to reinforce the idea that Iberian colonial society varied from region to region, and from century to century. We have no volume

[5] Leon G. Campbell, "A Colonial Establishment: Creole Domination of the Audiencia of Lima During the Late Eighteenth Century," *Hispanic American Historical Review,* 52 (1972), p. 20. Professor Campbell supports his interpretation with biographic sources. See his "Survey of Career, Data, Connections, and Property of the Judges of the Audiencia of Lima, 1777," ibid., pp. 21–25.

as yet comparable to Eileen Powers's *Medieval People* or S. E. Morison's *Builders of the Bay Colony*. Eventually our historians will go beyond lapidary phrases, if they follow the lead of Konetzke, Lockhart, and others. Magnus Mörner has already provided a realistic view of the eighteenth-century ruler Pombal's support for marriages in Brazil of Portuguese settlers with Indians.[6] He struck off a splendid phrase: "His Majesty does not distinguish between his vassals by their color but by their merits." But this "liberal" policy toward Indians was deeply rooted in political objectives including his relentless struggle against the Jesuits, whom he expelled in 1767, and it did not extend to Negroes in Brazil.

Similarly we probably will have to free ourselves of such easy generalizations as the famous one by Cervantes, who failed to get the job in America that he had hoped for but felt he knew enough to describe the people there in this fashion: "The refuge and haven of all the poor devils of Spain, the sanctuary of the bankrupt, the safeguard of murderers, the way out for gamblers, the pomised land for ladies of easy virtue, and a lure and disillusionment for the many, and a personal remedy for the very few." [7]

[6] Magnus Mörner, *Race Mixture in the History of Latin America* (Boston: Little, Brown and Company, 1967), pp. 50–51.

[7] As quoted by Charles R. Boxer, *Race Relations in the Portuguese Colonial Empire, 1415–1825* (Oxford: Clarendon Press, 1963), p. 86.

WOMEN

1. Spanish Women of the Second Generation in Peru

JAMES LOCKHART

Here Professor Lockhart uses evidence from notarial and judicial documents to challenge the myth that Spanish women took little part in the early settlement of Peru. As this selection shows, they in fact formed a large minority in the colony's population and exerted an even greater cultural influence than their numbers might suggest.

Spanish women constituted a large minority of the settlers in Peru in the conquest period, and their significance was even greater than their numbers, for although women from home were not numerous enough to give every Spaniard a wife, they sufficed to keep Spanish Peru from being truly a society without women. The analysis Gilberto Freyre made of Brazilian society, that in the absence of European women, Indian women largely determined early Brazilian culture insofar as it had to do with the household, cannot be applied to Peru. While Indian influence was important, both immediately and over time, Peru even in the first generation had enough Spanish women to preclude the simple loss of any important culture elements.

Nevertheless, assessing the role of Spanish women in conquest Peru is a delicate task. In view of the old tradition among historians of ignoring them, the cultural and biological contribution of Spanish women to the building of a European society in Peru requires emphasis. Spanish women were commonly present at almost all times and places during the early occupation of Peru, and therefore cannot be considered a rarity. On the other hand, there can be no doubt that in Spanish Peruvian society, as in any new community, women were greatly outnumbered by men. Tabulations for the Indies as a whole, based on the *Pasajeros a Indias,* have indicated a ratio of about ten to one. As suggested by Richard Konetzke, however, the actual proportion of women in the Indies must have been higher than it had been at emigration, because of

From *Spanish Peru, 1532–1560* by James Lockhart (Madison: University of Wisconsin Press, © 1968 by the Regents of the University of Wisconsin), pp. 150–169, passim. Reprinted by permission.

the higher mortality among men. For Peru this was a factor of more than usual significance, with the major Indian rebellion, twenty years of civil wars, and innumerable expeditions of discovery into surrounding jungle areas.

A list of Spanish and apparently Spanish women in Peru during the period of 1532–60, assembled from all sources used for the present study, reached a total of 550, but this figure is even more ambiguous raw material for arriving at an overall estimate than was the similar list of artisans, since women had little occasion to appear in notarial and official records. Therefore, it is reasonable to think that the list of 550 women, brought together from the same archival sources as the more than 800 artisans, is a much smaller fraction of the total than in the latter case; but there is no firm basis for even the rudest approximation of a statistical estimate.

A second element of uncertainty in the listing is the quite broad interpretation Spaniards were willing to give to the concept of a Spanish woman. Women were identified in legal records only as to their marital status, but Spanish women were recognizable as not being specifically called Negro, Indian, or mestizo. The Spanish secretaries were very consistent in specifying Negro and Indian women; with mestizo women, particularly daughters of prominent Spaniards, they were somewhat less so, but this group did not become important until the late 1550's. There was, however, hesitance and inconsistency, both in fact and in the matter of their explicit identification in documents, when it came to two groups who were in the process of being absorbed among the ordinary Castilian women: the *moriscas* and certain light-skinned, Spanish-speaking mulatto women. The moriscas, slave women of Muslim descent, were for the most part Caucasian, Spanish-born, and converted to Christianity, and they spoke Spanish as a native language. Fully acculturated mulatto women were also usually born in Spain or an older colony. Slave-mistresses of both types often obtained their freedom, and married Spaniards or in other ways took their places among the ranks of Spanish women, which they might well do, considering their birthplace. It is particularly hard to find reasons to deny full status as Spanish women to the moriscas who were simply undergoing a process familiar for centuries in Spain's Christian reconquest.

At any rate, one must keep in mind that Spanish women included a minority of moriscas and mulatto women with, after 1555, the addition of some mestizo women. To define the size of the minority is statistically impossible, but it can hardly have been more than a tenth of all ostensibly Spanish women. To make a rough commonsense estimate, then, of the statistical importance of Spanish women, including the women from ethnic minority groups who were accepted as Spanish, and taking into consideration the *Pasajeros a Indias,* Konetzke, and the implications of the list made for the present study, it appears probable that from the early 1540's on, Peru had one Spanish woman for every seven or eight men, in absolute numbers perhaps three or four hundred women by 1543 and a thousand by 1555.

Few Spanish women, except moriscas, took part in the actual conquest of Peru in the years 1532–35, but followed close behind the fighting. . . . The number of Spanish women would seem to have grown quite steadily until 1548, when, with the end of the great Gonzalo Pizarro rebellion, they came into the country at a much faster rate than before. By 1548 enough time had elapsed so that a very large number of Spanish Peruvians had roots in the country, were sure they wanted to stay, and sent for female relatives, such a summons being the principal mechanism for the entry of Spanish women.

As the relatives of the male Spanish Peruvians, the women shared the social and regional origins of the rest of the population. A sampling of the regional origins of Spanish women showed all the principal regions in their usual order, and close to their usual proportions of the total. Andalusia was at the head of the list, as was to be expected, but Andalusian women had already lost the overwhelming numerical superiority they apparently had in the Caribbean area in the early years of the sixteenth century. . . .

The social quality of Spanish women in Peru was as varied as that of the men, ranging from the sisters of fishermen to the daughters of counts. Just as with men, there took place over the years a rise in average social status on the Spanish scale, as the wealth of Peru attracted people from an ever broader spectrum of Spanish society. It would be hard to say whether social origin had more or less importance among the men than among the women. On the one hand, a woman who could buy fine clothes and learn to imitate polite behavior could make herself more nearly the equal of high society than could a man, who faced the barrier of literacy. For while some ladies could read and write and play keyboard instruments, such accomplishments were far from universal even at the highest level. On the other hand, the use of the "doña" drew a sharp line down the middle of the female population, based on Spanish peninsular distinctions. . . .

Many of the encomenderos' wives in the 1530's, having been married in Spain before their husband became rich, or picked from the generally plebeian women already in the Indies at that time, did not boast the title "doña." After the 1540's, the encomenderos married practically only doñas, and the older ladies' lack of title was sorely felt, but no change was possible. It could happen that their younger sisters, brought to Peru to share the family's good fortune and to make advantageous matches, would be allowed to assume the "doña" which was denied the rich and powerful patronesses. For the second generation, the "doña" was standard for the legitimate daughter of any encomendero, whether the mother bore the title or not, and was commonly allowed to the daughters of any prominent and wealthy man. . . .

Family and regional ties were even more important for women than for men. The great majority of women either arrived as part of a family, or were sent for by male relatives already in Peru. The motive was usually to seek marriage or join a husband. If the husband died, as could happen without a moment's notice in tumultuous Peru, the woman would be thrown completely on family and compatriots, for unless she was wealthy, a widow or single woman could sustain herself only with difficulty or loss of honor.

Probably nine-tenths of all adult Spanish women were married. Previous chapters have indicated how marriage was, though not universal, the rule among encomenderos and established artisans; it was common for lawyers, doctors, notaries, and shipmasters, and not unknown among merchants. All this added up to a formidable demand for marriageable women. The natural desire to form matches was given urgency among the Spaniards by their particularly strong drive to perpetuate and enhance their lineage, and by the importance of an honorable, legitimate wife in the Spanish ideal of life. The official threat to deport all those who, having wives in Spain, failed to have them brought to the Indies, cannot be considered a major factor. Most of the time, and for most people, it was a dead letter, though governors could rid themselves of troublesome individuals by invoking it, and the royal officials could use it to extort money.

There was only one area where official policy had a strong effect in encouraging marriage, though there it was admittedly of utmost importance. While an encomendero could hope to avoid the various royal ordinances threatening to take away the encomiendas of those who did not marry, he had no chance of passing his encomienda on to his heirs unless he married and had legitimate children. At this point official policy became a serious matter, for the deadly competition to secure encomiendas would allow nothing else. Many encomenderos had their mestizo sons legitimated to inherit their property, but legitimation was never allowed to include the right to succeed in the father's encomienda, except for the children of Francisco Pizarro and one other noted captain. The encomendero's incentives to marry were increased even more by the prospect, then still very much alive, that the encomienda could be converted into a perpetual fief and family possession. With these motivations, some encomenderos began to marry or bring their wives to Peru as soon as, or even before, the first phase of the conquest was ended. Ten years after the conquest, a large minority, perhaps a third, had their wives with them; in certain more settled areas like Lima, Trujillo, and Piura the proportion was no doubt greater. By the early 1550's two-thirds of the encomenderos of highland Cuzco were married; and in 1563 there were only thirty-two encomenderos left unmarried in all Peru, of almost five hundred.

Certain aspects of marriage were the same whether the man was an encomendero or an artisan, the wife wellborn or plebeian. Practically all marriages were strategic alliances arranged with a view to improving the partners' wealth or social standing; if a few Spaniards married for love, they were exceptions not indicative of any trend for the nature of marriage to change in the Indies. Both partners were seeking the greatest wealth and the highest lineage possible in the other party; but the classic type of match in the Indies was that in which the man had acquired wealth or power and now wanted to gain matching social prestige by marrying a woman of higher birth, though often poor. In these cases the man contributed a large dowry, perhaps many thousands of pesos, reversing the traditional process. Almost always the fiction was maintained that the dowry originated with the wife or her relatives, but occasionally the man, alleging the "custom of the Indies," would grant the sum openly, in consideration of the lady's virginity and high birth. However, if the higher lineage was on the man's side, the dowry reverted to its traditional form. Some encomenderos paid princely dowries, of 20,000 pesos and over, to have their sisters or daughters marry a member of the Spanish high nobility or a magistrate of the Audiencia.

The dowry had other uses as well. At times it simply represented the total property and money which a widow or wealthy spinster brought into a marriage, and meant to keep under her control. A dowry could also be a hedge against future indebtedness; sometimes husbands acknowledged receipt of a fictional dowry far in excess of the total worth of man and wife, so that if in the future the husband's property were seized for debts, or if claims heaped up after his death, the wife could always retain this large amount in the family as dowry goods.

Spanish Peru, as has been seen elsewhere, was not a place where social mobility was easy, but there were ways a man could, within certain limits, raise his position through his own activity in war or commerce. For a woman, on the other hand, there was hardly anything she could do independently to enhance her position, and much that she could do to lower it. Women took their original status from their family, and it could be altered only through marriage. Practically the only chance for a woman of humble birth to reach the top rank of Peruvian society was to marry an obscure man who later became an encomendero. After the 1530's this was a rare occurrence.

Except for the minority who had married in Spain before leaving, encomenderos chose their wives primarily from among the female relatives of prominent people, other encomenderos or churchmen, in their own Peruvian community. Marriage in the upper levels of society was the first area of life where a new Peruvian regionalism superseded the Spanish regionalism to which the settlers remained generally faithful when choosing friends and associates. Though it would not be unheard of for an encomendero of Cuzco to seek out a bride from his home town, he would be more likely to choose a sister or cousin of the richest and most powerful of his Cuzco colleagues who would deign to consider a match, regardless of the two men's regional origin in Spain. (Such marriages were often arranged while the brides were still in Spain.) In this way, the encomendero class in each Spanish Peruvian town had by 1560 become a closely interrelated group.

Other encomenderos made matches with the wellborn, and allegedly wellborn, ladies who were imported for that purpose almost as a speculative business venture. An impecunious father with three or four marriageable daughters and some claim to hidalgo status would set out from Spain to Peru with no other assets than the prospective marriages and, in some cases, royal cédulas recommending that the Peruvian governors show favor to whomever the daughters might marry.

The encomenderos' wives were the most important and influential women in Peru, their position as central in its way as that of their husbands. They were the heads of large households of dependents, servants, and slaves. (Alone of all the women in the country, some of them had the luxury of a Spanish woman head servant.) Aside from their household responsibilities, they were often left in charge of their husbands' encomiendas and general affairs. In this broader function they were not thought to perform well; there was general agreement that the most heartless, avaricious, and destructive tribute collectors were Spanish women.

Nevertheless, the encomenderos' wives, always maintaining their homes even when the encomenderos were absent at war, were an important force for social and economic continuity, a continuity which was not broken with the death of the encomendero. The mortality rate in the civil wars among prominent men was high, and one woman might retain the same house, servant staff, encomienda, and landed property through as many as three or four husbands. Because of the pressures of custom, the governors, and the dissatisfied pretenders, no woman who inherited an encomienda could stay unmarried. She might have a limited choice as to her next husband, but had to remarry almost immediately. Some governors merely implored and hinted at reprisal if compliance was not forthcoming, while others straightforwardly informed the ladies concerned that they had arranged their marriage; but all were adamant. The record for noncompliance was set by María de Escobar, a woman of immense wealth, seniority, and political power, who managed to place a three-year interval between her second and third husbands. In cases like these, the encomienda was juridically and in fact more the woman's than the man's. . . .

The wives of men who were not encomenderos, among whom artisans' wives were the largest group, could not live with as much magnificence as women in the upper rank, but they came nearer to that ideal than might be imagined. In a singular fashion, Spanish Peru preserved most of the social distinctions of the Peninsula, and even invented new ones based on seniority and the possession of encomiendas, yet at the same time, because of the fabulous wealth available to the intruders, and the presence of a large servile population, even those Spaniards who were thought of as poor and plebeian could afford things that in Spain were the perquisites of wealth. Most Spanish women dressed in fine stuffs; none were without servants. An artisan's wife could be expected to have a considerable staff, who would call her "señora" and relieve her of most of the burden of daily housekeeping. In Lima in 1546, the wife of one far from prosperous artisan was waited upon by a Negro woman slave, a freed Indian woman of Nicaragua, and a Peruvian Indian servant, aside from two slaves who aided her husband in his work. In the main, artisans' wives and encomenderos' wives lived in different circles, choosing their confidantes, comadres, and dining companions from among their equals. Yet there were points of contact; often a humble woman stood in a kind of client relationship to an encomendero's wife, and it could happen that the wife of an encomendero would serve as sponsor at the wedding of an artisan.

Independent economic activities of women, carried on either by married women from the base of their dowry goods, to which they retained rights, or by widows and spinsters who had to gain a living, were channeled into certain areas defined by convention. Women owned a great deal of city real estate, both for their own residences and for the purpose of renting out, but were not too often seen as the owners of agricultural land or livestock. A large proportion of Negro slave house servants were the personal property of women, and much speculative buying and selling took place. Like all other elements of Spanish Peruvian society, women who had achieved solvency invested as silent partners in merchandise and loaned money.

There were single women in Lima who over the years acquired great wealth and a solid position, though not much social prestige, through such enterprise. It was not that any stigma attached to these activities in themselves, being practiced by the most patrician of ladies, but if a woman was of humble origin, or had a less than honorable start, such facts were not subsequently forgotten.

Other fields open to women were more in the nature of feminine specialties, and had strongly lower class connotations. The baking of bread and biscuit, both for ordinary city consumption and for the provision of ships and armies, was carried out largely under the supervision of women. Spaniards spoke of the panaderas as if male bakers did not exist, which was not quite true, but there is no doubt that the business was mainly shared by Spanish women and free mulatto and Negro women, the bulk of the work in either case being done by Negro slaves and Indians. Women naturally monopolized the occupation of midwifery, which they combined with the general healing of ailments. Poor women, doing as they have always done, sewed and took in boarders. Hospitality by the rich was the principal method of housing and feeding transients in Peru, but some of the women who accepted boarders for a fee began, by the late 1540's and the 1550's, to evolve into regular innkeepers (who also sold odds and ends to the public), not only in Lima but as far into the highlands as La Paz. . . .

For their self-protection and for their honor, it was prudent for women who kept inns to marry, and those who could find willing husbands did so. In 1547 la Valenciana married an Antonio de Toledo, who thenceforth helped in the operation of her house. She became deeply committed to Toledo in more than a formal sense, giving him free management of her properties and supporting his relatives. But the relationship came to an end because of a difficulty that plagued marriage in the Indies. Toledo was a bigamist. Presumably la Valenciana's husband in Spain had died before the new match, but Toledo's first wife was still alive. He had succumbed to the temptation that overcame more than one Spaniard in Peru, that of forgetting a poor, distant wife in Spain for a new one who was rich and present. After a year the validity of the marriage was challenged in the ecclesiastical courts, only to be confirmed, until finally around 1554 Toledo's previous marriage was established beyond doubt, he was exiled from Peru, and his marriage with la Valenciana was invalidated.

There is no particular reason to think that la Valenciana's place was ever more than a boarding house. But it is possible; not all adventurers in the Indies were male. Already in 1537 Bishop Berlanga of Panama complained of the presence of too many single women of bad morals. There were always a certain number of women, not necessarily of the very lowest origin but certainly of low repute, who served the Spaniards as prostitutes, camp followers, and mistresses.

Full-fledged prostitutes definitely existed in Lima, the center of all amenities, and in rich Potosí, but there were not enough such women to be organized by the houseful. Nor was there anything like mass demand for the physical woman. Spanish men found Indian women attractive, and any Spaniard could have as many as he wanted. Spanish prostitutes catered more to the need of Spaniards to be near a woman who shared their language and culture. As much as anything else there were entertainers, who might, like María de Ledesma in Potosí, have a fine vihuela or guitar and know how to play and sing well. Jokingly, half in derision, these women were commonly called "doña" by their clients, and this usage has found its way into the chronicles of the civil wars; but they were not so termed in any serious context.

Far more common than true prostitutes were adventuresses who were prepared to form loose relationships, either temporary or quite permanent, with any man who would support them well. They were not averse to an advantageous marriage, but could expect marriage only under unusual circumstances. Often such a woman served in effect as interim or replacement wife for a man whose real wife was still in Spain, or, even more characteristically, for a man who was single and desired female companionship, but did not want to marry until he was in a position to make a match with a wealthy or wellborn lady who could do honor to his lineage. When that time came, if the relationship had been a meaningful one and the man was generous, he might give his former mistress a dowry and marry her to another, less ambitious Spaniard. . . .

At the opposite pole from the concubines were the feminine devotees of the church. Peru was slow to develop true convents of nuns, and the ones that began to be organized, as 1560 neared, already belonged to a new era. But they were preceded, in the late 1540's and 1550's, by the *beatas*. Beatas, a specifically Spanish phenomenon, were women living in pious retirement, sometimes individually and sometimes in groups, who wore the habit of an order with which they had some, usually formal, connection.

The Dominican beatas seem to have been the first to organize themselves; in 1548 the Dominican beata Mari Hernández de Pereda donated her house for the purpose, though she soon added the clause that a rival, Leonor del Aguilar, should not be allowed entry. Later the Dominican friars persuaded her to revoke the clause, and the formerly excluded Leonor, who had lived in her own small house with a mulatto slave girl and a mestizo child she cared for, came there to live. Discipline, one can see, was not what might be expected from regular nuns, but the Dominican effort was serious and sustained. Leonor del Aguilar remained a beata for at least ten years; the Dominican house was still in existence in 1557, and even had affiliated members in the coastal valley of Chincha, where the Dominican friars maintained a monastery.

The Dominican beatas were women of modest circumstances; another establishment started under Augustinian sponsorship around 1557 drew from a different stratum of society, its membership being prominent widows and daughters of encomenderos, all of them doñas. After some years the beatas became regular nuns and founded a convent of the same order.

Rich and poor, concubine and beata, Spanish women made their most basic contribution to the development of the country by educating those around them in the ways of the homeland. In their houses Spanish was spoken and learned. They taught their Negro and Indian maids to make beds, sew European clothes, and prepare Spanish foods in Spanish fashion. As irregular as some of their own private lives may have been, they taught religion to their slaves and servants, and encouraged them to form steady unions and marry.

But above all, this influence extended to the second generation, for whose upbringing the Spanish women were responsible, a generation which included not only their own fully Spanish children, but large numbers of mestizo children, fathered by Spanish settlers who were not content to see their offspring raised as Indians. The demand for people to care for such children was large, and any Spanish woman, whether she had children of her own or not, could expect to be importuned to raise mestizos and orphans. Once the children were taken in, personal attachment grew, whatever the original agreement had been. . . .

When it came to the wives of encomenderos, their collections of children were truly imposing. Isabel de Ovalle, twice married but childless, raised two orphaned Spanish girls, a mestizo girl who had been befriended by her first husband, and two more mestizo girls she had taken in on her own initiative (not to speak of two Negro slave orphans she meant to free). She planned to give them all substantial dowries. Childlessness was not, of course, the rule among encomenderos' wives, many of whom were notably fertile. Doña Francisca Jiménez had, by 1548, ten children alive and with her; two by her first husband, three by her second, and five by her third. She was also raising the mestizo daughter of her second husband, who acted as her maid. This was the fate of many mestizo children who were raised in Spanish homes; they received sustenance, education, and affection, but were seen in the light of servants.

There was, then, growing up in Peru during the 1540's and 1550's, a new generation whose cultural heritage was strongly Spanish, whether they were of pure Spanish blood or mestizo. For the future character of the colony, this group was of immense importance; but in the period before 1560 they remained little more than a potentiality. Hardly any representative of the second generation, either Spanish or mestizo, appeared in any kind of independent role during the whole thirty years from the time the conquering expedition set out for Peru, not even in the humbler fields of endeavor such as artisanry.

Mestizos and Spanish children were born in Peru from 1533 on, but the second generation had its true beginnings only after the Indian rebellion ended in 1537. By 1560 only a small minority of the second generation were over twenty years of age. The new generation also had to contend with the general Spanish reluctance to entrust anything important to the very young; in the Spanish legal tradition, very much in force in Peru, both men and women were minors and required guardians until their twenty-fifth birthday. Emerging into independence was rendered yet more difficult by the crushing prestige of the first generation of settlers, which kept them in command in all walks of life for an abnormally long time. . . .

There was in conquest Peru no one standard treatment or fixed social evaluation of the thousands of mestizo children born of Spanish fathers and

Indian mothers. Many, never recognized, grew up with their mothers as Indians and were reabsorbed into the indigenous population. In other cases, Spaniards went to great lengths to provide for mestizo offspring. Some Spanish fathers sent for their mestizo children to join them from as far away as Mexico and Nicaragua. Many made plans to send mestizo sons and daughters to Spain, to be raised at home by their own families, and though this did not come to fruition as often as intended, it was no idle thought.

For those who were in one way or another received among the Spanish Peruvians, their condition as mestizos was a handicap, but depending on other factors, did not preclude acceptance at a fairly high level. It is hard to separate the Spaniards' feelings about racial mixture, as it affected the mestizos, from their position on illegitimacy, for ninety-five per cent of the first generation of mestizos were illegitimate. To judge by the treatment accorded the few legitimate mestizos, who were accepted fully as equals, the Spanish may have considered illegitimacy to be a more serious blemish than mixture with Indians. Legitimate mestizos could and did inherit encomiendas, and one was considered for an appointment to the city council of Lima. Moreover, there were cases of Spaniards who had both Spanish and mestizo sons out of wedlock and gave them all equal treatment. . . .

The path was easier for the girls of this class, who could hope to marry within Spanish Peruvian society, perhaps not to their fathers' equals, but to substantial Spaniards of lower degree. To a Spaniard, such a marriage offered the advantages of an alliance with the girl's father, and a large dowry, which might be enough for him to live on. If the father was exceptionally rich and powerful, his mestizo daughter might be able to marry well by any standards. A daughter of the famous captain Lorenzo de Aldana married a large encomendero of Charcas. Diego Maldonado, called the Rich, married his daughter to a Spanish don, with a dowry of 20,000 pesos. Ordinarily, however, such girls married men from the second rank: majordomos, merchants, entrepreneurs, or gentlemen pretenders without encomiendas.

The pattern seen among the mestizo children of encomenderos repeated itself at the lower levels, but with alteration. Above all, the frequent presence on the scene of the Indian mother reduced the intensity of Hispanization. Ordinary Spaniards often succeeded in marrying their daughters to juniors or inferiors; a shipmaster to one of his sailors, or a merchant to his factor. But the point was soon reached at which the size of the dowry and the prestige of the father did not suffice to attract suitors. Many Spaniards fulfilled their duty to their mestizo children (both boys and girls) by making them a "donation." If the donation was large, perhaps a thousand pesos in value, the child could be assured of a future, but usually it was much less: two or three hundred pesos, or a mare with a colt, or a few goats. A child so endowed would probably succeed in being raised by some Spanish family, but the amount was not enough for a dowry or a start in life.

By the 1550's, therefore, a major problem in Peru was what to do with the many mestizo girls who were growing up Spanish, but were not wealthy enough to find Spanish husbands. It became a favorite form of charity to donate dowries to mestizo orphans. In Cuzco and Lima, philanthropic citizens established houses to shelter them. (Hardly ever did it occur to the charitable to arrange a marriage between two mestizos, partly, no doubt, because men did not marry as young as women, and few mestizo men had come of age). Philanthropy could not, of course, take care of all the Hispanized mestizo girls; apparently very many ended in purely servile positions, or took to loose living, or were abandoned entirely. . . .

All in all, the Spaniards must be judged to have shown an unusual amount of interest in the fate of their mestizo offspring. Even if many, possibly most, mestizo children suffered neglect, there were many hundreds who were protected, and grew up inside Spanish Peruvian society.

In order to explain the relatively good treatment of mestizos it is not necessary to imagine any unusually strong parental tenderness on the part of the Spaniards, though some had such feelings (they were often struck, it appears, by how much their mestizo children resembled them). Most important was the strong Spanish feeling for lineage, which emphasized solidarity with all one's relatives near and distant, as well as the necessity of carrying on the family name. Another factor was the strict Spanish machinery for legal guardianship. Finally, there was the special sense of responsibility which the Spaniards, in the Arab tradition, felt for the protection of females. At all levels, more care was lavished on mestizo girls than boys, with the probable result that a higher proportion of them were absorbed into the Spanish population, and indeed, with men more numerous in that population than women, they were more needed.

To sum up the substance of the chapter, there were among the settlers of Peru a large minority of Spanish women who, living in the cities, often as heads of the large households of encomenderos, were able to exert a cultural influence on the urban population out of proportion to their numbers. Even humble women had mixed servant staffs to whom they taught Spanish ways. The household of one almost indigent Spanish woman of Lima could stand as a paradigm of Spanish Peru: herself, her Negro slave, her Indian servant, and a mestizo orphan girl. Above all, the Spanish women were responsible for the existence of a second Spanish generation who were to inherit the encomiendas and other wealth of the first, and they provided the surroundings in which a generation of mestizos grew up to be primarily Spanish in language and culture.

2. Dowries Helped to Reduce Domestic Instability, Illegitimacy, and Prostitution in Bahia

A. J. R. RUSSELL-WOOD

The history of women in colonial Brazil remains largely to be written, for documentation appears to be scanty and what does exist has not been carefully organized or systematically studied. The British Brazilianist Dr. A. J. R. Russell-Wood has made skillful use of the available records of the Santa Casa de Misericórdia (The Holy House of Mercy) of Bahia to shed light on the attitudes of society toward women and their role in the life of this colonial capital. The Misericórdia was an important institution for social welfare developed in Portugal and transplanted in Brazil. As a charitable brotherhood it had an important role in connection with dowries and marriage, foundlings, prisons, hospitals, burials, and charity.

The Misericórdia of Bahia in the seventeenth and eighteenth centuries . . . maintained a hospital, a retirement house and a foundling wheel and its members visited the prison regularly. The Misericórdia also strove to assist people in modest circumstances by outright alms. Brothers were supplied with the names of needy citizens by parish priests and these were visited and assisted in so far as the resources of the brotherhood permitted. Dowries were granted to girls to enable them to preserve their honour and contract suitable marriages. In colonial Brazil even a girl of respectable parentage found difficulty in marrying unless she had a dowry. Without this aid from the Misericórdia there was a very real danger that she would slip into a life of prostitution. In the concession of dowries the Misericórdia was contributing on a private level to a national policy. . . . The concession of dowries had been regarded as politically expedient since the earliest days of the Portuguese expansion. . . .

The Misericórdia of Bahia played a valuable rôle in advancing the national policy of marriages and in affording some degree of protection to girls who might otherwise have been unable to marry or whose precarious financial position would have rendered them susceptible to prostitution. All records in the Misericórdia archives for the sixteenth century were destroyed by the Dutch, but for the seventeenth and eighteenth centuries the registers afford a complete record of bequests made to the brotherhood for the provision of dowries.

From *Fidalgos and Philanthropists: The Santa Casa da Misericórdia of Bahia, 1550–1755* by A. J. R. Russell-Wood (1968), pp. 173–200 passim. Originally published by the University of California Press; reprinted by permission of the regents of the University of California and Macmillan, London and Basingstoke.

The dowries for which testators provided in their wills fell in three categories. First, there were dowries granted by the testator to the daughters of a relative or of a friend. In such cases the Misericórdia was merely the executor of the will and passed on the dowry to the nominee after the estate of the testator had been settled. Secondly, there were dowries left to the Misericórdia for immediate distribution to orphan girls without the brotherhood incurring any further obligation. Thirdly, there were dowries left by the testator for administration by the Misericórdia. These were financed from the interest on capital placed on loan and were granted annually. Before discussing the last two types of dowry, I wish to dwell briefly on the attitudes of mind revealed by the terms of these wills towards the position of women in colonial Brazil because frequently these attitudes show social, religious and racial preoccupations.

Wills making legacies for the allocation of dowries have certain features in common. The testator was usually of the upper class and the main beneficiaries were his nieces. In all cases the concession of a dowry, be it to a relative or not, depended on the undoubted virtue of the nominee. These aspects have implications in the wider social context of colonial ideology.

Testators who provided dowries for their relatives were not all of the landed aristocracy of Bahia. Nevertheless they were sufficiently prominent in the social life of the city to be very conscious of class distinction. This preoccupation with social standing is very apparent in the clauses of a will stipulating the terms for the concession of a dowry. Jorge Ferreira, who had died in 1641 leaving 2,450$000 to the Misericórdia for the saying of masses, was of the landowning class and had just such a preoccupation. The owner of a sugar plantation in Sergipe, a provision farm in the Serra, a smallholding in Rio Vermelho and houses in the city of Bahia, he was not one to wish that his niece should marry below her station. Thus he had bequeathed the results of his sixty-three years' labour to his niece, Jerónima Ferreira, as a dowry "so that her husband may be ennobled thereby." . . .

Preoccupation with the maintaining of social prestige and with the hazards of marrying "below one's station" led many families of Bahia to send their daughters to convents in Portugal rather than risk the possibility of their contracting socially undesirable marriages in Bahia. Young girls and boxes of currency were constant features of any fleet from Bahia to Portugal in the late seventeenth and early eighteenth centuries. Dom João de Lencastre (Governor-General, 1694–1702) told the king of the social and economic evils of this practice. No longer were there any society marriages in Bahia, and large sums of money were being sent to the convents of Lisbon, Oporto and Viana to provide for the expenses of these girls. . . .

Not only was the practice of sending girls to Portugal prejudicial to the society and economy of Bahia. Frequently the girls themselves were the victims of parents who compelled their daughters to take the veil against their will. It was this human aspect rather than the financial and social well-being of Bahia which induced Dom João V to act. In a decree of March 1732, he ordered that in future no girl should be sent from Brazil to Portugal without the royal consent having been previously obtained. Before such permission would be granted, the viceroy and governors were to hold a full enquiry to determine all the circumstances of the petition made by a girl wishing to go to Portugal. In addition to this civil enquiry, there was to be an ecclesiastical report. The archbishop or bishop was to interview the girl and ensure that the petition was born of true religious vocation and not of parental intimidation. The penalties for non-observance of this decree were severe. The captain of a ship found carrying a girl against her will was liable to a fine of 2,000 *cruzados* and two months' imprisonment. This measure effectively curtailed the traffic in girls from Bahia to the convents of Portugal because the royal consent was granted on few occasions. It could not stop the traffic in coin from Bahia to Portugal for dowries for nieces and relatives of testators in Brazil. . . .

Religious feeling may have contributed on a sub-conscious level to the decision of many families to send their daughters to the convents of Portugal. The other characteristic of the wills recorded in the registers of the Misericórdia — that legacies to relatives were frequently confined to the nieces of the testator — had a purely physical basis. Barrenness among white women and infant mortality were frequent in the tropics. On the one hand was the case of the businessman Gaspar dos Réis Pinto who had been married three times but was still without offspring. On the other was Luzia Freire, widow of a brother of the Misericórdia, who had produced eight children of whom only two had survived. In his will of 1643 Gaspar dos Réis Pinto ordered his executor to sell his plantations in Sergipe and Rio Vermelho and distribute as many dowries as possible from the proceeds. For her part Luzia Freire stipulated in her will of 1685 that monies derived from the sale of her sugar plantation in Patatiba and her cattle ranches on the S. Francisco river be applied to the saying of masses for her soul. These purely physical factors obviously led many testators to send to distant relatives in Portugal the fruits of a lifetime's labour in the tropics.

Bahians who made legacies to nieces and the daughters of relatives in Brazil were guided by a different set of reasons. All testators were obsessed by the possibility of spurious claimants challenging their wills in an attempt to inherit lands or possessions. The wills of married couples and bachelors alike often began with the categorical statement that the testators had no offspring "natural or spurious." Such was the extent of this fear that many testators adopted a matrilineal attitude when making their legacies. Two Bahian bachelors of the early seventeenth century, Francisco Dias Baião and Diogo Fernandes, stipulated that only the daughters of their relatives could benefit from their wills. In no circumstances was a male relative to inherit. The philanthropist Felippe Correia, after making numerous legacies to the Misericórdia in his will of 1650, left his plantations in Pituba to his sister on the condition that in no way was her husband to enjoy part ownership of these properties. Possibly this condition may have been the result of personal animosity; if so, there was no reference to it, and Correia gave as his reason that he wished the property to remain in the Correia family. Other testators founded trusts to be enjoyed by the distaff side only. In the event of there being no more female descendants the trust was to be administered by a brotherhood for charitable purposes.

The attitude towards what might be called the "legitimacy of the womb" and even the practice of sending daughters to Portugal may have been influenced by the multi-racial nature of Bahian society. There was always the fear that a daughter might have an affair with a coloured man. In this there was one law for males and quite another for females. It was considered rather *macho*, or masculine, for a teenage son of a white family to have a coloured mistress: if she did conceive, so much the worse for her. On the other hand, for a white girl to have a coloured *amigo*, or lover, was tantamount to demanding social ostracism. This fear on the part of parents was rarely expressed but strongly felt. When the lawyer Jerónimo de Burgos and his wife had established a trust in 1664 for the saying of masses and charitable purposes, they had stipulated that after the terms of the trust had been fulfilled any additional income should be given to their heirs provided that "they do not marry anyone tainted with the blood of the forbidden races." In an age when race and creed were often equated, such a clause effectively ruled out coloured or New Christian partners.

The attitudes of Bahians towards the distaff side of their families have shown that many of the conditions attached to legacies were prompted by racial, religious and social prejudices. Bahia was a multi-racial society and the coloured population was infinitely larger than the white population. The enthusiasm felt by the early settlers for the Amerindian girls and Negresses continued even after there had been an increase in the number of white women available for marriage. The so-called *Minas* (probably Fulahs or Ashantis) were especially favoured because of their good appearance, dignified carriage, and their fame as mistresses of the culinary skills. The attitudes shown by testators in their wills towards their coloured slaves reveal the complexity of the racial issue.

Historians and anthropologists alike have dwelt on the manner in which the white masters exploited their female slaves. It is undeniable that the girls of the *senzalas,* or slave quarters, were often the concubines of the masters, the butts for the anger of jealous wives, and the playthings of adolescent sons.

But there was another side to the picture of inter-racial contact which is usually forgotten. Many slave owners appear to have taken a genuine interest in the welfare of their slaves. The receipt ledgers of the Misericórdia frequently recorded payments of up to 50$000 made by a plantation owner for the cure of a slave in the hospital of the brotherhood. João de Mattos referred in his will, with evident pride, to how he had arranged the marriage of one of his slave girls and had given her a dowry and some household possessions. Many slaves were granted their freedom as a reward for years of faithful service. A wealthy widow, Theodora de Góis, who died in 1693, granted her slave Luiza her freedom and ordered that a dowry of 100$000, clothing and gold trinkets be given her on marriage. This paternal attitude on the part of the white ruling classes towards the coloured population was not limited to slaves. Many families adopted coloured children. Pedro Viegas Giraldes and Felippe Correia, both benefactors of the Misericórdia in the seventeenth century, brought up mulatto children in their homes. The history of the relationships between masters and slaves, white and black, was not always a chronicle of cruelty and exploitation. There was often an undercurrent of Christian idealism among the authoritarian and domineering plantation owners of colonial Bahia.

On other occasions the attitude of the white man to his slaves was not paternal, but uxorious. One slave owner, Pedro Domingues, was consumed by jealousy at the prospect of his concubine marrying. In his will of 1676 he granted her her freedom, the ownership of his house, and three slaves on the condition that she should stay single. Other slave owners had had children by their slave girls and made generous provision for both mother and child. A smallholder, Diogo Fernandes, left detailed instructions in his will for the care and education of his son by a Negress: he was to be taught the Bible and trained as an apprentice in a mechanical trade. The bachelor Joseph Lopes, who had established a "chapel of masses" in the Misericórdia in 1656, also regarded his favourite crioula as more than a mere *peça de Indias* ("pieces of the Indies"). He granted the mother and her son and daughter their freedom. The little girl was to be placed in an honourable home and on marriage was to receive a dowry of 100$000 and furniture. Evidently the family of Joseph Lopes had opposed his recognition of paternity, because he stipulated that his daughter should not be boarded in the house of any of his relatives. This respect for the Negro slave was based largely on her rôle as the mother of the white man's children. The glorification of the wife in her maternal rôle still persists in Brazil and although a fickle husband may indulge in the enchantments of his concubine to the full, he will rarely leave his wife, simply because she is the "mother of my son."

Preoccupations of class, creed and colour were constant factors in the minds of Bahians of the seventeenth and eighteenth centuries. Anxiety for the preservation of class status was allied to an obsession with the maintaining of purity of blood. Members of an essentially male-dominated society were influenced by these two factors into adopting matrilineal attitudes when making their wills. The position of women in Portuguese colonial society is usually presented as insignificant. Travellers to colonial Brazil commented on the seclusion of females. The seclusion of women in colonial times has been considered by historians as indicative of the insignificant position they enjoyed, but it seems likely that the womanhood of colonial Bahia was a good deal more influential than is generally realised.

The attitudes to women and slaves illustrate to the full the almost paradoxical variety of outlook in colonial Brazil. The apparent contradiction of a male-dominated society adopting matrilineal attitudes had its counterpart in the attitude towards the coloured population. On the one hand was the brutality of the slave ships and slave markets. On the other hand was the Christian charity shown in the adoption of a coloured orphan, the emancipation of a slave, or the granting of dowries. A modern visitor to Bahia referred to the "Bay of all saints and of all devils." This would have been an accurate epigram for Bahia in colonial times when idealism and materialism, virtue and vice were so closely interwoven. . . .

The administration of dowries by the Misericórdia exemplifies all that was good and all that was bad in the brotherhood. Dowries were given to coloured girls as well as white girls, to girls of the city and to girls of the surrounding region. By so doing, the Misericórdia offered a social service without parallel in Bahia of the eighteenth century. Many girls who would otherwise not have married, or would have been degraded, were able to marry honourably. By this action the Misericórdia was to a small degree responsible for reducing the domestic instability, illegitimacy and prostitution for which Bahia was notorious. Unfortunately its powers of administration did not equal its idealism. Loans were placed on poor securities and lost. Legal disputes made others impossible to collect. Small sums were lost through the dishonesty of brothers or employees. The Misericórdia was affected by external factors: disruption of the economy; the decrease in the value of properties; lack of co-operation from the judiciary in law suits brought against debtors. It was pride which prompted the Mesas to continue granting dowries for as long as they did, without consideration for hard financial realities. Although it is easy to condemn the administrative deficiencies of the brotherhood, the important rôle played by the Misericórdia in the distribution of dowries can only command respect.

3. Sor Juana Inés de la Cruz: 'The Supreme Poet of Her Time in Castilian'

IRVING A. LEONARD

Professor Leonard, who was the Domingo Faustino Sarmiento Professor at the University of Michigan at the time of his retirement a few years ago, made an outstanding contribution in what might be best called cultural history. Of his many studies the best known are *Baroque Times in Old Mexico* (1959) and *Books of the Brave* (1949). His writings were always marked by a grace of style and detailed research that explain their readability and their permanent value.

The late Pedro Henríquez Ureña, probably the most distinguished Latin American literary critic of this century, termed Sor Juana's life "a prodigious tale of devotion and knowledge." * He emphasized the obstacles she faced, "the many censors who doubted the wisdom of so much learning in a woman who even succeeded once in inducing a mother superior — 'a very saintly and very foolish woman' — to forbid her the reading of books."

This prohibition lasted only three months: she faithfully gave up books, but this did not prevent her from thinking: "and so, though I did not study in books, I studied in all the things God created." This meant pondering on the many individual differences between people, even though they were of the same species. The geometrical figure of objects interested her: "She observes two girls playing with a spinning top and decides to find out what kind of curve it draws while it spins — she sprinkles flour on the floor and discovers that the curve is a spiral. In the kitchen, she remarks on the properties of sugar or eggs and adds: 'If Aristotle had known how to cook, he would have written even more than he did.' "

Henríquez Ureña also pointed out that her poetry reflects the conditions of her life in seventeenth-century Mexico:

> In a superb sonnet to the rose she draws from its brief life the traditional lesson — "thy life deceives and thy death teaches" — but in another sonnet she approves the rose's life — "happy it is to die while young and fair and not endure the insult of old age." This is an expression of her persistent fighting spirit, which led her to write the defiant lines: "If my displeasure from my pleasure comes, may heaven give me pleasure at the cost of displeasure" — lines strikingly coincident with a number of folk songs and proverbs in Mexico.

Sor Juana needed all the persistence and courage that she had. Archbishop Francisco Aguiar y Seixas (1632–1698), who was in power during the last

* All quotations in this headnote come from Pedro Henríquez Ureña, *Literary Currents in Latin America* (Cambridge, Mass.: Harvard University Press, 1945), pp. 75–82.

years of Sor Juana's life, helps us to appreciate the spirit of some of the dominant forces of the age. Professor Leonard discreetly terms him "misogynistic," but his hatred of women led him to shun all contact with them. He even refused to make the ceremonial visit on the Viceroy required by protocol, because he would meet the Vicequeen at the same time. He was a pious and hardworking prelate withal; he visited all parts of his enormous archbishopric and founded a seminary and a colegio as well as a "House for Demented Females" and a "House For Women Abandoned by Their Husbands."

Even though the times were against Sor Juana, she wrote on a subject always dangerous for women to take up: men. "Her best known poem is the one in defense of women; . . . it is her thesis that men are irrational in blaming women for their imperfection, since men constantly strive to make women imperfect. It is not great poetry, but it is a polemical masterpiece."

One August day of 1667 in Mexico City an attractive, talented girl, still some months short of her sixteenth birthday, entered the sternly ascetic Order of Discalced Carmelites as a chorister. The convent that received her was the one that had been the dream of those earnest nuns, Sister Inés de la Cruz and Sister Mariana Encarnación when they plied the fickle Archbishop García Guerra so assiduously earlier in the century with sweetmeats and seductive music. Though immediate success had eluded these efforts, it will be recalled, patience was triumphant in 1616, and the new religious community came into being. The young lady who, a half century afterwards, gained admittance to its holy precincts was Doña Juana Inés de Asbaje y Ramírez de Santillana, better known as Sister Juana Inés de la Cruz, . . . famed as the "last great lyric poet of Spain and the first great poet of America." Also musically gifted, her ecclesiastical name was possibly adopted in veneration of the instrument-playing hostess of Fray García Guerra and cofounder of the Carmelite convent, of which she was now a temporary inmate.

In an age when matrimony and religious reclusion were the sole careers open to respectable females, the act of taking the veil was a commonplace event in Mexican society. In most sisterhoods the discipline was not severe, and within the cloistered walls many comforts and amenities of secular life could be enjoyed, including the services of personal slaves. Indeed, for daughters whose matrimonial prospects were not bright, an immured existence of this sort seemed a desirable alternative, and a young woman whose parents or relatives

From *Baroque Times in Old Mexico: Seventeenth-Century Persons, Places, and Practice* by Irving A. Leonard (Ann Arbor: University of Michigan Press, 1959), pp. 172–191, passim. Copyright © by the University of Michigan, 1959. Reprinted by permission.

could provide the requisite dowry was regarded as fortunate. But the case of the adolescent Doña Juana Inés de Asbaje y Ramírez de Santillana seemed exceptional, and strangely obscure the reasons for her decision. Here was a maiden "that was far more beautiful than any nun should be," the darling of the viceregal court, and the favorite maid-in-waiting of the vicereine. Her personal attractiveness, her nimble wit in penning verse for any occasion, and her amazing knowledge of books, were all very nearly the talk of the town. In fact, the admiring Viceroy himself, on one occasion, had arranged that a group of the leading professors at the University of Mexico should examine the precocious girl in various branches of learning, and when she emerged triumphant from this ordeal, the learned gentlemen marveled at the erudition and composure of a maiden who hardly seemed more than a child.

Her rise and renown in the courtly circle of the capital had been truly phenomenal. A village lass, born in 1651 in a tiny hamlet called Nepantla, "the land in between," that looked up to the snow-crested volcanoes Popocatepetl and Ixtacihuatl, she had begun to read at the age of three, later devouring the small library of her gandfather. When eight years old she went to Mexico City to live with relatives. Soon this pretty child prodigy caught the eye of the vicereine who brought her to reside amidst the luxury and splendor of the viceregal Palace. In this sophisticated environment the young girl rapidly acquired a maturity that quite belied her years, and in the Court she soon found herself envied for her wit by the women and desired for her physical charms by the men.

Social success of this sort in such aristocratic circles was all the more extraordinary in the light of her illegitimate birth, though this circumstance was, perhaps, undisclosed to anyone save her confessor. Her mother, it was later revealed, had had two separate trios of children by as many men, and neither of these unions the Church had hallowed. It was not an uncommon situation at the time, even in families of some distinction, but it was hardly a genealogical asset for any one of patrician pretensions. That this lowly origin influenced the resolve of Juana Inés de Asbaje y Ramírez de Santillana, who thus bore the surnamcs of her progenitors, to become a nun is likely but, as the sole explanation of her choice, it is unlikely. Her deep passion for study, her stated "total disinclination to marriage," and the promptings of her zealous confessor, the Jesuit *calificador* of the Inquisition, Antonio Núñez de Miranda, had undoubtedly made a life of reclusion seem attractive to her troubled spirit, and finally moved her to abandon the pomp and glitter of the Palace social whirl, of which she was so conspicuously a part.

That this determination was attended by doubts, misgivings, and inner conflict appears evident in the fact that illness caused her to withdraw from the Carmelite order within three months. The transition from a worldly court to the harsh confinement of a convent proved too abrupt and severe. Early the following year, however, she took her first vows in the Jeronymite community, the milder discipline of which was better suited to the sensitive temperament and scholarly aspirations of the poetess. The remainder of her forty-three years of life she spent chiefly within the book-lined walls of her cell, to which she retreated as often as her conventual duties permitted. There she pored over her accumulating volumes, attended to an extensive correspondence within and outside of the broad realm of Old Mexico, and wrote the verses so widely known in her time and that have since won enduring fame.

Her poetry is varied in meter and theme, including love lyrics that occasionally border on the erotic, tender Christmas carols, morality plays, allegorical pieces, and even secular three-act comedies like those performed in the public theaters of Spain and Spanish America. Much of this metrical expression abounded in literary conceits and was clothed in the ornate, florid, and obscure style of prevailing Baroque fashion. Unlike most verse of her contemporaries, however, subtle meaning and profound feeling often lay hidden in the intricate foliage of words and clever figures of speech. . . . Yet many of her sonnets and shorter lyric poems have an almost limpid clarity and an exquisite beauty that mark her as the supreme poet of her time in Castilian.

As time passes the appeal of this Creole nun-poetess increases and the circle of her admirers enlarges. It is not merely the esthetic merit of so much of her verse which brings her this homage — though she is often regarded . . . as among the greatest poets in the speech of Spain — but, perhaps even more, the complex personality refracted in many of her writings. Her more intimate and spontaneous expression offers glimpses so fleeting and elusive of the inner life of an extraordinary woman that they serve to pique the reader's curiosity rather than to satisfy it. In certain lines her intention seems illumined for a bare moment, like a flash of lightning in the night, only to be followed by an obscurity more impenetrable than before. Thus it is that the enigmatic quality of Sister Juana's verses, even more than the technical perfection of the best of them, inspires a veritable cult and wins for her an expanding audience. . . .

In the multiplying criticism of the life and work of the Mexican nun-poetess there is increasing agreement that her intellectual distinction exceeds her eminence as a poet, and that her preoccupation with ideas was greater than with artistic creation. Without minimizing the deeply emotional and feminine nature of Sister Juana, she was basically a rationalist with a passion for knowledge, and the processes of analysis were stronger and more obsessive than any other of her psyche. Her extraordinary gift as a lyric poet was ancillary to her acutely rational mentality, and her supreme aspiration was the freedom of her mind to roam untrammeled and unimpeded through every realm of thought. To read, to study, to experiment ". . . just to see if, by studying, I might grow less ignorant . . ." was the consuming desire of her existence. Since earliest childhood she had experienced this powerful yearning and later she had begged her mother to permit her to attend the University of Mexico disguised in male clothing. "What is indeed the truth," she wrote in her famous *Reply to Sister Philotea,* a letter of much autobiographical significance, "and which I do not deny (in the first place because it is well known to everyone, and in the second place because, though it may be to my detriment, Heaven has bestowed upon me the blessing of a very great love of truth), is that, ever since the first glimmer of reason struck me, this inclination to learning has been so urgent and powerful. . . ." In her young innocence she had desisted from eating cheese in the belief that such food would make her unpolished and uncouth, hence ". . . the desire to know was stronger in me than the desire to eat, even though the latter is so strong in children. . . ." This "inclination" triumphed over every other urge, including the sexual — for marriage she had a "total negation" she had declared — and she candidly confesses that her decision to take the veil — her only other choice — was largely influenced by the relatively freer opportunity it promised for study. The more solitary practices of the Carmelites had induced her, perhaps, to select that Order first. She had thought to escape the tyranny of what almost seemed a vice by dedicating herself as a bride of Christ, but ". . . poor, wretched me! I merely brought myself with me, together with my worst enemy, this inclination!" Instead of extinguishing this passion for reading and cogitation she found that, once subjected to her vows, this thirst for learning ". . . exploded like a charge of powder.". . .

In the medieval atmosphere of seventeenth century Mexico where women could not dream of independent lives, where it was axiomatic that they possessed inferior intelligence, and where they were scarcely more than chattels of their fathers, brothers, and husbands, intellectual curiosity in Sister Juana's sex was not only indecorous but sinful. It might, indeed, be the workings of the Evil One and, therefore, imperil one's salvation, as her superiors in the convent more than once assured her. Though there were learned women in history, any emulation of them by a nun was not without an attendant sense of guilt. Sister Juana herself had not escaped this feeling, for she wrote: ". . . I have prayed God to subdue the light of my intelligence, leaving me only enough to keep His law, for anything more (according to some persons) is superfluous in a woman." But, even in these despairing words, one seems to detect in a parenthetical phrase, in which the masculine form is used, a veiled rancor against the man-made world of her time. But her obvious intellectual distinction also aroused the jealousy and antipathy of her companions in the convent, and over the years this hostility developed in her a persecution complex. Her brilliant, inquiring mind seemed always a source of vexation. "If my intelligence is my own," she wrote in one of her poems, "why must I always find it so dull for my ease and so sharp for my hurt?"

This avid curiosity and desire for knowledge, so at odds with her time, place, and sex, seemed only to bring down upon her head the criticism and censure of those about her:

> Why, people, do you persecute me so?
> In what do I offend, when but inclined
> with worldly beauties to adorn my mind,
> and not my mind on beauty to bestow?
> I value not a treasure trove, nor wealth;
> the greater measure of content I find
> in placing riches only in my mind,
> than setting all my intellect on wealth.
> And I esteem not beauty, for, when past
> it is the spoils of age's cruelty;
> nor faithless riches carefully amassed.
> Far better nibble, it seems to me,
> at all life's vanities unto the last
> than to consume my life in vanity.[1]

And again in one of her ballads she asks bitterly why her fondness for truth must always bring her punishment. "If this fondness I have is licit and even an obligation, why should they chastise me because I do what I must?"

These protests, indicating a sensitiveness to sharp disapproval around her, recur so frequently as to suggest a more disturbed state of mind than would result from eminence in the accepted forms of learning of her time, even after due allowance is made for the fact that such pursuits were deemed unsuitable for a woman, and particularly one bound by vows of perpetual submission. This exaggerated feeling of persecution was possibly generated in part by a growing sense of guilt engendered by the *kind* of knowledge that she was seeking and by the *kind* of methods that she was using to acquire it. In short, her learning might appear more secular than ecclesiastical — "What a pity it is that so rich a mind should so debase itself in the petty matters of this world!" the Bishop of Puebla was to chide her — and her procedures more

[1] Translated by Pauline Cook in *The Pathless Crook* (Prairie City, Ill.: Decher Press, 1951). Reprinted by permission [Ed.].

experimental or scientific in the modern way than scholastic and philosophic. Even more reprehensible than mundane knowledge were the unorthodox means of seeking it. "Experimentation tugged at Sister Juana from earliest childhood," comments a student of her life. Here, then, is the possibility of a conflict, intellectual in origin which, given her environment, profession, and sex, would inevitably be spiritual and emotional as well. This inner discord, with its concomitant overtones of heresy and disobedience, could well produce a brooding conviction of guilt and thus, through anxiety, accentuate a feeling of persecution. . . .

It was Sister Juana's fate to have her being in this age when, even in Old Mexico, though ever so slightly, the long accepted and sole approach to truth was beginning to be threatened by a new way, a new method. Almost imperceptibly the traditional scholastic and authoritarian concepts of revealed knowledge were yielding to the more sensate procedures of scientific observation and analysis. In the Mexico City of her time there was greater awareness of this intellectual revolution than commonly believed, and the capital had a tiny group of savants who were abreast of contemporary thought, even that of non-Catholic Europe. The comparatively free circulation of nontheological books during the sixteenth and seventeenth centuries, the frequent presence in the viceroyalty of transient men of learning from the Old World, and the personal correspondence of local scholars with thinkers abroad, had all contributed to a more vital mental climate in the New World centers than the contemporary dominance of a medieval Church was thought to permit. A small number of Creole *sabios* were already familiar with the ideas and writings of Erasmus, Copernicus, Kepler, and particularly Descartes, whose philosophies they discussed among themselves in comparative freedom and even cited in their published writings.

Most conspicuous of this intelligentsia of New Spain was Don Carlos de Sigüenza y Góngora. He was a professor of mathematics in the University of Mexico, renowned for his studies of astronomy, archaeology, history and natural philosophy, and also an intimate friend of Sister Juana. Living at the Hospital del Amor de Dios where he served as chaplain, he was a frequent visitor at the Jeronymite convent a few blocks away where the nun-poetess had her cell. It appears that these two intellectually gifted and lonely people enjoyed long discussions together in the locutory of the convent. Sigüenza, a very minor poet, was encouraged in these exercises by Sister Juana, while she in turn received his stimulation and training in scientific disciplines. It is likely that she acquired the mathematical instruments and some of the books said to have furnished her cell as a result of this association. Indeed, the attainments of these two figures working together have moved a discerning critic to comment that they were ". . . the first ones (in Mexico) in whom the modern spirit appears or manifests itself." It was Sigüenza who most often brought visiting savants to her convent, including the great mission-founder of the American Southwest, Father Eusebio Francisco Kino. And it was he who initiated the exceedingly intelligent nun into the new methodology propounded by Descartes, of which there are faint indications in her verse. Doubtless it was he who understood her enthusiasm for, and encouraged her in, the performance of such simple experiments in physics as she mentions in her *Reply to Sister Philotea*. And it was he who shared her love for the dawning Age of Enlightenment of which they both were unconscious pre-cursors in Mexico.

The inherent critical capacity of Sister Juana, coupled with omniverous reading, moved her to welcome a more pragmatic approach to truth. Latent in her mind was a healthy skepticism regarding the effectiveness of purely verbal rationalization, and her eager curiosity was insidiously drawn to ex-perimentation and direct observation. A scrutiny of Sister Juana's verse and prose tends to support the conviction that she felt an instinctive distrust of the scholasticism dominating the intellectual life of viceregal Mexico. Her deeper regard for observation and a more scientific analysis seems apparent when, in the *Reply,* she emphasizes the importance of varied studies and methods in throwing light on speculative learning, particularly theology, and her underlying preference is revealed when she adds: ". . . and when the expositors are like an open hand and the ecclesiastics like a closed fist." Her reactions to the specious learning and rhetorical ratiocination around her, characterized chiefly by polemical disquisitions with ostentatious displays of classical quotations and cloudy verbosity, emerge clearly in the ballad begin-ning with the pathetic verse "Let us pretend that I am happy." The wordy de-bates of bookish pedants and charlatans of the so-called intelligentsia filling the air about her with their din move her to exclaim metrically: "Everything is opinions and of such varied counsels that what one proves is black, the other proves is white.". . .

In the *Reply* she comments, with veiled scorn, on the affectation that passed as learning in the excessive number of quotations from authorities: ". . . and I add that their education is perfected (if nonsense is perfection) by having studied a little Philosophy and Theology, and by having a smattering of lan-guages, by which means one may be stupid in numerous subjects and lan-guages because the mother tongue alone is not room enough for a really big fool." Mindful, likewise, of the self delusion facilitated by the verbalism of scholasticism, Sister Juana believed that everyone should keep within his own mental limitations. If this were so, she tartly exclaims: "How many warped intelligences wandering about there would not be!"

Perhaps the most penetrating stanza of this same ballad is the one in which she puts her finger on the core of true wisdom, the development of sound judgment: "To know how to make varied and subtle discourses is not knowledge; rather, knowledge simply consists of making the soundest choices.". . .

Thus it appears that Sister Juana found herself not only torn between "reason" and "passion," but also between *two methodologies of reason.* The time-honored dialectics and syllogisms of scholasticism were still entrenched as the accepted means of rationalization in the Church of Christ which held her in its protective arms and to which she was irrevocably bound by vows. This great institution sheltered and loved her, and obedience to its authority and ways was her ineludible obligation. Yet, deep within, she could not reciprocate its love. Instead, she seemed possessed by a way of thinking that threatened to ˈundermine the assumptions on which the Faith rested. On the true object of her affections, the new concept of experimentalism relying· on the senses rather than on authority, her benevolent guardian, the Church, severely frowned. Such intellectual exercise might well be inimical to the divine science of theology, and it was potentially, if not actually, heretical. Adherence to such thinking could seriously jeopardize her eternal salvation, which was infinitely precious to her. In her religious play, *The Divine Narcissus,* she wrote: "Behold that what I yearn for I am powerless to enjoy, and in my anxious longing to possess it, I suffer mortal pangs.". . . But convent-bound in the medieval atmosphere of the ecclesiastical society of Mexico City she could only feel at war with it and with herself. The love and kindliness implicit in the Church's paternalism claimed her gratitude and, of course, her vows compelled obedience to it. Yet the persistent longing for a freer expression of her intuition and for another and more open avenue to truth and to God prevented complete reciprocation and submission. . . .

As the dawn of April 17, 1695 was casting a wan light over the troubled City of Mexico the wracked and broken spirit of Sister Juana quietly claimed its longed-for release from the prison of her aloneness. "See how death eludes me because I desire it," she had exclaimed in one of her poems, "for even death, when it is in demand," she had added, "will rise in price." Over the long years of her short life she had struggled against the viselike prejudices and incomprehension of her time and place. She had dreamed of a liberation from the shackles of static traditions and stultifying conventions. She had dared to rebuke the men of her society for their double standard of morality and had thus struck a first blow for women's rights.

> Which has the greater sin when burned
> by the same lawless fever:
> She who is amorously deceived,
> or he, the sly deceiver?

Or which deserves the sterner blame,
though each will be a sinner:
She who becomes a whore for pay,
Or he who pays to win her? [2]

But more than all else she had struggled for a freedom of thought for all. "There is nothing freer than the human mind," she had proclaimed to a world that could not comprehend these words, or could only hear them as subversive of a God-given truth. Against her the odds were too great and their relentless pressure brought at last a total renunciation of all effort and a complete submission of her intellect. The passionate woman in her capitulated to the devout nun and this surrender left her bereft of life. Physically she survived herself briefly.

To the unhappy nun-poetess during the last four of five years of her existence the world outside must have seemed a projection of her own inner turmoil and affliction. A series of disasters and phenomena were then plaguing the city and its environs, bringing suffering, fear and violence. Heavy rains in 1691 brought successively ruinous floods, crop destruction, famine, and pestilence, while a total eclipse of the sun stirred panic fear. Sullen discontent and mounting tensions erupted into mass riots that nearly toppled Spanish authority in the land. As these sinister events darkened the world without, the storm, so long brewing within Sister Juana Inés, broke.

In 1690 she inadvertently brought to a head the disapproval and hostility of her religious associates slowly gathering over the years. In some way she was induced to write a successful rebuttal of certain views set forth long before in a sermon by a famous Portuguese Jesuit, Father Vieira. Her skill in manipulating the methods of neo-scholasticism evidently pleased the Bishop of Puebla who took it upon himself to publish her paper. At the same time, in the guise of "Sister Philotea," he wrote her a letter chiding her alleged neglect of religious literature and her fondness for profane letters. "You have spent a lot of time studying (secular) philosophers and poets, and now it would seem reasonable to apply yourself to better things and to better books." Clearly, this was a reproof from a superior high in the hierarchy and it could not fail to distress a nun tormented by guilt feelings. Through months of declining health she brooded on a reply to the Bishop's censure. Finally, under date of March 1, 1691, it took form in her famous *Reply* in which, with many autobiographical details and with alternate humility and boldness, she defended herself from the prelate's strictures.

Obscure complications followed this epistolary exchange, chief of which

---

[2] Robert Graves, trans., "Against the Inconsequences of Men's Desires . . ." *Encounter*, no. 3 (December 1953). Reprinted by permission of Robert Graves [Ed.].

was the withdrawal of her confessor, Father Antonio Núñez de Miranda, who had influenced her decision to enter the convent and had counseled her over the years. Vainly he had urged her to turn from what he considered worldly matters and apply her great talents to things eternal. All her devoted supporters, it seemed to her, were falling away through absence, desertion, or death. And she had never enjoyed the favor of the misogynistic Archbishop Aguiar y Seijas, who had involved her in his frenzied almsgiving. In 1693, as if to remind everyone of her worldliness, a second edition of a volume of her poems, which the vicereine, her friend and patroness, had extracted from her, appeared in Spain, and copies doubtless reached Mexico City soon after. This intended kindness may have hastened her final surrender. On February 8, 1694, using blood from her veins as ink, she indited an abject reaffirmation of her faith and renewed her vows, which she signed: "I, Sister Juana Inés de la Cruz, the worst in the world." She renounced all her possessions, the gifts and trinkets of her admirers, the mathematical and musical instruments that she had so long studied and used, and — the most painful wrench of all — those silent and precious companions of her cell, her beloved books. All were sold and the proceeds given to charity. With this bitter deprivation, she gave herself to excessive acts of penance, self-flagellation, and mortification of the flesh. The coveted death of the body came at last during her tireless ministrations to sisters of her community decimated by a pestilence sweeping the city. . . .

4. Riots in Seventeenth Century Mexico City

CHESTER LYLE GUTHRIE

A large volume could be written on the tumults and disturbances in Mexico City from the time of Cortez until Spanish power was broken three centuries later. Here is a chapter on this subject by Dr. Chester Lyle Guthrie, one of the many scholars who received their historical training under Professor Herbert Eugene Bolton at the University of California, Berkeley.

When the Pilgrim Fathers were making their first settlement in America, indeed when Jamestown was still a struggling community, New Spain already possessed a world-famous metropolis, Mexico City. Time and two empires had established it as perhaps the greatest in the New World. Well-nigh a cen-

"Riots in Seventeenth-Century Mexico City: A Study of Social and Economic Conditions" by Chester Lyle Guthrie, *Greater America: Essays in Honor of Herbert Eugene Bolton* (1945), pp. 243–258, passim. Originally published by the University of California Press; reprinted by permission of the Regents of the University of California.

tury under Spanish control, Mexico City spoke of Hernán Cortés as a figure of the dim past, and had seen the children of the conquistadors grow white-haired.

In the aftermath of conquest, social and economic problems had arisen which were both grave and troublesome. The soldiers of fortune became less and less important, while the merchant, the artisan, the farmer, and other more stable if less romantic elements gained in influence. A man without a profession or trade, or without financial resources, was finding it harder and harder to make a living. Many were forced to accept public or private charity, or else had to depend on begging and the soup of the monasteries. Further-more, the large, conquered Indian population was still in the city and had to be absorbed into the body politic. The time had passed when the Indian prob-lem could be thrust aside by military repression, for the conquered natives had by now attained to a certain legal status. Also, free Negroes and a multi-tude of racial mixtures, each requiring a place in society, had arisen. Mestizos, mulattoes, *castizos, lobos, chinos, zambos,* to mention only a few of the blood combinations, had to be fitted into the social scale. Riots and unrest followed almost as a natural consequence from such numerous and varied social and economic stresses. The following brief discussion of the events surrounding the two major riots of the century may assist the reader to an understanding and evaluation of the underlying causes of the discontent.

The first outbreak occurred on January 15, 1624. On that day the people emerged from early morning Mass in the great cathedral of Mexico with one of the most dreaded edicts ever issued in New Spain ringing in their ears. The pronouncement had been to the effect that all churches would be closed under an order of *cessatio a divinis.* Furthermore, the viceroy, at that time the haughty and unpopular Diego Carrillo de Mendoza y Pimentel, Marqués de Gelves, had been called a heretic and excommunicated. Soon the populace were giving voice to their disapproval of the administration, which they held responsible for the course of events. Scattered at first, then from all sides, came shouts of "Long live the Church!" "Long live the Faith!" "Death to bad government!" "Death to this excommunicated heretic!"

At this unfortunate moment the viceroy's secretary, Cristóbal Osorio, drove into the square in an open carriage. He was recognized, and some urchins selling vegetables in the market raised the shout of "Heretic!" "Heretic!" Osorio ordered a halt and called to his retainers to discipline the youthful hecklers. It was a mistake. In self-defense the boys pelted the servants with stones and even directed some at the secretary himself. Soon other boys joined in hurling missiles, and before long they were assisted by their elders. Indians, mulattoes, mestizoes, and Negroes made up the mass of the first attackers. Even some poor whites joined the mob. Under such a barrage, Osorio had to make the best escape possible; there was not time then to uphold dignity and rank. Consequently, he shouted to the driver to whip the horses to a run, and the carriage thundered into the courtyard of the viceregal palace just ahead of a cloud of flying stones and debris. In haste the guards forced shut the ponderous doors in the face of the raging people.

From that moment the fury of the mob was turned against the palace. With each hour the position of the defenders grew more and more precarious, for the unrelenting pressure of thousands of milling, shouting rioters was more than the civil and military power of Mexico City could withstand. In vain did the viceroy make promise after promise to the people; in vain revoked, even, the edict which had brought about his excommunication. Vainly also did the Inquisition, the great councils, and even the influential citizens strive to calm the rioters. Not until hope of saving the palace was gone did the supporters of the viceroy, especially the audiencia, the greatest of the governing councils, withdraw its aid. By five o'clock in the evening the rioters had burned and sacked the palace. Viceroy Gelves escaped with his life only by the device of putting on servant's clothing and mingling with the crowd, shouting with the rest, "Death to this heretic viceroy!"

A series of events had contributed to this serious outbreak in Mexico City. In the first place, a critical food shortage had caused a virtual famine. Maize, which supplied the principal sustenance of most of the population, had more than quadrupled in price. The resulting misery was very great. And prices of other foodstuffs rose, thus adding to the discontent.

Perhaps second to hunger as a cause of unrest was the viceroy's unfortunate inability to make himself acceptable. By means of impolitic moves he had alienated almost every group in the society of the capital. To the official class he was an unjust and insulting taskmaster, whose arbitrary and retroactive punishments seemed quite out of proportion to the crimes for which they were inflicted. To the rich he was a dangerous reformer; to the poor, an implacable tax collector, law enforcer, and general meddler. Even in executing his reforms he allowed himself to be outmaneuvered and placed in the false position of favoring monopoly and oppression, while other men and institutions, particularly the Church, were credited with any betterments achieved.

Especially violent, however, were the viceroy's quarrels with the Church. After many disagreements, Gelves and the strong-minded archbishop, then a certain Juan Pérez de la Serna, clashed over the use of churches as asylums for fugitives from justice. Neither the archbishop nor the viceroy would give way in the matter. In the end, both parties resorted to their most potent weapons. The viceroy obtained a decree exiling the archbishop, and the archbishop in turn placed the city under an interdict and excommunicated the viceroy. Each made every effort to see his sentence imposed, with the result that the restless population improved its opportunity to riot against the government.

Thus the first riot of the century passed in violence and bloodshed, and for many years there were no great hostile outbreaks to disturb the administrative calm of the city, though other rumblings of discontent were heard from time to time. The danger of mob violence soon gave little concern to the minds of the representatives of the sovereigns of Spain. The old fundamental complaints against the colonial order remained, however, and in less than two generations the greatest riot of the century occurred in Mexico City.

Nature as well as society seemed to conspire to bring misery upon the people of the capital of New Spain. The summer of 1691 was an unusually wet season. Lake Texcoco, from which Mexico City was separated only by a dike and with which it was connected by canals, was changed from a dry, dusty plain into a large body of water. Roads became impassable; supplies ran low; pastures were flooded; and many of the adobe walls of the poorer houses melted, leaving the inhabitants wet, shivering, and hungry. To add to the general distress, the following winter was unusually severe, with snow blanketing the surrounding hills and making it impossible to bring supplies into the city. As a result of the inclement weather, the summer crops in the vicinity of Mexico City were so weakened and rotted that they fell victim to a blight, called by the Indians *chahuistle*. The winter and spring crops were failures, also. Prices began rising, as in 1624.

Under such conditions, the public granary, or *alhóndiga,* was called upon in greater and greater measure to allay the distress. At first it was an agency for stabilizing prices, but soon it became one of the most important sources of food supply. From dispensing a normal amount of six to eight hundred *fanegas* of grain a day (a *fanega* being about one and six-tenths bushels), the *alhóndiga* was soon called upon to dole out as much as six thousand *fanegas* a day. Under pressure, the government strove frantically to keep enough grain on hand, both by public means and through private initiative, but to little avail.

As famine increased, the lower class became more and more restless and intractable. Not only was food scarce, but more and more the wheat-eating, Spanish-descended part of the population was forced to turn to maize as the principal stay of its diet. This, as it happened, provided a new employment for the Indians since maize was most generally eaten by them in the form of tortillas, and they were the ones who best knew how to make that substitute for wheaten bread; and, impressed by their new importance, they became difficult to control. At the *alhóndiga* there was bedlam. Each Indian woman strove to obtain as much maize as possible before the supply should run short, in order to be the first to get her wares to market. Much of the newly found opulence, so far as the men were concerned, went for pulque, which happened to be plentiful that season. Soon in the smoke-filled, dimly lighted *pulquerías,* as the native liquor shops were called, Indians were giving vent both to their old irritations and to their new feeling of superiority. Did not the laws of the land state, said they, that the natives should be served first at the *alhóndiga?* Certainly the Spaniards had grown afraid of the noble Aztecs. Encouraging these beliefs were the mestizos, the mulattoes, and the other malcontents. As a result, to the increasing restlessness in the city, growing out of the misery and discontent of all the lower class, was further added a combative spirit on the part of what was usually the most humble of the social elements in Mexico City, the once-conquered Indian.

As the year 1692 progressed, the scarcity of food became greater and greater. The government of the viceroy looked on all sides for supplies, in a desperate effort to curb the growing discontent. Only by keeping the city quiet until the new harvest should be reaped could the crisis be passed peacefully. The attempt was a failure. An adequate food supply was nowhere to be found.

Early in the afternoon of June 6, word was given out that the maize had been exhausted, and in the ensuing disorder an Indian child was suffocated. This, of course, aroused the anger of the native population. Next day, the crowd at the grain market was sullen and quarrelsome, with the result that the viceroy appointed two of his high-ranking officials to watch over the transactions and keep order. All went well until the maize was once more exhausted and the officials had finally left the market. Then the crowd again became unmanageable; and in the uproar which followed, word flew from mouth to mouth that an Indian woman had been whipped to death by one of the *alhóndiga's* attendants. The *alhóndiga* was promptly deserted as the angry Indians and their supporters marched to the palace, there to seek redress. They were turned away by the palace guards, and consequently went to the palace of the archbishop, where again they were refused a hearing. From there they swarmed back to the government palace, where rioting began in earnest. The Indians were soon joined by Negroes, mulattoes, mestizos, and poor whites, called *saramullos.*

Even more terrible, perhaps, than the riot of 1624 was this new uprising of the lower class. With few weapons other than sticks, stones, fire, and their bare hands, the rioters laid siege to the palace. The outbreak found the administration of the viceroy unable to protect itself. The military forces of the city had become greatly reduced in man power and efficiency during the two generations of peace following 1624, and, as chance would have it, this lack of preparedness was made even more disastrous to the administration by the fact that the crisis came on a church holiday, when many of the officers and men, including even the viceroy, were absent from the palace.

"Long live the Virgen del Rosario!" "Long live the king!" "Long live pulque!" cried the mob as they strove harder and harder to break into the palace. At the same time, and with even more zest, they howled "Death to the viceroy!" "Death to his wife!" "Death to the *corregidor!*" "Death to the Spaniards!" "Down with bad government!" To these cries they added curses of such ingenuity and expressiveness that even the Spaniards were astonished. Shouts of "Death to the Gachupines who eat up all our maize!" did not reassure the onlookers, who, afraid to oppose the mob, had gathered in the streets leading into the square. It soon seemed impossible that the palace could hold out much longer. Especially was the mob successful in setting fires. Most of the palace was blazing, and some of the other government structures, such as the buildings of the *cabildo,* or town council, in which was the *alhóndiga,* were fired. Before the rioters were halted, they had even tried to burn the palace of Pedro Cortés, Marqués del Valle, heir to the title of the famous conquistador.

The mob was diverted only by the action of the clergy and — perhaps more effectively — by the opportunity offered to the rioters for looting the rich market in the Plaza Mayor. While the Indians were trying to take the palace, many of the *saramullos,* and others of the lower class, broke into the *cajones,* as the shops in the plaza were called. First, the stores containing axes, bars, swords, and knives were ransacked for arms and tools. Then the shops with weak doors or roofs were forced open. When the Indians and those besieging the palace saw what was going on, they promptly left what they were doing and joined the plundering of the market. . . .

Among the clergy, the tardily aroused archbishop was the one who took the initiative. He had at first paid little heed to threats of mob action, but once violence occurred he realized the seriousness of the situation. His first move was to call all the churchmen together to plan a course of action, but it was not until nine o'clock in the evening that the forces he organized were ready to act. Two processions, one of Jesuits and the other of friars of Our Lady of Mercy, bravely entered the square singing, praying, and carrying saintly images. . . .

Although a few stopped to listen to the Jesuits and the friars, it was one of the secular clergy who was most successful in diverting the rioters from their purpose. The treasurer of the cathedral, Manuel de Escalante y Mendoza, accompanied by two priests and a friar, took the Holy Sacrament and went into the plaza. The viceregal palace seemed to be beyond help so he forced his way to the palace of the Marqués del Valle, where the Indians had started a fire against the portals. The flames were mounting fast, but the padre was able to persuade the rioters to desist and to put out the blaze. Then the mob turned to the house of one of the important officials, with the intention of burning it, and once more the treasurer prevented them. In fact, he succeeded in keeping them from starting more fires anywhere. Other priests came to his assistance, and soon one was preaching in the native tongue, persuading the Indians to go home, and was heeded.

The destruction caused by this second riot was very great both in lives and property. Undoubtedly, scores were killed and many more were injured, though casualties were never counted since every attempt was made to keep the identity of the rioters secret from the avenging officials. As for the material losses, they were staggering. The great viceregal palace was so badly burned that it had to be rebuilt. The shops in the square had been thoroughly ransacked, and the buildings of the *cabildo* in large part demolished. In all, it was estimated that damage amounting to some three millions of pesos had been done.

For an understanding of the causes underlying the riots, one must delve into the social history of the period. There were at least three reasons for unrest in Mexico City in the seventeenth century. First, there was great social inequality, produced by sharply marked class distinctions which were mainly racial. Second, there was the precarious economic status of the largest part of the population, the part which in the main suffered most from the irritations and restrictions of differences in caste. Finally, administrative weaknesses offered an opportunity for major demonstrations to break out; for, as events showed, the viceregal government was unable to defend itself quickly and effectively against a determined domestic disturbance.

Three fundamental class divisions, based upon likenesses of interest and occupation, were discernible in colonial Mexico City. The first of these, the upper or ruling class, was composed of the rich and the nobility of Spanish extraction. Associated with them were the great merchants and others of the wealthy middle class, between whom and the nobility there was very little social differentiation. Even for a gentleman of noble birth, trading on a large scale was considered a satisfactory occupation. If any cleavage existed, it was between those born in Spain and those born in the New World.

Fallen from high estate, and now perhaps more properly to be considered as of the middle class, was a small, clannish group, the impoverished descendants of the conquistadors. Turbulent and haughty, they usually engaged in some trade or minor occupation. Sometimes, our of deference to the services rendered by their ancestors, the most needy of these were appointed to minor positions in the government.

Aping the nobility, but for the most part economically nearer to the masses, was the lower middle class, including the artisans and poorer shopkeepers. This group, however, was few in numbers and of little influence in the direction of the city's affairs. Instead of absorbing many of the masses, it kept its ranks closed by means of exclusive guild regulations, with the result that a large and restive lower class remained unaccommodated in the community. Consequently, the city's class struggle was essentially between the two extremes, and was emphasized by the great size of the lower class.

By far the most numerous and restless social group was this lower one. In an estimated population of a quarter million, its members represented from three to five times the total of those above them. Most of the viceroys had already been aware that they poverty, their vices, and the hopelessness of their position in the social scale might ripen them for crime and violence.

Among the more difficult to control were those outcast whites, together with some Indians and mixed-bloods, who were called vagabonds. Petty thievery and chicanery were their stock in trade, and any untoward disturbance would at once enlist them as rioters.

Of the non-Spanish elements which helped to form the lower class, the one which ranked the highest in the social scale was that composed of the mestizos, those who had a mixture of Indian and Spanish blood. Their number was quite large. It was admitted that they were presumptuous and almost as troublesome as the other groups among the masses, but the officials pointed out that they showed more promise of development than others of the racial mixtures.

Many and diverse were the strains which included Negro blood. The Negroes, both of mixed and of pure descent, formed a sizable part of the population of the seventeenth-century Mexico City. As a rule they were considered untrustworthy by the rest of the citizens.

Outnumbering the mestizo and Negro elements were the Indians. They were the ones upon whom fell the chief burden of manual labor in colonial society. If an aqueduct had to be repaired, Indians were promptly assigned to the job. If a load was to be moved, or any other task of similar nature was to be performed, Indians were always called upon. Consequently, their very low position in the scheme of colonial life, as well as the fact that their interests, by the same token, were so widely separated from those of the ruling class, made them especially inclined to join subversive movements. . . .

For the most part, members of the lower class depended upon wages for their livelihood. Trade and industry employed a large number in the lesser capacities, while personal service and government projects accounted for another sizable group. Ordinarily, the wages paid were just enough to meet the needs of the laborer.

In industry, the lower class suffered many restrictions. Although a large proportion was employed in the trades, the rules of the guilds were so formulated that persons of non-Spanish origin, of which the lower class was mostly composed, could never hope to rise higher than the unskilled, low-paid levels. Even the very poor whites could hope for little from the guilds, for the expense of going through the period of apprenticeship, and of paying the fees and fulfilling the requirements attendant upon examination for entrance into one of the trades, made such a course a practical impossibility. In fact, restrictions were so stringent that Viceroy Linares complained that there was a marked lack of opportunity even for Spanish youths to enter a trade.

For those who were not absorbed into industry, domestic service, or governmental activities, there was little left to do but to peddle fruit, vegetables, flowers, grass, and similar goods in the public markets. Should this fail, only begging or crime was left.

Unemployment and partial unemployment added greatly to the problems of the wage earners. Many of the Indians, especially, worked at seasonal occupations in the country. Out of season, they spent almost their entire time in idleness; or so said Viceroy Juan de Mendoza y Luna, Marqués de Montesclaros. Furthermore, the presence of so many vagabonds of all races and mixtures in the city indicated that there was a great deal of unemployment. To Giovanni Gemelli Careri, a noted Italian observer, it seemed as if almost all the Indians were idle and therefore reduced to cheating in order to make a living. Viceroy Linares complained of the great number of idlers who lived by doing occasional odd jobs and, the rest of the time, by dishonesty. . . .

Under such circumstances a fluctuation in the price of any basic commodity, such as maize, was a matter of great importance. There were a number of times when the price of maize became very high, notably in 1624 and in 1692, the years of the two riots, when it rose to four and five times its normal figure, or about ten *reales*. In several other periods of scarcity, high prices caused unrest and demonstrations among the poor — without violence, however.

To counteract the fluctuating cost of living, the government felt obliged to give some aid to the poor. This help, together with direct charity, was one of the characteristics of colonial Mexico City. It was believed that without governmental regulation the price of the fundamental necessities would rise so high that none but the well-to-do and the rich could live comfortably, or perhaps even exist at all. Besides, charity was not only a civic duty; it was an important part of the religious life of the time. The poor, the widows, and the orphans found a place in the financial budgets of the government, institutions, and private individuals. Nevertheless, in spite of these mitigating influences, the fundamental problem of a low standard of living, barely at the subsistence level, helped to keep society unstable.

Many means of price fixing were tried. Perhaps most noteworthy was the supervision and operation of the public grain market, the *alhóndiga*. For the institution the government established numerous and complicated rules, which somewhat alleviated the general situation. The difficulty was that during the years of plenty most of the rules and regulations would fall into disuse and the market would be practically abandoned as a major activity of the government. When a time of scarcity arrived, this shortsighted policy left the *alhóndiga* too badly crippled to act as efficiently as it should have done. Besides grain, almost all other commodities, such as meat, fruit, vegetables, and bread, were carefully regulated in price, in an attempt at fairness both to the consuming public and to business.

As the social and economic conditions of the era were basic factors in the development of movements of unrest, so in turn was the failure of the government to provide itself with adequate forces to suppress those outbreaks which led to rioting. When uprisings threatened the capital, three forces of protection were available to the viceroy: the regularly constituted police authority, the guard of soldiers kept in Mexico City, and the citizen militia, which was supposedly ready to answer a call to arms in case of an emergency. Twice in the seventeenth century all three of these agencies failed. . . .

There remains the question why the great tumults of the century occurred only in the years 1624 and in 1692. Two reasons present themselves. First, there was the difference in the degree to which scarcity in foodstuffs was felt. In 1624 and in 1692 the suffering was much greater, and continued over longer periods of time, than during other crises which developed in the seventeenth century. Hence the people were driven to extremes of desperation. Second, there was the difference in the administrative ability of the persons in authority. Several times the poor were so far aroused that many of them went in a body to the palace, and each time obtained satisfaction quickly and with a minimum of irritation because the viceroys proved equal to the occasion. This was not true in 1624 and in 1692, when the potentially dangerous conditions in Mexico City ended in uprisings.

The tumults achieved few permanent results, by reason of their nature. In the first place, although the riots were exceedingly violent, they lasted only for very short periods, thus quickly relieving the government from pressure for reform. Second, they were spontaneous outbreaks without plan, program, or leadership, and flared up from immediate resentment. Consequently, the riots prompted administrative reform in the city but brought about no permanent social or economic improvement. Once quiet was restored, and there was no longer any reason for the government to be alarmed, most of the new regulations were relaxed until another period of crisis arrived. The importance of the riots, then, lies in the light which they throw upon social and economic conditions under the viceroys, and not upon the reforms which followed close upon them.

5. Tensions Between Spanish- and Spanish-American-Born Friars in Seventeenth-Century Peru

ANTONINE TIBESAR

Father Antonine Tibesar of the Academy of American Franciscan History has carried on research for a number of years on the ecclesiastical history of Peru. Here he describes the growing tension between friars from Spain and those born in Peru, based on a wide variety of sources.

Serious trouble eventually came, which led to fire, tumultuous scenes, and death. The long-range consequences were unfortunate for the Church: "the clergy suffered a continuing loss of both prestige and numbers. . . . The alternative seems to have been a mistake for both Church and State."

Within recent years there has been increasing interest in those aspects of Spanish American history which represent a growing political consciousness

From "The Creole Inheritance," in *Miners and Merchants in Bourbon Mexico 1763–1810* by D. A. Brading (Cambridge, England; Cambridge University Press, 1971), pp. 208–216, passim. Reprinted by permission.

among the inhabitants of those lands especially during the seventeenth and eighteenth centuries.

Perhaps nowhere can the growth of this sentiment be studied with greater ease than in the religious orders. By their development, the religious orders, the Augustinians, Dominicans, Franciscans, Jesuits, and Mercedarians, came to consist almost exclusively of *criollos* (descendants of Europeans born in America) and *Chapetones* (friars born in Europe, in particular in Spain): the two groups which were to be the leaders of the two contending parties in the wars of independence. The ultimate estrangement of these two groups developed during the colonial period in the course of which the rising creole desire to manage their own affairs encountered increasing opposition from the Spanish Crown. The encounters were not always peaceful. The participants, on both sides, in good faith held to their principles with a deep conviction of which the incidental vehemence is perhaps the clearest proof. Neither side yielded readily. This is true also of the friars.

By their constitutions, most religious orders held elections every three or four years in which the friar-delegates freely elected their provincials and his council. Of course, these elections afforded the creoles, and the Spaniards too, a perfect opportunity to voice their sentiments regarding the type of candidate which they preferred with comparative freedom and immunity. Thus the chapters of the religious orders may in a certain sense be regarded as the first forum in which the creole was able to state for the first time his preference in regard to his ruler. There was perhaps little political significance, at least in the beginning, in the decisions of these chapters. The friars were not revolutionaries seeking to overthrow Spanish authority, though they may well have wished to restrict the extent of the Spanish monopoly of positions and power. Neither were these chapters wholly without political significance. Many friars in the seventeenth century were members of powerful creole families. Their relatives, who did have political ambitions which were regularly thwarted by the royal policy of preferring *Chapetones* exclusively for the highest offices, regarded these chapters with more than passing interest. In them their unspoken protests found voice. This was realized by the royal officials and in an effort to curb creole aspirations the Crown imposed the *alternativa:* the forced alternation in the higher offices of the respective provinces of Spanish and Peruvian friars.

The first friars who arrived in Peru were, of course, almost exclusively Europeans. The bulk of these were Spaniards, though we do find Portuguese, French, and even Germans in their ranks. The Dominicans and the Mercedarians came with Pizarro in 1531 with the Franciscans following their example after a few months. The Augustinians came in 1551 and the Jesuits in

1568. From the very beginning, the Dominicans do not seem to have received any Indians or those with Indian blood in their ranks, and all available evidence today points to the conclusion that the Dominicans as a rule received only Spanish or creoles. The Mercedarians at an early date, certainly before 1548, had already established the policy of admitting Indian and mestizo boys — a fact which may help to explain the attitude of that order towards the Pizarros and also its loss of social acceptance by the Spaniards which resulted in its royal suppression in 1568. The Franciscans seem to have adopted in the beginning the Dominican attitude, although there are some indications that they may have admitted Indians as lay brothers, though not as priests. In general also the Augustinians accepted the Dominican policy and at a comparatively early date, 1571, forbade the reception of mestizos. The attitude of the first Jesuits towards the mestizos is not clear but after the arrival of Father Joseph de Acosta in 1572, the Jesuits, for a time, became the devoted protectors of the mestizos and admitted a number into their Order, among them the famous Blas de Valera. The experiment, however, did not prove happy and in 1582 the Jesuits also excluded them. From that time, until possibly the middle of the eighteenth century, the religious order in Peru with the exception of the Jesuits were to be made up almost exclusively of creoles and *Chapetones*. After their sad experiences with the mestizos, the Jesuits proceeded to limit also the numbers of creoles who might join their company. This limitation was not removed until late in the eighteenth century.

The other Orders had placed no limit on the reception of creoles and accordingly as the century advanced an ever greater proportion of the total number came to be drawn from this class. The desire to manage their own affairs grew apace with their numbers and importance and before the end of the sixteenth century encountered considerable opposition from the Spanish friars who had founded the provinces in Peru and had enjoyed a monopoly in their government for a number of decades. In particular was this true of the Dominicans who had been the first religious to organize a province in that country and apparently also the first to receive candidates. It is understandable therefore that this problem would become acute first of all among them. As early as 1565, Castro informed the Crown of the existence of factions among them. Castro did not specify the cause of the division but in 1588, Viceroy Villar reported that the desire of the creole Dominicans to govern themselves was the cause of internal difficulties. At the same time, the viceroy added that the Spanish Dominicans were few in number. By 1592, the creoles were so firmly entrenched among them that they were able to pass a law which prohibited the entrance of any Spaniard into the Dominican Lima province. The situation must have been very similar in the other Orders for by 1593, the majority of the friars in all Orders in Peru were creoles, though none of the others is known actually to have forbidden the reception of Spaniards.

The situation occasioned by the emergence of the creole friars to positions of power disturbed the royal officials both in Peru and in Spain. It would simplify the problem if we could state that this uneasiness was merely the reflection of the usual antagonism of the metropolis versus the colony. However the matter is not quite that simple. The Spanish officials and the Crown just did not feel at this time that the creole friars were quite ready to manage their own affairs and they feared that under continual creole control the state of the religious orders would decline or deteriorate. Fairness demands that this writer state that he found no responsible Spanish official whose uneasiness over creole control at this time was motivated by racial or political implications. Their opposition was based at the end of the sixteenth century not on discernible political motives but on the lack of personal qualifications by the creole class in general.

Actually it is somewhat difficult to comprehend the need for Spanish concern because at this very time when the authorities were worrying about creole competence, the Church in Peru was being or was about to be blessed with a series of men and one woman of extraordinary virtue. However that may be, the official reason for Spanish opposition to creole control at that time was the widely held belief that the creoles just were not then fit for the job. Strange to say, creole resentment against continued Spanish monopoly seems to have been based at this time on the same grounds. The creole friars felt that the Spanish friar who came to Peru or the Spanish boy in Peru who wished to be a friar were usually the misfits or the laggards from Spain and the creoles did not want them. Besides they felt that even the best Spanish friars frequently were unable to view with sympathy and equanimity the innovations which the circumstances of life in the New World had rendered necessary. Here again, therefore, the personal qualifications seem to have been the prime consideration, not the racial or political. This was to change both for the Spaniards and for the creoles in the course of the next century, as we shall see. But in the early years of the seventeenth century, the creole-Spanish problem does not seem to have been rooted in either racial or political considerations and suggestions made at that time by the viceroys and others which might have tended towards that development were either ignored or expressly prohibited, perhaps in the hope that the problem might somehow finds its own solution.

If such were indeed the desire of the Crown, it was doomed to be frustrated. The problem would not disappear and the solution which was evolved during the ensuing decades of the seventeenth century — if solution it may be called — was in essence racial. This solution was called the *alternativa*. The *alternativa* signified the forced alternate election of Spaniards and creoles to the main offices in the provinces irrespective of superior qualifications or superior numbers. The reason for selection, therefore, was primarily the place of birth. . . . Despite the great numerical superiority of the creoles, the Spanish friars maintained an almost complete monopoly of the higher offices in the Lima province down to almost 1650 with relatively little creole dissent. However, by 1630, there is evidence of an awakening creole consciousness of their power. . . . On the basis of numbers . . . the Spanish friars were receiving a fair representation in the election of the provincial — the highest office in the province filled by direct and free election of the members of the province. However, the disturbing element in the picture was the constant trend against the Spaniards, and these had little hope for improvement in the ratio. This disquieted the Europeans and rumbles of their dissatisfaction with the turn of events are discernible in their letters to the Crown beginning already in the 1640's. The ready made equalizer was the *alternativa*. . . .

The motives which led the Spanish friars to seek the *alternativa* may be reduced to three: (1) distrust of creole capabilities and perhaps also of their loyalty; (2) a feeling that the creoles owed such consideration to the Spaniards because of their services in the past; (3) a vague certainty of Spanish superiority. Nowhere do the Spanish friars assert that they seek the *alternativa* because of ambition, just as nowhere do the creoles admit that they wish to reject the *alternativa* for the same reason. It is evident that the creoles, or Americans and Peruvians as they were frequently called during the debate, could not agree completely with the views advanced by their Spanish brethren. Nor apparently was there any neutral ground upon which to base a compromise. The argument therefore would have to continue until either one side or the other was adjudged the victor. In 1666, this meant that the Peruvians would have to appeal since the 1664 decree had been adverse to their wishes. . . . [All appeals failed, and by 1680 the Americans seemed to be ready for open revolt.]

On Sunday evening, December 29, 1680, at about eleven o'clock a fire was discovered at one of the five doors leading to the private quarters of the Commissary General, Father Marcos Terán. Though both Terán and the viceroy-archbishop claim that this fire was begun by the creoles, neither of them investigated its origin. The city council of Lima which "conducted a thorough investigation uncovered nothing concerning either the authors or the origin of the fire." Their conclusion was that "it might have been started by some student friars or by others to throw blame on them." At any rate no harm was done and the remaining four doors permitted Terán free egress.

As soon as the alarm was given by a lay brother who chanced to pass on his way to bed from the convent chapel, a Spanish friar of most curious ancestry and habits and five men in lay clothes, all fully armed, rushed from the quarters of Terán and roamed the cloisters while Terán made his way to the chapel of La Soledad. When asked later what these armed men were doing in his quarters, Terán answered that he had been warned a few days before that the creoles were plotting to kill him and the Spanish friar had organized an armed guard.

At the time the alarm was first given some of the younger friars were just rising to go to church for their regular midnight prayers. Some of these began to toll the church bells to give the alarm and this was soon taken up also by the bells of the cathedral — the official sign of an enemy attack. The confusion both within San Francisco — which is three blocks long by about a block and a half wide — and in the city was indescribable. In the city itself perhaps matters were worse than in the convent because the people had just passed through a series of alarms due to the pirates along the coast and their first thought was of course that the pirates had returned.

The viceroy was informed at 11:30 P.M. of the happenings and immediately ordered the *alcaldes* and their infantry to the monastery to search for weapons and to quiet the people now gathering there. The search continued until 2 A.M. though no weapons were found anywhere except in the quarters of Terán, which in the words of the *maese de campo* were "many and good ones too." Terán was escorted by some of the soldiers to the viceregal palace while three companies patrolled the streets outside the monastery and another company was garrisoned within to control the main doors. The majority of these soldiers were Spaniards.

Monday, December 30, passed in this fashion. "It was a day of shots and confusion within and without the monastery." No friar was permitted to leave and all doors remained under the control of the soldiers. Under the circumstances, of course, tension mounted between the Spanish soldiers and the creole friars especially the young students as insults were shouted back and forth. Terán issued a statement laying all the blame on the Peruvian friars and placing all of them under excommunication. During the late afternoon about 2,400 soldiers were concentrated around the monastery in obedience to the viceroy's orders to the astonishment of the people. The *alcaldes* were again sent in to search for arms with no more success than on the preceding night, even though the entire monastery was searched room by room.

Tuesday, December 31, came with a company of soldiers still camped in the monastery and others on the outside. The viceroy had sent them into the convent on Sunday night perhaps without much thought and the problem now seemed to have been how to withdraw them without losing prestige. Some reason had to be found to justify this extreme measure. In the palace, the viceroy and some of the members of the audiencia agreed with Terán that this was the occasion to exile fifteen more friars to Chile: nine of them priests and six student friars. Among the priests was Father Cristoval de Contreras, the nominal leader of the creoles. Accordingly at 5 P.M. the *alcalde de corte,* D. Gaspar de Cuba, came to San Francisco and asked to see the nine priests. When the priests came and were informed of the purpose of the visit, they merely requested permission to return to their rooms to get some clothes. Thereupon, without protest or other difficulty, all nine were put in coaches drawn up outside the monastery and driven under guard to Callao preparatory to their shipment to Chile. After seeing the nine priests driven off, the *alcalde* returned to call for the six students. As he knocked at the door of the students' quarters, he heard a shot from within and a terrible scream. Without fulfilling his mission, the *alcalde* departed as soon as he heard that a friar deacon, Francisco Manrique, had been shot and instantly killed by a shot in the heart by a soldier of a Basque company which was on guard. What seems to have happened was that the students were panic-stricken when they heard the *alcalde* had come to take away some of their number. They tried to escape by fleeing through a *puerta falsa* which they mistakenly thought was unguarded. As they opened the gate, one of the guards fired and Manrique fell mortally wounded. The tension of three days on the guards and on the friars had reached its climax.

Pandemonium now broke loose. The people in the streets hearing the shot and the ensuing screams and shouts broke open one of the doors of the church to enter the monastery. The friars at the same time tried to get out of the monastery but the soldiers resisted their efforts until one of the priests brought the Blessed Sacrament from the students' chapel. Thereupon one of the captains, the only creole captain, ordered his men who were guarding the door to the church to permit the friars to leave. Lima now saw what was most probably the strangest procession in its entire history emerge from the church of San Francisco. A huge mulatto had picked up the body of the slain deacon and carried it cradled in his arms with the blood oozing to the ground. Most of the friars followed the Blessed Sacrament to the College of the Jesuits of San Pablo, while the mulatto carried the body across the *plaza mayor* in front of the viceregal palace to the church of the Dominicans, while the bells of the churches tolled in mourning. Only those of San Francisco were silent because the guards would not permit the few friars who remained to ring them. The viceroy issued a *bando* to clear the streets, but that was not necessary. Stunned by the happenings of the afternoon, the people dispersed rapidly, each one rather anxious to get home. . . .

It was quite evident that events had gotten out of hand. The people of Lima, submissive and rather timid, were greatly disturbed and it may well have been true, as the viceroy stated, that only good fortune prevented a bloody outbreak. Certainly a more virile race would have done something long before that. The Augustinian, Jesuit, and Mercedarian superiors in Lima protested not only against the tyranny of the viceroy and of the commissary general but against the *alternativa* as well. Among the people, aroused nationalistic loyalties divided husband from wife, parents from children. Some wives even asked to be separated from their husbands. More to be feared were the rumbles of discontent among the Indians of the sierra and of unrest among the miners. Now it was the turn of the authorities to be dismayed at the effects which their imprudent measures had provoked. With a complete lack of a sense of responsibility for the chaos to which the Franciscan Order had been reduced, Terán blithely announced that he thought that he could no longer do anything with the creoles and hence he would take the first ship to leave the country. Apparently he did so too, and from the north finally sent a letter appointing the Spaniard, Father Diego Phelipe de Cuellar to handle the situation. Liñán also suddenly decided that he had never wanted to support Terán's efforts anyway. Instead on January 1, 1681, he decided to permit the *alternativa* to lapse and to withdraw the troops from San Francisco. As he wrote to the king:

> Although the disobedience and rebellion of these creoles galls me greatly, it is almost impossible to punish it as it deserves because of the general support they receive from the entire kingdom because of family ties and because of the sympathy [por la pasión] of all the other Orders.

Liñán then passed the problem to Madrid by recommending that the Crown should punish the friars by taking away their *doctrinas* and by appointing the provincial in the future from Madrid. . . .

The tensions engendered by the *alternativa* affected both State and Church in Peru. Politically, this struggle helped to emphasize the fact that while in law the Peruvians and Spaniards were equal vassals of the same kind, in fact the Peruvians were regarded by the Crown as colonials. Hence, there is reason to agree with those who profess to see in the *alternativa* one of the factors which fostered the growth of a Peruvian national consciousness and thereby, at least indirectly, of a desire for independence. Certainly at the time when other factors rendered the decision in favor of national independence feasible, the *alternativa* would have done much to prepare the minds of the Peruvians to concur in and to favor that decision.

More pronounced, perhaps, were the effects, both direct and indirect, upon the Church itself. Directly, to judge from the records of the Franciscans, the clergy suffered a continuing loss of both prestige and numbers. During the decade, 1680–1690, relatively few Peruvians entered the Franciscan Order in Lima, while before that date the annual increase averaged nearly twenty-four. At the same time, the young men after 1690 who did become Franciscans seem definitely to have belonged to a lower social class than had those who had been received before that decade. Also the average of the annual entrants never seems to have reached the volume maintained earlier. . . .

It is possible that the Church may have suffered also indirectly from the *alternativa*. At that time, there was union of Church and State. In the earlier decades of Peruvian history, the Church had undoubtedly profited from this union. Now the State demanded its payment. At a time when Spanish prestige was declining throughout the world, the Crown needed all the support it could muster. In this effort, it forced the Church, at least in the *alternativa* affair, to identify its interests with those of the State. Perhaps any other position at that time would have been unthinkable. It would seem to be just as unthinkable, although at this time there is little concrete proof for or against this theoretical conclusion, that the later revolutionary political leaders should have cherished the Church while hating the State with which it was identified.

In the long run, therefore, the *alternativa* seems to have been a mistake for both Church and State. The creole friars tried to persuade the royal officials to adopt this belief. They had failed. Accordingly, on January 6, 1686, the *alternativa* was finally imposed on the Lima Franciscans by explicit royal order.

THE TEXTURE OF URBAN LIFE

6. *The Imperial City of Potosí, Boom Town Supreme*

LEWIS HANKE

The history of the mining city of Potosí in colonial Peru, now part of Bolivia, might be reduced to a series of graphs recording the amount of silver produced each year. Such a statistical report would tell the economic story of Potosí, and someday when the archives have been more thoroughly searched a chart of rising and falling production to indicate the curves of prosperity and decline in Potosí's history will surely be made. The following sketch, however, emphasizes the human aspects of the vicissitudes of this legendary silver city.

No city in all of the vast territory of America won for the King of Spain — save perhaps Mexico City — has had a more interesting or more important history than Potosí, located in the Viceroyalty of Peru. The colorful story of this great mountain of silver began when the Inca Emperor Huayna Capac started digging almost a century before the Spaniards arrived. He was halted — so legend has it — by a terrible noise and a mysterious voice which commanded, in the Quechua Indian language: "Take no silver from this hill. It is destined for other owners." The *conquistadores* heard no such prohibitory voice in 1545 when they were told of the rich silver ore by Indians who had accidentally discovered it, and indeed, if they had, would doubtless have considered themselves the rightful owners. They immediately began to develop Potosí, which was to become one of the most famous mines in the history of the world.

Treasure seekers flocked from Spain and many other parts of the world to this bleak and uninviting spot high up in the Andes, to exploit the silver in the *Cerro,* or sugar-loaf mountain, which rises majestically over the plateau to a height of almost 16,000 feet above sea level. The first census, taken by Viceroy Francisco de Toledo about twenty-five years after the news of the lode first burst upon the world, showed the unbelievable total of 120,000 inhabitants. By 1650 the population had risen — we are told — to 160,000 and Potosí was incomparably the largest city in South America. At a time when Virginia and the Massachusetts Bay Colony were puling infant colonies, unsure of their next harvest, Potosí had produced such quantities of silver that its very name had become so common a symbol for untold wealth that Don Quijote quoted to it Sancho Panza. *Vale un Potosí,* the Spaniards expressed it. The phrase "as rich as Potosí" became current in English literature as well, for within a generation of its discovery the astronomical quantities of silver mined there had become known to Spain's enemies and to others in far corners of the world. Potosí was soon marked on maps by the Portuguese, always the vigilant rivals of Spain, and even on the Chinese world map of Father Ricci, where it was placed in its correct position and called Mount *Pei-tu-hsi.*

The flush times of Potosí lasted for almost two centuries, and during this period the Imperial City (as it was officially designated by the Emperor Charles V) developed a wealthy and disorderly society. The vice, the piety, the crimes, the *fiestas* of these Potosinos, all were on a vast scale. In 1556, for example, eleven years after the founding of the city, the inhabitants celebrated the accession of Philip II to the throne of Spain with a party which lasted twenty-four days and cost eight million pesos. In 1577 three million pesos were spent on water works, an improvement which ushered in a period of even greater prosperity. By the end of the sixteenth century, miners in

From *The Imperial City of Potosí: An Unwritten Chapter in the History of Spanish America* by Lewis Hanke (The Hague: Martinus Nijhoff, 1956), pp. 1–42, passim. Reprinted by permission of the publisher.

search of recreation could choose among the fourteen dance halls, the thirty-six gambling houses, and the one theater, the price of admission to which ranged from forty to fifty pesos. Later, one of the governors organized a "grandiosa fiesta," to celebrate an ecclesiastical event, which included the establishment in one plaza of a circus "with as many different kinds of animals as in Noah's Ark, as well as fountains simultaneously spouting wine, water, and the native drink *chicha.*" The seventeenth-century ecclesiastical chronicler Antonio de la Calancha declared: "In Potosí the signs of Libra and Venus predominate, and thus most of those who live there incline to be covetous, friends of music and festivities, zealous in the pursuit of riches, and somewhat given to venery." The scanty literature now available emphasizes about equally the carnal pleasures obtainable in the silver-rich mining camp, and the curious, awe-inspiring, and stupendous events of its uproarious history. Our knowledge of Potosí may be said to be still in the folklore stage.

For many years Potosí was boom town supreme and full of turbulence. Treachery, assassination, and civil war flourished as the natural result of the gambling, the intrigues, the antagonism between Peninsular Spaniards and American born Creoles, and the rivalries for the favor of women. Fighting became a pastime, a recognized social activity. Even the members of the town council came to their meetings armed with swords and pistols, and wearing coats of mail. The Dominican friar Rodrigo de Loaysa described the "accurséd hill of Potosí" as a sink of iniquity, but the Viceroy García Hurtado de Mendoza declared that the mine was the *nervio principal en aquel reino,* "the principal support of that realm."

At one time, in the early part of the seventeenth century, there were some 700 or 800 professional gamblers in the city and 120 prostitutes, among them the redoubtable courtesan Doña Clara, whose wealth and beauty, the chroniclers assure us, were unrivalled. The most extravagant woman in Potosí, she was able to fill her home with the luxuries of Europe and the Orient, for her salon was frequented by the richest miners, who competed enthusiastically for her favors. Vagabonds abounded, and royal officials indignantly reported that there ne'er-do-wells did nothing but dress extravagantly and eat and drink to excess. So high were the stakes that one Juan Fernández dared to start a revolution in 1583, by which he hoped to make himself king of Potosí. He and his brothers planned to seize the city and, "despite the fact that he was a married man, Fernández had selected a widow, María Alvarez, to share the throne of his kingdom-to-be." The government learned of this plot and captured Fernández before his revolution could erupt, but this was not the last time that the wealth of Potosí engendered a fever of boundless hope and all-consuming desire among the bold spirits attracted to that cold and windy city.

A thick volume could be compiled on the plots that were hatched. One was the conspiracy led by Gonzalo Luis de Cabrera and the *relator* of the Audiencia de La Plata named Juan Díaz Ortiz. They caused royal officials much trouble in 1599 because they tried to smuggle in hundreds of Englishmen through the port of Buenos Aires to help them with their plans to take over Potosí.

When other mines were discovered, particularly after 1640, production began to slacken at Potosí. It continued to decline steadily throughout the eighteenth century, despite frantic efforts to improve the methods by which the silver was exploited, and at last the glory departed. The War for Independence was a decisive influence in the final decline of Potosí under Spanish rule. During this agitated period the Indians practically stopped working in the mine, and it was difficult to obtain materials needed for its operation. Up to 1816 Potosí was lost and won by the opposing forces three times. After 1816 Upper Peru was wholly occupied by royalist forces despatched by the Viceroy in Lima, and continuous guerrilla warfare was the rule. . . .

The citizens of Potosí early felt the growing pains of greatness and from the earliest years demanded royal recognition of their city's value to the crown. The Emperor Charles V bestowed upon Potosí the title Imperial City, and placed upon its first coat of arms the words: "I am rich Potosí, the treasure of the world, and the envy of kings." His prudent son Philip II devised the scarcely less modest legend on the shield he sent them, which is used to the present day: "For the powerful Emperor, for the wise King, this lofty mountain of silver could conquer the whole world." Here was a slightly veiled royal hint that it took money to make the wheels of empire turn around. Besides the royal cut of one-fifth of all silver mined there was also the possibility of "gifts" or "loans" by individual Potosinos to a succession of ever necessitous kings whose coffers held too little for their needs. A number of documents in the archives attest to the fact that Potosinos did assist the crown in this way.

The Potosinos naturally expected some return for their assistance. As the old Spanish proverb has it: "You trim my whiskers and I'll do your topknot." Therefore the Villa Imperial regularly sent representatives to the court thousands of miles away to make known their desires. Potosí early became irked at the fact that the City of La Plata, some 150 miles away, held jurisdiction over it. The miners at Potosí struggled to throw off this yoke and by 1561 had gained their independence.

The *cabildos* or municipal councils in America were relatively weak creatures in the Spanish colonies, but not so the group that ran the affairs of rich Potosí. Their representatives enjoyed real bargaining power, and they presented their demands in well-executed and detailed documents. Antonio de León Pinelo, one of the most outstanding administrators, lawyers, and bibliographers of the seventeenth century, drew up briefs and petitions on behalf of Potosí. Sebastián de Sandoval y Guzmán was particularly active, and his *Pretensiones de la Villa Imperial de Potosí*, printed in excellent fashion in Madrid in 1634, was typical of a whole literature which might be labeled "Pretensiones de Potosí."

What did the miners want? A steady supply of Indians for the *mita*, mercury at a low price, and freedom from bureaucratic interference by royal officials were some of the demands; and loud and insistent complaints of the miners on these and other problems fill many volumes in the archives. They resisted the drawing off of miners to fight as soldiers in Chile or other threatened parts of the empire. They felt that the regulation of Viceroy Toledo, establishing that miners should never be imprisoned for debt or their property sold to satisfy debts, was a wise law which should never be revoked, because it assured a steady production upon which depended the economic health of Potosí and consequently a steady revenue to the crown. The Real Banco de San Carlos was designed to help the miners, too, and the history of this bank will doubtless provide a valuable chapter in the fiscal history of Potosí.

The Potosinos agitated for an exemption from the *alcabala*, or sales tax, and also urged the crown to see to it that merchants in Panama and Peru sent sufficient merchandise to the ever-thirsty markets of Potosí. Above all, the Potosinos wanted the royal share of silver mined cut down from one fifth to one tenth of production.

All these and other privileges and exemptions were clamored for by a city conscious of its power and aware of the king's constant need for funds. Sometimes these requests were granted in part and for limited periods, but the Potosinos were never completely satisfied. As late as 1783 we find the king decorating the Villa Imperial with the title of "Fidelísima" or "Most Faithful," in another royal attempt to assuage some of their feelings with fine words. The struggle between a succession of hard-pressed monarchs and Potosí was in fact a continuous seesaw, ending only with the successful revolution against Spain. . . .

The wealth of Potosí drew to this Andean mining center Indians from many parts of Peru, a forced migration movement of great proportions that had never before been seen in the land, for under Inca rule only Indians on royal business had moved along the Inca highways. Negroes were also brought to Potosí, despite the doubts concerning their usefulness in the cold, rarefied atmosphere of Potosí. Spaniards from most parts of the peninsula and from all walks of life participated in the rush to explore the mine, and it does not seem strange to learn that one of the miners was a descendant of Columbus.

Foreigners were so numerous that the crown became alarmed at the dangers of their presence. A document dated 1581 lists the foreigners then in the city, and many other censuses of foreigners and reports on what they were doing, and whether their presence was "inconvenient" or not, were prepared by the hard-working representatives of the crown. The Inquisition documents provide information on suspected heretics and also on various Portuguese, who seem to have prospered in Potosí.

Another concern of the crown was the large number of vagabonds and ne'er-do-wells that flourished in the city. Not only did these lazy fellows not produce silver, but they might even be potentially dangerous, as a rebel group. Orders were despatched regularly for the "vagabonds that infest the city" to be punished and summarily ejected. These measures failing, the crown suggested that they be discreetly encouraged to engage in new discoveries and colonization attempts. If not killed in the frontier battles, at least they would be drawn away from Potosí and established far away, perhaps never to return!

The whole round of social life in this ebullient community has a sort of wild-west atmosphere. It was a vast melting pot, even more so than some other parts of the empire, for few white women could stand the climate; childbirth was particularly difficult because of the altitude. By 1586 enough *mestizos* or mixed bloods were present to provoke a riot, and the history of Potosí is well laced with disturbances which probably derived, in part at least, from the tremendous mixing of peoples that went on steadily. One little-known rebellion was attempted in 1599 with the help of the English.

This mixing of racial strains produced some interesting results. From time to time legal documents are found in the archives concerning the action of an individual who wishes to be recognized legally as a *mestizo,* because otherwise he would be forced to work in the mines as an Indian. And at least one legal process relates to a person who stated that he was an Indian and did not want to be considered a *mestizo.*

Tailors went berserk in 1604 over an election of their guild officers and even Augustinian friars once had to be reproved by the government for resisting the law with swords. Some ecclesiastics engaged in commerce or led loose lives, the crown interested itself in sending married men back to their wives in Spain or in other parts of the empire, excess ostentation in funerals had to be reproved, bull fights held in holy years were frowned upon, Indians who had fancy merchandise forced upon them against their will protested, priests quarrelled about preferential places in processions, and the descendants of Diego Huallpa, the discoverer of the mountain of silver, claimed special rights and privileges they considered due them. The detail on the social life of Potosí is rich, copious, and unexploited. . . .

Even if all the thousands of pages of manuscripts on Potosí were to be organized and made available for study, and even if monographs were prepared on all the topics listed above, problems of interpretation would still remain.

One great pitfall to be avoided is that of exaggerating everything connected with the mine. Historians writing on Potosí have not infrequently fallen victims of the boom spirit so typical of the city itself. . . Américo Castro reaffirms the belief in the overriding importance of American treasure in the history of Spain in Europe, and Víctor Andrés Belaunde has remarked that the entire colonial epoch in Peru might be designated as a "vast religious and political organization for the exploitation of the mines." The Cerro was the most noted of these mines and just as the Portuguese classic seventeenth-century historian Francisco Manoel de Melo referred to that "inestimable Potosí," other writers old and new, Spanish and foreigner, beat the drum on behalf of Potosí. The belief in the opulence of Peru generally began when Atahualpa in 1532 paid over to Francisco Pizarro a roomful of gold and two more of silver. And even after New Spain began in the seventeenth century to produce more silver than Peru, the Viceroy of Peru still received a higher salary than the Viceroy of New Spain, whose position was considered an inferior one. Was this due, in part at least, to the influence of Potosí and the general belief in its supposedly inexhaustible wealth? Myths about Potosí still influence the historians who study its past.

We know that Charles V and Philip II were usually hard pressed for cash, but did Potosí really provide funds for running the empire, in the splendid way it is supposed to have done? Or were the undramatic and mundane factories in the Low Countries the solid economic base for Spain, as R. H. Tawney stated years ago? If so, was not the revenue from Potosí still a fairly steady flow which permitted the Spanish crown to act more independently than if it had to rely on Spanish revenue alone?

Did Potosí also affect the economy of the other parts of Europe? Did its cheaply produced silver cause the collapse of such mining centers as those directed by the Fuggers in Tyrol? We know, from the classic study of Earl J. Hamilton, of the influence of American treasure on prices in Spain. G. N. Clark is even more emphatic and has this to say, in commenting on the discovery of Potosí and the fact that in a few years silver was flowing to Europe in quantities that had never been imagined before: "This might in other conditions have affected silversmiths and ladies more than anyone else; but coming at this time it played a part, and perhaps a very great part, in changing the hunger for the precious metals as money into a surfeit of them. All over

Europe metallic money became easier to get; in other words there was a great rise in prices, which is called 'the price revolution.' . . . Some men became suddenly rich. All those who were entitled to fixed sums, whether as rents or as taxes or dues, could buy less with these sums than before; all those who were free to demand what prices they could exact had new and rising opportunities. So, broadly speaking, the old world of landlords and peasants found it harder to carry on; the traders and bankers found it easier, and capitalism advanced."

What was the influence of Potosí in America itself? Did mining play a progressive role, as Bailey W. Diffie believes, through which "an urban civilization came into existence, a middle class was created, the buying power of the people increased . . . and in general America was able to grow?" Or did Potosí help to fasten upon the Viceroyalty of Peru a pernicious economic and social system which exacted quick profits from the mines, and kept agriculture in such a secondary place that its growth was dangerously retarded and a feudal society prolonged for centuries? If the answer is "yes" to this last question, can one escape the conclusion that some of the present desperate problems of Bolivia constitute, in part at least, a heritage from Potosí? Or, perhaps, did the mountain of silver rather help to develop a Bolivian nationality by establishing an economic, governmental, and social nucleus around which a nation could be organized, as that energetic historian of La Paz, Humberto Vásquez Machicado, has suggested? Or is it possible that each proposition contains some measure of truth? . . .

One final observation must be made which affects all the problems of interpretation raised above. Potosí was a part, albeit a particularly important and flamboyant part, of a vast empire and functioned within the structure which Spain established in America. Its history, therefore, must be written with one eye on the rest of the empire. Potosí was necessarily influenced by the legislation, policies, and foreign entanglements of Spain just as the mountain of silver exerted an influence on other parts of America and the mother country as well. The history of Potosí is a broad and complicated story, and therefore a tale which cannot be told adequately from the vantage point of the Cerro alone. If its historians are to avoid myopia, they must always remember that Potosí, although physically isolated from most of the other New World possessions of Spain, was in fact an integral part of lands governed by the crown of Spain from its capital thousands of miles away. Potosí was unusual, of course, in some ways. The rapidity of its growth, for example, sets Potosí apart from Mexico City, whose population grew rather slowly until recent years, and from Lima, which never suffered the spectacular decline that came upon Potosí in the eighteenth century.

The truly unique aspects of Potosí, however, were its size and dramatic history. Other mining centers existed in the empire and developed somewhat similar societies and sets of institutions. But Potosí came to exhibit those common characteristics of all mining societies in such a theatrical way that it became symbolic of the process that was going on everywhere. Perhaps herein lies the real justification for assigning to Potosí a long and significant chapter in the history of Spain in America. Just as the vociferous and learned Dominican Bartolomé de Las Casas, although not the only defender of the Indians, most persistently captured the imagination of his contemporaries and later generations as The Defender, so Potosí exemplified, in the gaudiest and most memorable colors, the passion for wealth that drew many Spaniards to the New World. Bernal Díaz del Castillo, the famous and articulate footsoldier of Cortez, exhibited the remarkable combination of *Gott und Gewinn* which characterized the Spanish conquest of America when he exclaimed: "We came here to serve God, and also to get rich." As the mountain of Potosí towers above the surrounding peaks, so will this mine, once its story is adequately told, stand as the towering symbol for the spirit of all Spaniards who came to the New World to get rich.

Alexander von Humboldt. This energetic German naturalist, accompanied by French botanist Aimé Bonpland, traveled through Central and South America between 1799 and 1804 recording geographical measurements; collecting mineral, botanical and zoological samples; visiting centers of education; and befriending the local learned creoles. His accounts of his experiences published in numerous books and essays are an indispensable source of information about Spanish America on the eve of independence.

SECTION VIII

Crisis and Climax
in the Eighteenth Century

The century before the Portuguese and Spanish colonies in America won their independence brought considerable cultural, economic, and political change. Tensions between the mother countries and the New World increased, despite or perhaps because of the many improvements in the lot of the overseas colonists. The Iberian empires were no longer so isolated from the world, and the increasingly determined attempt of Spain and Portugal to keep their American citizens more efficiently under peninsular control led to resistance rather than acquiescence. Portugal administered a shock to Brazil when she expelled the Jesuits in 1759, even before Spain took the same decisive step a few years later. The causes for what many considered a harsh and wrong attack in both Brazil and Spanish America upon this powerful order were many and complicated, as Professor Magnus Mörner has ably shown in a volume on this controversial event.[1] Whatever the real causes for the expulsion of the Jesuits, this action helped to loosen the ties that bound the colonies to the mother countries.

A different set of circumstances in Mexico created another kind of problem. Spain decided to organize a colonial militia to protect the land from foreign incursion, such as Havana and Manila had both suffered in 1762 at the hands of the British. The well-born young men in Mexico displayed no great enthusiasm for military service until granted the *fuero militar,* which conceded such privileges and immunities as to create an officer class largely exempt from civil responsibility. Thus came into being a significant inequal-

[1] Magnus Mörner, *The Expulsion of the Jesuits from Latin America,* Borzoi Books on Latin America (New York: Knopf, 1965).

317

ity that laid the basis for the nineteenth-century military dictators. Yet relatively speaking, Mexico appeared to be advanced. Alexander von Humboldt, in his classic overview of Mexico about 1800, lauded Mexico City: "No new city of the new continent, without even excepting those of the United States, can display such great and solid scientific achievements as the capital of Mexico." He added, however: "Mexico is the country of inequality. Nowhere does there exist such a fearful difference in the distribution of fortune, civilization, cultivation of the soil, and population" (Reading 1).

Eighteenth-century Peru was the locale of probably the most significant Indian rebellion in the whole colonial period. Led by the mestizo José Gabriel Tupac Amaru, Marquis of Oropesa but also descended from the Inca leader Tupac Amaru who had been beheaded by Viceroy Francisco de Toledo in 1572, its history "is intricate and obscure." Was the revolt primarily aimed at ending the oppression of the Indians, as many have. asserted, or was it an attempt to throw off the Spanish yoke completely and achieve an independent Peruvian Indian state? Few accept this view: "The Indians wished to capture Spanish institutions, not destroy or displace them by others." [2] Whatever the true causes, and research is still going forward, the rebellion of 1780–1781 failed despite widespread support of Indians and the aid of the leader's intelligent and vigorous wife. But the bloody affair shook Spanish officialdom somewhat; in 1787 an audiencia was established in Cuzco, which was designed to afford greater protection for the Indians against exploitation by their Spanish governors and Indian chiefs alike.

One action, this time by the crown, did have considerable influence on economic, political, and religious life in Upper Peru — the expulsion of the Jesuits. Though this sudden operation struck a blow at Jesuit power throughout the Iberian colonies, the way it was carried out reveals the practically absolute power of the Spanish king even in the far corners of his vast empire in America.

Another problem in Peru was declining mineral production, upon which its economy had been based ever since the Potosí silver mines were discovered in 1545. Silver production depended upon mercury, which the Huancavelica mine had provided in great quantities since about 1570. The crown devised many plans to revive Huancavelica during the eighteenth century without much success. Stagnation and decay did not characterize the Spanish American Empire generally in the eighteenth century, however, and the late Professor C. H. Haring stated in his fundamental work that "at the end of the colonial era

[2] George Kubler, "The Quechua in the Colonial World," *Handbook of South American Indians*, 2, ed. Julian H. Steward (Washington, D.C.: Smithsonian Institution, 1946), pp. 331–410.

most of the American provinces enjoyed greater prosperity and well-being than ever before." [3]

Professor R. A. Humphreys concurs with this view and presents an excellent general analysis and description of the fall of the Spanish Empire in America, which stretched "in unbroken line from California to Cape Horn. From Stockholm to Cape Town is less distant, and within the area ruled by Spain all western Europe from Madrid to Moscow might lie and be lost" (Reading 4). But other interpretations flourish, too, as may be seen from an "essay on economic dependence in perspective" (Reading 2) by Stanley J. and Barbara H. Stein in their stimulating volume *The Colonial Heritage of Latin America,* and Professor Philip W. Powell's defense of Spanish rule in America (Reading 3).

Some Brazilian historians have reached dismal conclusions on Portuguese colonial rule. Caio Prado, Júnior, has recently written: "The panorama offered by colonial society may be summarized as follows: settlement, scattered and unstable; economy, poor and miserable; mores, dissolute; administration, both lay and ecclesiastical, inept and corrupt." A nineteenth-century Brazilian, Capistrano de Abreu, penned a famous description of the colonial family in Brazil: "Taciturn father, submissive wife, cowed children." [4]

These divergent modern interpretations point to an important aspect of the study of Latin American history — the sharp and apparently irreconcilable disagreements over the true nature of Portuguese and Spanish rule. Characteristically there is more written on Spanish America than on Brazil. The dispute goes back to the earliest part of the Conquest when Bernal Díaz del Castillo, indignant at the pro-Cortez version of the Conquest, wrote his *True History of the Conquest of Spain.* Today the questions foremost in the minds of many historians relate to the social and economic impact of conquest on the conquered Indians and enslaved Negroes. Comparative history has become a flourishing growth industry today among an ever-widening circle of historians who grapple with problems involving factual, moral, and nationalistic considerations.

Comparative cruelty and questions of comparative oppression are almost impossible to discuss in such a way as to satisfy many historians, because facts are difficult to obtain and moral indignation is often present. Alexander von Humboldt in his classic work on Mexico at the end of the colonial period believed that the condition of the Indians was not much worse than that of

[3] C. H. Haring, *The Spanish Empire in America* (New York: Harcourt, Brace, and World, 1963), p. 322.

[4] Caio Prado, Júnior, *The Colonial Background of Modern Brazil* (Berkeley and Los Angeles: University of California Press, 1969), p. 414.

the serfs of the time on the rural estates of the Baltic. Stanley J. and Barbara H. Stein acknowledged that it might be valid to state that the existence of West European peasants, craftsmen, and miners was as wretched as that of the lowest stratum of society in Spanish America in the sixteenth and seventeenth centuries. But they go on to ask: "Were West Europeans forced into mines and kept there in the seventeenth century without surfacing from Monday to Saturday? Was there in operation in western Europe an annual labor draft which forced unwilling laborers to move hundreds of miles to pitheads along with their families, supplies, and pack animals?"[5] One wonders whether anyone can really compare the lives of the wretched, because of the inherent problems and prejudices involved. Yet the comparisons go on. In the April 1972 issue of the *American Historical Review* we find a review of a monograph by the Dutch historian J. G. Van Dillen on the economic and social history of the Dutch Republic in which Charles R. Boxer remarks: "He does not ignore the widespread poverty among many sections of the lower classes during the 'Golden Century' [1580–1650]. The textile workers of Leiden, for example, seem to have fared little better than the Amerindian laborers in the *obrajes* or textile sweatshops of colonial Spanish America."[6]

The selections (Readings 2 - 4) by the Steins, Powell, and Humphreys are designed to afford students an opportunity to sample representative views of historians and to encourage further meditation on these basic controversies that color much of the writing on Latin American colonial history.

Finally, in discussing Spanish American economic ills, we should not forget that there has always existed in Spanish-speaking lands a not unimportant segment of society that maintains that economic matters are of minor significance. Américo Castro has expressed it this way: "Religious faith as a basis for life and the monarchy as social horizon" are the two fundamental facts of Spanish life. "Those who attribute the troubles of Spaniards to the poverty of their land are perpetuating a myth."[7] Another eminent Spanish historian, Claudio Sánchez Albornoz, violently disagrees with Castro on many points, but both are convinced, as were many Spanish writers of Spain's Golden Age in the sixteenth century, that economic affairs were only minor determinants in Spanish history. How far Spanish Americans today are moved by these attitudes is a moot question, as is the question of to what extent those countries with large Indian populations have inherited the noneconomic attitudes of the pre-Columbian peoples. These considerations of values may be debatable, but they cannot be ignored by the historian.

[5] Stanley J. and Barbara H. Stein, *The Colonial Heritage of Latin America* (New York: Oxford University Press, 1971), p. viii.
[6] *American Historical Review*, 77 (1972), p. 531.
[7] Américo Castro, "The Spanish People," *Texas Quarterly*, 3 (1960).

A NINETEENTH CENTURY OBSERVER

1. *Problems and Progress in Mexico*

ALEXANDER VON HUMBOLDT

The first non-Spaniard of stature to be allowed to visit the empire in the last years of Spanish rule was the German scientist Alexander von Humboldt, whose detailed and discerning descriptions enabled the world to see what Mexico was like about 1800. He compiled much useful data on the geology, rainfall, soil, and other physical characteristics of the land, but we value him today for his honest and informative view of economic, political, and society life on the eve of the revolution.

Mexico is the country of inequality. No where does there exist such a fearful difference in the distribution of fortune, civilization, cultivation of the soil, and population. The interior of the country contains four cities, which are not more than one or two days' journey distant from one another, and possess a population of 35,000, 67,000, 70,000, and 135,000. The central table-land from la Puebla to Mexico, and from thence to Salamanca and Zelaya, is covered with villages and hamlets like the most cultivated part of Lombardy. To the east and west of this narrow strip succeed tracts of uncultivated ground, on which cannot be found ten or twelve persons to the square league. The capital and several other cities have scientific establishments, which will bear a comparison with those of Europe. The architecture of the public and private edifices, the elegance of the furniture, the equipages, the luxury and dress of the women, the tone of society, all announce a refinement to which the nakedness, ignorance, and vulgarity of the lower people form the most striking contrast. This immense inequality of fortune does not only exist among the cast of whites (Europeans or Creoles), it is even discoverable among the Indians.

The Mexican Indians, when we consider them *en masse,* offer a picture of extreme misery. Banished into the most barren districts, and indolent from nature, and more still from their political situation, the natives live only from hand to mouth. We should seek almost in vain among them for individuals who enjoy anything like a certain mediocrity of fortune. Instead, however, of a comfortable independency, we find a few families whose fortune appears so much the more colossal, as we least expect it among the lowest class of the people. In the intendancies of Oaxaca and Valladolid, in the valley of Toluca,

From *Political Essay on the Kingdom of New Spain* by Alexander von Humboldt, trans. John Black (London: Longman, Hurst, Rees, Orme, and Brown, 1811), vol. 1, pp. 134–217, passim.

and especially in the environs of the great city of la Puebla de los Angeles, we find several Indians, who under an appearance of poverty conceal considerable wealth. When I visited the small city of Cholula, an old Indian woman was buried there, who left to her children plantations of *maguey* (agave) worth more than 360,000 francs. These plantations are the vineyards and sole wealth of the country. However, there are no caciques at Cholula; and the Indians there are all tributary, and distinguished for their great sobriety, and their gentle and peaceable manners. The manners of the Cholulans exhibit a singular contrast to those of their neighbors of Tlascala, of whom a great number pretend to be the descendants of the highest titled nobility, and who increase their poverty by a litigious disposition and a restless and turbulent turn of mind. Among the most wealthy Indian families at Cholula are the Axcotlan, the Sarmientos and the Romeros; at Guaxocingo, the Sochipiltecatl; and especially the Tecuanouegues in the village de los Reyes. Each of these families possesses a capital of from 800,000 to 1,000,000 of livres. They enjoy, as we have already stated, great consideration among the tributary Indians; but they generally go barefooted, and covered with a Mexican tunic of coarse texture and a brown colour, approaching to black, in the same way as the very lowest of the Indians are usually dressed.

The Indians are exempted from every sort of indirect impost. They pay no *alcavala;* and the law allows them full liberty for the sale of their productions. The supreme council of finances of Mexico, called the *Junta superior de Real Hacienda,* endeavored from time to time, especially within these last five or six years, to subject the Indians to the alcavala. We must hope that the court of Madrid, which in all times has endeavored to protect this unfortunate race, will preserve to them their immunity so long as they shall continue subject to the direct impost of the *tributos.* This impost is a real capitation tax, paid by the male Indians between the ages of ten and fifty. The tribute is not the same in all the provinces of New Spain; and it has been diminished within the last two hundred years. In 1601, the Indian paid yearly 32 reals of plata of *tributo,* and four reals of *servicio real,* in all nearly 23 francs. It was gradually reduced in some intendancies to 15 and even to five francs. In the bishopric of Mechoacan, and in the greatest part of Mexico, the capitation amounts at present to 11 francs. Besides, the Indians pay a parochial duty (*derechos parroquiales*) of 10 francs for baptism, 20 francs for a certificate of marriage, and 20 francs for interment. We must also add to these 61 francs, which the church levies as an impost on every individual, from 25 to 30 francs for offerings which are called voluntary, and which go under the names of *cargos de cofradias, responsos* and *misàs para sacar animas.*

If the legislation of Queen Isabella and the Emperor Charles V appears to favour the Indians with regard to imposts, it has deprived them, on the other hand, of the most important rights enjoyed by the other citizens. In an age when it was formally discussed if the Indians were rational beings, it was conceived granting them a benefit to treat them like minors, to put them under the perpetual tutory of the whites, and to declare null every act signed by a native of the copper-coloured race, and every obligation which he contracted beyond the value of 15 francs. These laws are maintained in full vigour; and they place insurmountable barriers between the Indians and the other casts, with whom all intercourse is almost prohibited. Thousands of inhabitants can enter into no contract which is binding (*no pueden tratar y contratar*); and condemned to a perpetual minority, they become a charge to themselves and the state in which they live. . . .

Amongst the inhabitants of pure origin the whites would occupy the second place, considering them only in the relation of number. They are divided into whites born in Europe, and descendants of Europeans born in the Spanish colonies of America or in the Asiatic islands. The former bear the name of *Chapetones* or *Gachupines,* and the second that of *Criollos.* The natives of the Canary islands, who go under the general denomination of *Islenos* (islanders), and who are the *gerans* of the plantations, are considered as Europeans. The Spanish laws allow the same rights to all whites; but those who have the execution of the laws endeavour to destroy an equality which shocks the European pride. The government, suspicious of the Creoles, bestows the great places exclusively on the natives of Old Spain. For some years back they have disposed at Madrid even of the most trifling employments in the administration of the customs and the tobacco revenue. At an epoch when every thing tended to a uniform relaxation in the springs of the state, the system of venality made an alarming progress. For the most part it was by no means a suspicious and distrustful policy; it was pecuniary interest alone which bestowed all employments on Europeans. The result has been a jealous and perpetual hatred between the Chapetons and the Creoles. The most miserable European, without education, and without intellectual cultivation, thinks himself superior to the whites born in the new continent. He knows that, protected by his countrymen, and favored by chances common enough in a country where fortunes are as rapidly acquired as they are lost, he may one day reach places to which the access is almost interdicted to the natives, even to those of men distinguished for their talents, knowledge and moral qualities. The natives prefer the denomination of *Americans* to that of Creoles. Since the peace of Versailles, and, in particular, since the year 1789, we frequently hear proudly declared, "I am not a *Spaniard,* I am an *American!*" words which betray the workings of a long resentment. In the eye of law every white Creole is a Spaniard; but the abuse of the laws, the false measures of the colonial government, the example of the United States of America, and the influence of the opinions of the age, have relaxed the ties which formerly united more closely the Spanish Creoles to the European Spaniards. A wise administration may reestablish harmony, calm their passions and resentments, and yet preserve for a long time the union among the members of one and the same great family scattered over Europe and America, from the Patagonian coast to the north of California. . . .

The Spanish laws prohibit all entry into the American possessions to every European not born in the peninsula. The words European and Spaniard are become synonymous in Mexico and Peru. The inhabitants of the remote provinces have therefore a difficulty in conceiving that there can be Europeans who do not speak their language; and they consider this ignorance as a mark of low extraction, because, everywhere around them, all, except the very lowest class of the people, speak Spanish. Better acquainted with the history of the sixteenth century than with that of our own times, they imagine that Spain continues to possess a decided preponderance over the rest of Europe. To them the peninsula appears the very centre of European civilization. It is otherwise with the Americans of the capital. Those of them who are acquainted with the French or English literature fall easily into a contrary extreme; and have still a more unfavorable opinion of the mother country than the French had at a time when communication was less frequent between Spain and the rest of Europe. They prefer strangers from other countries to the Spaniards; and they flatter themselves with the idea that intellectual cultivation has made more rapid progress in the colonies than in the peninsula.

This progress is indeed very remarkable at the Havannah, Lima, Santa Fe, Quito, Popayan, and Caraccas. Of all these great cities the Havannah bears the greatest resemblance to those of Europe in customs, refinements of luxury, and the tone of society. At Havannah, the state of politics and their influence on commerce is best understood. However, notwithstanding the efforts of the *patriotic society of the island of Cuba*, which encourages the sciences with the most generous zeal, they prosper very slowly in a country where cultivation and the price of colonial produce engross the whole attention of the inhabitants. The study of the mathematics, chemistry, mineralogy, and botany, is more general at Mexico, Santa Fe, and Lima. We everywhere observe a great intellectual activity, and among the youth a wonderful facility of seizing the principles of science. It is said that this facility is still more remarkable among the inhabitants of Quito and Lima than at Mexico and Santa Fe. The former appear to possess more versatility of mind and a more lively imagination; while the Mexicans and the natives of Santa Fe have the reputation of greater perseverance in the studies to which they have once addicted themselves.

No city of the new continent, without even excepting those of the United States, can display such great and solid scientific establishments as the capital of Mexico. I shall content myself here with naming the School of Mines, directed by the learned Elhuyar, to which we shall return when we come to speak of the mines; the Botanic Garden; and the Academy of Painting and Sculpture. This academy bears the title of *Academia de los Nobles Artes de Mexico*. It owes its existence to the patriotism of several Mexican individuals, and the protection of the minister Galvez. The government assigned it a spacious building, in which there is a much finer and more complete collection of casts than is to be found in any part of Germany. We are astonished on seeing that the Appollo of Belvidere, the group of Laocoon, and still more colossal statues, have been conveyed through mountainous roads at least as narrow as those of St. Gothard; and we are surprised at finding these masterpieces of antiquity collected together under the torrid zone, in a table-land higher than the convent of the great St. Bernard. The collection of casts brought to Mexico cost the king 200,000 francs. The remains of the Mexican sculpture, those colossal statues of basaltes and porphyry, which are covered with Aztec hieroglyphics, and bear some relation to the Egyptian and Hindoo style, ought to be collected together in the edifice of the academy, or rather in one of the courts which belong to it. It would be curious to see these monuments of the first cultivation of our species, the works of a semibarbarous people inhabiting the Mexican Andes, placed beside the beautiful forms produced under the sky of Greece and Italy.

The revenues of the Academy of Fine Arts at Mexico amount to 125,000 francs, of which the government gives 60,000, the body of Mexican miners nearly 25,000, the *consulado,* or association of merchants of the capital, more than 1,500. It is impossible not to perceive the influence of this establishment on the taste of the nation. This influence is particularly visible in the symmetry of the buildings, in the perfection with which the hewing of stone is conducted, and in the ornaments of the capitals and stucco relievos. What a number of beautiful edifices are to be seen at Mexico! nay, even in provincial towns like Guanaxuato and Queretaro! These monuments, which frequently cost a million and a million and a half of francs, would appear to advantage in the finest streets of Paris, Berlin, and Petersburg. M. Tolsa, professor of sculpture at Mexico, was even able to cast an equestrian statue of King Charles the Fourth; a work which, with the exception of the Marcus Aurelius at Rome, surpasses in beauty and purity of style everything which remains in this way in Europe. Instruction is communicated *gratis* at the Academy of Fine Arts. It is not confined alone to the drawing of landscapes and figures; they have had the good sense to employ other means for exciting the national industry. The academy labours successfully to introduce among the artisans a taste for elegance and beautiful forms. Large rooms, well lighted by Argand's lamps, contain every evening some hundreds of young people, of whom some draw from relievo or living models, while others copy drawings of furniture, chandeliers, or other ornaments in bronze. In this assemblage (and this is very remarkable in the midst of a country where the prejudices of the nobility against the casts are so inveterate) rank, colour, and race is confounded: we see the Indian and the Mestizo sitting beside the white, and the son of a poor artisan in emulation with the children of the great lords of the country. It is a consolation to observe, that under every zone the cultivation of science and art establishes a certain equality among men, and obliterates for a time, at least, all those petty passions of which the effects are so prejudicial to social happiness.

Since the close of the reign of Charles the Third, and under that of Charles the Fourth, the study of the physical sciences has made great progress, not only in Mexico, but in general in all the Spanish colonies. No European government has sacrificed greater sums to advance the knowledge of the vegetable kingdom than the Spanish government. Three *botanical expeditions* in Peru, New Granada and New Spain, under the direction of MM. Ruiz and Pavon, Don Jose Celestino Mutis, and MM. Sesse and Mocino, have cost the state nearly two millions of francs. Moreover, botanical gardens have been established at Manila and the Canary islands. The commission destined to draw plans of the canal of *los Guines,* was also appointed to examine the vegetable productions of the island of Cuba. All these researches, conducted during twenty years in the most fertile regions of the new continent, have not only enriched science with more than four thousand new species of plants, but have also contributed much to diffuse a taste for natural history among the inhabitants of the country. The city of Mexico exhibits a very interesting botanical garden within the very precincts of the viceroy's palace. Professor Cervantes gives annual courses there, which are very well attended. This *savant* possesses, besides his herbals, a rich collection of Mexican minerals. M. Mocino, whom we just now mentioned as one of the coadjutors of M. Sesse, and who has pushed his laborious excursions from the kingdom of Guatimala to the north-west coast or island of Vancouver and Quadra; and M. Echeveria, a painter of plants and animals, whose works will bear a comparison with the most perfect productions of the kind in Europe, are both of them natives of New Spain. They had both attained a distinguished rank among *savans* and artists before quitting their country.

The principles of the new chemistry, which is known in the Spanish colonies by the equivocal appellation of new philosophy (*nueva filosofia*), are more diffused in Mexico than in many parts of the peninsula. A European traveller cannot undoubtedly but be surprised to meet in the interior of the country, on the very borders of California, with young Mexicans who reason on the decomposition of water in the process of amalgamation with free air. The School of Mines possesses a chemical laboratory; a geological collection, arranged according to the system of Werner; a physical cabinet, in which we not only find the valuable instruments of Ramsden, Adams, Le Noir, and Louis Berthoud, but also models executed in the capital, even with the greatest precision, and from the finest wood in the country. The best mineralogical work in the Spanish language was printed at Mexico, I mean the Manual of Oryctognosy, composed by M. del Rio, according to the principles of the school of Freyberg, in which the author was formed. The first Spanish translation of Lavater's Elements of Chemistry was also published at Mexico. I cite these isolated facts because they give us the measure of the ardour with which the exact sciences are begun to be studied in the capital of New Spain. This ardour is much greater than that with which they addict themselves to the study of languages and ancient literature.

MODERN INTERPRETATIONS

2. *"The Pre-eminent Social Legacy of Colonialism Was the Degradation of the Labor Force, Indian and Negro, Everywhere in Latin America"*

STANLEY J. and BARBARA H. STEIN

The Steins are one of the few husband and wife teams writing on Latin American history. Though Professor Stein of Princeton University first established his reputation by two outstanding monographs on Brazilian nineteenth-century history, he afterward turned to investigating the roles of merchants in Mexico and Spain in the last half century of the colonial period, and with Mrs. Stein, also trained in history, has carried on prolonged archival research on this theme. The present selection is taken from a volume on *The Colonial Heritage of Latin America* and has a frankly economic and social focus in which they treat "certain basic institutions, patterns of behavior and attitudes which have had impressive continuity in Latin America: hacienda, plantation and associated social patterns, mining enclaves, the export syndrome and related trade mechanisms and mentality; elitism and racism; nepotism, clientilism, and a tradition of private right in public office."

Revolution in America occurred in 1810 because the criollo elite finally provided the leadership that the castas and the lower even more oppressed strata of colonial society had long awaited. To those who have examined the process of economic development and social change in a historical context it is clear that social systems appear to have extraordinary powers of cohesion, flexibility, adaptation. The cohesion of Latin American colonial social structures was maintained, if transformed, during three centuries largely because no viable alternative system appeared. Fidelity to Spain, sanctified by religious injunction, cemented the structure of colonial society, economy, and polity. The principle of hierarchy, of superordinate and subordinate social groups tied to the European metropolises, was accepted since it satisfied the interests and aspirations of an elite which, in effect, had the monopoly of force to maintain it.

In deciding to break with metropolitan controls, the colonial elite found natural allies in the mestizos, mulattoes, and castas in general; the Indian masses they handled gingerly. The Indians recognized their exploitation under the colonial system, but their bitterness had never successfully found effective expression. The criollo leaders now feared the masses, who often erupted in urban and rural violence, and they rationalized their repression and exploitation of them with the myth that they were inferiors. Undoubtedly some of the colonial elite believed that the Indian masses might remain inert in case of rebellion or, if mobilized intelligently, could be controlled to aid in the elimination of the handful of Spanish bureaucrats and merchants. Support by the castas strengthened the elite's position and promised assistance in controlling the Indians. With the backing of the castas, who were perhaps even more irked by the Spanish-imposed social hierarchy and by restrictions on "passing" and upon economic activity, some of the colonial elite probably saw the possibility of a rather peaceful transition toward independence. In allying with the castas, they co-opted a small but influential social group whose role was magnified by the expansion and diversification of the eighteenth-century colonial economy and by demographic growth.

Put another way, one detects in eighteenth-century Latin America the transformation of the older bases of colonial hierarchy, estates and corporations, into something approximating economic classes based upon wealth and income. The castas seem to have grown proportionately faster than the other social groups, and the lighter-skinned castas moved upward into the group of what were now called American Spaniards. In a word, "passing" became easier and more widespread. Castas were accepted in the colonial militia where criollo officers predominated. The large and growing intermediate group of mestizos and mulattoes spilled over from the hacienda and the Indian communities to fill the expanding number of occupations a diversifying economy requires. They resented the social stigma a colonial regime fastened upon them because of their "inferior" social origins. They bribed local priests to register their children as Spaniards rather than as light mulattoes or light mestizos, or they later had parish records changed. European officials at the end of the eighteenth century complained of the difficulty of registering people as castas for tax purposes. Nor could castas be kept out of artisan guilds nor even kept from pursuing artisan production outside them. They became weavers who established their own weaving shops; they became shopkeepers and itinerant merchants; they entered the church in large numbers; they flowed into the lesser bureaucracy. In colonial areas of heavy slave importation in the eighteenth century the number of free Negroes and mulattoes increased proportionately. It is not that racial prejudice declined: it is simply that rigid maintenance of status based upon color and ancestry became too difficult. To some extent the sheer number and diversity of castas tended to create a new basis of hierarchy, wealth, at the end of the colonial period. Those able to break away from the status of slave, those who abandoned the Indian communities or indigenous enclaves of Amerinds, became a middle group which could survive only by ruthless pursuit of self-interest. The Hispanized Indian or ladino, the mestizo, the free Negro, became in many cases a more ruthless exploiter of his social inferiors than the White elite. This was becoming evident before the wars of independence; it was to become even clearer afterward.

If the major legacy of colonial society was degradation and social conflict, what basis exists then for the often heard view that the Iberians had a policy toward Indians and Negroes which was more humanitarian and more tolerant than that of the non-Catholic west Europeans in America? It is true that there were sensitive, articulate, and hard-headed churchmen in the colonies who perceived the deculturizing, brutalizing, and exploitative aspects of culture-contact and imperialism in the sixteenth century. Such a man was Las Casas. One must, however, recall that other clerics who left posterity detailed ethnographic accounts of the social, political, and religious history of the conquered peoples of America studied the major institutions and values of dominated peoples in order to make colonial rule enduring. They were applied anthropologists. This, after all, was the aim of Las Casas' clerical contemporaries, Landa and Sahagun. If they often admired the institutions described, the admiration was given grudgingly.

Iberian colonialism did not exterminate subject peoples. It did accept the people of miscegenation. It did tolerate a degree of slave manumission. Yet the direction of colonial rule was not toward social uplift, toward integration; colonial rule was predicated upon separation, not integration, whether one examines tax systems, access to political or military office, even the church. Limited social integration and racial toleration were by-products of special conditions, in particular, the shortage of free labor available for interstitial occupations, those between field hand and elite. Since few Europeans were available to fill these jobs, the colonial society had to supply them. Hence the number of mestizos and mulattoes accepted at certain levels of society, in certain occupational roles. The fact that access to high status and occupation was rigidly controlled permitted the absorption of some newcomers.

The pre-eminent social legacy of colonialism was the degradation of the labor force, Indian and Negro, everywhere in Latin America. This is the abiding significance of debt peonage and chattel slavery. That occasionally members of the mixed groups were incorporated into the ruling group during the colonial period or distinguished themselves in the struggle for independence is not a persuasive argument for the racial integration of either colonial or post-colonial society. To argue in this fashion is to raise random sexual activity to the level of planned parenthood and to consider the growth of a mestizo or mulatto population a reliable index of racial integration and equality. On the contrary, it might be argued that the rigor of the barriers to upward social mobility — the barriers of birth, color, and economic deprivation in both colonial and post-colonial Latin America — permitted the elite to absorb an insignificant percentage of the more aggressive mixed groups and thereby to preserve the essence of social stratification. Absorption into the elite meant that newcomers accepted the social values and aspirations of that group; in striving for higher status, they lost contact with the disadvantaged groups which they abandoned and simultaneously removed themselves as leaders of the struggle for the amelioration of the lot of the illiterate, impoverished masses of color.

To be sure, social aspects of colonialism cannot be divorced from the economic matrix, and the heart of that matrix in Latin America remained privilege in the form of access to property and occupation, to ownership of mines, large farms, cattle ranches, to trade, and to the bureaucracy. A stratified and hierarchical society meant that a small group closely interrelated by marriage and kinship controlled wealth and income. Failure to diversify the colonial economy meant that economic opportunity remained limited. For the masses there was no role other than that of field hands or urban proletariat. And those who labored as dependents, debt peons or chattel slaves, were stigmatized as inferior. Rationalization buttressed inferiority. Indians were ignorant, superstitious, docile, lacking intelligence and initiative, not because society made them so, but because they were Indians — so thought the elite. Similarly they rationalized the maintenance of Negro slavery on the grounds that Christianity saved the Negro from barbarism and tribal warfare. To educate such elements of congenital backwardness was an exercise in futility. The colonial legacy of social degradation and racial prejudice surfaced in the nineteenth century in the form of acute racial pessimism, in the belief that only the immigration of European Whites via colonization could supply the industrious labor force capable of effectively transforming Latin America.

Social realities have a habit, however, of proving rationalizations of the *status quo* inadequate. We are now beginning to realize that much of the social unrest of Latin America in the past century was a continuation of conflicts over access to property and occupation that the lower classes touched off in the eighteenth century, that flared up briefly in the struggles for independence and which the elite suppressed after 1824. It is in the twentieth century that the long struggle for social vindication, rooted in the colonial past, is again re-emerging.

3.   The Three Centuries of Spanish Rule in America Should Not Be Characterized as a "Tyranny" or as "Oppressive"

PHILIP W. POWELL

The late Professor Philip W. Powell of the University of California, Santa Barbara, long defended Spain from what he believed to be unjust attacks on her rule in America and the charge that all of the ills of Spanish America today are colonial legacies. Students who compare his interpretations with that of the Steins (Reading 2) will see how fundamentally professors of history can disagree!

The standard simplistic version of Spanish rule in America as a slavocracy, filled with tyranny, looting, bleeding taxation, and suffocating obscurantism, does not conform to the facts. Spanish rule through all this period was generally more benign than much or even most Spanish American government has been since separation from Spain. Had this not been so, Spain's rule would not have lasted as long as it did.

One of our leading authorities in such matters, Professor Lesley Byrd Simpson, writes:

> It seems to me that the average stature of the viceroys of New Spain [Mexico] was so great that no country to my knowledge was ever more fortunate in its rulers. New Spain had plenty of things the matter with it, . . . but it enjoyed a long life (three hundred years!) of relative peace, stability, and prosperity, in marked contrast to the squabbling nations of Europe. Some of the men who made this possible are worth our knowing.

And an English scholar, Ronald Syme, recently implied something similar, in broader context:

> In spite of the handicaps of geography and of distance, Spain was able to hold her wide dominions for three centuries and set upon them indelibly the stamp of her language, thought and institutions. That achievement deserves more honour than it has commonly earned — and a more searching investigation. . . .

One finds, at times, the curious paradox that taxation overseas was not as onerous as it was in some parts of the mother country. One also finds that American life was often easier, or more prosperous, than in much of the mother country, where poverty was commonplace. In food availability, for example, Spanish Americans, of whatever level, were apt to fare as well or better than their European counterparts, Spanish or otherwise. Even the lower classes of Spanish America were likely to live somewhat better than much of the European peasantry.

There were, of course, many abuses of governmental authority, and all the many and varied evils of a vast bureaucracy, cholesterol of empire. Crimes of all sorts were committed, as one might expect in an empire of such size and long life. But there was also judicial machinery and legislation for punishment of abuses. The important point is that the norm was legality and law enforcement, just as in other civilized societies. In general, Spaniards did not try to

From "Spain in America: The Real and the Unreal," in *Tree of Hate: Propaganda and Prejudices Affecting United States Relations with the Hispanic World,* by Philip Wayne Powell pp. 23–29. © Basic Books, Inc., Publishers, New York, 1970.

impose upon America something hypocritically foreign or inferior to what they lived with at home. Taxation, municipal practices, university statutes, criminal and civil legislation, judiciary, artistic endeavors, social welfare agencies, commercial practices, etc., were, *mutatis mutandis,* close approximations of Spanish usage and norms in European territories. For example, in governmental and private welfare practices alone, there is abundant testimony to the comparatively advanced concern and practices of Spaniards in the New World. Moreover, this is a subject that merits much more attention and honor than it has received. . . .

The one great innovation was, of necessity, in Indian affairs. Spain's three centuries of tutelage and official concern for the welfare of the American Indian is a record not equaled by other Europeans in overseas government of peoples of lesser, or what were considered lesser, cultures. For all the mistakes, for all the failures, for all the crimes committed, and even allowing for Crown motives of practicality and self-service, in its overall performance Spain, in relation to the American Indian, need offer no apology to any other people or nation.

Spain's Inquisition and her State-Church structure are usually blamed for an oppressive obscurantism that supposedly blighted the three centuries in America and entrenched so many of the ills that today beset Spanish American nations. Anti-Catholic prejudice in our own country makes this myth particularly attractive, and nineteenth- and twentieth-century Latin Americans are fond of reiterating it. But no scholar having acquaintance with Spanish educational and other intellectual achievement in America — e.g., Indian education, encouragement of literature, history, scientific investigations, university instruction — would subscribe to such a judgment. The Spanish record of some twenty-three colleges and universities in America, graduating 150,000 (including the poor, mestizos, and some Negroes) makes, for example, the Dutch in the East Indies in later and supposedly more enlightened times, look like obscurantists indeed. The Portuguese did not establish a single university in colonial Brazil nor in any other overseas possessions. The total of universities established by Belgium, England, Germany, France, and Italy during later Afro-Asian colonial periods assuredly suffers by any fair comparison with the pioneering record of Spain.

In this vein, let us observe a few comments by Professor John Tate Lanning, of Duke University, our leading authority on the subject of Spanish American colonial culture:

> Up until a generation ago the view that all intellectual products of Europe were excluded from America by a zealous monarch and Inquisition went almost without question. No careful scholar would now pro-

nounce upon the availability of books in America upon the exclusive basis of the estimable *Recopilación de Indias* or the *Index of Prohibited Books*. The bibliographical avenue of Enlightenment to Spanish America was at no time so thoroughly barricaded as the statutes and indexes indicate.

Again:

An effective and relatively unhampered literary contact with the whole world of thought is implicit in the propositions defended in the [Spanish American] universities toward the end of the eighteenth century. The censorship of the Inquisition, well established though it was in law, was even more than many other somnolent colonial institutions, essentially bureaucratic and ineffectual.

He also said:

A grandiose and tenacious injustice springing from the traditions and emotions of the early national historians [of Spanish America] is the sweeping condemnation of Spanish colonial culture as "three centuries of theocracy, obscurantism, and barbarism!"

Along the way, let us notice also that barely more than one hundred persons were executed in Spanish America as a result of Inquisition action during its some 250 years of formal existence. This would seem, I think, to compare rather favorably, as these things go, with the torture and execution of Roman Catholics in Elizabethan England (130 priests and 60 laymen, or a total of 250 killed by the state if one includes those dying in prison). And estimates of deaths for witchcraft in the German states during the sixteenth and seventeenth centuries run well into the thousands. . . .

The substantial scholarly literature on American institutional development under Spanish rule continues to increase, but this fact usually comes as a surprise to many university students and intellectuals in the United States. It seems incredible to some that achievement worthy of later intellectual consideration could have taken place in an inquisitional Spanish-Catholic environment; but, if one applies a bit of logic to the situation, there should be no such astonishment. Spain, as should be well known, was enjoying a Golden Age during most of the first two centuries of her empire-building in America, and there was no reason for the mother country to withhold this intellectual activity from her colonies. And the answer is that she did not. Spaniards in America, and their progeny, had access to Spain's great intellectual achievements, and what's more, American universities were modeled on that of Salamanca, one of the most famous in Europe. Through the mother country came the intellectual currents of the rest of Europe. This was as true of the eighteenth century as it was of the sixteenth or seventeenth.

Almost all of Spanish and Spanish American history is a testimonial to the fact that people of Spanish descent do not long acquiesce to any tyranny that the majority, or even much of a minority, finds unbearable. Spain ruled in America for more than three centuries without professional soldiery or standing·military forces except in a few places where they were needed mainly to repel foreign attack or guard against frontier Indian depredations. And in all that time there was not a single rebellion that indicated widespread dissatisfaction with the Crown's rule. There were, of course, local disturbances, conspiracies, and uprisings, which made some mark on this history; but in virtually every case, except the few strictly Indian rebellions, there were apt to be Peninsulars and Americans on both sides and the circumstances were local, with little or nothing to indicate significant separatist spirit. Even when Napoleon invaded the mother country, usurped the throne, and "shook the tree of independence" by pushing Spanish Americans to extraordinary measures of self-government, most Spanish Americans did not initially aim at separation from Spain; independence from the mother country was a slow-growing idea even in that heady atmosphere of crumbling traditions. Independence was almost an accidental outcome, and there were far more important factors in this achievement than any popular rebellion against Spanish tyranny or obscurantism. The strong anti-Spanish propaganda inspired within relatively limited circles did not achieve wide popularity until years of it and abrasive fighting had crystallized dogmatic hatred into war for independence. The war period and subsequent decades spawned a literature of justification with strong hispanophobic twists.

In summary, the evidence so far presented in scholarly monographs, articles, and in documentary publications, does not allow any fair-minded observer to characterize those three centuries as a "tyranny," as uniquely "oppressive," as purposefully or generally cruel, or as "obscurantist." There is still much to be studied concerning those centuries, but it is already clear that they were too complex to fit such generalized epithets. Above all, it is completely fallacious to consider them as merely a continuation of the initial conquest patterns. . . .

4. *The Fall of the Spanish-American Empire*

R. A. HUMPHREYS

Professor R. A. Humphreys almost single-handed has created a school of Latin Americanists in Great Britain during the last quarter century. As a Commonwealth Fellow he became attracted to the field while in the United States, and after his appointment to the first Chair of Latin American History in University College, London, in 1948, he steadily and systematically fostered a sound development of teaching and research. It was largely his influence that led to the establishment of several Latin American centers in British universities, the excellent *Journal of Latin American Studies,* and the Institute of Latin American Studies in London, of which he serves as Director. His publications on modern Latin American history have been distinguished for their balance and style.

At the time of the Napoleonic invasions of the Spanish peninsula in 1807–8, the Spanish empire in America stretched in unbroken line from California to Cape Horn. From Stockholm to Cape Town is less distant, and within the area ruled by Spain all western Europe from Madrid to Moscow might lie and be lost.

A hundred years earlier, at the beginning of the eighteenth century, Spain had been a major battlefield of Europe. That experience was now to be repeated, and this time foreign invasion spelt imperial destruction. The French Revolution in its Napoleonic aspect was the occasion, if not the cause, of the emancipation of Spanish America. But in the years between the war of the Spanish Succession and the wars of Napoleon, Spain herself had risen with remarkable resilience from the decrepitude into which she had fallen in the seventeenth century. Her economic decline had been first arrested and then reversed, and under Charles III and during the early years of Charles IV she enjoyed what seems in retrospect to have been an Indian summer of prosperity.

What was true of Spain was true also of her empire. Of the empire during the long years of Spain's weakness and decay we know all too little. But of its material and intellectual advance during the so-called century of enlightenment there is abundant evidence. And Spain, like Britain, undertook in the eighteenth century the task of imperial reorganization and reform. At home

From "The Fall of the Spanish American Empire" by R. A. Humphreys, *History* (October 1952), pp. 213–227, passim. Reprinted by permission.

and in the empire the administrative system was overhauled. New viceroyalties and captaincies-general were created. The establishment, in the very year of the North American Declaration of Independence, of the viceroyalty of the Río de la Plata, covering the whole, indeed more than the whole, of what is now Argentina, marked a period in the history of Spanish America. And the attempt to systematize and centralize colonial government by the division of the colonies into intendancies — "to unify the government of the great empires which God has intrusted to me," as Charles III expressed it in the Great Ordinance of Intendants for New Spain — was scarcely less important.

The reforms in the imperial economic system were equally radical. The Spanish system of colonial and commercial monopoly differed not in kind from the colonial policy of other powers, but in the extraordinary rigour with which it was applied. There were special reasons for the severity and minuteness of these economic regulations, and special reasons for the quite disastrous consequences that followed. But though the policy of colonial monopoly was never abandoned, it was, in the eighteenth century, liberalized. Slowly and cautiously the natural trade routes of the Indies were opened up. Where once Cádiz and Seville had enjoyed a monopoly within a monopoly, and the fleets and galleons had divided between them the commerce and treasure of Mexico and Perú, step by step the ports of America and the ports of Spain were opened, the age-old restrictions on inter-colonial commerce were lightened, and the tariffs and duties hampering trade revised. The so-called Decree of Free Trade of 1778, by which all the more important ports of Spain and of Central and South America were allowed to trade, if not freely at least directly, with one another, was as much a landmark in the economic history of the later empire as was the establishment of the viceroyalty of the Río de la Plata in its political history.

The reasons for these striking innovations were, in the broadest sense of the word, strategic. Efficiency in administration, the rehabilitation of colonial trade, were not so much ends in themselves as means to an end; and the end was imperial defense, the protection of the empire against foreign aggression, particularly English aggression, the elimination of foreign economic competition, and the restoration of Spanish maritime and military power in Europe. And as in British colonial policy after 1763, so in Spanish, the financial problem was paramount. Defence demanded revenue, "it being necessary," as Charles III instructed his visitor-general to New Spain,

on account of the large sums needed in attending to the obligations of my royal crown, to exhaust all means which may appear conducive to increasing as much as possible the income from the revenues.

This was a dominant consideration both in administrative and in economic reform. And what Britain in part proposed to effect by tightening up the acts of trade, Spain in part proposed to effect by their relaxation.

The results, or the apparent results, were remarkable. The volume of imperial trade notably increased. At Buenos Aires, now the capital of the viceroyalty of Río de la Plata and no longer a dependency of Lima, the economic life of the colony was transformed. Its customs receipts, its exports, its shipping, its population, all alike rapidly increased. At Havana, Cuba, where six vessels had sufficed for the trade of Spain in 1760, two hundred were insufficient in 1778, and more than a thousand, Spanish and foreign, entered in 1801. New Spain, or Mexico, repeats the same story — a larger volume of shipping, swelling revenues, greater exports. In Perú, when the legislation of 1778 first came into effect, "speculations were multiplied to so extraordinary a degree" in the first fervour of novelty that the merchants resorted to the now familiar device of destroying their goods in order to maintain the price level. And even remote Chile experienced a new and vigorous impulse of economic change.

Whatever truth, therefore, there may be in the legend of the stagnation and decay of Spain and of the Spanish American empire in the seventeenth century, it does not hold for the eighteenth. Within Spain's transatlantic dominions the signs of an expanding economy and of a growing prosperity were everywhere, or almost everywhere, writ large. "It is just . . . to observe," wrote a competent British observer, that Perú, during the late eighteenth century

> was not only in a flourishing state both in respect to her mines and to her commerce, but also as referable to the capitals possessed by individuals, to the comparative extent of her manufactures, and to her navigation. Between the years 1790 and 1800 there existed in Lima a *commercial* capital of above 15 millions of dollars; whereas in the present year [1826] it is under one million.

Humboldt, in Venezuela, noted that "everything seemed to announce the increase of population and industry." In New Spain the public revenues increased more than sixfold in the eighteenth century, and so also did the produce of the mines. And though more than half of the world output of the precious metals still flowed from Spanish America, and though there is a lively superstition that the Spanish American colonies were made of gold and silver and nothing else, agriculture as well as mining, as the great Gálvez tells us, were the basis of their prosperity. The value of the gold and silver of the Mexican mines, says Humboldt, was less "by almost a fourth" than that of the agricultural produce. Of Venezuela and Cuba he observes that agriculture "founded more considerable fortunes" than had been accumulated by the working of the mines in Perú, and in southern South America, where the mines were few, but where Buenos Aires and even Montevideo were rapidly rising in importance, the pastoral and agricultural industries, then as now, were the economic staples.

It is reasonable to conclude, with Professor Haring, that as the eighteenth century closed the peoples of Spanish America were probably more prosperous than at any time in their history. True, in a colonial and developing area, there was no considerable growth of manufactures. Nor was there in the English colonies. But domestic manufacturing was in fact more widespread than is commonly supposed. True, also, the whole population of Spanish America was certainly not greater than that of the British Isles in 1811. But its increase in the eighteenth century was remarkable. In 1800 Mexico City was the leading city of the western hemisphere, larger than any city of Great Britain and Ireland except London and Dublin. Its rival, Lima, compared with Bristol and was itself outstripped by Havana. Even long-neglected Buenos Aires was as large as New York or Philadelphia in 1790. And the growth and embellishment of the cities (not merely the capital cities) illustrates the same expansionist trend. Here, at least, in public buildings and public display, were the marks of opulence; and it is no accident that here also, at the end of the century, there was an efflorescence of intellectual activity, in the universities and academies, in the growth of a periodical press, in literary societies and in clubs. In Santa Fé, Perú and Mexico, observed an English merchant in 1804, there was not only a greater degree of knowledge and a greater degree of progress in civilization than was commonly supposed in Europe, but, he added, though perhaps with prejudice, "much more than exists in Old Spain."

The disruption of this society by a violent cataclysm which would, within a few years, destroy much of its wealth, would seem, at first sight, an improbable event. The Conde de Aranda, one of the more far-sighted of Spanish statesmen, indeed foresaw it. "We must imagine" he wrote in 1782 "that sooner or later in [Spanish] America there will occur revolutions like those of the English colonies." And Canning's retrospective judgment, on the effect of the American Revolution, that "the operation of that example" was "sooner or later inevitable," is well known. The influences of eighteenth-century rationalism and of the French Revolution were equally powerful dissolvents. The continent, despite the censorship of the Inquisition, was not closed to ideas. Forbidden literature is always the most enticing of literature. A cultivated minority was certainly acquainted with the writings of the *philosophes,* of Rousseau, of Locke, even of Adam Smith. These were to be echoed, along with the Declarations of Independence and the Rights of Man, in the pronouncements and charters of revolutionary leaders and revolutionary governments. Yet despite the activities of an adventurer like Francisco de Miranda, who knew the "brace of Adamses" and had seen the French Revolution at first hand, despite occasional conspiracies and even outright rebellion, there was little specifically revolutionary activity in Spanish America before Spain herself fell a prey to Napoleon. The revolution, when it came, rose like a sudden tide from still, or comparatively still, waters.

Yet Spain's colonies were lost before the revolution began. The Bourbon reforms came too late, they did not go far enough, they were given insufficient time, to save the empire. And politically at least they contained no concession to the newer movement of ideas.

> "Instead of considering its colonies as a place of refuge for the idle, the profligate, and the disaffected, where they might learn to amend their lives, and, if possible, forget their errors," wrote the *Edinburgh Review* in 1806, "the Spanish Crown has watched over its foreign settlements with the solicitude of a duenna, and regulated their government as if they were to be inhabited by Carthusians."

The quotation, perhaps, is mainly interesting for the light it throws on the value placed on colonies in early nineteenth-century Britain. But it contains a solid grain of truth. The empire, from first to last, was built on paternalist and absolutist lines. It could not, in point of fact, be quite so centralized as theory might imply. The royal will was always limited by circumstance. But the price of paternalism was procrastination and inefficiency, a tradition of legalism and a disrespect for law, a class system which almost, but not quite, became a caste system, and a mounting jealousy between Spaniards born in Spain and Spaniards born in America, between, that is, the governors and the governed. "The most miserable European" wrote Humboldt "without education, and without intellectual cultivation, thinks himself superior to the whites born in the new continent." The creoles, excluded generally from the higher administrative posts, found almost their sole representation in municipal institutions. "Even in the most despotic states" says Robertson in his famous *History* "this feeble spark of liberty is not extinguished." But even here it was the local, not the representative, character of the *cabildos,* or town councils, too often closed corporations, petty oligarchies, which caused them to play so prominent a part in the events of 1808 to 1810.

There was no relaxation of this paternalistic system in the eighteenth century. On the contrary, enlightened despotism sought to rationalize and simplify the machinery of imperial administration both in Spain and in America in the interests of order, uniformity, centralization, efficiency. And though, for a time, a new life was breathed into the imperial system, the political aspirations of the creoles were forgotten, or ignored. In so far as the newly appointed intendants, invariably Spaniards, superseded minor, but creole, officials, and trespassed, moreover, on the functions of the *cabildos,* the Spanish American creoles were, in fact, still further removed from the work of government. "We were left" Bolívar was to say "in a state of permanent childhood."

And, paradoxically enough, the measures designed to secure a still closer integration between Spain and her colonies had precisely the opposite effect. In Spanish America, as in Spain, local and regional loyalties were always strong. Customs, conditions, varied enormously. Cities and squares, law and administration, might be drawn to a pattern, but the life of the colonies flowed in its own individual channels; and at a time when the Bourbon economic reforms gave to the several regions of Spanish America a new economic autonomy, the creation of new viceroyalties and captaincies-general promoted and consolidated a growing sense of regional nationalism. Colonial self-consciousness was directly stimulated. It can be no accident that the revolution, when it came, gained its first successes in those areas whose economic and political status had thus been raised. The origins of the new Spanish American nations must properly be sought in the developing life of the eighteenth century.

Apart from a small minority, an intellectual *élite,* it is possible that the rising creole middle class of lawyers, merchants, landowners and soldiers might have reconciled themselves for some time longer to their political inferiority, however much they resented their social inferiority, to the Spaniards. The loyalists, or royalists, were always far more numerous during the Spanish American revolutions than they were during the revolution for North American independence. But whatever the prosperity of Spanish America, whatever the rehabilitation of Spain, in the second half of the eighteenth century, the economic foundations of the empire had been irretrievably undermined. The recovery of Spain had failed to keep pace with the expanding economy of her colonies, and the imperial economic reforms of Charles III were no more than palliatives of a condition imperfectly understood. The trade of the empire was still a closed monopoly of Spain, but the monopoly was imposed by a country which could still not successfully apply it, a country outstripped in financial and technical resources, in facilities and skills, by its greatest colonial rival, Britain. The empire, Professor Whitaker has observed, "fell not so much because of decay within as because of pressure from without"; and from this point of view its fall was no more than a corollary of the commercial expansion of Europe and particularly of England.

What really stimulated the economic expansion of Spanish America in the eighteenth century, perhaps, were not so much the imperial economic reforms as the European search for Latin American markets and the European demand for Latin American products. And for the continued growth of European interest in Spanish America there were, apart from considerations of strategy and politics, three main reasons. First, Spanish America provided dollars, the gold and silver coin and specie which was the lubricant of international trade. The bullion supply was as interesting to the continental as it was to the British and North American merchant. Secondly, Spanish America supplied a number of raw materials, such as drugs and dyewoods, hides and skins, increasingly important for industrial and commercial purposes. Thirdly, it afforded a market for manufactured goods, particularly textiles and hardware. The market, perhaps, was not infinitely extensible as was sometimes imagined, but its potentialities were great, some English and some continental merchants knew it far better than might be supposed, and it was undoubtedly profitable.

There were, also, two ways of tapping the resources and trade of Spanish America. The first was to do so indirectly by way of Cádiz and, still more indirectly, by way of Lisbon and Rio de Janeiro. The second was the direct or contraband trade. Both had long been practiced. At the end of the seventeenth century everybody knew that the fleets and galleons at Cádiz were stocked with foreign, principally French and English, not Spanish goods, that the Spanish merchants were little more than agents or shippers, and that the returns which flowed to Spain immediately flowed out again.

> "We owe to Divine Providence," Philip V complained, "the special blessing of vast dominions in America, the centre of abundant precious metals; [yet] the Crown has always seen that . . . this is the kingdom which retains the least."

Or, in Pufendorff's phrase, which Mr. Christelow has recently quoted, "Spain kept the cow and the rest of Europe drank the milk."

Spain, in short, could not supply her colonies herself. But she maintained the pretense of so doing. What was more, she insisted that colonial products should flow only to Spain. Since the tonnage of the galleons fell by three-quarters in the seventeenth century, it is obvious that the volume of imperial trade had seriously contracted. Not only this, high duties and restrictive freights combined with the monopolistic interests of the merchant houses in Seville and Cádiz to raise the price level in America to fantastic heights. An increase of two to three hundred per cent above the prices in Spain was not uncommon. And if Spain could not herself supply her colonies with enough or cheap enough goods, neither could Europe obtain from Spain all that she wanted of colonial products. The result was an enormous contraband trade. This was the second method employed by the French, the English and the Dutch, the direct or contraband trade; and the more debilitated Spain became, the greater grew the contraband, the more the contraband, the greater Spain's debility, and the weaker her empire. . . .

The effect on Spain can partly be measured in the continuing decline in the tonnage of the fleets and galleons and in the irregularity of their sailings. When the galleons sailed for the last time in 1737 they were unable to dispose of their goods because the markets were already overstocked. Royal decree after royal decree complained of the presence of foreigners and foreign goods in the Indies. Foreigners must be expelled. Officials who connived at contraband trade should be punished with death. Even their immortal souls would be imperilled, for in 1776 the Church was recommended to teach that contraband was a mortal sin. Finally, of course, the great series of economic and commercial reforms which began in 1740 with the permission given to register ships to sail round Cape Horn and culminated in the legislation of Charles III, reflected the acute anxieties of the crown.

The reforms could alleviate, but they failed to remedy the situation. It is true that they did much to rehabilitate Spanish commerce. Though the old monopolists protested, new and more enterprising Spaniards and Spanish Americans entered trade. Shipping and revenue increased. But the contraband continued. To tap the trade of the Gulf of Mexico and the Spanish Main, the British, in 1766, established free ports in Dominica and Jamaica, extending the system, after 1787, to other strategic points in the West Indies. And there is no doubt that, despite temporary vicissitudes, the free port trade, encouraged in time of peace and specially licensed in time of war, was, as the board of trade found it, when reviewing the Free Port Acts themselves, highly "beneficial." The Spaniards might properly complain. But it was no part of British policy to enforce the Laws of the Indies. And whatever may have been the prospects that the imperial reforms of Charles III could have arrested foreign economic pressure upon the walls of the empire and that Spain herself could have been brought successfully to compete in the swelling volume of international trade, the doom of Spanish hopes was sealed by two events. The first was the death of Charles himself in 1788 and the accession of the incompetent Charles IV. The second was the entry of Spain into the French revolutionary wars.

The war of 1779 to 1783, when Spain had actively promoted the independence of England's colonies, had been costly enough. For the first time in Spanish history the crown was forced to issue paper money, soon to be inflated. The brief war with France, from 1793 to 1795, was a further blow. But when, in 1796, Spain again went to war with England, and, with a brief interval of only two and a half years, remained at war for twelve years more, the result was disaster. This was the crisis of the empire. Spain and her colonies were severed. The Spanish economy was seriously deranged. The Spanish navy was almost destroyed. And the colonies were thrown upon their own and foreign resources.

There had been occasions, in earlier years, when Spain had been compelled to tolerate the trade of friends or neutrals in Spanish America. In 1782, for example, Louisiana had been allowed to trade with France. Cuba, in 1793, was permitted to trade with the United States. In the years after 1789, moreover, the slave trade had been thrown open and foreigners allowed to engage in it. But when, on November 18, 1797, the crown opened the ports of Spanish America to neutral shipping, the measure was one of desperation. The order was indeed revoked in 1799 because it had "redounded entirely," as the decree of revocation complained, to the injury of the state and of the interests of its subjects. But what the law forbade, local regulation continued to tolerate and the crown itself to license; and though the old system was restored at the peace in 1802, with the renewal of the war once again the ports were opened.

The result, or partial result, was the rapid growth of North American trade, from Cuba to Buenos Aires and Buenos Aires to Chile. And more than one American, perhaps, like the young Richard Cleveland of Massachusetts, carried in his cargo a copy of the Federal Constitution and of the Declaration of Independence, conveniently translated into Spanish. But it was not only American trade, legitimate and illegitimate, that grew. So also did British trade. The contraband flourished at the free ports in the West Indies. It flourished at Trinidad, which alone was said to supply the Spanish colonies with goods to the value of one million pounds a year. It flourished at Vera Cruz, as Viceroy Marquina bitterly complained. It flourished at Buenos Aires. And, even on the Pacific coast, where the South Sea whalers were actively engaged in it, it extended and strengthened its hold.

There was still to be fought out in Spanish America the battle between monopoly and free enterprise, between the beneficiaries of an old order and the partisans of a new. But the issue was already resolved. It was impossible to re-enact the Laws of the Indies. The economic emancipation of Spanish America was determined before its political emancipation began.

And so far as political emancipation was concerned, the years from 1796 to 1808 were equally decisive. As Britain had formerly wavered between plundering the Spanish American colonies and trading with them, so now she hesitated between their conquest and their emancipation. In 1797 the governor of Trinidad was specifically instructed to encourage revolution on the Mainland. The invasion of Buenos Aires was prepared, and cancelled, in the same year. And there were other plans, in the mind of the British government as well as in that of Francisco de Miranda, so long plotting in England and America the emancipation of Venezuela. But fundamentally Britain was more interested in trade than territory. Her designs were commercial and strategic rather than imperial, and when, in 1806, Sir Home Popham captured Buenos Aires, it was at his own responsibility. *The Times,* indeed, rejoiced. It knew not, it said, how to express itself in terms adequate to the national advantage obtained. But the government vacillated. It did too little and that little too late. Buenos Aires was recaptured and Montevideo lost. The whole affair, said *The Times,* was "a dirty, sordid enterprise, conceived and executed in a spirit of avarice and plunder," and the chief source of the calamity was the unauthorised beginning of it.

But for Spanish America its end was all important. The viceroy of Río de la Plata had fled. It was the creoles who defeated the British, deposed the incompetent viceroy and appointed a new one. Spanish America had seen the deposition and imprisonment of the legal representative of the king. It had seen a creole militia defeat a European army. It had seen a colonial port crowded with British ships and flooded with British goods. It was not a revolution that took place at Buenos Aires as a result of the British invasions. But it was a political and economic transformation that contained the seeds of revolution.

Suddenly, however, the situation changed. Napoleon invaded Spain. The crown fell into captivity. A usurper sat upon the throne. From an enemy Britain became, overnight, the ally of Spain, and the army which Wellesley was preparing in Ireland for the liberation of Spanish America sailed, not to emancipate Spanish America from Spain, but to liberate Spain from France.

The news of the fall of the monarchy, and of the invasion of the mother country, stirred the loyalty and moved the indignation of the colonies, and, superficially, the resistance movement in Spain was almost exactly imitated in Spanish America. As juntas sprang up in Spain in the name of Ferdinand VII, so in Spanish America juntas and *cabildos* assumed the powers of viceroys, presidents and captains-general, the agents, now, of an authority which had ceased to exist. Extraordinary circumstances called for extraordinary measures. The colonists took thought for their own protection and their own future. Power reverted to the people, though by "the people" nothing more can be meant than a small but active creole minority: the revolutions in Spanish America were the work of the few, not of the many.

But that a movement which began as an assertion of independence from France should have ended as an assertion of independence from Spain was due quite as much to Spain herself as to the creole minority in her colonies whose thwarted aspirations in government and trade were thus fulfilled. For though the monarchy had collapsed, though the Peninsula was overrun, the Spaniards still clung to the principles of imperial monopoly and colonial subordination. Crown, Regency, Cortes, showed themselves equally blind, equally determined. The colonies, declared the Junta Central, in 1809, were an integral part of the Spanish monarchy, and the deduction soon followed that they owed obedience to the extraordinary authorities erected in Spain. That was not the Spanish American view. Nor had it been the Habsburg view. "Estos y esos reinos," "these and those kingdoms," was the famous phrase used to define the royal possessions in Spain and the Indies. The Indies had never belonged to Spain. They were the property of the crown of Castile, united to the kingdoms of Spain merely by a dynastic tie. The Bourbons forgot, or ignored, this Habsburg view; and so did the Spaniards. But the creoles remembered it. Just as the English colonies, in the eighteenth century, refused to accept subordination to the sovereignty of parliament, so the Spanish Americans refused to accept subordination to the people of the Peninsula. And in both cases what reason failed to arrange, force was left to decide.

SUGGESTIONS FOR FURTHER READING AND VIEWING

Section I
The Transit of Civilization

BOOKS

Brandon, William. NEW WORLDS FOR OLD. Athens, Ohio: University of Ohio Press, 1986. Traces the impact of the discovery of the New World on the development of European social thought.

Crosby, Alfred W. THE COLUMBIAN EXCHANGE: BIOLOGICAL AND CULTURAL CULTURAL CONSEQUENCES OF 1492. Westport, Conn.: Greenwood Press, 1972. Stimulating essays that analyze the exchange of plants, animals, people and disease between Old and New Worlds.

Diffie, Bailey W. and George Winius. FOUNDATIONS OF THE PORTUGUESE EMPIRE, 1415–1580. Minneapolis: 1977. Comprehensive survey of Portuguese expansion in Asia, Africa and America.

Elliott, John H. THE OLD WORLD AND THE NEW, 1492–1650. Cambridge: Cambridge University Press, 1970. Noted British scholar surveys the impact of the New World on the mind of the Old.

Lunenfeld, Marvin. 1492: DISCOVERY, INVASION, ENCOUNTER: SOURCES AND IN-TERPRETATIONS. Lexington, Mass.: D.C. Heath, 1991. Useful anthology of documents and secondary accounts assessing Columbus as man and legend and the impact of his voyages on the Old and New Worlds.

Parry, J. H. THE ESTABLISHMENT OF THE EUROPEAN HEGEMONY: 1415–1715. New York: Harper and Row, 1961. Readable introduction to the history of European expansion.

Sauer, Carl Ortwin. THE EARLY SPANISH MAIN. Berkeley and Los Angeles: University of California Press, 1966. Historical geographer describes people and setting of the Caribbean islands before the arrival of the Spanish and the impact of the conquest.

FILMS AND VIDEOTAPES

COLUMBUS AND THE AGE OF DISCOVERY (Color, WGBH-TV Documentary Series, 1991)
Distributor: VHS video—Films for the Humanities & Sciences

Seven 58-minute programs produced for public television to mark the sesquicentennial of Columbus's discovery of America. Topics include: "Columbus's World"; "An Idea

347

Takes Shape"; "The Crossing"; "Worlds Found and Lost"; "The Sword and the Cross"; "The Columbian Exchange"; and "In Search of Columbus." Excellent photography and meticulous scholarship make these documentaries an outstanding series. The "Columbian Exchange" program is especially appropriate for this section.

THE BURIED MIRROR: REFLECTIONS OF SPAIN AND THE NEW WORLD (Color, Smithsonian Institution Documentary Series, 1992)
Distributor: VHS video—Films Incorporated Video

Five 59-minute programs to mark the sesquicentennial of Columbus's discovery of America. Based on an original idea by historian Peggy K. Liss; written and presented by Mexican author Carlos Fuentes. Survey of the history of the Hispanic world on both sides of the Atlantic. Topics include: "The Virgin and the Bull"; "Conflict of the Gods"; "The Age of Gold"; "The Price of Freedom"; and "Unfinished Business." Viewer guides available. Can be purchased with either English or Spanish soundtracks.

Section II
Was Inca Rule Tyrannical?

BOOKS

Bingham, Hiram. LOST CITY OF THE INCAS: THE STORY OF MACCHU PICCHU AND ITS BUILDERS. New York: Atheneum, 1963. Bingham's account of his discovery of Macchu Picchu in 1911. For a rapid survey of Inca culture, see pp. 3–33.

de la Vega, Garcilaso. ROYAL COMMENTARIES OF THE INCAS AND GENERAL HISTORY OF PERU. Trans. by Harold V. Livermore. 2 vols. Austin: University of Texas Press, 1966. Classic history of the Incas written by a mestizo in the seventeenth century.

Hanke, Lewis. ARISTOTLE AND THE AMERICAN INDIANS. Bloomington: Indiana University Press, 1970. Discusses the efforts of the Spanish to understand the nature of the Indians in the sixteenth century.

Hemming, John. THE CONQUEST OF THE INCAS. New York: Harcourt Brace Jovanovich, 1970. Detailed, colorful narrative of the conquest of Peru with special emphasis on Indian resistance.

Katz, Friedrich. THE ANCIENT AMERICAN CIVILIZATIONS. New York: Praeger, 1974. Survey of Inca and Aztec civilization based on classic sources.

Métraux, Alfred. THE HISTORY OF THE INCAS. New York: Pantheon, 1969. Still the best brief introduction to Inca society.

Wachtel, Nathan. THE VISION OF THE VANQUISHED: THE SPANISH CONQUEST OF PERU THROUGH INDIAN EYES, 1530–1570. New York: Barnes & Noble, 1977. Presents the Indian view of the conquest and also discusses the conflicts between Spaniards and Indians in fringe areas.

FILMS AND VIDEOTAPES

HORIZON: LORDS OF THE LABYRINTH (Color, 54 minutes, BBC, 1978)
Distributor: 16 mm film—Films Incorporated Video

Investigates the history of the city of Chan Chan in the Peruvian desert close to the Pacific Ocean that was conquered by the Incas only seventy years before Pizarro landed with his conquistadors. Scenes of massive pyramids, huge courtyards and vast complexes of irrigation canals which brought water to the city from distant valleys. A good introduction to the history of ancient Peru before the Incas.

THE INCAS (Color, 55 minutes, PBS/BBC TV Odyssey Series, 1979) Distributor: 16 mm film—Documentary Educational Resources

John Murra introduces the work of three archaeologists—John Hyslop, Craig Morris, and Ann Kendall—who are studying the extensive network of Inca roads, towns and agricultural regions. Although the main focus is on archaeological methods, the film provides much insight into the nature of the Inca empire as well as spectacular photography of the Peruvian sites.

Section III
Relations Between Spaniards and Indians

BOOKS

Clendinnen, Inga. AMBIVALENT CONQUESTS: MAYA AND SPANIARD IN YUCATAN, 1517–1570. Cambridge: Cambridge University Press, 1987. Revisionist view of Mayan proselytization by Franciscans, stressing Indian efforts to retain their pre-Christian beliefs.

Farriss, Nancy. MAYA SOCIETY UNDER COLONIAL RULE. Princeton: Princeton University Press, 1984. Analyzes the mental and material worlds of the Maya, using ethnological as well as historical methodology.

Gibson, Charles. THE AZTECS UNDER SPANISH RULE: A HISTORY OF THE INDIANS IN THE VALLEY OF MEXICO. Stanford: Stanford University Press, 1964. Groundbreaking study of Indian city-states and their points of contact with the Spanish world.

Hanke, Lewis. THE SPANISH STRUGGLE FOR JUSTICE IN THE CONQUEST OF AMERICA. Philadelphia: American Historical Association, 1949. Analyzes the efforts of Bartolomé de Las Casas to defend the Indians from Spanish exploitation.

León Portilla, Miguel, ed. THE BROKEN SPEARS: THE AZTEC ACCOUNT OF THE CONQUEST OF MEXICO. Boston: Beacon Press, 1961. The events of the conquest as set down in Indian manuscripts.

Lockhart, James. SPANISH PERU, 1532–1560. Madison: University of Wisconsin Press, 1968. Draws on notarial records to examine key groups in Spanish conquest society.

Stern, Steve J. PERU'S INDIAN PEOPLES AND THE CHALLENGE OF SPANISH CONQUEST: HUAMANGA TO 1640. Madison: University of Wisconsin Press, 1982. Focuses on Spanish-Indian relations in Peru, showing the ability of each group to manipulate the other.

FILMS AND VIDEOTAPES

AGUIRRE, THE WRATH OF GOD (German-made but filmed in Peru, color, 94 minutes, German dialogue with English subtitles, 1973)
Distributor: 16 mm film—New Yorker/VHS video—Facets

Werner Herzog directed this fictional portrayal of the real-life exploits of Lope de Aguirre, a sixteenth-century Spanish conquistador. While searching for El Dorado in the Amazon jungle, Aguirre rebelled against Gonzalo Pizarro and went on a rampage of terror and destruction through northern South America. Herzog's film strays far from the actual historical events, but the superb photography, authentic costumes and presentation of Spanish-Indian relationships offer real insight into the nature of the conquest of America.

THE MISSION (Filmed in Argentina and Colombia, color, 126 minutes, 1986, English dialogue). Directed by Roland Joffee; screenplay by Robert Bolt. Starring Robert DeNiro, Jeremy Irons and Ray McAnally.
Distributor: VHS video—Facets

Prize-winning, epic film about the conflict between Spain, Portugal and Jesuit missionaries when the Treaty of Madrid in 1750 required that seven Jesuit missions in formerly Spanish territory be turned over to the Portuguese. The film centers on the crises of conscience faced by two very different priests. By posing the question of whether the priests should take up arms against the crown to defend the natives, the film draws a parallel between the eighteenth century and the late twentieth century, when many priests in Latin America have found themselves at odds with Rome.

Section IV
Population Questions

BOOKS

Borah, Woodrow and Sherburne F. Cook. THE ABORIGINAL POPULATION OF CENTRAL MEXICO ON THE EVE OF THE SPANISH CONQUEST. Berkeley and Los Angeles: University of California Press, 1965. Estimates size of pre-conquest population of Mexico.

Cook, Noble David. DEMOGRAPHIC COLLAPSE: INDIAN PERU, 1520–1620. Cambridge: Cambridge University Press, 1981. Examines the rates and reasons for the decline of Indians in Peru.

Denevan, William M., ed. THE NATIVE POPULATION OF THE AMERICAS IN 1492. Madison: University of Wisconsin Press, 1976. Original essays on aspects of indigenous demography in several geographic regions.

McNeill, William H. PLAGUES AND PEOPLE. Garden City, N.J.: Doubleday, 1976.

Sherman, William L. FORCED NATIVE LABOR IN SIXTEENTH-CENTURY CENTRAL AMERICA. Lincoln: University of Nebraska Press, 1979. Shows how oppressive labor conditions contributed to decline of Indian population.

Super, John C. FOOD, CONQUEST AND COLONIZATION IN SIXTEENTH CENTURY SPANISH AMERICA. Albuquerque: University of New Mexico Press, 1988. Discusses colonial patterns of food consumption and Indian adaptation to European foods.

FILMS AND VIDEOTAPES

COLUMBUS AND THE AGE OF DISCOVERY (see Section I for complete profile) The fifth program in this series, "The Sword and the Cross," discusses the diseases brought to the New World by the Europeans as well as the impact of the conquistadors and the Church on the indigenous population.

Section V
The Introduction of African Slavery in Spanish America

BOOKS

Bowser, Frederick. THE AFRICAN SLAVE IN COLONIAL PERU 1524–1650. Stanford: Stanford University Press, 1974. Most complete survey of slavery in Peru.

Cohen, David W. and Jack P. Greene, eds. NEITHER SLAVE NOR FREE: THE FREEDMAN OF AFRICAN DESCENT IN THE SLAVE SOCIETIES OF THE NEW WORLD. Baltimore: Johns Hopkins University Press, 1972. Collection of essays discussing patterns of manumission and the role of free blacks in various regions of Latin America.

James, C.L.R. THE BLACK JACOBINS. New York: Vintage, 1963. Marxist account of Haitian plantation society and the 1791 revolt led by Toussaint L'Ouverture.

Klein, Herbert S. AFRICAN SLAVERY IN LATIN AMERICA AND THE CARIBBEAN. New York: Oxford, 1986. A modern, comprehensive comparative study of African slavery in Spanish, Portuguese, and French-speaking regions of America.

Palmer, Colin A. SLAVES OF THE WHITE GOD: BLACKS IN MEXICO 1570–1650. Cambridge: Harvard University Press, 1976. Important contribution to study of black slavery in Mexico.

Price, Richard, ed. MAROON SOCIETIES: REBEL SLAVE COMMUNITIES IN THE AMERICAS. Baltimore: Johns Hopkins University Press, 1979. Collection of essays describing communities of escaped black slaves in various regions of the Americas.

Rout, Leslie B. THE AFRICAN EXPERIENCE IN SPANISH AMERICA: 1502 TO PRESENT DAY. Cambridge: Cambridge University Press, 1971. Still a good introduction to the topic.

FILMS AND VIDEOTAPES

THE LAST SUPPER (Cuba, color, 110 minutes, 1977, Spanish dialogue with English subtitles). Directed by Tomás Gutiérrez Alea.

Distributor: 16 mm film—New Yorker

Cuban feature film based on an incident that actually occurred at the end of the eighteenth century when a pious slaveholder decided to improve his soul and instruct his slaves in the glories of Christian humility by inviting twelve of them to participate in a reenactment of the Last Supper. Alea exploits this specific event to describe the nature of economic, social, political and cultural life on a plantation. There is careful attention to detail; an authentic recreation of a late eighteenth-century plantation setting.

THE OTHER FRANCISCO (Cuba, black and white, 97 minutes, 1975, Spanish dialogue with English subtitles). Directed by Sergio Giral.
Distributor: 16 mm film—New Yorker

Based on the nineteenth-century Cuban anti-slavery novel *Francisco,* written by Anselmo Suárez y Romero in 1839 but published posthumously. The film offers a critical analysis of the novel, showing how the author's social background led to the use of a melodramatic plot to convey his liberal, humanitarian viewpoint. The result is a compelling drama about an era when politicians, intellectuals and slaves fought to destroy slavery—but each with different purposes in mind.

Section VI
The Crises of Seventeenth-Century Brazil

BOOKS

Alden, Dauril, ed. THE COLONIAL ROOTS OF MODERN BRAZIL. Berkeley: University of California Press, 1972. Essays on socioeconomic topics.

Boxer, Charles R. THE DUTCH IN BRAZIL, 1624–1654. Oxford: The Clarendon Press, 1957. Readable survey of the Dutch occupation of Pernambuco.

————. SALVADOR DE SA AND THE STRUGGLE FOR BRAZIL AND ANGOLA, 1602–1686. London: The Athlone Press, University of London, 1952. Biography of an energetic governor of Rio de Janeiro.

Burns, E. Bradford, ed. A DOCUMENTARY HISTORY OF BRAZIL. New York: Knopf, 1966. Anthology of key primary documents. About one-third pertain to the colonial era.

Freyre, Gilberto. THE MASTERS AND THE SLAVES: A STUDY IN DEVELOPMENT OF BRAZILIAN CIVILIZATION, second English-language edition, revised. Berkeley: University of California Press, 1986. Study of race relations by renowned Brazilian sociologist-historian that provided much factual support for the Tannenbaum thesis.

Hemming, John. RED GOLD: THE CONQUEST OF THE BRAZILIAN INDIANS. Cambridge: Harvard University Press, 1978. A history of Brazil from the Indian perspective, incorporating documents and secondary sources.

Prado, Caio, Jr. THE COLONIAL BACKGROUND OF MODERN BRAZIL. Berkeley and Los Angeles: University of California Press, 1967. Synthesis from a Marxist perspective based on materials from the eighteenth century.

Queirós Mattoso, Katia M. de. TO BE A SLAVE IN BRAZIL 1500–1888. New Brunswick: Rutgers University Press, 1986. Well-written, up-to-date survey of all aspects of slave life.

Schwartz, Stuart B. SUGAR PLANTATIONS IN THE FORMATION OF BRAZILIAN SOCIETY. BAHIA 1550–1835. Cambridge: Cambridge University Press, 1985. Study of a society that was based on sugar and slavery.

FILMS AND VIDEOTAPES

HOW TASTY WAS MY LITTLE FRENCHMAN (Brazil, color, 80 minutes, 1971, Portuguese and Tupi dialogue with English subtitles). Directed by Nelson Pereira dos Santos. Distributor: 16 mm film—New Yorker

This Cinema Novo film tells the story of a Frenchman who is captured by Brazilian Indians in the sixteenth century and lives for more than a year as their slave. The contrast between his attitudes and theirs vividly reveals what happened when different cultures met and interacted in the early years of South American colonization. Director dos Santos based his plot on the true adventure of Hans Staden, a German who sailed as a gunner on a Portuguese ship on two voyages to Brazil in 1548 and 1549. The sets and costumes are authentic, and the whole atmosphere derives from paintings and writings of the period.

QUILOMBO (Brazil, color, 114 minutes, 1984, Portuguese dialogue with English subtitles). Directed by Carlos Diegues. Distributor: 16 mm film—New Yorker/VHS video—New Yorker

Lavish musical that tells the story of the life and death of Palmares, the fugitive slave settlement, or *quilombo*, whose existence between 1605 and 1695 became a threat to Portuguese rule in America. This is epic cinema with great heroes, terrible events, self-sacrifice and victory of the spirit, but Diegues uses authentic costumes and recreates the sixteenth-century ambience. The result is a vivid film that traces the African roots and customs of modern Brazil.

Section VII
The Development of Society

BOOKS

Bakewell, Peter J. SILVER MINING AND SOCIETY IN COLONIAL MEXICO: ZACATECAS, 1547–1700. Cambridge: Cambridge University Press, 1971. Analyzes the technical and institutional aspects of Mexican silver mining in the sixteenth and seventeenth centuries.

Henderson, James and Linda Henderson. TEN NOTABLE WOMEN OF LATIN AMERICA. Chicago: Nelson-Hall, 1978. Biographies of women representing major themes in Latin American history. Colonial subjects include Malinche, Inés de Suárez, Catalina de Erauzo, Sor Juana de la Cruz, and Leopoldina, wife of Pedro I of Brazil.

Lanning, John Tate. THE UNIVERSITY IN THE KINGDOM OF GUATEMALA. Ithaca: Cornell University Press, 1955. Pioneering study on an important colonial institution.

Lavrin, Asunción, ed. LATIN AMERICAN WOMEN: HISTORICAL PERSPECTIVES. Westport, Conn.: Greenwood Press, 1978. Essays collected by the leading scholar on Latin American women.

Leonard, Irving A. BAROQUE TIMES IN OLD MEXICO. Ann Arbor: University of Michigan, 1959. Delightful study of cultural and intellectual movements of seventeenth-century Mexico.

Martín, Luis. DAUGHTERS OF THE CONQUISTADORES: WOMEN OF THE VICEROYALTY OF PERU. Albuquerque: University of New Mexico Press, 1983. Colorful survey of Spanish women in colonial Peru from the sixteenth through the eighteenth centuries.

Mörner, Magnus. RACE MIXTURE IN THE HISTORY OF LATIN AMERICA. Boston: Little Brown, 1967. Succinct introduction to an essential topic.

Phelan, John L. THE KINGDOM OF QUITO IN THE SEVENTEENTH CENTURY. Madison: University of Wisconsin, 1967. Biography of Antonio de Morga, president of the Audiencia of Quito from 1615 to 1636, but covers other aspects of the development of the colony.

Sweet, David G. and Gary B. Nash. STRUGGLE AND SURVIVAL IN COLONIAL AMERICA. Berkeley: University of California Press, 1981. Anthology of biographies describing the lives of ordinary people.

FILMS AND VIDEOTAPES

CHUQUIAGO (Bolivia, color, 87 minutes, 1977, Aymara and Spanish dialogue with English subtitles). Directed by Antonio Eguino.
Distributor: 16 mm film—New Yorker

Analyzes race and caste barriers in La Paz, Bolivia, by presenting separate but interlocking stories of four residents in the capital: Isico, a young Indian boy; Johnny, a *cholo* teenager; Carlos, a middle-aged, middle-class government bureaucrat; and Patricia, an upper-class university student. Ranging from satire to tragicomedy, each of the episodes dramatizes the frustration of the personal dreams of its protagonist by a social system that seems to have him or her trapped. Set in contemporary Bolivia, the film says a good deal about the legacy of the colonial past.

Section VIII
Crisis and Climax in the Eighteenth Century

BOOKS

Fisher, J. R. GOVERNMENT AND SOCIETY IN COLONIAL PERU: THE INTENDANT SYSTEM 1784–1814. London: The Athlone Press, University of London, 1970. Case study of Bourbon reforms in Peru.

Fisher, Lilian E. THE LAST INCA REVOLT, 1780–1783. Norman: University of Oklahoma Press, 1966. Narrative of the Tupac Amaru rebellion.

Humphreys, Robin A. and John Lynch, eds. THE ORIGINS OF LATIN AMERICAN REVO-LUTIONS 1808–1826. New York: Knopf, 1965. Still useful anthology of essays on politi-cal and economic factors contributing to the outbreak of the war of independence.

Lafaye, Jacques. QUETZALCOATL AND GUADALUPE: THE FORMATION OF MEXI-CAN NATIONAL CONSCIOUSNESS. Chicago: University of Chicago Press, 1976. Surveys the efforts of the creoles to refute European charges of their inferiority.

Lanning, John Tate. THE EIGHTEENTH-CENTURY ENLIGHTENMENT IN THE UNI-VERSITY OF SAN CARLOS DE GUATEMALA. Ithaca: Cornell University Press, 1956. Institutional and intellectual study of a Spanish American university.

Phelan, John Leddy. THE PEOPLE AND THE KING: THE COMUNERO REVOLUTION IN COLOMBIA, 1781. Madison: University of Wisconsin Press, 1978. Study of one of the major revolts against Spanish rule in the late eighteenth century.

Russell-Wood, A.J.R., ed. FROM COLONY TO NATION: ESSAYS ON THE INDEPEN-DENCE OF BRAZIL. Baltimore: Johns Hopkins University Press, 1975. Collection of essays analyzing the causes and course of Brazilian independence.

FILMS AND VIDEOTAPES

THE BURIED MIRROR: REFLECTIONS ON SPAIN AND THE NEW WORLD (see Section I for complete profile)
Program IV, "The Price of Freedom" in this series explores the causes and courses of the revolutions for independence in Latin America.

THE GREEN WALL (Peru, color, 110 minutes, 1970, Spanish dialogue with English subtitles). Directed by Armando Robles Godoy.
Distributor: Films Incorporated Video

Godoy's autobiographical story concerns a young family that decides to abandon life in Lima to build a home in the lush, overgrown Peruvian jungle frontier. Their idyllic life is suddenly threatened when the Land Reform Commission challenges their claim. While the father journeys to the city to fight for their home, their six-year-old son is bitten by a poisonous snake. His mother, alone and on foot, must race through the jungle to save his life. THE GREEN WALL is a well-made Peruvian feature film that dramatizes timeless joys and perils of frontier life.

FILM AND VIDEO DISTRIBUTORS

Documentary Educational Resources
5 Bridge Street
Watertown, MA 02172
(617) 926-0491

Facets Multimedia, Inc.
1517 West Fullerton Avenue
Chicago, IL 60614
(312) 281-9075
(800) 331-6197

Films Incorporated Video
5547 North Ravenswood Avenue
Chicago, IL 60640-9979
(800) 323-4222, ext. 43

Films for the Humanities
   and Sciences
Box 2053
Princeton, NJ 08540
(609) 452-1128
(800) 257-5126

New Yorker Films
16 West 61st Street
New York, NY 10023
(212) 247-6110